OTHER BOOKS BY DANIEL P. MOYNIHAN

The Politics of a Guaranteed Income

On Equality of Educational Opportunity (editor, with Frederick Mosteller)

On Understanding Poverty: Perspectives from the Social Sciences (editor)

Toward a National Urban Policy (editor)

Maximum Feasible Misunderstanding:
Community Action in the War on Poverty

The Defenses of Freedom, the Public Papers of Arthur J. Goldberg
(editor)

Beyond the Melting Pot: The Negroes, Puerto Ricans, Jews,
Italians and Irish in New York City (with Nathan Glazer)

Coping

Essays on the Practice of Government

Coping

Essays on the Practice of Government

Daniel P. Moynihan

RANDOM HOUSE  NEW YORK

Grateful acknowledgment is made to the following for permission
to reprint previously published material:

The American Institute of Architects: "Architecture in a Time of Trouble," by Daniel P. Moynihan. Reprinted from the *AIA Journal*, September, 1969. Copyright © 1969 The American Institute of Architects.

American Council on Education: "On Universal Higher Education," by Daniel P. Moynihan. Reprinted from *Education Record*, Winter 1971 issue.

America: "The Case for a Family Policy," by Daniel P. Moynihan. Reprinted from *America*, September 18, 1965. All Rights Reserved. Copyright © 1965 by America Press, Inc., 106 West 56th Street, New York, N.Y.

Communications/Research/Machines, Inc.: "Liberalism and Knowledge," by Daniel Moynihan, previously titled "Eliteland," reprinted from *Psychology Today* Magazine, September 1970. Copyright © Communications/Research/Machines, Inc.

Library of Congress Cataloging in Publication Data

Moynihan, Daniel Patrick.
Coping: on the practice of government.

CONTENTS: Introduction.—"Bosses" and "reformers."—
The case for a family policy.—[Etc.]
1. United States—Social conditions—1960-   —
Addresses, essays, lectures. I. Title.
HN17.5.M68   309.1'73'092   73-3983
ISBN 0-394-48324-3

Manufactured in the United States of America

9 8 7 6 5 4 3 2

First Edition

For Paul Horgan

Contents

INTRODUCTION
3

1. "BOSSES" AND "REFORMERS"
53

2. THE CASE FOR A FAMILY POLICY
69

3. TRAFFIC SAFETY AND
THE BODY POLITIC
79

4. THE AUTOMOBILE AND THE COURTS
100

5. NIRVANA NOW
116

6. THE CRISES IN WELFARE
134

7. THE EDUCATION OF THE URBAN POOR
167

8. THE POLITICS OF STABILITY
185

9. THE NEW RACIALISM
195

10. THE CITY IN CHASSIS
210

11. ARCHITECTURE IN A TIME OF TROUBLE
233

12. MARIA REGINA MARTYRUM
243

13. POLITICS AS THE ART OF THE IMPOSSIBLE
248

14. LIBERALISM AND KNOWLEDGE
259

15. POLICY VS. PROGRAM IN THE 1970s
272

16. ON UNIVERSAL HIGHER EDUCATION
285

17. THE PRESIDENCY AND THE PRESS
314

18. THE DEEPENING SCHISM
344

19. *CUI BONO?*
370

20. ON THE EDUCATION OF ENGINEERS
395

21. ADDRESS TO THE ENTERING CLASS
AT HARVARD COLLEGE, 1972
405

22. "PEACE"
420

Coping

Essays on the Practice of Government

Introduction

Midway through the *Education* Adams tells of the great expectations with which he encountered the theories of Darwin and others of the grand synthesizers of Victorian London. "The ideas were new and seemed to lead somewhere," he wrote, ". . . to some great generalization which would finish one's clamor to be educated."

A century has passed. Ever more commanding generalizations have made their appearance and now, one gathers, we may be approaching the "great generalization" as to the biological nature of life itself. But even as knowledge approaches such grand achievement, experience seems to foreshorten our view. Increasingly it is what is *known* about life that makes it problematical. The dictum of Ecclesiastes 1 : 18, "For in much wisdom is much grief and he that increaseth knowledge increaseth sorrow," seems more fitted to our time; and education is more and more a matter of coming to terms with this less optimistic vision.

Even those who might still share Adams's expectations hardly do so with any sense that to be part of this time is a mark of privilege not a little touched with daring. Ours is more an age of complaint, rising at best to a certain cheerful resignation, as in the story of the man who says, "They told me if I voted for Goldwater in 1964 there would be half a million troops in Vietnam in a year's time, and I voted for him and, by God, they were right."

The unexpected, the unforeseen: the public life of our age seems dominated by events of this cast, while the task of intellect seems increasingly that of imposing some measure of order on this less than cosmic chaos. After a period of chiliastic vision we have entered a time that requires a more sober assessment of our chances, and a more modest approach to events. Large theory continues to attract persons of large ability. Long-range forecasting steadily becomes more rigorous and more valuable. And yet the here-and-now and the close-at-hand are the dominant facts of public life, and the proper study of those who would take part in it. That the people must have vision I do not doubt; but what leaders need is foresight. That at least is the sum of my experience. Those I have respected most and most tried to emulate have not tried to think immensely far ahead, but only a little way ahead: their art is not that of prophesying, but of coping.

This is no timorous exercise, much less a surrender to expediency. The "great generalizations" of any age serve a purpose, and it may be that in time everything *will* come together. But until then the work of the world will be to keep things from coming apart. Of such hope these essays are made. The subjects vary, but there is a single theme, that of coping with specific public issues by anticipating the directions they will take. To cope is an old verb that has acquired a new meaning: "to strive or contend on equal terms with a measure of success." The original sense was "to buy," later "to exchange or barter," and some of this sense persists in modern usage, for the ability to cope is indeed an exchange relation. In exchange for analytic competence, sometimes accompanied by a willingness to take risks, opportunities open, dangers diminish, things desired become attainable, things feared are avoided. There is nothing grand about any of this, yet there are worse things than commonplace competence addressed to near-term issues, concentrating on what is likely to happen in two and three and five and ten years' time. As one learns more of the world, one comes to value any "measure of success."

Judgments in such matters reflect expectations, and here it seems that generations differ. I was shaped by experiences that were still common to my generation of persons who have been active in public business, but not so common to the cohorts now beginning to succeed us. I was raised in chancy circumstances in an already sufficiently threatening world. The first major public event of my life after childhood was Pearl Harbor. I learned about it from a man whose shoes I was shining on Central Park West, somewhere in the seventies. I knew little of such matters, but was not much surprised. My normal beat was Times Square. (On Sundays and holidays, one worked uptown in the Museum area.) Two years watching the ribbon of news going round and around *The New York Times* building had got across to me the point that the Japanese had a way of starting wars. The afternoon wore on, and I continued shining shoes. No resolve formed in the young man to grow up and teach foresight to the Republic. It seemed there wasn't much in the great affairs of government, but then there wasn't much in the affairs of the ordinary people one knew. A normal condition.

Life went on. Twenty-two years later, as Assistant United States Secretary of Labor, I was in the White House when the word came that President Kennedy was dead. There were perhaps a dozen of us gathered in Ralph Dungan's office on the southwest corner of the West Wing, waiting. The knowledge came silently. Somehow in the same instant everyone in the room knew. Hubert Humphrey arrived. A strong, good man. He opened his arms, embraced Dungan, eyes blazing and wet, and exclaimed: "What have they done to us?"

Which they? No one asked; it was obvious. No one did anything, save McGeorge Bundy who moved to a telephone in the next room: "This is Mr. Bundy. Get me Mr. McNamara, please." By ones and twos we drifted off. As Bill Walton and I left, the flag atop the mansion was coming down. I noticed and said to Walton he probably ought to watch, and finally it was too much. Cameras came crowding. Wherewith he straightened up and said, "Let's walk out the way he would have expected." When he chose Walton for a friend he had chosen well.

But the death of a President requires more of his men than that they maintain their dignity. John F. Kennedy, dead, had a right to expect that those of us still alive would *think* about what had happened, and not simply in terms of what it meant to us as individuals. Kennedy had been "my" President in a way that happens only once. He had the right especially to expect that the likes of me would think. In a not altogether absurd sense it could be said I had spent my life preparing for his presidency and had done so rather as he had done. We had been officers in the same Navy, had learned something of that; he, obviously, more than I, but I had learned also. Surely I had learned that one man's death does not bring an end to things.

You would not necessarily have known this from the way I behaved. I wandered over to the Department of Labor and then wandered back to the White House, doing and thinking nothing. It occurred to me to take one last look at the Oval Room, which I did not expect to see again. I had hardly been a regular visitor, but even so I had been there, with him in the rocking chair, and had once, even, corrected his arithmetic; and now this was all finished. (I have never seen it recorded that on the day of the assassination they were fixing the rug or something, and furniture from the Oval Room was piled out in the corridor, with the rocking chair on top, as if the occupant was moving.) I picked up a picture of him from Mrs. Lincoln's desk and went round to the center door that opens from the corridor, where, on sudden impulse, I saluted, turned, Officer of the Deck style, and marched off. A guard asked for my Secret Service pass, and I asked, "What difference does it make?"

Well, for one thing, it made all the difference there was. The point of discipline is to make it possible to act when it is difficult to concentrate.

But Walton had made his point and I came to later in the afternoon on learning that the Dallas police had arrested a left-wing, pro-Castro sympathizer. It flashed: which "they" had done what? It did not surprise me that such a man might be arrested, and I was not disposed to think it impossible he was guilty. But I knew the Nation better now. I knew Dallas just well enough to assume the police would be incompetent. I knew Texas well enough to think someone there would try to shoot the man who was said to have shot the President. I knew the rest of the country would never believe it. It was clear: *We had to get custody of Oswald.*

Washington was empty. There was almost no one to tell this to save men too stricken to care, or too stupid to understand. Air Force One returned, but there was no way to speak to the new President or his men. The Cabinet had been halfway across the Pacific, en route to Japan, when the assassination occurred.

Its plane got back to Andrews Air Force Base at midnight, and here commenced a decisive experience. I made my way up and down the hierarchy of those waiting, and then those arriving, pleading: *We had to get custody of Oswald.* But with no success. I kept it up until Oswald was shot. I then realized it is possible to grow enormously successful and powerful in America without knowing that the world is a dangerous place.

I suppose I had always realized this, but never in a way that made any difference to me. In the weeks that followed it sank in. It seemed to me that unless the murder of Kennedy and of his accused assailant was remorselessly investigated, a penumbra of suspicion would grow around the American national government such as would darken its moral authority for a generation to come, and who could say what might happen in the interval? John Macy, then Chairman of the Civil Service Commission, shared this view. Together, and singly, we went round the capital much as I had made my way among the throng at Andrews Air Force Base. At best we encountered incomprehension; at worst, the suspicion that *we* thought there had been a conspiracy. We did not; we were merely convinced that significant portions of the public *would* believe there had been one *unless* the inquiry went forward with this preeminent concern in mind. I went to New York. *Commentary* and *America* published powerful editorials affirming my point. But all for nothing, as we learned later from Edward Jay Epstein's *Inquest,* and from the public opinion polls that preceded and followed his study.*

And so I failed, and at some cost. I was never, thereafter, quite trusted by the new Administration. This sank in and at length I left.

I began once again to write. My subjects varied, but looking back I find the consistent purpose—I hope I do not delude myself in this—of calling attention to situations of potential difficulty that could still be resolved by analytic competence and the willingness to try to think ahead just a little ways. This might seem a fatuous comment: what is government about save the exercise

---

* My fears as to the consequences of a too cautious investigation of the assassination may have been exaggerated, but I am not yet ready to concede the point. As I write (August 27, 1972) the front page of *The New York Times* reports "Mystery Cloaks Fate of Brain of Kennedy." The issue has not died.

of such faculties? Fair enough. That is the minimum we expect. And yet I had lived through a crisis of the most intense kind possible to politics—the murder of a head of state—in which I, a minor figure, had made sense; while men high above me had not. For one thing, they had taken their competence for granted. For another, they had an exaggerated sense of that competence. There had been, I now think, a serious misreading of the Eisenhower years. The national government had *seemed* to be in the hands of men of weak intelligence, low energies, and hardly any aspirations. It had *seemed* that men of vigor and purpose could not but do infinitely better than such a crowd of Rotarians and press agents. Well, of course, this wasn't so. Eisenhower was a man of great skill at governing. One of his skills—a lethal one— was to encourage his opponents to underestimate him. Another was not to try things that would fail. (It appears that he regarded the Interstate Highway System as the most important domestic achievement of his Administration. I had written savagely about the program when it began, but I came to realize that like it or not it was indeed a massive event, the equivalent in ways of the building of the railroads.) I grew out of patience with intellectuals opining that "nothing" happened during the Eisenhower Administration. What they meant was that nothing happened that interested them, a different matter. But what Eisenhower undertook to do *was done*. No small thing to say about a President. I came slowly to this judgment, but in the mid-1960s, when I began writing again, I had considerably scaled down my expectations of what government could do about most things— in the early 1960s in Washington we thought we could do anything, and we found out different—and had acquired the discipline of not being too much impressed by clever-seeming people. I no longer took competence in government or politics for granted. I had once. I no longer did. The assassination was that kind of event. It changed many people, and it changed me. I slowly learned to expect trouble.

I suppose I was in any event inclined to this view. Years earlier, in the space of a few hours, I had watched men of large experience and high position utterly undo themselves for the lack of just a little foresight. This was at the New York State Democratic Convention of 1958 when the party tore itself apart over the nomination of a candidate for United States senator and went

down to ruin at just that moment when almost everywhere else
the Democratic Party was surging to power, indeed was only two
years away from winning back the presidency. Considering events
since, this may seem a small matter, yet another view is possible.
For the past generation American politics has been notable for
the relative absence of influence from the State of New York,
during most of this period the largest state, with the largest
Democratic Party, the cultural, intellectual, financial, business,
and journalistic capital of the Nation. From the time of Alfred
E. Smith through that of Franklin D. Roosevelt the influence of
New York in national politics corresponded to its influence in
these other areas. Then it faltered. First came the failure of
Franklin D. Roosevelt, Jr., to carry on what was seen to be a
succession. He had been joined by a whole cohort of young men
returned from the Second World War who by every appearance
were destined for national prominence, but who faded away in
a succession of futilities. Yet the New York Democratic Party
had great vitality still. In 1953 Robert F. Wagner, Jr., was
elected mayor of New York City, ending a period of dissident
and independent officeholders. In 1954 Averell Harriman was
elected governor, ending the long Republican rule of Thomas E.
Dewey. Wagner immediately became a potential U.S. senator;
Harriman, a potential President. A major political force was in the
making that would have influenced the 1960s. All this came
crashing down in the space of four or five hours at the state
convention of 1958; and, again, I had watched as a minor figure
nonetheless privy to the more important events. I had written
speeches for the young Roosevelt, campaigned for Wagner,
worked for Harriman, and was Acting Secretary to the governor
at the time of the convention. In the weeks preceding I had been
vaguely aware that there seemed to be no agreement as to who
would run for senate on the ticket with Harriman, but busied myself with State matters, confident that more experienced and
certainly more powerful men were looking after the matter. I
arrived in Buffalo to learn they had not. Wagner had decided
against running, and the "reformers" were deadlocked with the
"bosses" over who the candidate would be. I considered myself
part of the reform element in the party, but was appalled at the
situation it had got itself into. The "bosses" wished to nominate
Frank S. Hogan, District Attorney of New York County. Re-

formers desired Thomas K. Finletter, former Secretary of the Air Force. Both were distinguished men. That choices might differ seemed understandable, but I was startled by the contempt in which the liberals, almost exclusively a middle- and upper-class group, many new to Democratic politics, held the judgment of party leaders who had spent their lives working at such politics. One might have supposed that anyone would recognize Hogan as a man of large achievement in law enforcement. But liberals did not seem to regard this as an achievement of any importance. Indeed, their principal argument against him, when they deigned to go beyond the fact of who sponsored him, was that he only knew about cities. *Only knew about cities!* Finletter was a man of the capital and the Cold War. Things that mattered. That cities mattered in 1958, and would be *seen* to matter well before a senatorial term would expire, was something simply beyond the comprehension of reformers who nonetheless viewed themselves as primarily concerned with issues in politics and only incidentally with personalities. Anyone who knew anything of New York City in 1958, would have *had* to know that urban problems, and notably that of public safety, would make up much of the agenda of the 1960s. Without conceding more to the regular Democratic leaders than they have claimed for themselves, it seems to me *they* were living in the future, while the "advanced" elements of the party were living in the past and choosing to do so. Finletter represented what they "knew," Hogan, what they did not know, and were not prepared to learn. It ended in the loss of Harriman, a world figure, who could have led New York liberals to genuine national influence of the kind they clearly most wanted. For hour after agonizing hour on the evening of August 26, 1958, the television cameras, stationary in those days, played on an empty platform and half-empty auditorium, broadcasting the news of the deadlock in a hotel room a few blocks away. In the end Hogan was nominated anyway, but while he ran well ahead of most of his running mates, he was defeated in November. Harriman left the convention already defeated, his party a wreck. It is now fourteen years since Democrats have elected a true New Yorker to statewide office, save the controller who was first elected with Harriman in 1954. At one point even the mayor of New York City was Republican. All because of the failure to foresee that there might be a split at the convention, to recognize that urban affairs had a claim on the party, to perceive the disastrous impression that would be made if agreement was not quickly reached. (The impression was that of "bossism," of decisions being made not by the delegates but by a few men hidden in a hotel room far from the convention floor. In reality the decision *had* to be made in a hotel room inasmuch as the Liberal party, by definition not represented in the convention, was nonetheless entitled by usage to participate in the decision. An ironic outcome for a splinter party that began ostensibly to put an end to smoke-filled rooms, but in any event a point too subtle for journalism to convey.) In that I lost my job when the election was lost, the event made an impression.

One gained a not dissimilar impression at this time from a quite different set of events involving the automobile industry. The Harriman years in Albany, 1955–58, were a time of considerable creativity in government. Arthur M. Schlesinger, Jr., not without reason, has referred to his administration as a "little New Deal," and in truth Harriman anticipated and prepared the way for much of the legislation of the Kennedy-Johnson administrations, in the way Smith had done for Roosevelt a generation earlier. Harriman, for example, on the advice of his Industrial Commissioner, Isador Lubin, began the first systematic attention to the problem of poverty in postwar America. Civil rights, under the prodding of Charles Abrams, was made a central issue. A consumer counsel was appointed, an adviser on the aged. Heroin use came under scrutiny, as did problems of juvenile delinquency under the leadership of Mark McCloskey. But very possibly the most important conceptual breakthrough of the administration was in the field of traffic safety. It was just that. Before the Harriman administration the problem was seen in one way; thereafter, in a wholly different way. It was no small problem. (To this day American government has more direct contact with citizens through the management of the motor vehicle transportation system than through any other activity.) But the solution was simplicity itself. Before Harriman it was assumed that the most effective safety activity of government involved efforts to influence the behavior of drivers so as to minimize the consequences to vehicles: i.e., crashes. After Harriman, it was seen that the most effective safety activity of government would be on the first order to influence the behavior of vehicles so that operating them would result in fewer crashes and crashing in them would result in fewer or lesser injuries. That is to say, to regulate and develop the safety features of the car.

A prime lesson was to be learned from this experience: *the crucial stage in solving a problem in government is that point where one defines what kind of problem it is.* Such small homilies will seem anemic to the trained scientist, and perhaps to any professional mind, but the reality is that this perception is not nearly so common in public affairs as it needs to be. The process of careful definition can have a quality of revelation, and the experience becomes all the more intense when it emerges that others cannot or will not follow. This was the case with the automobile industry, and the safety movement then allied to it. Men of considerable position and achievement, whose manifest interest it was to follow the argument, failed to do so. This was not, as is sometimes the case, because the argument was presented in a hostile or threatening manner. To the contrary, as officials formally charged with dealing with the issue in the State of New York, we approached the industry with an air of glad tidings: the problem had been *solved*! But the industry officials could not comprehend. In 1959 I published the first paper stating, in explicit terms, that if the industry did not regulate vehicle design itself, it would end up regulated by the Federal government. This took seven years. (The history is recounted in *Traffic Safety and the Body Politic,* written the year regulation was imposed. My debt to William Haddon, Jr., which began during the Harriman days, will be evident in the article written almost a decade later.) Such near-term events—in this instance, the imposition of Federal safety regulation on motor vehicles in the second half of the twentieth century, much as similar regulation was imposed on steamboats and railroads in the first and second halves, respectively, of the nineteenth century—are not hard to foresee, and yet those with the most interest in seeing them seem quite often to have the most difficulty in doing so.

A similar experience arose when Nathan Glazer and I published *Beyond the Melting Pot* in 1963. The book had been some years in the making and did not pretend to great authority. It began "This is a beginning book." We asserted that ethnicity, race, and religion continued to be major forces in American life and were likely to become more so. It ended: "Religion and race define the next stage in the evolution of the American people." It was not especially well received. Religion and race were supposed to be ending as influences in American life. Here was a tract asserting that they had only just begun.

One began to sense that a price was to be paid even for such mild dissent from conventional liberalism. Having contended that Frank Hogan would make a good senator, that ethnicity persisted, and that race would not quickly go away, having contended that government regulation could not affect driver behavior, one came to be regarded as a person of somewhat questionable belief. If any of these propositions had been genuinely heretical, or had represented a major intellectual achievement, it would be understandable that they might arouse uneasiness and hostility. But they involved no more analytic competence than did the premonition that Oswald might be shot. If it were otherwise, the point would not be worth making. There is a certain amount of genius in the world, and it goes its way, usually where few can follow. But the practice of government involves quite ordinary people of ordinary powers. In most circumstances such powers are adequate to the tasks at hand, given—such is my contention—a simple openness to alternative definitions of problems and a willingness to concede the possibility of events taking a variety of courses. This ought to be the preeminent mode of liberalism, and yet somehow it is not. If my first traumatic encounter with this rigidity was at the New York State Democratic convention of 1958, I grew even more confirmed in the impression at the national Democratic convention of 1960, where I was a member of the New York delegation. I found those who had opposed Hogan now also opposing Kennedy, and with much the same disdain. He was not liberal. His brother was illiberal. His supporters, worse yet, grew uneasy with such persons, the more so when they flocked to Washington after the election to displace the Buckleys, Sharkeys, O'Connells, and Crottys, who had been with Kennedy from the first, who had nominated, and more than any group helped elect him. These may appear to be loose categories, and they are; and yet to anyone who was caught up in these matters, such tendencies are as currents in the ocean, as powerful as they are hidden.

One of the difficulties in writing about such matters of late has been the extraordinarily shifting course which these currents have taken. Left has exchanged positions with right, liberal with conservative. (Consider the puzzlement which must occasionally have overwhelmed Frederic Coudert, Jr., in his last years. As the ultraconservative congressman from the Silk Stocking district of Manhattan's East Side, he had years earlier sponsored legislation which would have required congressional approval before troops could be sent abroad and would have limited the power of the President to initiate foreign wars. "All of these measures," the *New York Times* noted in his obituary in 1972, "were assailed at the time by liberals.") A considerable list could be compiled involving shifts of position by both political tendencies, but quite the most volatile have been those of liberals positioning themselves in ways presumed to be advantageous. In all this I have discerned only one persistent theme: the steady displacement of working-class Democrats, in the main Catholic, from positions of leadership and legitimacy in their party. This is the theme of the first essay in this collection, "Bosses and Reformers," written just after the 1960 Democratic National Convention, and the only one written before 1965. It is the background for many of those that follow. It has seemed to me this is part of a general development in Western democracies where mass-based, egalitarian but culturally conservative parties are being taken over by their "class enemy" and don't know what to make of it. The educated, often wealthy, and invariably affluent heirs-presumptive to a high conservative political tradition in countries such as Britain and America prefer, in sufficient numbers, the more lively politics of the liberal left and in this generation have sought not only to influence but to control the party of that persuasion. The Labour front bench in Britain, as an example, is every bit as much an "old boy" network as anything the Tories could muster. In the whole of the Labour Shadow Government at this moment, there are but two men without university degrees. There was a time, not far back, when half the group would have been coal miners. It has seemed to me this may mark a shift toward culturally rather than economically defined politics; but whatever the case, it has made liberal politics more complex. It has also made it less consistent and at times less honorable: a characteristic, or so it seems, of periods when one class is displacing another and exploiting every advantage that comes to hand. To have served in the past three administrations is to have watched this with pity and terror.

There now remains no question in my mind that the calamities of the Democratic administration-of-all-the-talents in the early 1960s were owing to hubris. I had watched this destiny, if you will, develop in the 1950s from the vantage point of New York State government. That party, then, had more than its share of talent and ambition drawn from the educated and prosperous classes, and to such persons the Eisenhower Administration made government seem easy. The Republicans were "colorless," clearly of moderate intelligence at most, manifestly low on aspirations, and of limited energy. Who could not improve on *their* performance! Liberal journalists agreed. Things were not perhaps so bad, but *think* of how much better things would be with better men in office. The "regular" Democrats were not so sure: if Eisenhower was so incompetent, their instinctive judgment ran, how come he got so many votes? Kennedy probably shared a little of both views, but in his Administration the former predominated. It was scarcely an assembly of men whose style was to allow their abilities to be underestimated. And so they found out the hard way that government is not easy at all, especially if you expect it to be.

The Eisenhower years had led us—for I surely was one—to overestimate our own abilities at government. There was an historical appropriateness to this. One of the military arts, surely, is to induce overconfidence on the other side. One has the impression that Eisenhower occasionally encouraged others to underestimate him. No such influence, however, accounts for the soft state into which liberal doctrine had declined by this time, for it had been declining a long while; and Lionel Trilling had beseeched us, had fair to pleaded, that we pay heed. In the wake of the much too seemingly complete victory of World War II he wrote in his collection of essays, *The Liberal Imagination:*

> In the United States at this time liberalism is not only the dominant but even the sole intellectual tradition. For it is the plain fact that nowadays there are no conservative or reactionary ideas in general circulation.

Trilling saw well enough in 1949 that this condition of seemingly unchallenged hegemony was in fact the primary challenge liberalism faced: a formula for decline. And yet not inevitable.

We cannot very well set about to contrive opponents who will do us the service of forcing us to become more intelligent, who will require us to keep our ideas from becoming stale, habitual, and inert. This we will have to do for ourselves. It has for some time seemed to me that a criticism which has at heart the interests of liberalism might find its most useful work not in confirming liberalism in its sense of general rightness but rather in putting under some degree of pressure the liberal ideas and assumptions of the present time.

This is a role that seemed ever more appropriate following the death of President Kennedy. It was too obvious a need not to have beckoned even before that, but the assassination turned a tendency into a purpose. I do not want to exaggerate this. I swore no oaths; took no vows. But I did become less respectful of caution. I had been right that night at Andrews Air Force Base. Others of vastly greater reputation had chosen to be wrong. I came to feel there *had* been an element of choice at work: a decision not to get involved. There is a fragment of Lippmann which sympathizes with the discretion of public men who judge "It is safer to be wrong before it has become fashionable to be right." I understood that, I think. In any event, no one ever *knows* when he is wrong, and at best has only a feeling about being right. Even so it seemed to me that risk avoidance was just the wrong lesson to learn from so great a loss, and I proceeded, I suppose, with less prudence than before.

This, I see now, was no small thing. "Prudence," Fielding writes, "is indeed the duty which we owe to ourselves, and if we will be so much our own enemies as to neglect it, we are not to wonder if the world is deficient in discharging their duty to us. . . ." When Kennedy died I had said, "I don't suppose there is any point in being Irish if you don't know the world is going to break your heart eventually," and I now proceeded to act out this somewhat maudlin proposition. I asked for and got my share of abuse, although not, I think, for speaking untruth, but rather for speaking of unpleasant things, that most willful form of imprudence. But more was involved than merely willing my own discomfiture, for I passed through this mood at a time when the culture was passing through a sudden and stormy period of leftist radicalism that either rose up from near-forgotten demonic depths, or rained down as the vengeance of heaven, or came God knows from where; but that it came none who lived through the time will ever doubt. It came as a surprise; this is almost the first point about it all. Trilling knew well enough that this was within the range of American political sensibility. He had written brilliantly on the subject as late as 1946 in his novel *The Middle of the Journey,* one of the subjects of the final essay in this collection. Yet three years later it all seemed a thing of the past, an overreaction, perhaps, to the depression of the 1930s, or an epiphenomenon of the curious military alliances of World War II. He had noted the dominance of liberalism in postwar America. Conservative and reactionary impulses he thought still to be at work, although not manifesting themselves in the world of ideas. But he does not even mention leftist views as a present or prospective force. Norman Podhoretz, Nathan Glazer, and others have recorded how widespread this assumption was in those years when the Stalinist cast of literary criticism and intellectual politics seemed finally to have been broken. And then, of a sudden, the 1960s saw it all revive, and with it the curiously impersonal *ad hominem* attacks of that particular political style. We are still much too close to this experience to understand it; indeed, it is by no means necessarily over. The difficulty is implicit in even so commonplace a statement, for I write as of a transient matter, a pathology of the political system. The radicalism of the 1960s deserves far more respect, not least for having rid itself of that enslavement to the national interests of Russia which was the outrageous if pathetic condition of so much of the radicalism of the period 1920–50. Even that statement betrays a condescension not in the least called for. "Rid itself" I write, as if there was a continuity of individuals and organizations. Yet there was some continuity—and for some of the individuals and organizations involved the old attachments seem never really to have been broken—but the overwhelming fact of the radicalism of the 1960s was that it was indigenous. The leftist movements of earlier periods were an immigration phenomenon. This was not. Indeed, typically, it manifested itself in the oldest and most elitist of our institutions rather than otherwise. The president of Yale toyed with it; the president of the AFL-CIO wouldn't touch it. The matter had its origin in a hateful and absurd war. Hateful because of what the war entailed; absurd because of the disproportion between the effort involved and the objective hoped for. Because it was so manifestly liberalism's war—this was the theme of my address to the National Board of Americans for Democratic Action—it was, I suppose, impossible to mount a serious opposition from within liberalism. Conservatism was too inert: too dense to perceive the cunning and wisdom of Eisenhower's remark, let drop in the manner of the rambling Old Soldier, that "When Lee was down in Virginia nobody could touch him, but the minute he got up to Pennsylvania he was in trouble." And so radicalism once again had its day, organizing the political energies of a great cohort of mostly young, and most not especially radical, opponents of the war. Even close up to the experience, as obviously we still are, a certain symmetry with the preceding liberal experience seems evident. The liberals of the first half of the 1960s seriously misread the performance of the conservatives who preceded them. The radicals of the second half of the 1960s just as seriously misread the conduct of the liberals in the 1960s. In each instance—such is my view—the error arose from the interaction of ambition with an historically formed mindset. The liberals wanted to govern—surely an honorable aspiration in a democracy—and they helped to persuade themselves and others that they ought to by invoking endless variations of the central psychological proposition of liberalism, which is that for every problem there is a solution. Well . . . *almost* every problem. It is an activist and somewhat unreflective faith. It seemed to me at the time that the new radicals did not so much want to govern as to impose on society their view of what government was about, and this was merely an extension of their own primal conviction of the historically necessitated corruption and decline of capitalist democracy. They saw Vietnam as a symptom. In the preceding period radical faith had been badly shaken by the seeming success of American society in coming out of the Depression, winning the war, and reestablishing a reasonably decent world order. But now America was seen to be failing again —war abroad, riots at home—and the old faith revived. I hope that friends on the left will not take this to suggest that they have been mere automatons, pronouncing programmed texts. Much less do I wish it to be thought that the objects of radical protest were spurious. The war, certainly, was a hideously real problem; and there was substance aplenty to many of the domestic issues which they raised. Nor were they alone in their preference for extreme explanations of the day-to-day difficulties of democratic government. I recall a luminary of the Johnson Administration reading through a news story about some development in the Justice Department of the time and mumbling that America was becoming a police state. The theme of imminent rightist encroachment on liberties is as much a liberal cliché as it is a radical doctine. But for all this I cannot accept the great debasement of language and the fantasizing of politics that accompanied the reaction to the war. The movement—it was that—involved much larger objectives, and much less attractive ones. The dominant theme was that of democratic decline; and the dominant tactic was to hasten it. Benjamin DeMott is witness to the claim, by "an admired academic political scientist" in 1968, that it was better to be for Nixon than for Humphrey "because as President, Nixon will bring fascism to America sooner." There was, as Arnold Beichman has shown, so much *lying*. And so much of it such poor stuff. *Nach Hitler uns* indeed! The wife of a Harvard colleague has described the incredulity and displeasure with which a young Cambridge historian greeted her unwillingness to accept as a self-evident fact that the Nixon Administration had "ordered" the shootings at Kent State University in May 1970. I was in the White House at that moment, too, desperately telephoning the campus and places near it: Did *anybody* know what was happening? Was there anything we could do? Ordered indeed! And then there was the matter—taken most seriously at about this time—of the Administration planning to cancel the 1972 elections. Such a list could go on to great length, but already it seems part of the past rather than the present. Yet this is not so! The vast decline of language—a fault on all sides—remains with us, and also the calculated use by the left of violence and the threat of violence to silence opposition. In "Nirvana Now" I forecast the onset of nihilism among elite youth—this was 1967—and it has come to pass. Hardly a month passes at Harvard University, for one place, without some outrage: a building "trashed," a professor's house emptied by bomb threats. In the main the authorities respond by evincing ever more intense identification with youth's quest for social justice.

I have not, myself, experienced much of this, but enough to have acquired a considerable contempt both for those who threaten violence and those who countenance it. In the course of the Cambodian crisis in the spring of 1970, while I was in Washington, a student at the Harvard Divinity School announced he was making a bomb to use on my house across the way, while a mob at Soldiers Field was told off for the same purpose. My wife and children went into hiding and the President sent Secret Servicemen to keep an eye on them. (As it turned out, the raiding party got diverted; and the divinity student never did get his bomb going. But they tried.) For the rest, however, it has been verbal assault. A psychology professor writing recently in a journal of some stature related how in the course of a scrap in the mid-1960s it was thought my work had been "demolished and left for dead." "As one of the alleged assassins," he recalled the "self-congratulatory victory celebrations"* among the vaguely frenzied activists with whom he travels. Alas, he continued, it turns out I had not perished. There is something sad in all this. ("One of the alleged assassins," indeed. Oh the fantasy life of academe! Imagine dreaming of being Oswald rather than Kennedy!) Yet it is also serious. The cause of my attempted assassination was a study of family structure prepared for President Johnson which said that trouble was coming in the black slums of the North reflecting conditions of unemployment and poverty that had as much claim on our concern as did the issues of civil rights in the South. If we moved quickly, I argued in the White House at the time, we could turn danger into opportunity. Martin Mayer has described this analysis (correctly, as I now believe) as merely a first approximation concerning a condition that quickly billowed into a genuine social problem. And if I thought the analysis would be a spur to action—as indeed I did—I was simply hopelessly wrong. So there it is: both right and wrong, as I suggested, I hope, in "The Deepening Schism." I was right, to put the barest meaning to the term, in forecasting which way the social statistics would move through the middle and end of the 1960s and into the early 1970s. I believe it fair to say that this was not generally anticipated. A number of the issues that grew out of these developments, e.g., welfare dependency, moved from near obscurity to the center of national politics in an often ugly and divisive way. But I was altogether

* William A. Ryan, *Social Policy*, May/June 1972, p. 54, "Postscript: A Call to Action."

wrong in thinking the issue would be dealt with more wisely and generously if it were understood better. To the contrary, demons without number were loosed on the world.

Walter Miller, in the collection *On Understanding Poverty: Perspectives from the Social Sciences,* has described what happened in terms of the ideology of what he called "The Poverty Movement." He notes the *"elaborate"* care I had taken to avoid "even the tiniest implication" that the poor were in any way to blame for their plight. To the contrary, I had "insisted repeatedly that their plight was an absolutely predictable consequence of prevalent policies of the dominant society—its selfish support of slavery, its racial bigotry, its criminal neglect of the newly urbanized." Alas, he continues, to no avail, for "the merest suggestion that some part of The Problem of the Poor might be attributable to causes other than Power-Structure villainy" was enough to make my name a code word for "grievous heresy."

Now came the time to learn from one's own assassination, however abortive it may have proved. I *had* been prudent that time. Exceedingly prudent. Prudent to the point almost of misstating evidence in order to avoid any implication of blame. This required no great effort. I was surely a liberal and partly a determinist. I didn't *think* anybody was to blame save perhaps political leaders who failed to perceive that here was a problem to be solved. (And even here I had few grounds for complaint. It took from March to June to translate a research paper in the Department of Labor into a major presidential address on the principal domestic issue of the time.) But in the fury that followed I came to sense the limits even of prudence as a charm to ward off misfortune. I had spent much of my adult life working for racial equality, had helped put together the antipoverty program, had set the theme and written the first draft of President Johnson's address at Howard University, which he was to describe as the finest civil rights speech he ever gave, only to find myself suddenly a symbol of reaction. I survived, thanks more than any one thing, to a short story of Sean O'Faolain's and a telephone call from Reinhold Niebuhr, but I emerged changed. I was no longer in thrall to a doctrine I had scarcely been aware of, and I came to view the thralldom of others with a distance and a lack of sympathy that frankly surprised me. I came to feel that American liberalism had created its own version of a *politique du pire;* that preferring the presidential candidate who would most quickly bring "Fascism" and gutting an effort to deal with substance rather than symbol in a matter such as poverty were not unconnected events, but rather manifestations of a general retreat from responsibility.

This seemed to me the logical outcome of a political culture that rewarded the articulation of moral purpose more than the achievement of practical good. It had puzzled me as a young man in city and state politics. Why was it that "regular" congressmen with impressive ADA voting records were nonetheless deemed bad men who had to be destroyed in the name of reform? An errant radical impulse told me this was merely the bourgeois consolidating its gain. It was representatives of working-class culture that usually went to the wall. But I had grown too suspicious of others' theories to embrace any of my own making. I settled for trying to expect neither too little nor too much of the world and to pay attention to work, which in my case is the near-term analysis of issues in American government.

Since Trilling wrote two decades ago, the circumstance of American liberalism has changed. It is no longer the sole intellectual tradition in the land. The left has revived. More importantly, conservative writers and polemicists have begun to make themselves heard and are showing some of the toughness of mind and spirit associated with persons willing to persist in an unpopular cause. Liberalism has produced a certain amount of the internal critique Trilling hoped for, notably in journals such as *Commentary* and *The Public Interest,* where many of the essays in this collection first appeared. But in the main it continues in that most perilous intellectual condition: a safe view professed by a secure majority. Trilling's premonition has come about in the most painful circumstances. Political liberalism ruled unchallenged through the 1960s and was accompanied by a succession of political disasters. In the aftermath those who were then only giving orders find themselves incapable of explaining what went wrong, or even, in instances, of acknowledging that anything did go wrong. It must have been like this along Wall Street in 1931. Surely there was the same suppressed fury that a despised and putatively defeated politician from the theretofore impotent opposition had come along and, to most appearances, restored reasonable order. But then, if liberalism is unable to learn from its own failures, it may be it can learn from the opposition's success, for, at least in his first years in office, Richard Nixon mostly opted for liberal policies, merely clothing them, as David Broder and some others have seen, in conservative rhetoric. A self-indulgent liberalism which pays more heed to words than to reality will miss this point, but it need not do so indefinitely. It can respond to criticism from within, and needs that criticism as much now as ever. Such criticism cannot expect always to be right. Certainly I have not been. But it can be reasoned, it can be civil, and it can impose some test of probable truth, put "some degree of pressure" on "the liberal ideas and assumptions of the present time."

To repeat, the heart of the matter is the process whereby problems come to be perceived and defined. The term "problem" does not of itself denote trouble. I use it in the Greek sense of "anything thrown forward, a question proposed for solution." Webster's *New International Dictionary* (2nd Edition) defines the mathematical usage as "Anything that is required to be done," which is yet more general, and even more my meaning. (That things "required to be done" by government are so widely understood to arise from troubles rather than opportunities is a matter to be dealt with presently.) There is more at issue here than accuracy or elegance of solution. Public affairs invariably involve coercion by the state: a seemingly inescapable condition. But this can be an acceptable and creative process when it is democratic *and* competent, that is to say when those who are to be coerced—who will pay taxes, stop at red lights, go to war—have had some part in the decision, by rules agreed to in advance, *and* when the decision is framed in terms of a reality to be dealt with, and not an imagined or fabricated condition. This goes to the issue of competence, which to my view includes that of honesty, for a competent person does not long permit himself to be deceived or allow himself to be confused. Georges Bernanos captured the essence of this proposition in a lecture given in Geneva in 1946. ". . . The worst, the most corrupting lies," he wrote, ". . . [are] problems poorly stated."* It may be noted

---

* I am indebted to Barbara Burke who dug up the original quotation, slightly misquoted from memory in "Politics As the Art of the Impossible." Bernanos published the lecture in *La Liberté pour quoi faire?* (Paris, 1953.)

that Bernanos was not writing of theological issues but of public ones. His lecture was entitled "L'Esprit européen et le Monde des machines." The impact of technology on civilization: the primary subject of public affairs, and a principal subject of the essays in this collection.

The reader will ask, "How are problems correctly defined?" and the answer, unavoidably, will be tautological. Social scientists are at work developing methodologies that may clear up some of the mysteries. Thus Jay W. Forrester writes that "With a high degree of confidence we can say that intuitive solutions to the problems of complex social systems will be wrong most of the time." A useful caution, and a goad to the further development of nonintuitive solutions. And yet surely it is the experience of science that causal sequences cease to be nonintuitive once they are understood. What will come if we do ever develop a dependable social science is a matter of some mystery. One takes heart that men such as Harold Orlans are not much troubled. He foresees, for example, a time when economists will enjoy about the same social standing as accountants; not because they will be less competent, but rather because their competence will have been filled out, become codified, and made replicable at a level decently below that of genius. But if this is to come, it has not yet. Economists, if anything, seem to grow less certain of their grasp of economic reality, while other social sciences for all their methodological advances are still patchwork affairs. I have seen something of government, have served in capacities from speech writer to Cabinet member, on levels from Manhattan's First Assembly District Middle to the United Nations. I would be hard put to recount a half dozen instances in which "experts" have come forth with confident advice as to the course social or economic policy should take.

Indeed, an increasingly common source of failure in social policy derives not from ignorance as such, but from the failure to recognize and acknowledge it. I have suggested that in this respect it is crucial to distinguish between political problems and knowledge problems in the initial process of definition. Political problems are no more than the term implies: different persons want different things, and cannot always agree. Political problems are solved by aggregating agreement to a certain course of policy until a sufficient preponderance is achieved. Often political problems are mistaken for knowledge problems, as in the familiar formulation of the 1960s that "if we can develop the know-how to get to the moon, we can develop the know-how to save our cities." But the one was a knowledge problem, and the other political. Going to the moon was a goal for which there was near universal political support in the United States. There was no one crucially involved in the operation who did *not* want to go. By contrast, the outcomes intended by the term "saving the cities" are frequently not outcomes which a preponderance of those who will have to cooperate actually desire. (Which is not to say the cities can't be "saved," but only that rescue has often been absurdly defined.) Pondering this, some may just recall that President Kennedy in his special message to the Congress of May 25, 1961, proposing that we go to the moon, also proposed that we go to Vietnam.

An ambitious society such as ours generates a fair number of political problems by continually adding new items to the political agenda which require the assembling of sufficient agreement. Lessons follow from this, of which the first is that a political structure in which it is difficult to aggregate power is not well adapted to clearing a heavy agenda of social issues. Hence, a prime inconsistency of "reform" politics in American cities in recent years has been the tendency to diffuse political power while lengthening the political agenda.

Knowledge problems are of a different order. One resists stating that they are new: what is the history of the world if not ignorance in action? But of late they are different: *increasingly it is possible to know what you don't know*, especially with regard to efforts to change human behavior, an objective which underlies so many of the social initiatives of modern time, from those of the most tolerant liberalism to those of the most intolerant totalitarianism. When the Bolsheviks set out to create the New Soviet Man, they thought they knew how to do so. They didn't. Moreover, it is possible to explain in what way they didn't (indeed Raymond A. Bauer has done so), especially with respect to the ways that institutions such as schools and police do or do not affect conduct. This is what that endlessly revealing problem of automobile safety was about. The problem had been defined as one of driver behavior. But those in charge of the problem implicitly agreed that certain measures with a high probability of actually changing behavior, for example greatly reducing the driving population leaving only cohorts that consistently drive successfully, would create political problems that could not be solved. That is to say, state legislatures would not pass such legislation. On the other hand, devising interventions that would change driver behavior in ways that were politically acceptable presented *knowledge* problems that apparently could not be solved either. Driver education was politically acceptable, but no one knew how to "educate" drivers so that they would drive differently. The same could be said of traffic law enforcement. It made no difference, or not enough. And so it went. (Happily, in the case of traffic safety, there was an alternative solution deriving from an epidemiological, as against behavioral, definition of the problem; but such alternatives are rarely readily at hand.)

In some ways the first emphatic demonstration of this general condition was the study by Andrew Greeley and Peter Rossi, *The Education of American Catholics,* which demonstrated how extraordinarily weak was the effect of parochial school education on religious practices, especially when compared with the influence of family. For a century and a quarter and more American Catholics had maintained at great expense and sacrifice a system of education which apparently did not do the one thing all had assumed it would do. The 1960s saw a succession of such social science findings, so many as virtually to transform the relationship of the social scientist to politically progressive movements. (See "Liberalism and Knowledge.") The Social Science Research Council put the matter thus in its report for 1968–69.

> The difficulty we as a nation face in solving our problems is not will but knowledge. We want to eliminate poverty, crime, drug addiction and abuse; we want to strengthen family life, but we do not know how.

More recently Amitai Etzioni, surely by temperament an optimist in such matters, delivered himself of an avowedly "unjoyful message" on this development and "its implications for social programs."

> We have come of late to the realization that the pace of achievement in domestic programs ranges chiefly from the slow

to the crablike—two steps backward for every one forward—
and the suspicion is growing that there is something basically
wrong with most of these programs. A nagging feeling persists
that maybe something even more basic than the lack of funds or
will is at stake. Consequently, social scientists like myself have
begun to reexamine our core assumption that man can be taught
almost anything and quite readily. We are now confronting the
uncomfortable possibility that human beings are not easily
changed after all.*

To be sure, from an only slightly different vantage point such
a possibility is not at all disconcerting. To the contrary, it is one
of the few circumstances that seem to limit the capacity of a
seemingly ever more manipulative state. In the workaday world
of social policy, however, the most important thing is for policy
makers, from the President down, to know what is not known,
and to have some feeling for the probable accuracy of what is
thought to be known. The malaise of overpromising derives almost wholly, in my experience, from the failure of executives
and legislators to understand what is *risked* when promises are
made. With a more homogeneous people, as for example the
British, the risks are fewer. Governments take chances, hope for
the best, and if things do not work out it is not normal to assume
sinister motives. We are different; an immensely diverse people.
We really don't know one another very well. When things don't
work out as promised it is all too easy to suspect that someone
intended that they should not. (Elsewhere I have recounted a
conversation, circa 1968, with a lady seeking money for a poverty-
related program in a central city area already crowded with equiv-
alents. Told that such programs were already being "funded"
she replied, "But do you notice they only fund programs that
don't succeed?") The point is central to these essays, and bears
repeating, for if I am wrong in this I am right in little else. The
polity must take care what it undertakes to provide, for failure
to do so is likely to be attributed to malevolent purpose.† This is

* Amitai Etzioni, "Human Beings Are Not Very Easy to Change After
All," *Saturday Review*, June 3, 1972.

† Some while after this was written, Philip Abelson made just the same
point with respect to the "excessive confidence in the power of technology" to cope with comparable difficulties. He wrote, there is "great

not to say expectations should not be raised, but only that they should not be raised indiscriminately. Has this not been painfully evident in foreign affairs? The war in Vietnam was begun by men who thought they were defending liberty. When it did not succeed, the war was judged to have been begun as an act of imperialism. John Roche, who served in the White House during those years, has noted how many members of the Johnson Cabinet have come retroactively to denounce in the most savage terms an effort they once deemed to be exalted and honorable. Others saw the war as a conspiracy of the right. Earlier on, in the McCarthy era, the seeming failure of similarly ambitious foreign policy was held to have come about through a conspiracy of the left. The charges are not really different. Social elites, as represented, say, by Ivy League students, tend—such is the political illogic of the time—to regard the right as bad. Working-class and lower-middle-class cadres, such as sustained McCarthy, view the left as evil. In each case the most damaging possible charge was made. And why? Because too much had been attempted, and the society was not cohesive enough to accept failure with calm. (It is possible to conceive of the Vietnam response as *in part* a diversionary effort by the social class that started it. There was, of course, great and genuine opposition to the war within this same social class, and from the beginning; but there was also a need to dissociate itself from failure, and in the face of the egregious behavior of some of those directly involved, it is difficult to discount altogether the simple impulse of self-preservation.) The McCarthy phenomenon was vertical rather than horizontal, which is to say the resentment and suspicion were directed from groups lower in the social hierarchy to groups higher. Even so, there was an element of class defensiveness involved, for it was becoming clear at the time that the American elite was growing increasingly contemptuous of the

---

impatience with the failure of science to solve many social problems, and it is implied that the failure is due to lack of good-will and a proper sense of priorities." One finds, as is not infrequently the case, that Alfred North Whitehead has best joined the technical with the ethical imperative: "Duty arises from our potential control over the course of events." I would merely call attention to the obverse: where no such control is possible, or where it is weak, duty either does not exist, or is conditional.

working-class virtues which had been celebrated in the 1930s and 1940s. (In his 1972 Labor Day statement, George Meany, head of the American labor movement, denounced the Republican President in traditional terms of economic interest, but accused the Democratic candidate of the more grievous fault of representing a political force that held working men in disdain.) The events are not fully comparable, but *something* of this kind was involved, and much the same is true of domestic initiatives which have ended ingloriously or, as is most often the case, merely indeterminately. Accusations and suspicions follow which the society can do without. To take this as an argument for doing less, rather than simply for promising less, is a mark of disingenuousness or inexperience, or both. It is merely an argument for competence.

Maurice Cranston, in his 1971 inaugural lecture at the London School of Economics and Political Science, offered a definition of politics that clarifies a matter normally subject to much confusion. Politics, he observed, is first of all "an argument about values between men who agree about some values but disagree about others." Second, politics is *"an argument about the future, or, more narrowly, about the future consequences of proposed lines of action."* (My emphasis.) One can discern in this partitioning an essential element of the liberal-conservative dichotomy. There are, perhaps, few writers who have not at one or another time heartily wished to be rid of these designations. They are at times surpassingly fuzzy. And yet the categories do help to sort out experience. There is, surely, a disposition among "liberals" to be concerned with values, and a corresponding tendency among "conservatives" to think about consequences. There is *also*, just as surely, a tendency for events to force a successful liberalism to pay more heed to experience. It is this, I contend, and not some hardening of the moral arteries, that gives a seemingly conservative cast to the thinking of persons who have been much in government. This is the perspective in which I hope these essays may be seen. They concern the practice of government, which is to say that point in the political cycle when the matter at issue is less what *should* happen than what *will*. Persons in perfect accord on values may differ profoundly in their estimate of how matters will go. Differences on the latter point tend to be greatest as between those of little experience and those of much. There is obviously such a thing as too little experience, and doubtless there can be such a thing as too much, but on balance experience is instructive and directs one's thoughts as much to what may go wrong as to what may go right. This judgment in turn depends on an assessment of the knowledge and the determination that will be applied to achieving a given goal.

To sense what can or cannot be done in terms of the state of knowledge or the possibility of collecting sufficient support is only a form of foresight. Not vision: nothing so grand as that. Merely a certain talent for sensing what is up ahead, and the discipline to keep the matter in mind amidst the great distractions —and, for those in power, the considerable pleasures—of the moment. It, too, is a form of prudence, the pride of Aristotelian virtues, nicely stated in Alfred E. Smith's maxim: "Never promise anything you can't deliver." Intelligent observers can with effort acquire a sense of how political issues of the moment will work themselves out: the limits, the probabilities. A corollary exercise seeks to form a judgment as to which relatively quiescent situations of the moment are likely to become political issues of the near future. It is no great feat. In a chess master it involves considerable intellectual elegance, but politics is mostly checkers. It is no great thing to estimate the various possibilities for the next move but one.

The essays in this volume attempt to do just this with respect to a number of issues of the present and the recent past. They will have, I hope, some intrinsic interest as the issues dealt with are still unresolved, or ill-defined, or in some cases not as yet even widely perceived. But I present them in the main to suggest that there is some method in this particular form of madness, which is to say the description of innate difficulty, and the likelihood of small or incomplete success in virtuous undertakings. A writer takes no great risk in bearing bad news *if* he can connect it up with bad men. To the contrary, this is a near-certain formula for success. But it is just that: a formula, and more often than not a means for avoidance of reality in the guise of raw confrontation. The risk comes with getting to the heart of a matter and discovering, not wrongdoing—with its ever-present prospect of repentance—but rather ambiguity and irony. This threatens what little sense of mastery we may have hoarded up against a foretold fate. But, perhaps more seriously, such findings, when they assume the status of a generalized expectation, tend to deprive politics of its moments of moral exaltation, and there are few other spheres of life in which such exaltation can any longer be had. There is only one political poem of the twentieth century I consider worth remembering, and that is Yeats's "Parnell."

> Parnell came down the road, he said to a cheering man:
> "Ireland shall get her freedom and you still break stone."

There it is, but who save a poet who has been a senator will say so? This is the knowledge life gives us, and it is indispensable to politics. And yet how alien to it. How irredeemable. Such an understanding can sometimes win respect, but it has virtually no power to inspire. Think of that stirring passage from Kennedy's inaugural address:

> Let every nation know, whether it wishes us well or ill, that we shall pay any price, bear any burden, meet any hardship, support any friend, oppose any foe, to assure the survival and success of liberty.

Supposing he had said:

> Things are complicated over here, not least because we are a liberty-loving people and allow one another a very great deal of it. This limits what a prudent government will try to do to protect the liberty of other peoples. We do not like totalitarianism, especially when it is Communist, the only kind that is currently expansionist, and we will be disposed to resist its expansion: this most assuredly when it threatens us directly, and just possibly when it does so indirectly and we can act by indirect means. But open warfare even on a "limited" scale is another matter. If there is a warlike tradition in American history, there is also, and this is the more unusual fact, an antiwar tradition. Nothing so much animates this sentiment as the spectacle of a great power seeking to crush a small one, and no matter what the facts, this will be the appearance if the United States openly involves itself in such a "limited war" against expansion on the Communist periphery, a war which our traditions of liberty will ensure is fully covered by television, which will seek out that

which is most characteristic in war, brutality and death. This in turn will arouse a yet more potent American fury at the spectacle of force seeking to crush ideology, and in this instance that fury will be turned on the American government itself. No President will be able to explain why the nation is involved with killing poor peoples in a faraway land of which we know little. There is, further, the possibility that we may not be able to achieve our military and political objectives quickly save by escalation, which forfeits the object of limited war. This introduces the prospect of prolonged public anger transmuting itself into permanent alienation. Moreover, while there is a social-democratic tradition on the American left which is persistingly anti-Communist, accounting in some measure for the energy the American labor movement displays in such matters, there is also, especially among intellectuals, a Marxist-Stalinist element which is dormant now but is certain to be aroused by such a war to all its dreary, manipulative rage. The vast proportion of Americans, including the vast proportion of those who will hate the war, have nothing whatever to do with this element. Most Americans, including my Vice President, are hardly aware that it exists; and those who once did have mostly forgotten; but I keep in touch with intellectuals, and I have not forgotten. On university campuses the question of the war will be raised to a moral issue, for indeed it will be a moral issue. This happened in Oxford and Cambridge in the 1930s, a period I have studied. Dissent, which is an exercise of liberty, will billow, fed by motives ranging from stark ambition to unsullied instances of moral witness. The police powers will begin, tentatively, to be employed against the dissenters where seeming violations of law occur, and there will be much dissembling, bad faith, and bumbling on both sides. The country will become increasingly difficult to govern. Institutions will be drained of authority, and will begin to change character. One of the first upheavals will be within the Democratic Party itself, the present character of which I happen to value for reasons both obvious and perhaps not so obvious.* Hence in the effort to secure the liberties of others we could well end up impairing our ability to defend our own. So let every nation know that we would be crazy to undertake to pay any price, bear any burden, meet any hardship, support any

---

* This hypothetical John F. Kennedy would surely have been distressed, could he have known that only twelve years hence his name would not even be mentioned in the acceptance speech of the Democratic nominee for President.

friend, oppose any foe to assure the survival and success of liberty. This will be especially so in countries which we haven't dealt with much, and which cannot be conceived of as doing as much on our behalf if we were to find ourselves similarly threatened. Small countries attacked by big countries should go to the United Nations. When that fails they should try to get the best terms they can. The more the Communist hegemonies expand, absorbing dissident nationalisms, the more internal trouble they will have, and they are welcome to it.

No, there would have been nothing inspiring in this.

There might also have been no Vietnam. Men such as Harold Macmillan foretold for Kennedy much of the trouble that would come. And so there is something to be said for the prudential mode, including, again, a passing reference to the fact that it is not always as safe as it might seem. I came late to opposition to the war: 1966–67, thereabouts. Friends such as David Riesman and Nathan Glazer were onto the issue as early as 1962: they could see ahead. But to do so at the time was to invite scorn, even vilification—I do not exaggerate—in the Washington of the early to mid-1960s. For to foresee certain kinds of trouble is bad news indeed. It involves a larger risk than most men with anything to lose are willing to take. To have been much in government is to know this for a fundamental limitation on the possibilities of politics. The men who did not want to know about what might happen to Oswald, who did not want to know that the makings of an enduring conspiracy theory were at hand, had reasons for not wanting to know. One got in real trouble that way. Not pretend trouble. Not the trouble of defying the Establishment, of daring to be different, of challenging the interests. Almost always such postures are transparently docile: the kind one encounters among professors who have never in their lives deviated five degrees from the views of their colleagues, but who collectively contrive to see themselves as nonconformists. Real trouble is different. To be seriously suspected, genuinely disliked, is different. There are good reasons to avoid it.

The essays in this volume deal with issues of lesser prominence, but they also would have profited, and will profit, from comparable efforts at forehandedness. Almost all have moved up on the political agenda and have become national issues, subject to national legislation. Thus by a narrow margin the Senate in

August 1972 voted to sidetrack a bill to set up a national no-fault system of automobile insurance, but the issue will be back in the next Congress. Automobile manufacturers recall defective models and wonder what happened to a once proud reputation. "Bosses" and "reformers" tear at one another in the Democratic Party, still uncomprehending of the lessons of the 1950s. The onset of nihilism among the youth of the educated elite which seemed inevitable in 1967 has come and may now be somewhat receding. Even so, the International Association of Chiefs of Police reports that 1971 was the worst year in the United States history for domestic bombings. (The bombers would say it was also the worst for overseas bombing, and they would also be right.) In 1971 a study at the Institute for Social Research of the University of Michigan found "over 65 percent of . . . men questioned mentioned some form of violence when asked about the things in this country which 'nowadays concerned them.' " Their anxiety was not directed to the issue of crime nearly so much as to the forms of civil disorder and protest discussed in "Nirvana Now." Similarly, the education of the urban poor has moved to the center of national politics, and on the worst possible terms, those of busing, a divisive form of compensatory education. Sides are being taken on the general subject with ever greater passion, but seemingly none of it informed by knowledge that has been available to us for almost a decade. Theodore R. Sizer, former Dean of the Harvard Graduate School of Education, speaks of the "persistent unwillingness [of the education profession] to face the implications of recent research." The plain fact, he continues, is that "American education in 1972 *is* afraid." This need not have been the case if only enough men and women of competence and fortitude had tried to face up to the facts concerning the nature of the education process that began to be evident in the mid-1960s.

Indeed, the presidential election of 1972 has become almost an object lesson in the cost to both parties and to the polity of such slackness. Charges concerning welfare, busing, quotas, income redistribution, and the like, are hurled back and forth between inexcusably ignorant armies. Both sides, mostly, have their facts wrong. Both sides, mostly, appear just this moment to have discovered issues that have been in the making for most of the previous decade and about which a good deal of reasonably confident knowledge *is* available. Until recently the electorate has responded to blowsy argument mostly by not paying attention. But this may change, and the time may be coming when candidates find themselves losing votes rather than attention when they garble an issue beyond the point of happenstance. In the present election this appears already to have happened to the Democratic candidate as a consequence of his confusing proposals for income redistribution and welfare reform. The plain fact is that these issues have been looming ever larger for at least the past four years, and no one, or no one of consequence, in the Democratic Party has taken the trouble to learn enough about them to present an intelligent and persuasive case. The voters are entitled to impose a cost on what is in effect misconduct. (This is scarcely to suggest that anything like a permanent "Republican majority" is in the offing. To the contrary. The Republicans cannot govern on a sustained basis in America. They simply do not have the intellectual or moral basis on which to build consensus. It can sometimes do what has to be done, and even on occasion improve on liberal performance, but it has never, as Gertrude Himmelfarb has remarked, been able to internalize the ethic of modern liberal government. It does what it does because it has to, and its periods in office have been and are likely to continue to be little more than interludes brought on by Democratic internal dissidence.)

The failure to face the clearly emerging issue of group rights in that period may be more excusable, but in the end it is likely to prove even more costly. It was clear years ago that a wrenching dilemma was in the making. In the summer of 1964, months following the passage of the Civil Rights Act on which the current "quota" directives of the Federal government are based, I raised the subject in a review of a study by Lucy S. Dawidowicz and Leon J. Goldstein, sponsored by the Institute of Human Relations of the American Jewish Committee. Their discussion of group political behavior led directly to the larger question of group status. I concluded:

> The most perplexing problem . . . is that of group rights. Groups do not *have* rights in America; only individuals do. But

groups have interests, have problems, have identities, and ought to have responsibilities.* Mrs. Dawidowicz and Mr. Goldstein observe that "the predominant political philosophy of the English-speaking countries is individualistic and rationalistic; it understands how individuals can act in their own interest, but is not able to deal with the impact of groups and group traditions." In accordance with this tradition, the best we have been able to do is prohibit discrimination against an individual because of membership in a group. It may be there is no need to go further; it may even be that much harm is to be had from going further. On the other hand, group rights certainly precede individual rights in human history, and perhaps the relation between them is not antagonistic or mutually exclusive. Perhaps there is a sequential relationship: until a people has obtained the strength that comes from collective rights, individual prerogatives will not be able to take its members very far. The relevance of this problem to our present situation is only too obvious; and if we do not cope with it properly, it will end by tearing us apart.

Eight years later we are certainly in the midst of a crisis with respect to government-imposed racial, ethnic, and sex quotas on university faculties and other real or asserted realms of meritocracy. In the spring of 1972 representatives of the major Jewish organizations of the nation met with the Secretary of Health, Education, and Welfare to discuss the issue. In August 1972 the American Jewish Committee obtained statements from the Democratic and Republican presidential candidates opposing "quotas." (An action promptly denounced by the chairman of the Congressional Black Caucus as "high-handed at best and racist at worst.") Across the land university faculties are discovering that government bureaucracy really does have the power to coerce and increasingly faculties act just so: as if *coerced*. "The New Racialism" was delivered as the Commencement Address at the New School for Social Research in 1968 and published in the *Atlantic Monthly*. By then it seemed inevitable that we were heading for a needless and sharply divisive clash between just those groups most concerned with social equality, and that it could only be prevented by confronting this potential then and there. This was not done. Four years later,

* I suppose I would not write today that "groups ought to have responsibilities." I just don't know.

Trilling himself in the first Jefferson Lecture in the Humanities, sponsored by The National Endowment for the Humanities, raised the subject in terms that suggest how far the matter already has gone.

> [T]here will be serious consequences for the academic profession if it is required to surrender an essential element of its best sense of itself, its belief that no considerations extraneous to those of professional excellence should bear upon the selection of its personnel. These consequences, we must know, will be felt not alone within the academic community but within the cultural life of our society as a whole, not least that part of it to which the excluded groups will themselves look for cultural sustenance.
>
> This issue I do not mean to debate, my point being only that the academic profession does not debate it. The profession must have noted that, by way of justifying the drastic sanctions which are being invoked against it, its traditional standards have been explicitly and as it were officially impugned, actually charged with being exclusionary or discriminatory. Surely it says much about the status of mind in our society that the profession which is consecrated to its protection and furtherance stands silent under this assault, as if divested of all right to use the powers of mind in its own defense.*

To which I would only add that the powers of mind include that of minimal understanding of what is inescapably ahead. Here was the Nation, or at least the Federal government, embarked on an effort to increase minority employment. Handled with sensitivity and foresight, a permanent improvement in our social condition was at hand. It took no great powers to see, however, that, pressed to the point of quotas, a harsh reaction was almost certain, from which the social loss would be considerable. "No Jews, White Males Need Apply" runs the headline in *The Village Voice,* while the ambivalence of the accompanying story attests once again to the failure of foresight.

Most of these essays are concerned with trouble, and a reader might conclude that these were unusually troubled times. I sup-

---

* Lionel Trilling, "Mind and the Modern World," The Jefferson Lecture in the Humanities, Washington, D.C., April 26, 1972. Mimeographed, pp. 24–25.

pose this is so. But are there any untroubled times? In retrospect some appear less disturbed than others, but this is rarely perceived at the time. Already it is common to refer to the 1950s as a *belle époque,* although living through that decade one was made to feel the Fascists would be taking over any moment. Even Trilling, in 1949, hedged. Conservatives and reactionaries might be "bankrupt of ideas," he notes, but that did not mean they were at the end of their powers.

> [I]t is dangerous for us to suppose it is so, as the experience of Europe in the last quarter-century suggests, for in the modern situation it is just when a movement despairs of having ideas that it turns to force, which it masks in ideology.

(A thought: could it be *this* that happened to radicalism on American campuses?) The more important point is that the work of democratic government is routinely concerned with matters defined as troubles. In "The Presidency and the Press" I make the point, familiar to anyone who has flown about the world much, that the best quick test of the political nature of a regime is to read the local papers on arrival. If they are filled with bad news, you have landed in a libertarian society of some sort. If, on the other hand, the press is filled with good news, it is a fair bet that the jails will be filled with good men.

There is a difference between forecasting trouble and prophesying doom. There has of late been a goodly share of such prophesying, but it has seemed to me suspect in its origin. Twenty years ago Robert Warshow wrote that "So much of 'official' American culture has been cheaply optimistic that we are likely almost by reflex to take pessimism as a measure of seriousness." In Warshow's context "we" meant for the most part a New York cultural elite primarily involved with literature, but caught up also in politics, especially as these involved the interpretation of texts. Harmless pursuits in the hands of qualified persons. The difficulty began when the elite style diffused, downwards and outwards, as is the American custom. A generation later the cheap optimism of Warshow's age had been replaced by a not less commonplace despair, generated in the first instance by the war, and perhaps justified by it; but still much too generalized. Established institutions insisted upon it. Fashionable university presidents, forward-looking churchmen, prestigious columnists reveled in it. It had become the mark of the middling mind. To be sure, there is an element of class aggression in such assertions. The politics of our time are not always easily explainable in terms of traditional class economic interests, but they are not very far removed from the traditional struggle over who is to rule. Norman Podhoretz has done us all a service by pointing to the unvarying political content of the proclamation of impending doom. The person making such a statement is asking that power someone else has be given to him or to her. In the United States at this time such persons are commonly members of social elites: wealthier, better educated, better off, than those whose power (real or imagined) they desire. It is understandable that such persons don't always see it this way, but equally understandable that others should. (In *Commonweal,* Michael Novak writes, "radical politics is so much the province of the affluent and the educated . . . that it fairly reeks of class bias.")* It is a bias against "middle America." It affects an extraordinary attachment to the dispossessed but, as Glazer and I have contended, this attachment is in essence tactical. From first to last the issue, in Richard F. Schier's formulation, has been "Power to the (Best) People."

There is a cost to ignoring such issues, uncomfortable as it may be to raise them. In 1970, toward the end of his life, so unhappily cut short, Richard Hofstadter described the 1960s as "The Age of Rubbish." A man of the democratic left, he was depressed by the rise of a vulgar—but "irresistibly chic"— radicalism among the well-educated and well-to-do. He found "Almost the entire intellectual community . . . lost in dissent." There was almost no dialogue left "between those who are alienated from society and those who are prepared to make an intelligent defense of it." One can agree with Trilling that "it is not conducive to the real strength of liberalism that it should occupy the intellectual field alone," while agreeing equally with Hofstadter's implication, that a liberalism Finland-ized by an elite left is likely also to be weakened. The posture of disdain is not unknown among those who would call attention to their status.

* Michael Novak, "The Ethnic Democratic Caucus," *Commonweal,* June 30, 1972.

I do not wish to be understood as dismissing out of hand the protests and alarms of recent years. They have concerned issues that did indeed cry out for attention, issues involving the most real and present dangers. And yet there remains the question of manner and purpose.

A generation ago Schumpeter described the mind-set of a type of intellectual endemic to bourgeois democracy which avoids having to acknowledge any evidence that the society has successfully undertaken and achieved certain objectives, by dismissing the objectives as trivial: "A sneer will serve as well as a refutation. . . ." It sometimes seems we have gone beyond this to the point where evidence is not so much trivialized as politicized. Facts become a kind of code which, seeming innocuous to the uninformed, reveal sinister realities to the initiated. In 1970, still in government, I came upon the rumor, widespread, and by every indication widely believed, on campuses (and in publishing houses!) that the Administration was intent on canceling the 1972 presidential election, and that even then the Rand Corporation was at work on a "game plan." It was no small matter at the time, involving the more prestigious "underground" press and seriously entertained at surprising levels of society. In a series of addresses, I tried to counter the rumor only to find that nothing so much confirmed the "truth" of the matter to those who wished to believe it as evidence assembled to argue its untruth. *Why else* would such evidence be assembled? Erving Goffman has taught us to appreciate the delicate balance between normalcy and lunacy in the perception of events, and such outbreaks are to be expected. Still, the apocalyptic style of recent politics has been costly. It wears out its welcome. Already one can sense the Nation turning away from important matters which it was patiently and on the whole successfully working at. If nothing is ever achieved, what then is the point of trying?

This is the danger of writing only, or mainly, about troubles. I present these essays as examples of near-term analysis of an everyday, feasible sort in the practice of government. They pretend to no larger achievement, and will not, I hope, be much faulted for failing in what they have not undertaken. Yet there is a failing, and a serious one. Success is too little acknowledged. Here and there it is suggested that things could be worse, or that they will get better; but precious little that approaches celebration will be found in these pages. And yet how much the Nation deserves praise, and how much it needs it! To recognize and acknowledge success, however modest, is fundamental to the practice of government. It is a first principle of leadership in a democracy, where loyalty must be directed more to institutions than to individuals. One is hard pressed to explain why this should be so, but surely it is. Robert C. Tucker notes that charismatic leadership derives in considerable measure from the ability to "accentuate the sense of being in a desperate predicament." This is rarely a climate in which liberties flourish. It perhaps accounts for the unease with which many view the relentless emphasis on social failure and corruption that characterizes the New Politics. It too readily follows that a system that could tolerate so much wrong, must itself be wrong. In any event, it is no way to summon the social energies that are needed to set things right. Albert O. Hirschman has shown how in underdeveloped countries a major barrier to progress can be the failure to perceive it when it does occur.

> [W]hen there are special difficulties in perceiving ongoing change, many opportunities for accelerating that change and taking advantage of newly arising openings for change will surely be missed. The obstacles to the perception of change thus turn into an important obstacle to change itself.*

"Developed" nations are not exempt from this rule. Our resources may be greater, but there is a limit to them also. A speculative point: if economic resources tend to grow at geometric rates—"the miracle of compound interest"—political resources advance in arithmetic progression, if at all. (Anyone who has been much involved in international matters will report this. Representatives of the weakest nations are rarely the weakest negotiators.) Consider, as one example, how much more easily we might now be dealing with the issue of school busing to achieve racial balance if there had just been a *little* notice that in late

* Albert O. Hirschman, *A Bias for Hope*, New Haven, Yale University Press, 1971, p. 337.

August and early September 1970 the dual school system of the South, virtually intact fourteen years after the Supreme Court decision in *Brown,* all but disappeared in the space of three weeks.

This success has been so little noticed that it is probably necessary to expand on the point. In the fall of 1968 something like six out of seven students in the South entered schools which were not only racially "imbalanced," but were units of separate, *de jure,* dual school systems. There was by then a cumulation of court decisions and administrative rulings prohibiting such arrangements, but the arrangements persisted. In the next two years a number of forces were set in motion—deliberately—such that when school opened in the fall of 1970 the dual school system virtually disappeared. The Department of Health, Education, and Welfare was able to report that for the school year 1970–71 the schools of the South were more integrated than those of the North. It could well be argued, and has been, that more change took place in the American public school system in those few weeks than in the preceding century. Yet relatively little notice was taken. A not uncommon political situation prevailed. The Administration in office, which had worked to bring about the end of the dual school system, did not especially want to take "credit" for it, while its opposition did not in the least want to give it "credit." The result is that a true achievement, the resolution of almost two decades of strife which at one point had involved that most ominous event, the use of the military to maintain civil order, passed all but unacknowledged. An immense stride toward a unified society, which had taken place without a single gun pointed at a single person, wholly without epithet, and practically without protest, was lost as a symbol of what the Nation is capable of achieving. Almost immediately thereafter, the issue of school busing arose in Northern cities. If *only* it had done so in the context of a widely acknowledged success in the South, might not public attitudes have been different? If Mississippi had risen to its responsibilities, surely Michigan could and would. And so would the national government. That order of argument. And yet no such argument was made. Not least, or so it would seem, because those who might have made it had denied the achievement in the South and, in so doing, grievously diminished their prospects for success in the North. This was a loss.

It is something of a loss also that so few seem able to perceive that the "urban crisis," the subject of many of the essays that follow, has considerably eased. As the 1960s came to a close, mass urban violence seemed to have become endemic. Something like mass hysteria on the subject was epidemic. And yet here we are with the memory of those years already fading. Mayor Kevin H. White of Boston appeared at the Democratic platform hearings to declare himself "startled, disappointed, and angry" that neither Senator George McGovern nor Senator Hubert H. Humphrey even mentioned the need of cities in their television debate at the outset of the California primary contest. Mayor John V. Lindsay of New York deplored the fact that in the three speeches climaxing the Democratic National Convention that year, including those of the nominees for President and Vice President, "there was no mention of the cities or of the central problem of the country domestically, which is urban America, by any one of them." One may sympathize with the mayors. Things aren't *that* much improved. On the other hand, things were never quite as *bad* as they were depicted when the mayors and their crisis were the center of attention. This, too, bears on the subject of success. When situations of considerable but not impossible difficulty are described in apocalyptic terms, responses tend to be erratic, even convulsive, and even if, by fortune or design, the difficulties lessen, there is no vocabulary at hand by which to describe such incremental change. Any number of forces combine to encourage the apocalyptic view, starting with the fact that it sells newspapers and absorbs TV audiences. (Capitalism has never hesitated to make money by prophesying, or proclaiming, its demise.) A politician of the late 1960s who dared suggest that urban conditions were not in fact out of hand, were deteriorating in certain respects but improving in others, would have been despised as well as defeated. This is perhaps a normal condition of politics, but it was, in this instance, passionately reinforced by the generality of academic comment. The collections of readings which professors assemble and publish for use in general-purpose courses are a reliable index of general academic opinion, given a time lag of two to three years which publication usually requires.

I find myself glancing through a recent arrival entitled *Metropolis in Crisis*. An introductory section sets the tone with articles such as:

> *An Unending Chain of Crises*
>
> *The Nation's Response to the Crises of the Cities Has Been Perilously Inadequate*
>
> *Confrontation between Poor and Affluent Is Explosive . . . It Must Be Resolved*
>
> *It Is Too Late in Our History to Restore Order or Reestablish Authority*
>
> *To Each Generation It Has Always Seemed That It Really Can't Happen Here — I Think It Can*

The articles are notable in that each was written by a person of avowedly Republican politics, two of them members of the Nixon Administration. By the late 1960s the apocalyptic assertion was practically universal.

It happens I became Assistant to the President for Urban Affairs (the first, and I should imagine, the last person to hold such a position) at about the time this rhetoric peaked. It had all but traumatized the Johnson Administration in its last years. The men in the White House, decent, competent and well-meaning, had nonetheless ended up dazed and indecisive. Hoist on their own petard is, for once, no bad image. In response to the rhetoric and appearance of crisis, they had, for example, established the Kerner Commission (The National Advisory Commission on Civil Disorders) in the summer of 1967. Within a year the Commission came back with such a stark assertion of imminent disaster that the President judged he could not even accept the report of his own Commission. And this only seemed to confirm the thrust of the Commission report! This was the condition the new Administration inherited in the aftermath of the presidential election of 1968. Four years later, the subject has all but disappeared from the pronouncements either of the White House or of political leaders aspiring to it. Allowing for the problem of attention span, there would seem little doubt that the main reason for this is that the urban riots of the 1960s ceased. These had been the symbol and the substance of the perceived crisis. When the riots went the rhetoric of crisis at least diminished. When and if they return, so, presumably, will that perception of crisis; but for the moment it would seem to have passed. Without asserting any final judgment on events that are still too close for comfort, some points on the question of coping can be noted. The first is that neither the national government nor any state or urban government knew enough, or had the resources, political and otherwise, to attempt any definitive response. It was from first to last a matter of dealing with near-term probabilities as best one could. A second point is that events occurred on their own; they were not in any significant sense the consequence of policy. On the other hand, the crucial role of policy was to facilitate what was going to happen, or in any event, to try not to prevent it. In this the role of analysis was fundamental.

The analysis—it was my analysis, obviously, and is of interest primarily because it was a basis of government policy in a brief but intense period—began with the assertion that the situation was not as abnormal as was generally thought. The Kerner Commission report depicted a situation of impacted crisis that would only worsen. Given the times, it was easy enough to accept this argument. Indeed, it seemed illiberal and mean-spirited *not* to. And yet the argument was wrong. To begin with, the situation was *not* without precedent. To know this it was helpful to have been around during the Harlem riot of 1943, or, more importantly, to have read Harold Orlansky's (now Orlans) study of the event published that year by the Social Analysis group.* Social Analysis was a group of young scholars, with mentors such as Selig Harris, that hoped "to apply the techniques of social anthropology to studies of the contemporary American scene." Their first project was the riot that had occurred near to their base at the City College of New York. On his own, with no research support, no assistants, Orlans produced an incisive account of the event (29 pages, 25 cents) in terms of the frustration-aggression hypothesis. He anticipated, idea for idea, fact for fact, the multimillion-dollar product that appeared a quarter century later. To read Orlans in the later context was to see that not much had changed, neither in social

---

* Harold Orlansky, *The Harlem Riot, A Study in Mass Frustration*, Social Analysis, Report No. 1, New York, 1943.

analysis, nor in the rhythms of urban life. The one difference was that while the Social Analysis group was on the political left, Orlans' assessment of the situation was essentially calm. He hoped for continued pressure for social justice, but he anticipated no social holocaust, and he was right.

There were grounds, then, for assuming that none would follow the events of the 1960s, or rather that the seemingly ever-mounting incidence of violence would not continue. This hypothesis was strengthened by contemporary evidence. The Kerner Commission had depicted a society moving toward irreconcilable division along racial lines. The Commission report was published in March. Four months later, in a volume entitled "Supplemental Studies," the Commission published its evidence, or at least the bulk of it consisting of a study, "Racial Attitudes in Fifteen American Cities," carried out at the Survey Research Center of the University of Michigan. Lo and behold, the polarization was not there! The research, even though preliminary, simply did not detect the movement the Commission had proclaimed. (One of the researchers later observed that wherever the Commission got its information, it certainly did not do so from data.) There was racial feeling aplenty in the cities studied, but clearly the strongest tides were running in the direction of a nonracially demarcated society. Nor did continued violence appear inevitable. This view was strengthened by a study of the 1967 outbreak in Detroit carried out by Elliot Luby which depicted such violence as essentially aversive behavior. Those involved would not wish to become reinvolved. In epidemiological terms—for the violence had an epidemic quality to it—the event was autoimmunizing. This was an impression easily enough gathered in Detroit in the summer of 1967, but Luby brought to the question a psychiatric perspective that was all the more persuasive.

This was perhaps not much information on which to base a national policy, but it was good information; and the decision process was not obstructed by *mis*information. Given what was known, the policy implication was obvious. Strategy would be based on the assumption—a bet, no more—that mass violence would trend downward of its own accord. A simple-seeming statement, but almost the opposite of the standard wisdom of the time, which is to say the winter of 1968–69. Tactics followed from strategy. As little as possible should be done to reward violence, and as much as possible to discourage it. This may also seem a simple statement, but it involved rather complex judgments as to who had benefited from violence and how to minimize such benefits. It was clear, for example, that by the end of 1968 the Federal government had got into the bad habit of letting itself be threatened with urban violence, in many instances actually inducing the threats, and, generally speaking, rewarding them. The White House would receive half a dozen emergency telephone calls a day from cities across the land reporting that if such-and-such a grant, concession, appointment, or whatever was not immediately forthcoming, the city in question would "blow." As a matter of policy the callers were now told that this was too bad, but that given the emergency conditions of the time resources could only be applied to situations where some hope remained and that a situation as advanced as that of the city in question was obviously hopeless. Accordingly, the grant, the concession, the appointment was to be considered out of the question. A kind of urban *triage* was developed. Cities which by their own report were mortally wounded were told they would be left on the field to die. By spring remarkable recoveries were being reported, which is not to be arch, but simply to record the plain fact that while the Federal government cannot always, or even frequently, control events, it can control the terms on which it negotiates. A corollary of this principle is that government must abide by the outcome of negotiations, even those conducted under previous, unfavorable circumstances. The 1960s had given rise to a jumble of social programs, some of which were direct responses to violence, others of which came to be perceived as such. (The antipoverty program was the most important of the latter.) Some of the programs were evident successes: many were not. A new Administration would have been within its right to clean house. Yet to have done so would have been unsupportable in the circumstances. The programs had created a *nouveau bourgeois*. To terminate the programs would have been to declass a whole cadre of persons, many of whom, for the first time in their lives, had something to lose. They had won their new status in the context of real or threatened violence. Faced with the prospect of losing it, they would inevitably seek the restoration of violence, which for the first time would be induced and not spontaneous, a wholly different situation. And so the Great Society programs were continued by the first Nixon Administration. Funding levels were maintained, or increased; in truth a sharp increase in domestic spending followed. Happily, however, through most of 1969 the press was filled with reports of such programs being closed down, cut back, or sabotaged. Most of these reports were untrue, but almost certainly they were believed by some who hoped this would happen, and also by some who feared it would. This eased the political pressure on the Administration from its own supporters, and may well have imposed a certain sobriety on the new bureaucracies scattered across the nation.

For the rest it was a matter of coming forward with Administration proposals new enough and impressive enough to reassure the "liberal audience," which, as James Q. Wilson notes, had rather approved of the violence and certainly saw it as a stimulus to desirable social change. This is a close point. It may at first have been true, but by 1969 it seemed no longer true. For what it is worth, my judgment was that the rhetoric of violence—and the reality—had already overreached itself and that this had begun to move politics in a conservative direction that would take a decade or so to run *its* course. Inevitably the last groups to recognize such changes would be those who perceived themselves as having benefited from violence or who, in a general way, approved it. These groups had to be dealt with, with as much sensitivity as any other. It was important that no one see the decline of violence as a loss. This was at least one consideration that led to the proposal of the Family Assistance Plan in August 1969, a measure far more radical in its basic aim—a guaranteed income—than any of the "riot" programs. It was assumed that those who would benefit from a guaranteed income would only very slowly, if at all, learn that one had been proposed; but the political world would have to react, and promptly, to this extraordinary turn of events suggesting that far from lapsing into stagnation, the country might be moving ahead faster than ever. And who could say but that in the process a guaranteed income might come about? For it was proposed in earnest and had a reasonable "mathematical" probability of enactment. It was further the case that by the end of the 1960s the social science prognosis for most Great Society programs was anything but cheering. The near-term probability for the early 1970s was a succession of reports and studies which would cast doubts on the strategies of compensatory education and such-like as a means of obtaining greater social equality. All the more, then, was the need to have in place when that time came a viable alternative in the form of a direct income supplement program. It was necessary in 1969 not simply to deal with the immediate need to reassure the "liberal audience" that the Nation had not entered a period of political reaction, but also to anticipate the onset of mild-to-severe disillusionment concerning the efficacy of programs that had previously been seen as the vanguard of political progress. Family Assistance served both purposes, and in concert with revenue sharing for state and local government— both proposed in the same Presidential address on August 8, 1969—maintained both the appearance and the substance of intelligent political innovation during a delicate transition from a period of overexcitement and unreason to a more normal condition of relative calm and mild optimism.

That there was nothing grand, certainly nothing heroic, in this policy will be evident; and yet it had one virtue. It worked. This is only to say that mass violence came to an end and did so in almost precisely the manner hoped for. The government contribution to this outcome was marginal at best, but it did try not to make things worse and did try to reinforce trends that had evolved "on their own." The policy developed in 1969 toward the problem of urban violence was, in this respect, rather like economic policy. Only limited influence was possible, but this could be crucial if it was brought to bear in something like synchronization with larger movements. As with economic policy, it dealt with near-term events. The object was to bring to a close a particular period of disorder: nothing more. There was no expectation of changing the world. And yet it remains the case that the national government was able to cope, on this near-term basis, with a perceived crisis of serious proportions.

This is no small achievement. It would be an even larger one if it were seen as such. American society would do better to pay somewhat more attention to its successes, for it needs the reserves of morale which this kind of awareness brings. But this is not our present disposition, and those engaged in the practice of government should probably accept the cold comfort that it hardly ever has been.

Derrymore, West Davenport, New York
September 1972

ADDENDUM

The introduction to a book of essays is commonly apologia masquerading as perspective. The Introduction to *Coping*, written in the summer of 1972, was no different. At a time when public affairs seemed to have entered a period of comparative stability, I sought to account for the persistent theme of crisis and unsuccess which runs through this collection. The first essay described— "anticipated" may be the better word—the failure of working-class politics in New York which would, as it did, shatter the liberal coalition that depended on everyday persons, especially those who have come to be known—God preserve—as "ethnics" feeling at home, if not predominant, in the Democratic party. What was to have been the last essay suggests that in the end the left extreme may have succeeded in ways it never dreamed: driven from the rude bastions of proletarian militancy that seemed its destined stronghold, it had regrouped and, of all things, found refuge, and at length a kind of prevalence, on campus. The essays in between, successive accounts of things done and un-done, were scarcely celebratory. And yet my own mood in that summer of 1972 was optimistic.

This was more than a little personal. For the first time in my adult life a Presidential campaign was in full swing, and I had not the least part in it. A Democrat, I had served in the Cabinet of a Republican President, and I judged this to impose an obligation of neutrality and silence. I had managed even to persuade myself there was a tradition to this effect. I made no speeches, signed no advertisements, attended no rallies. This, and the thought that once out of such activities it is difficult ever to get back, was enough to cheer anyone up. I had been of some service to the state, and whether or not "they" knew it: that time in my life, was past.

A fairly well-defined period in the nation's life also seemed past. The world, in the meantime, went on, and was in some respects better. Things had been learned that would be of use in the future. My simple purpose and sole excuse for presenting this volume was the thought that this needed saying and illustrating, albeit it seemed that the new period into which we were entering would be less an ordeal than the immediate past. (I have now added a further essay, given as a lecture in January 1973, which sets out the grounds for this expectation.) All in all, things were looking up. I dared to conclude the Introduction by suggesting a parallel between workaday social science and economics: both useful, if limited, contrivances.

I write this postscript as I correct galleys, eight months later and far from the United States, at the moment the Watergate disclosures are hemorrhaging back in Washington. Revulsion and depression alternate in enervating antithesis: It has happened yet again. Disaster.

In his presidential address to the American Economic Association delivered at the turn of the year, John Kenneth Galbraith began by speaking of economics as "a subject which features defeated expectations." Such at minimum must be the mood of anyone who thought government was a craft that could be improved by attentive experience and abetted by a sufficiently inobtrusive social science.

And yet, viewed from halfway round the world, the events seem less discontinuous than otherwise. Can it be that disaster just never let up? In "Nirvana Now," the Phi Beta Kappa Oration given at Harvard in 1967, I am to be found quoting a then recent *Letter from Washington* by Richard Rovere: "This city is awash with lies and deceptions. . . ." In "The Education of the Urban Poor," written at about the same time, there is this passage:

> The plain fact is that the United States had best look to its standards of conduct, or face the prospect of being discharged from the decade of the 1960s under conditions less than honorable.

If, from a distance, any comment is to be offered, mine would be of this order: Recent politics have encouraged many groups to set their own standards of behavior by reference to what they believe to be the standards of opposing or contending groups. The result has been an almost competitive depreciation in such standards, first in a Democratic administration, next in a Republican one. The most recent revelations may seem to us more shocking as they are more personal, which is to say they involve men doing things they will acknowledge were wrong. And yet, it was precisely the impersonal quality of the events of Vietnam that seemed so terrible. Sufficient unto the day is the banality thereof. The legitimation of lawlessness is not readily confined to one subject or one set.

Life will go on, and things will appear to improve. Indeed, the recent events as such provide no great ground for pessimism. There are, if you like, two kinds of political regimes: those whose crimes you read about in history books, and those whose crimes you read about in newspapers. Ours is of the latter, less common kind. The self-corrective mechanisms of the system would seem to be in good working order. The strong and moral men of the present administration—the Leonard Garments, the Elliot L. Richardsons, the Raymond K. Prices—are coming to be valued for the integrity they sustained in murky times. Strong and ethical men in other institutions—the Congress, the courts, the press— are seen for what they mean. Dignity is acquiring meaning, not least with respect to those who for the moment keep silent, for there is noise enough.

Let us, indeed, consider the possible gain. Persons with an excessive sense of their worth have been having a difficult time. From the moment those men in the White House of whom we now read so much first started putting replicas of the American flag in their lapels, it was probable they would end by disgracing it. They had begun to think themselves better than they were, and ended worse than they were. There is a lesson here. In the meantime we must endeavor to cope.

New Delhi, India
May 1973

"Bosses" and "Reformers"
A Profile of the New York Democrats

1

The morning John F. Kennedy spoke to the New York delegation prior to the voting at the Los Angeles convention, he reminded the New Yorkers that the Democratic party was founded in the course of a botanizing expedition up the Hudson River valley, which had brought Thomas Jefferson and Aaron Burr together to talk politics. By almost any calculation, this would make the New York Democratic party the oldest political organization on earth: the British Tories, the American Republicans, the French Radicals are all venerable institutions, but the New York Democratic party was in the second half of its first century before even the oldest of these others was established as a permanent organization.

Of all the institutions that Jefferson helped to found, there is surely none that would please him more, in its freedom from the burdens of tradition, than the New York Democrats. They have no ceremonials, no mace, no ancient customs; it is unlikely that anyone could say for certain just where, if anywhere, the records of fifteen or twenty years back are stored. (But would even Jefferson have dared hope that after one hundred and sixty-odd years of continuous existence, the oldest political party in the world would still have its offices in a hotel room?) To be free of tradition, however, is not to be free of the past. In the months since Los Angeles, the New York Democrats, after helping Ken-

" 'Bosses' and 'Reformers' " was first published in *Commentary* in May 1961.

nedy to carry the state by 375,000 votes, have been torn apart
by a controversy—involving the related efforts of the "reform"
Democrats to get rid of Carmine De Sapio as leader of Tammany,
and those of the Kennedy administration to get rid of Michael
H. Prendergast as state chairman—that has its roots in the very
origins of the party.

It is helpful to think of the dichotomy that shaped those
origins: Jefferson and Burr, aristocratic idealist and Tammany
politician. (But this is helpful only if one avoids stereotypes concerning which type knows most about getting on in the world:
consider the outcome of Jefferson's career as against that of
Burr.) The more immediate source of the present controversy,
however, can be found in the choice of Franklin D. Roosevelt
over Al Smith for the Presidential nomination in 1932. Smith's
defeat was a sharp blow to the dominant Irish Catholic group
in the party, but it was nothing compared to the shock of the
New Deal politics that followed. The "regulars," the old-time
Democrats, were "out on a limb," Smith told a 1936 campaign
audience, "holding the bag, driven out of the party, because
some new bunch that nobody ever heard of in their life before
came in and took charge of things and started planning everything." James A. Farley's break with Roosevelt in 1940 left the
New York Democratic party completely in the hands of the
"regulars," mostly conservative Irish Catholics who felt little
enthusiasm for what was going on in Washington. The leaders of
this group were not necessarily poor men, but their constituencies
were emphatically made up of the Catholic working class which
produced the great bulk of the Democratic vote.

During this period a change of profound consequence took
place that was to give the present controversy its distinctive
coloration. The great mass of the New York Jews emerged from
the slums to become middle class almost in one generation.
However, they remained loyal to the Democrats in far larger
numbers than might have been expected from their new economic
position, while at the same time a fair number of middle-class
Protestants were also developing attachments to the New Deal.
Thus was created the special feature of New York politics: the
existence of a large, middle-class Democratic vote.

Neither the Jews nor the Protestants entered the party leadership in New York; in a sense they did not even apply for admission, for their main interests and loyalties were concentrated

on national politics. It was not really until the New Deal era came to an end in 1952 that the attention of these groups was turned, *faute de mieux,* to state and local politics, where they found in control people with views remarkably different from their own.

The first shock involved Adlai Stevenson. The liberals gave their hearts completely to the 1952 Democratic candidate; the regulars considered him soft on Communism. ("Like sending the cabbage patch to the goat," said James A. Farley, at a later date, concerning the prospect of Stevenson negotiating with Khrushchev.) Besides, it was obvious to the regulars that Stevenson was going to lose. At that point the "reform" movement began to erupt in Manhattan. Significantly—symbolically—the leaders of the reform group were Roosevelt's wife, his Lieutenant Governor (Herbert Lehman), and a former special assistant to his Secretary of State (Thomas K. Finletter).

The nature of the reform movement is best seen by the neighborhoods in which the new clubs have taken hold. They are concentrated in Manhattan because that is where the very young, or the very well-to-do, of New York live. The archetype is the Lexington Club, an alliance of millionaires and law clerks, located in the "Silk Stocking" district of the East Side. Typically the reform clubs have succeeded in districts which have a Republican (i.e., middle-class) majority, or in heavily Jewish districts which are middle class but vote Democratic. Generally the reform clubs have replaced old Irish organizations which have outlived their neighborhoods.

Although the reform movement now controls a quarter of the votes on the Tammany executive committee and has elected a Congressman, two Assemblymen, and a State Senator, its success has so far been limited. The main obstacle is geography. Given their choice, liberals live in Republican neighborhoods, and they tend to have virtually no connection with the working class. Therefore, so long as the Democrats remain a basically working-class party, the reform group will remain a decided minority within it.

This in itself is unexceptional; the middle class is always a minority—but it almost always runs things. Here is where the real source of conflict lies: for so long as the Democratic party in New York remains as well a predominantly *Catholic* party, the reformers are not going to run things either. Their perfectly natural inability to understand this has led to much of the present discord.

The divergence in the party between "regulars" on the one hand and "liberals" on the other, operates on three levels. First, there is the difference in class. The regulars tend to be working class or lower middle class in origin and, in a curious way, in outlook. The liberals tend to be middle class in outlook, if not always in origin. (The Jewish working class in New York, while decidedly liberal, is to a considerable extent organized in the Liberal party and its influence is therefore hardly felt in the Democratic ranks.) The liberals have been fighting for the class interests of the workers for half a century, but of late—as their efforts have borne fruit—this has resulted in a certain impairment of their own interests as members of the middle class. In any event, they do have class interests distinct from those of the mass of the Democratic party, and their actions have recently been demonstrating this fact. A case in point is their penchant for Governor Rockefeller, whose program is aimed directly at what might be called the first-generation bourgeoisie. When liberal Democrats say that Rockefeller has had the "courage to face up to the tax problem," what they perhaps mean is that his revenue program has added one million workers to the income-tax rolls.

On the second level there is the religious difference. The regulars include every religious and ethnic group in the city except white Anglo-Saxon Protestants. (There is a small group of elite Protestants who will work with the regular party, but they usually do so as a result of a deliberate decision on each side to vary the normal pattern.) Similarly, the liberals include every *middle-class* religious and ethnic group in the city except Catholics. (Again there are calculated cross-overs, but these only emphasize the pattern.) In terms of predominance, the Catholics can be said to run the "regular" party, just as the Jews can be said to run the liberal movement. Jews have great influence, as they have great numbers, within the regular party, but their most vigorous types tend to avoid the role of party bureaucrats. The Women's Division of the Democratic State Committee, however, is dominated by the energetic wives of Jewish businessmen. When the ladies are rewarded for services it is commonly in the form of honorary positions for their husbands.

The main problem on this level is that the Catholic Democrats —as Catholics—no longer have any distinct political purpose in New York State. Catholic legislators from Brooklyn and the Bronx are dependably liberal in their voting records, in fact are hardly to be distinguished from the most ardent member of Americans for Democratic Action on that account. But their energies are immobilized by two equally powerful and contradictory impulses: almost any large, new program that would appeal to the secular interests of the Catholic population involves an increase in the functions of the state, which almost necessarily involves a diminution in the functions of the church. At the very least, it diverts yet more resources to the public domain. The problem for Catholic politicians is further complicated by a harsh streak of anti-liberalism which is to be found on every level of Catholic society, and which has produced a considerable body of extreme conservatives who nonetheless remain Democrats. Just as serious, until recently the Catholic intellectual community has been too small and too weak to prod Catholic legislators into a concern with the more important political problems of the day.

All this has greatly strengthened the tendency of the regulars to avoid issues altogether. The regular Democrats in the state legislature, for example, are practically an inert mass. What patronage they get from the Republicans is mainly used on bartenders and coleaders. For a legislative program, the leaders get out a press release at Christmastime calling for stricter rent control and lower taxes. (By contrast, the Liberal party, which does not elect a single legislator, and cannot hope to do so, comes forth each year with an exhaustive legislative program.) The New York electorate knows what it might expect from a Democratic legislature: it has sent a Democratic majority to Albany for only three years of the twentieth century.*

The liberal Jews and Protestants, on the other hand, have no great problem with the secular state—they more or less invented

* The Johnson landslide of 1964 gave New York its fourth Democratic-controlled legislature of the century. It was not a disaster. It was . . . nothing. That is to say, nothing happened. The renowned Roosevelt coalition had not shattered, but it was no longer able to achieve a sustained political purpose. There was nothing it wanted to do *together*.

[Publisher's note: Throughout this volume the author has added comments which were not in the original. These footnotes are set in this type face, to distinguish them from the original text.]

it. They are extremely program-minded, and marvelously adept at devising new ways to spend money. In the regular party, conferences on issues are regarded as women's work. Once each year the Women's Division has a meeting in Albany which is on the whole well done—but there it ends. By contrast, among liberals, conferences abound on every conceivable issue. Such gatherings, however, are rarely conducive to party unity. For example, the New York Committee for Democratic Voters recently held a large, day-long conference on state legislative issues at which the featured luncheon speaker warned that a higher-education bond issue being proposed in Albany would permit building loans to *parochial* colleges. The regulars react to this much as the liberals would respond to a speech by a Bronx Italian protesting that an increase in competitive state scholarships for higher education would only give further advantage to the children of middle-class Jews—a view not unknown in Albany, but emphatically not expressed. This is not the way regular Democrats conduct political business.

The third level of divergence is cultural in a broad sense. The liberals are people with what is called a high rate of upward mobility. Not so the regulars, who incline to stay near the old neighborhoods, speaking with the old accents, even after they have become rich and successful. This makes for quite different views of what constitutes proper conduct in the political game. To be upwardly mobile means to be successfully aggressive—a preeminent trait of liberals, for all that their aggressiveness tends to be of the sophisticated variety. The regulars generally view such liberals as persons without enough manners to wait their turn.

The liberal combination of energy and ability has been an invaluable asset in appointive politics; when an elected Democratic (or Republican) official comes to choose his staff, he chooses liberals. Thus President Kennedy has appointed a host of New Yorkers to his cabinet and sub-cabinet—from the Secretary of State on down—but these have almost without exception been liberals with, at best, a fleeting and embarrassed relation to the regular party organization. But there were no organization candidates *for* Secretary of State. Neither were there any Catholic candidates. Although any number of highly educated and intelligent persons can be found among the conservative Catholics in the party, Catholic education does not, it would seem, produce the kind of excellence American society wants.

This, however, is not the whole story; the success of the liberals in private life and in appointive politics is balanced by their relative failure in elective politics. Politics is a neighborhood business, and liberals are not neighborhood people. Consequently, while they have been getting all the glamorous jobs, the party organization has remained solidly in the hands of the conservative regulars. The sixty-two Democratic county chairmen in New York are as unrepresentative in one direction as are the members of the Lexington Democratic Club in the other. There are, for example, only two Jews in the entire lot, and these are relative newcomers. (Invariably a majority of the county chairmen are Irish Catholics.) The Democratic party in New York City does not send a single white Anglo-Saxon Protestant to the state legislature, or to the United States Congress. And the five county leaders of New York City are normally all Catholics, either conservative or apolitical.

At the risk of simplifying a most complex subject, it can be said that the liberals, accustomed as they are to success in every other sphere of life, simply do not understand how and why people like the regulars should have come to dominate them in the party offices and legislative posts, and therefore they have resorted to "bossism" as an explanation. On the other side the party regulars regard the liberals as pushy, arrogant newcomers who do none of the work in turning out the vote and yet get all the gravy. This feeling—aggravated by the liberal habit of impugning the motives of anyone they disagree with—has led many of the regulars to the point of high irrationality. Men who started out as perfectly sensible practical politicians in Morrisania and Greenwich Village and the like, have ended as snarling monomaniacs who go about proclaiming that they would prefer to lose every judgeship in the city before taking a solitary vote from "that ADA crowd." And since many of the regulars are men of capacity (which tends to be overlooked because their abilities are not marketable in midtown New York), their opposition to liberal encroachment has been effective.

Yet, in order to put together a majority of the votes at the state level, neither group can do without the other and both together must have the support of the Liberal party. Since World War II, out of all the elections that have been held, Democratic candidates have carried the state only six times, and only four men (Herbert Lehman, Averell Harriman, Arthur Levitt, and John Kennedy) have been able to pull off the trick. Of these, two—Lehman and Kennedy—won largely on personal appeal. Only the election of Harriman and Levitt in 1954 was a genuine party victory, brought about by a successful coalition put together by Carmine G. De Sapio.

De Sapio is incomparably the most able politician the New York Democrats have produced since Farley. He is just that, a politician. The extent of his *ideological* commitment may be measured by his pronouncement to the Holy Name Society Communion Breakfast of the New York Sanitation Department that "there is no Mother's Day behind the Iron Curtain." This is, of course, the source of his ultimate failure: he is not in the least interested in government, only in politics. It is simply too bad that he should have come to power in a world in which this was no longer good enough.

Having grown up as an Italian among the "outs" of an Irish Catholic party, De Sapio was always perfectly aware that the party executive committee does not recessarily reflect the exact composition of the party constituency. When he took over the leadership of Tammany his position was quite clear. He already had the votes of the conservative Democrats; the next step, therefore, was to win the liberals. This he accomplished by making liberal speeches and nominating liberal candidates: Robert Wagner, Averell Harriman, Franklin D. Roosevelt, Jr., and so on through the list—an approach that worked extremely well once it got organized. Tammany had touched bottom in 1952. In 1953 De Sapio elected Wagner Mayor of New York. In 1954 he sent Harriman and Levitt to Albany. By 1956 he even had a candidate for the Presidential nomination. But here his downfall began.

De Sapio's support for Harriman against Stevenson at the 1956 convention alerted the Roosevelt-Lehman-Finletter group to the fact that there were limits to De Sapio's liberalism. These limits were definable as the point where the gain in liberal votes at one end of the spectrum was outweighed by the loss of conservative votes at the other. De Sapio knew his party; in 1956 Stevenson lost the state by 1,589,571 votes, but the New York Democratic party itself—having supported Harriman at the convention—did not suffer a grievous defeat.

A similar situation brought about the debacle of the 1958 Democratic state convention, which led to the downfall of almost everyone concerned. The significant feature of De Sapio's 1954 slate had been that for the first time in memory there was no Irish Catholic among the candidates, and therefore the 1958 nominee for United States Senate had to be an Irish Catholic— unless Wagner, who is Catholic and half-Irish, were to be chosen. When Wagner declined after the two-day convention got under way, a bitter dispute arose over which Irish Catholic candidate the party should offer.

The New York City party chairmen wanted Manhattan District Attorney Frank Hogan—a man who was living evidence that there existed able and distinguished party regulars who had stayed at home, as it were, but had yet rendered service of the highest order to American government. (Farley's gibe that Hogan's knowledge of foreign affairs was limited by the Battery on the south and the Harlem River on the north, was in a sense a recommendation.) Wagner and Harriman had nothing whatever against Hogan, but felt that liberal sentiment would demand a candidate more closely indentified with foreign affairs, and thus they backed Thomas E. Murray of the Atomic Energy Commission. Lurking in the background of this move was the fear that Hogan's candidacy would be labeled as an attempt by Tammany to get rid of the one man who had maintained a modicum of law enforcement in Manhattan over the previous decade and a half.

No one present in the hotel room during this argument was behind Thomas K. Finletter for *that* nomination, and when the meeting broke up in an impasse—the tempers of proud men having been lost—the party leaders went off to nominate Hogan, and Wagner (with Harriman's support) went off to nominate Murray. On the way to the convention hall, however, Wagner was persuaded by Finletter supporters not to announce a preference for *either* Murray or Finletter, at the risk of incurring the wrath of the liberals. Since the party leaders had the votes anyway, Wagner let it go at that. He spoke for no candidate and a free contest ensued. Hogan got 772 votes, Murray 304, and Finletter 66.

Despite this emphatic evidence that Finletter, although widely respected and esteemed, was the choice of hardly anyone for the 1958 Democratic nomination for U.S. Senator, the liberal group in the party decided that Hogan's victory had been dictated by bosses, which in turn produced the impression that Harriman had been for Finletter, but had been unable to enforce his wishes.

In Connecticut at this time a strikingly similar situation arose with, however, very different consequences. Thomas E. Dodd, an Irish Catholic party regular, and Chester E. Bowles, a foreign policy-oriented Protestant liberal, were both candidates for the Democratic Senatorial nomination to run with the liberal—and in this case, Jewish—Gubernatorial candidate, Abraham E. Ribicoff. The Catholic party leaders made exactly the same decision as in New York, with Ribicoff's approval. Dodd was nominated for the Senate, Bowles was persuaded to accept an unlikely Congressional nomination as a gesture of unity and support. In the upshot, everybody won. By contrast, in New York, liberals deserted the Democratic ticket in hordes. Harriman lost to Rockefeller by 593,034 votes. Significantly, Hogan lost by only 132,992 votes, and the Jewish candidate for Comptroller, Arthur E. Levitt (a most able man by any standards), ran 600,000 votes ahead of the ticket and managed to win.

Having been beaten, De Sapio completely lost his standing among the liberals. Where they had once praised him as the new-style political leader, they now denounced him as an old-style political boss. The Roosevelt-Lehman-Finletter group was formed to rid the party of the "image of bossism" (Harriman, who had the most to complain about, did not join in), and soon the battle was on. Prevented now from exercising his special talent for balancing liberals and conservatives, De Sapio had no choice but to side with the old guard. And once under attack, his judgment began to go wrong. In return for some kind words of support from former President Truman, he toyed with Symington's candidacy for the 1960 nomination long after it should have been evident that Kennedy was the one man both his party and the voters would support. Other county leaders came out for Kennedy, and only at the last moment did De Sapio follow suit.

His final act of folly was the attempt to exclude Herbert Lehman—the most respected and distinguished Jewish political figure in New York—from the 1960 Democratic delegation. This move involved De Sapio in a conflict not only with liberal Jewish

Democrats, but with all Jewish Democrats—probably a quarter of the party following. The effort collapsed almost the moment it was announced, it being evident to the dimmest clubhouse denizen that here were the makings of party disaster. The state chairman, Michael H. Prendergast, who had at first joined in the move to exclude Lehman, gave up his own seat to make room for the elder statesman. At this point, Prendergast's troubles began.

"Mike" Prendergast is the quintessential regular. Politics is his profession—his only profession. As if by design, he was born in Jim Farley's home town of Grassy Point in Rockland County, just up the Hudson from New York. He graduated from Haverstraw High School and was in politics before he was old enough to vote. He got his first patronage job (with the Democratic National Committee) at the age of twenty-two, served on the Rockland police force, went to work for the National Catholic Welfare Conference, and in time became county chairman, a post he filled very successfully. In 1955, Harriman, the newly elected Governor, chose him as state chairman to work at building the party organization in upstate New York.

Politics, Prendergast style, is a decent, quiet, family affair, and the highest priority is assigned to those things which keep it so: patronage, small and not-so-small favors, the strict observance of the complex prerogatives of party members on various levels. "Issues" in the world of Prendergast are viewed as essentially divisive influences that one would hope to do without.

The Democratic party is the life of men such as Prendergast, and—resembling nothing so much as old-time radicals in their passion for the One Big Union—they have a sharp dislike for those who disrupt its orderly, hierarchical functions. Although Prendergast had opposed De Sapio at the Buffalo convention, after the 1958 election he had no recourse but to turn to the Tammany leader for support. When the liberals began to include him in the list of bosses who must go, he responded by trying to act like a boss, although this was not by any means his normal manner.

Prendergast's difficulty with the Kennedy administration was inevitable. During the Presidential primaries, the Kennedys had worked out a highly effective technique for moving into a territory and setting up a campaign organization. This included the brilliant political invention of having the Kennedy representative in any given area be a man from an altogether different state, as often as possible someone with a personal relation to Kennedy himself. The brilliance of this technique was that in one stroke it cut through the tangle of jealousy, interest, and intrigue which normally surrounds the campaign chairman and frequently drains the energy from the operation itself. Accordingly, three of Kennedy's best men were sent to New York. They promptly set about establishing "Citizens for Kennedy" organizations designed to bring into the campaign the great range of groups who were attracted to Kennedy but were not part of the regular Democratic organization, and to serve as a vehicle for reaching others who were not even necessarily Democrats. In New York City the object was largely to reach liberal Jews. Upstate the target was conservative Catholics. In between, there was the usual wonderful mixture of all shapes and sizes.

To Kennedy's men these methods seemed the essence of a rational, dispassionate approach to a political problem. Armed with Lawrence O'Brien's masterful campaign manuals, the citizens' groups got under way with much vigor—only to find the Democratic state committee opposing them at every turn. Or so, at least, it seemed. (There is no such thing as objective truth in party politics.) One party, one organization, said the regulars. The Kennedy men pleaded, cajoled, warned. Prendergast's reaction was to try to get one of them removed. By mid-campaign the Kennedy men had concluded that Prendergast simply did not understand how to win an election and would himself have to go.

As the campaign neared its conclusion in New York, the only remaining question was how many Jews could be brought out to vote for the man who had vanquished Adlai Stevenson. At the penultimate moment of the campaign, a great rally was held in New York City with Kennedy on hand. Either deliberately, or through a misunderstanding, Lehman was not permitted to speak, although Kennedy had expected he would. Thus a doubt as to Prendergast's integrity was added to the doubts about his good judgment in the mind of the future President, and Prendergast was in deep trouble with the new administration even before it took office.

Shortly after the election, it was made clear that the administration wanted a new state chairman in New York—one not disposed to face the future with a loss of 25 percent of the

Democratic vote. The difficulty in bringing about a change is that the very people who would have to persuade Prendergast to step down—the county leaders—do not in their hearts feel that he has done anything wrong. The most conspicuous example is Congressman Charles A. Buckley, the Bronx leader. If splinter organizations are distasteful to Prendergast, they are anathema to Buckley. Fighting them is *the* passion of his life. Thus, with the rarest exceptions, no Bronx Democratic candidate is permitted to accept the Liberal party endorsement, even if it means losing the election. Buckley regards Prendergast as a slow but honorable man, and though he and the other leaders would like to see "Mike" step aside in order to please the President, they can rouse no passion in insisting that he do so. Prendergast, for his part, feels that his integrity was insulted when the administration offered him a federal job if he would resign: if his political decisions could be affected by offers of money, he would not, he declares in private, need a job.

In resisting the President, Prendergast was presumably supported by De Sapio, who carries on his now hopeless fight with dignity and courage. Tammany did without the help of Grover Cleveland, Woodrow Wilson, and Franklin D. Roosevelt. It can, in fact, do without John F. Kennedy, but it will most likely in the near enough future prefer to do without Carmine De Sapio instead. But the New York Democratic party cannot easily do without either. Unless there is a dramatic reversal of the present trend toward complete fragmentation, the 1962 elections will go by default. The party leaders know this—one of the best-informed estimates of the moment is that, barring such a reversal, Rockefeller will be returned to office by a million votes. Probably Kennedy's best strategy would be to write off the election, rather than to have it appear a test between him and a likely Republican opponent in 1964. But this is not the Kennedy style. He wants to see the New York Democratic party rebuilt.

The *logical* man to unite the New York Democratic party, as the President realizes, is a Catholic liberal. (A working description would be an Irish Catholic county leader who reads *Commonweal*.) A number of such already exist, and each year sees more of them appearing: typically, they have come to power in suburban counties where an old-line Catholic party membership has been augmented by a flood of middle-class liberals from the city. William F. Luddy in Westchester and John F. English in Nassau are excellent examples. Both are vigorous, intelligent young men who have ethnic, religious, or intellectual ties with all the elements in their party. Each has brought large numbers of middle-class workers into the party bureaucracy.* Neither Westchester nor Nassau has yet gone Democratic, but the Republicans no longer take them for granted.

In casting about for a Catholic liberal to succeed Prendergast, the President chose Peter J. Crotty of Buffalo. Crotty is a working politician from a big, ugly, turbulent city, where tens of thousands of Democrats but very few liberals live. He has managed to bring together a baffling collection of Democratic factions to produce an effective party organization in Buffalo. He is a man of intellect, a diligent student of Catholic social theory, a formidable labor lawyer, and a passionate believer in racial equality. (He once resigned as county chairman when the party balked at making the first major Negro political appointment in Buffalo. The party gave in and he withdrew his resignation.) Given all this, Crotty should have been acceptable as state chairman both to the regulars and to the liberals. But the depth of the Democratic division turned out to be deeper than anyone knew, and the New York reform movement promptly announced that Crotty was unacceptable. The reason was visceral rather than logical, much as was the Liberal party's refusal to endorse Crotty when he ran for state Attorney General in 1958. Organized liberals cannot help being suspicious of the liberalism of Irish Catholic county leaders who are at ease on city councils and who get along with police chiefs.

Catholic liberals also have their difficulties with the regular party organization. Such Catholics are almost invariably Irish,

---

* In Nassau 50 percent of English's committeemen are Jews, 40 percent are Catholics, and 10 percent are Protestants. Some 73 percent have one —or more—college degrees. This, of course, is not a statistically representative group. It is much too middle-class—in Great Neck, English says, he probably hasn't a single committeeman who makes less than $15,000 a year. There is also a disproportionate number of Jews, who account for only 17–18 percent of the population. But the high percentage of middle-class people and Jews does give an accurate reflection of the distribution of Democratic energies in a suburban county with no party patronage to dispense.

which gives them a certain tribal acceptability to the (still largely Irish) Democratic leadership, but they do not generally fire the enthusiasm of the Italians, who (with the Poles coming along) are far the most vigorous of the rank-and-file Catholic Democrats. Of all the ethnic groups active at the moment in New York State, the Italians have the strongest political purpose: they are fighting for social equality. De Sapio's demise would be a setback for them, especially since he himself has systematically cut short the careers of a number of promising Italian leaders. (They were usually sentenced to life on the state Supreme Court bench.) Thus if De Sapio goes, there will be a gap in Italian leadership, which is not likely to be filled—in Italian eyes—by yet another Irishman.

In any event, the present Catholic leadership of the party is doomed. It is the fag-end of a succession which made some social sense in the mid-nineteenth century but which knows no purpose today other than to persist in the joyless distribution of increasingly empty emoluments. (What, after all, is achieved by becoming the 116th Irishman to get on the Court of General Sessions? The ennui is even showing among the Italians.) The one honorable course open to the present leaders, to elect a brilliant Congressional delegation and keep it there, has not, with but a few exceptions, been followed. The only power left to the city Democratic leaders is to keep the party impotent at the state level— which they may or may not choose to do.

For the moment, all is stalemate. Prendergast, with about fifteen months of his term to go, refuses to resign, and he cannot be made to do so. (He is elected under the election law and has as much right to his job as, say, the Governor does to his.) A good many upstate county leaders refuse to turn on him for acting as they themselves would have acted (there is a high content of honor in American politics—most politicians, if they only knew it, have a right to feel morally superior to their constituencies), and the Kennedy administration will presumably come for a time to deal with these leaders through Prendergast. But this will hardly change matters. Prendergast is the victim of a deep misunderstanding, but he is not for that reason any the less a victim.

Though the logic of the party's situation now demands a Catholic liberal like Crotty to succeed Prendergast, all the signs are that the New York Democrats are heading ultimately for a period of Jewish leadership. The Jews have heavy influence in the regular organization and predominate in the reform movement and the Liberal party. Unlike the members of other ethnic groups, Jews in different factions are able to talk to each other and to respect each other. The most hard-bitten Jewish district leader in Brooklyn, for example, thinks of himself as a liberal, and consequently there are no *semantic* gulfs to separate him from the reformers and the Liberal party. A liberal Catholic, then, or a conservative Jew: one or the other seems likely in New York before long. The winds of change are blowing, and the New York Democrats are moving into an era of the balanced party bureaucracy—a device that may prove as formidable in the future as was the balanced ticket in the past.

The Case for
a Family Policy

2

The United States is very possibly on the verge of adopting a national policy directed to the quality and stability of American family life. It would mean an extraordinary break with the past. This could be the central event of our new era of social legislation.

In the course of the past several months, in a series of specific events that mark the transition with a precision almost unknown to social history, the United States concluded one era of domestic politics and embarked upon another. Nearly a quarter century after the event, the legislative agenda of the New Deal was finally completed. The reason for the delay could not have been more simple: the New Deal lost its majority in Congress in 1938 and did not really get it back until 1965. But once it was back in power, as it were, bills were passed one-two-three-four; President Johnson, of course, was there to sign them. The Education and Medicare Acts were perhaps the most significant, but a host of measures accompanied them. At long last, the social insurance and public welfare proposals of the 1930s have become law.

In about this same period, less dramatically but more sig-

"The Case for a Family Policy" was first published in *America*, September 18, 1965.

nificantly, the other great objective of the New Deal has also been achieved: it is now fairly clear that the United States has at last learned how to make an industrial economy operate at a high level of employment and a steadily rising level of production. The goals formally set forth in the Employment Act of 1946 are closer to reality today than at any time in history.

The components of this economic revolution have been so complex, and the results so persuasive, that it is easy to overlook it. The United States is now in the fifty-third month of unbroken economic expansion—the longest and strongest in peacetime history. During this brief, fleeting period—not two thousand days, not nearly that—we have raised the level of Gross National Product by some $160 billion. In 1946, the year the Employment Act was passed, our total GNP after two centuries of growth and the enormous spurt of World War II was only $211 billion. In June of the present year, the number of industrial jobs surpassed the historic peak of November 1943, and in July the unemployment rate for white workers dropped to the interim goal of 4 percent.

All in all, it has been a magnificent achievement. As a result, the general quality and decency of life in the United States is incomparably greater than in years past, just as it is in almost all the industrial democracies that have been going through the same process as we.

On the other hand, there are two sets of problems very much before us. The first concerns that segment of our population whose lives have somehow not been touched by the general success— except to the extent they have fallen even farther behind the rest of the nation. The second concerns those problems brought on by success itself.

It is growth, not decline, that is turning America ugly: ride into town from any airport in the country if you have doubts about it. It is a superabundance of goods and services and gadgets, rather than lack of them, that gives us the feeling of being hemmed in. (New York City, for example, is surrounded by water and covered by air, but somehow running out of both.)

Because it is entirely possible that many of the processes that are producing prosperity are also producing much of our poverty, it may be that both sets of problems are in fact part of a single phenomenon: the pathology of post-industrial society. It is to this continuum of issues that the next period of social policy-making in the United States must address itself.

One could hardly ask a more agreeable challenge. The resources available are unprecedented—the level of GNP is expected to rise by something like $235 billion in the next five years—and the receptivity to new ideas in Washington can hardly ever have been greater. Richard N. Goodwin, of the White House staff, spoke in a recent address of the challenge of a great society that "looks beyond the prospects of abundance to the problems of abundance" and to the reality that, for all our success, "we find discontent with what we have, dissatisfaction with the life we created, unhappiness and restlessness." The President has set moving a series of task forces pursuing just such issues.

In one sense, what is involved is a search for new definitions. It is here that the possibility of a national family policy most clearly emerges.

American social policy until now has been directed toward the individual. The individual—and the various circumstances relating to him—has been our primary unit of measurement: men, women, and children are all lumped together. Thus, our employment statistics count as equally unemployed a father of nine children, a housewife coming back into the labor market in her forties, and a teen-ager looking for a part-time job after school. The minimum wage required by law to be paid to any of these persons is exactly the same. If they should somehow have the same level of earnings—which would be easy enough—and were to lose their jobs, the amount of unemployment insurance paid to each would be exactly the same. The examples are numerous; the point does not change. American arrangements pertain to the individual, and only in the rarest circumstances do they define the family as the relevant unit.

This is a pattern that is almost uniquely American. Most of the industrial democracies of the world have adopted a wide range of social programs designed specifically to support the stability and viability of the family. Except in the United States, family allowances are practically a hallmark of an advanced industrial society. In France, for example, a worker with a wife and three children, earning the average factory wage, receives about as much in family allowances as in his pay packet. Typically, the money is paid to the man, not the housewife.

It would be useful to learn more about the reasons for this situation. To state that it is in the tradition of American individualism does not explain the process, but simply restates it. I would venture that it has something to do with the extraordinarily diverse pattern of family systems in the United States, which results from the no less extraordinary pattern of immigration. About one-third of our population is descended from migrants from Great Britain and Northern Ireland. The rest came from all parts of the globe. With them they brought family structures ranging from the extremes of patriarchy to the outer reaches of matriarchy—combined with every known variant of stability and instability.

With such confusion, it was impossible to prescribe family programs that would meet the needs or desires of all groups, and all the more so since the Anglo-Saxon families were heavily concentrated in rural areas, which were opposed to all such measures on general conservative principles. (The problem is perhaps still reflected in our complex adoption procedures.)

One has the impression that a Catholic problem was also involved. Catholics made much of families, were said to have enormous ones, and—in a view that was and may still be widely held—could be counted on to compound the enormity if public funds began to subsidize "indiscriminate reproduction." And European bishops talking about *patrie, famille, et travail* didn't help.

It is also quite possible that events of the New Deal era, until now the most creative period of modern American social policy, were much influenced by the anthropological orientation of American sociology at that time. Family structures could be vastly different, one from the other, but who was to say which was better or worse? They were simply different.

The sociologist Nathan Glazer has pointed out that this amiable tolerance began to break down during World War II. If the family structure of the European middle class produced personalities that were peculiarly susceptible to Fascist and Nazi ideologies, was that a matter of indifference to the world? Moreover, when the colonial areas of the world began to achieve independence, the new rulers were often far less satisfied with the results of the traditional ways of life than the colonial administrators, who often carefully preserved them.

More recently, however, American social scientists have been revising their views. More and more the family is seen, as Glazer puts it, "as not only the product of social causes but as itself a significant and dynamic element in the creation of culture, social character, and social structure."

As society, in the form of government, more and more acknowledges its responsibilities to the poor and disadvantaged, it follows that it must be concerned with family patterns that help or hinder efforts to bring people out of poverty and into the mainstream of American life.

The different effects of different patterns are also becoming more clear. Of the many peoples who have come to the United States, some have prospered much more than the general run, others much less. Without any question, family stability and values account for much of the difference. No people came to our shores poorer than did the Chinese and Japanese. Yet in terms of census data, they are today incomparably the highest social and economic group in the nation. Thus, twice as many Japanese and Chinese go to college as do Americans as a whole. American Jews as a group are probably even better off in socio-economic terms than the Chinese and Japanese, although the census does not classify persons by religious faith. And what have all three groups in common? A singularly stable, cohesive family life.

It would be wrong to suggest that there is a very great deal of systematic knowledge on this subject. There is not. Typically, Catholic "teaching" abounds in moralisms about family values, but Catholic sociologists seem hardly to have touched on the question. Once again we find ourselves with a surplus of opinions, but few facts, on a subject of profound moral significance about which we should be helping to shape national policy.

Even so, general impressions surely cannot be far wrong: the stability and quality of family life are a prime determinant of individual and group achievement. This is not to argue for any one pattern—any more than to declare that there can be only one form of achievement. But what evidence we do have argues that social conditions ought to enable the general run of families to succeed in whatever arrangements fit their fancy. American social policy, however, ignores the question altogether: the individual rather than the family is the object of concern.

The shortcomings of this approach are beginning to be manifest. For several reasons, they have become most clear with regard to the problems of Negro Americans. This being the most pressing and grave social problem facing the American people today, it has begun—only just begun—to attract a degree of serious inquiry. Invariably, the problem of family life emerges as one of the most deep-rooted of Negro problems. Because census data distinguish between white and nonwhite families, it is possible to trace the experience of the Negro family over the past several decades and to see the effect of various economic and social developments on a group of persons of whom a high proportion live in or near to poverty. It is almost certain that many or most of the same effects would be found to occur among white families in similar circumstances, but the experience of poor whites is concealed in the affluent mass.

Our experience of unemployment in the postwar period gives perhaps the best example of how our traditional way of looking at events from the point of view of the individual has concealed many of the most important things we ought to have known. For a quarter century, the nation has been keeping ever more detailed and accurate accounts of the number of persons working and not working. For most of this period, we have had a relatively high level of unemployment. And throughout there has been a disastrous unemployment level for Negroes. It has been universally agreed that this is a bad thing. All administrations have deplored it. It has been generally depicted, however, as a bad thing for the individuals involved. Not until President Johnson rose to deliver his historic address at Howard University last June has anyone in high office in the United States even suggested that it was a catastrophe for the *families* involved.*

The main outlines of the President's speech are well known to the nation. Despite spectacular progress in some areas of the Negro community, for the great majority of Negro Americans, "the poor, the unemployed, the uprooted, and the dispossessed,"

---

* For what it may be worth, President Johnson in the spring of 1972 was of the view that the Howard University address was the finest civil rights speech he ever made. By them he thought I had written it, which was not the case. I wrote the first draft, but the second and final draft was the work of Richard Goodwin. This article, written for a Jesuit journal shortly after the Howard address, will be seen as a bit self-serving.

he reminded us, ". . . the walls are rising and the gulf is widening."
"Only a minority—less than half—of all Negro children," the
President reported, "reach the age of 18 having lived all their lives
with both of their parents." He added: "Probably a majority of
all Negro children receive Federal public assistance sometime
during their life."

Behind the President's speech was a body of data that reveals
how the persistent, savage unemployment of the Negro male
worker had contributed to this breakdown. I should not think
there is another nation in the free world in which anything comparable could have occurred without the fullest national awareness and outcry. President Johnson spoke to a nation that
seemed almost never to have heard of the idea—save for the
leaders of the Negro community, who hailed his forthrightness
and courage, and in doing so revealed not a little of their own.

The absurdities of our exclusively individual-oriented approach are also becoming clear. The most striking example is
our experience with the Aid to Families of Dependent Children
program. This New Deal measure, part of the Social Security
Act, was primarily designed to provide income for families in
which the father had died or become permanently disabled. But
families in which the father was simply absent—having deserted
or whatever—were also included. By 1940, there were a quarter
of a million children in this latter group of families—some 30
percent of all AFDC children. Today this figure has grown to
almost 2 million children: two-thirds of the total.

In New York State, the average number of persons receiving
AFDC payments rose from 177,889 in 1954 to 497,038 in 1964
—nearly three times as many. Two-thirds of the children are
Negro or Puerto Rican; two-thirds of all fathers are absent
from the home.

In New York City, the average number of children per AFDC
case rose from 2.2 in 1950 to 3.1 in 1963.

What the AFDC program has amounted to for most of its
history is a family allowance program for *broken* families. Each
family is given a sum of money according to its needs, as measured by its size. But only *after* the family breaks up. (Since 1961,
unemployed men can receive AFDC payments, but these are still
fewer than 10 percent of the cases.)

I venture to say that in Canada—not to mention Britain or

France—such an arrangement would be viewed as a form of social insanity.

Typically, such imbalance in social values produces further contortions. Project Headstart, a program in the war on poverty, is one of the most imaginative and promising efforts to bring hope to slum children that we have seen in this generation. Even so, it must be stated that we are paying women—well-qualified, professional women to be sure—up to $9.20 an hour to look after the children of men who can't make $1.50. If the working-class fathers of the city earned a steady $3.00 or $4.00 an hour, would we need a Project Headstart? Clearly we need one today, but are we going to change the system that produced the need, or merely cope with it as in the AFDC program?

The urgency of this question is compounded by a special fact of demography: as perhaps never in history, while the rich of America do whatever it is they do, the poor are begetting children. Again, the statistics about Negro Americans, because they are separated out and contain so large a proportion of poor persons, give a clue. In 1960, 1 person in 10 in the United States was nonwhite. Today it is 1 in 9. By the end of the decade, it will be 1 in 8. Of persons under fourteen today, it is 1 in 7. Of persons under the age of one, it is 1 in 6.

Given the opportunity for a stable family life, with all that this means in the way of family income, family housing, and family services, there is no reason for anything but rejoicing at the prospect of an increasing number of Americans not utterly bound to middle-class rigidities. But given the course of events that we have pursued until very recently—the policy of paying little or no attention to any such question—one could grow profoundly alarmed. From the wild Irish slums of the nineteenth-century Eastern seaboard, to the riot-torn suburbs of Los Angeles, there is one unmistakable lesson in American history: a community that allows a large number of young men to grow up in broken families, dominated by women, never acquiring any stable relationship to male authority, never acquiring any set of rational expectations about the future—that community asks for and gets chaos. Crime, violence, unrest, disorder—most particularly the furious, unrestrained lashing out at the whole social structure—that is not only to be expected; it is very near to inevitable. And it is richly deserved.

Although the Labor Department's report on August unemployment shows that the Negro jobless rate fell fairly sharply to 7.6 percent of the Negro labor force, still the unemployment rate among adult Negro males remains deplorably high. It remains about twice that of whites. These are the very men we are expecting to rear stable, orderly, well-behaved children, and to do so in what is just about the worst urban housing in the Western world.

We are expecting the impossible, and will end up with an impossible situation unless we seriously and promptly address ourselves to the issue of what it takes for a working man to raise a family in an American city today, and then see to it that what it takes is available. What this comes to is a national family policy.

In itself, a national family policy need not be any more complex than were the provisions of the Employment Act of 1946. The point is not what answers are provided, but what questions are posed. The Employment Act said nothing about how to achieve the fullest measure of employment, but rather declared that the national government should be continually concerned with just that question, and should be constantly seeking answers.

A national family policy need only declare that it is the policy of the American government to promote the stability and well-being of the American family; that the social programs of the Federal government will be formulated and administered with this object in mind; and finally that the President, or some person designated by him, perhaps the Secretary of Health, Education, and Welfare, will report to the Congress on the condition of the American family in all its many facets—not of *the* American family, for there is as yet no such thing, but rather of the great range of American families in terms of regions, national origins, and economic status.

Taxation is a good example of an area of government policy in which a general pronouncement would have considerable specific relevance. General impressions to the contrary, during the postwar period indirect taxes, which bear heaviest on the families of the poor, have been *rising* as a proportion of all tax receipts. The "value" of the income-tax exemption for wives and children has steadily eroded since its present level was set in 1948. Recent tax cuts certainly have not improved, and may have further worsened, the relative tax burden of poor families. All these imbalances could easily be righted, however, if the tax reductions of the coming five years or so are deliberately designed to do so. The tax cuts are coming: a national family policy would help shape them in a direction they might not otherwise assume.

Whatever the specific form a national family policy might take, it is clear that President Johnson raised just such large possibilities in his Howard University speech. "The family," he said, "is the cornerstone of our society. More than any other force, it shapes the attitude, the hopes, the ambitions, and the values of the child. When the family collapses, it is the children that are usually damaged. When it happens on a massive scale, the community itself is crippled."

As we enter a new era of social policy, the opportunity to overcome the one great shortcoming of the past is almost in our grasp.

Traffic Safety and
the Body Politic

3

I

A series of converging events make it likely that the United States is, at long last, going to come to terms with a gigantic domestic problem that has attracted enormous attention but almost no interest: traffic safety. It is not at all clear how much will be made of the present opportunity. But much more is at stake than is generally perceived. To grasp this, it is necessary to have some idea of the dimensions and the ramifications of the problem.

Automobile injuries and deaths began to cause concern before the First World War. In the nineteen-twenties, when the automobile became a standard family possession, it also created what is by now an endemic public health problem. The National Health Survey indicates some 4 or 5 million persons are injured each year, involving perhaps 100,000 permanent disabilities. Another 50,000 injuries are fatal. In Korea the Air Force found that automobile injuries were generally more serious and required

"Traffic Safety and the Health of the Body Politic" was read as a Monday Evening Paper before the Fellows of the Center for Advanced Studies of Wesleyan University in March 1966. A version appeared in *The Public Interest* in Spring 1966.

longer hospitalization than battle casualties. One can be fairly certain the same is true in Vietnam.

The economic costs are considerable, of course. A disproportionate number of the persons killed or permanently disabled represent an almost complete loss on a heavy investment: they are persons with twenty years of nurture behind them and presumably forty years of productive work ahead. The cost estimates are surpassingly fuzzy, but something like 2 percent of the Gross National Product seems about right, if property damage accidents are included.

Little attention has been given to the indirect social costs of traffic accidents, although these are probably the more serious ones. American adults probably have more direct relationship to government through the management of the motor vehicle system than in any other way. There are some 90 million persons who are licensed to drive. Nothing like that number pay taxes, vote, engage in "participatory democracy," or know that the mainland of China is controlled by Communists. A driver's license is close to a necessity of life for many, perhaps most, Americans, and the power of government to grant or deny it, or to suspend or withdraw it, is, of course, considerable. Oddly enough, it does not seem to have led to a very great deal of corruption, perhaps because it is so near to indispensable. (It may be that corruption arises in areas where something more like privilege is dispensed.) On the other hand, because the traffic laws are not observed, the system has made lawbreakers of just about everyone and has resulted in the arrest and trial of vast numbers of persons. I should not be surprised if, as a consequence of the management of the system, the incidence of police arrest in American society is the highest of any in history. I am not clear that it is good for a society for the persons in it to become accustomed to being arrested. The darkest aspect of this development is that we seem to have become reconciled to being arrested in this manner and no longer seem to think much of it. George Orwell, of course, kept insisting that oppression comes on little cat's feet and that once it has happened it no longer seems like oppression.

The most important impact of traffic-law enforcement has been on the courts and the legal profession. It is probably true that the judicial and legal profession of the United States devotes almost one-half its time to the adjudication and adjustment of automobile matters and earns perhaps a third of its fees that way. An editorial in *The New York Times* reports that "automobile negligence suits make up from 50 to 90 percent of the case loads of civil courts throughout the country." This appears to be true in the appellate divisions as well as in the lower tribunals. It inevitably has led to a startling backlog of cases in American courts. In New York, for example, it takes *over four years* to get a jury trial convened. In the measure that justice delayed is justice denied, it would seem there are clear implications of such delays for a society that wishes to be a just one. The advantages that the wealthy have over the poor in such a system are obvious. Whether or not this situation will bring about an eventual erosion of respect for the judicial process is a related question.

Now, these are a familiar assortment of sorrows: life is expensive; justice, elusive; death, inevitable. There is little to be said for or against them unless it can be seriously argued that, in this particular case, they are unnecessary, or at least meliorable. But not only can such an argument be made; increasingly, it is not even disputed. There is a considerable body of empirical evidence—of which the different accident experience of different road systems is the most striking—that automobile accidents can be reduced without substantially compromising the essential transportation system by which they are generated.

It should be noted on the other hand that there is not much evidence that the number of accidents can be substantially reduced by altering the behavior of drivers while maintaining the present, near-universal, driver population. It may be this can be done, but it has not been done. This leads to the basic strategy of crash injury protection: it is assumed that a great many automobile accidents will continue to occur. That being the case, probably the most efficient way to minimize the overall cost of accidents is to design the interior of the vehicles so that the *injuries* that follow the *accidents* are relatively mild. An attraction of this approach is that it could be put into effect by changing the behavior of a tiny population: the forty or fifty executives who run the automobile industry.

It would also seem obvious that the legal problems of adjudicating the consequences of traffic accidents could be considerably reduced. Most accidents are probably not worth adjudicating: a simple claims procedure as proposed by various judges, and most carefully by O'Connell and Keeton, would eliminate a large part of the case load (as would, of course, a reduction in accidents). More significantly, a careful enquiry might well reach the conclusion that in many cases it is simply not possible to establish by testimony and similar evidence just how an accident occurs, much less who is to blame. The system has failed, and that is about all that is to be learned with finality. With the best will in the world on the part of persons testifying, it is probable that for many high-speed accidents the essential events are beyond the threshold of perception of the persons involved. (Suppose murder trials were conducted on the basis of demanding to know of witnesses which way the bullet was traveling when the victim was hit!)

II

If the reduction of accidents and injuries—and of the social costs they give rise to—is possible, how is it that this has not been done? More to the point, why has it not been seriously attempted?

It is not that no one has noticed the problem. On the contrary, there are few public issues which have been so consistently the subject of comment by government officials, communications media, service organizations, and the like. There is every reason to suppose the public is highly sensitive to the subject and that it can be a rewarding political issue. (In a recent survey by *The Economist,* British voters were asked to name what they thought was the single most important issue in the then forthcoming British general election, "without any prompting." More named "road safety" than taxes.) Why, then, so few results?

I am persuaded there are at least three clusters of reasons that explain this failure.

FIRST: THE VENALITY OF THE AUTOMOBILE INDUSTRY

After a decade of intermittent involvement with the problem (in 1958, as Acting Secretary to the Governor, I was Chairman of the New York State Traffic Safety Policy Committee; in

Washington in the early nineteen-sixties, I represented the Department of Labor on the President's Committee for Traffic Safety and the interdepartmental body concerned with this subject), I have come to the conclusion that for brute greed and moral imbecility the American automobile industry has no peer.

The industry is, for its size, incomparably the most profitable enterprise in the world. These profits are drenched in blood. In 1960 Dr. William Haddon, Jr., and I made tentative calculations that something like one-third of the automobiles manufactured in Detroit actually end up with blood on them. I understand a Canadian group has raised this estimate to the level of every other car.

To a perhaps surprising degree, the profits of the industry are related to these accidents (although not, of course, to the injuries). Much attention has been paid to the concept of "planned obsolescence" (which itself may account for a fair number of vehicle failures), but almost no interest has been shown in the role of accident damage in creating a market for the products of the industry. There are anywhere from 15 million to 40 million accidents a year. While in the Department of Labor, I made some rough estimates that as much as 20 percent of the total production of the automobile industry is required to replace or repair damaged vehicles. This estimate may be high, of course.

I believe it can no longer be doubted that within the higher executive levels of the industry there has been a conviction that an excessive concern with safety is bad for business. Ford made a serious effort in 1956 to sell a safer car; this was accompanied by a bad sales experience that has apparently frightened off the entire industry ever since. Chrysler, at a time of management troubles, made some important statements on the subject and has kept a highly competent man on as its safety engineer, but has not gone much beyond that. On balance, the impression anyone following the subject must have is that General Motors, which dominates the industry, has been consistently opposed to any systematic concern with safety design and has had its way.

This is the hardest possible case to prove, of course, but there is evidence. One of the few glimpses inside the industry came from testimony in the 1959 case of *Comstock v. General Motors Corporation*, heard in the Supreme Court of Michigan. Anyone concerned with the morality of American business organizations would have to be appalled by *Comstock*. The uncontested facts of the case are that the 1953 Buick Roadmaster had a defective power brake system (involving a ring sealer in the hydraulic-brake master cylinder which allowed the brake fluid to escape from the cylinder). Having manufactured this car and having discovered that the brakes did not always work, the manufacturer's response was as follows, in the words of the Michigan Supreme Court:

> The matter was judged serious enough by General Motors to require the issuance of 2 separate kits for replacement of the defective parts. . . .
>
> The agencies were instructed to make repairs on the power brake system at General Motors' expense whenever 1953 Buicks came into the shops. These repairs were made without notice to the owners and even if there was no complaints about the brakes. No warning to owners of 1953 Buicks equipped with these power brakes was given either by General Motors, or by the agency which sold this Buick as far as this record reveals.
>
> Wentworth, the Lawless Buick agency service representative, testified on this point:
>
> *A.* Because I was not allowed a campaign to call these people or mail anything to them.
>
> *The Court:* They asked you to call them.
>
> *A.* They said to get these cars whenever you could get your hands on them. When a customer didn't come around I couldn't look up the thing. I thought it was Buick's responsibility. Most of the time on things like that owners were sent registered letters. I was not allowed to do that.
>
> *The Court:* Who said you couldn't send letters?
>
> *A.* The service department at Buick. It was a hush thing. They didn't want the public to know the brakes were bad and they were very alarmed.

Mr. Krause, the general service manager of Buick, testified somewhat differently:

> *Q.* Mr. Krause, did the Buick Motor Division ever contact the owners of these cars?
>
> *A.* No, sir.
>
> *Q.* Didn't advertise what the conditions were?
>
> *A.* No, sir.

Q. Were any parts ever sent to a dealer as replacement parts unless he asked for them?

A. No, sir.

Q. I take it nothing was done at all by the Buick Motor Company or Buick Division of General Motors unless and until the parts were asked for and then they were given, if possible?

A. The parts were ordered by the dealer and shipped to the dealer by us.

Q. That is all the Buick Company did?

A. Well, other than put out the technical information such as the bulletin you just read there.

The Court: You didn't call them up and say, get all these cars in and have them repaired?

A. No, sir.

Q. Why not?

A. Well, in the first place that is the obligation of the dealer, and in the second place we don't know who all the owners are or where they are.

Q. Did they ever do anything to find out?

A. We have no right to tell the dealer how to run his business. He is an independent businessman.

Q. But did you do anything to find out?

A. No.

Just how general such conduct has been in the industry is an open question, but the attitude underlying it has been common and manifest. When the possibility first began to be raised that the impurities in automotive exhausts might cause cancer as well as smog, the response of the industry was one of utter unconcern and flat refusal to do what would have been easy and cheap to do (install blow-by devices as standard equipment) until forced by legislation.*

There is a resistance to reasonableness in this field that is at once baffling and revealing. It was soon enough evident that the executives and engineers in the industry simply would not comprehend the idea of designing their machines so that the injuries that result from accidents would be minimized. This at least could be explained: these were one-subject-at-a-time men who would not accept the inevitability of accidents, or in any event were not trying to design machines that would not have them as a

---

* Well, sort of cheap.

result of mechanical failures. If the fools driving them wished to collide with one another, that was not the engineer's lookout. But recent congressional hearings have produced evidence that the incidence of design failure *known to the industry* is much greater than anyone suspected. Meanwhile evidence of failure in the obsolescent stage is mounting. (Nonwhites have much higher fatality rates than whites, owing presumably to being forced by economic pressures to drive older and hence more dangerous vehicles.)

But beyond the unwillingness to face up to the persistence of accidents, there is an obtuseness on the overall subject of traffic safety that is bewildering, coming as it does from men of un-questioned probity and manifest rationality in the management of their affairs in general.

On April 5, 1966, for example, Mr. John Bugas, Vice-President of Ford, speaking for the industry before the Senate Commerce Committee, asking that the industry be given a chance to police itself, said, "If you assume that we haven't gotten the message before on the importance of safety, we have got it now, believe me." Yet ten days later, on April 15, Mr. Henry Ford, 2d, made it just as clear that this was not so. In an otherwise candid and positive statement of intention to make cars even safer than they were, Mr. Ford went on to criticize Mr. Ralph Nader, one of the most forceful critics of the industry, in terms that do no one any good: "He can read statistics and he can look up a lot of facts that are in the public domain, but I don't think he knows anything about engineering safety into automobiles," said Mr. Ford. "I think that, if these critics who don't really know any-thing about safety will get out of our way, we can go ahead with our job—and we have a job to do. We have to make our cars safer." This in itself is an understandable enough attitude for a manufacturer and would not merit comment save for the remarks that preceded it. Pointing out that "the driver is the most im-portant factor [in safety] because, if you drive safely accidents won't happen," Mr. Ford noted that laws signed by Senator Abraham Ribicoff when he was Governor "cut the deaths on Connecticut roads by about 50 percent" without any changes being made in automobiles.

If in truth there are laws which when enacted cut the number of highway deaths in half, it will surely be seen that this is an immensely important fact. And if the Chairman of the Board of Ford Motor Company says it is a fact, we should have every reason to assume it is. What is, then, to be made of the discovery that it is not a fact? In the four years 1951–1954, the average number of highway deaths in Connecticut was 254 per year. In the four years of Governor Ribicoff's term, which followed, the average was 286. In the years since the average has been 323. In the period since 1955 the number of accidents per year in Connecticut has more than doubled, the *rate* of accidents per hundred million vehicle miles has gone up 43 percent, and the rate of injuries up 29 percent.

It has been these frustrating, stubborn realities, among others, that have led Senator Ribicoff, for whom no praise could be too great in this area, to his present line of enquiry.

Mr. Ford's confusion is not an isolated event. It is the pattern of events. Moreover, the message the crtics of the industry have sought to deliver goes precisely to this point. If the companies will not respond fairly to information that *is* in the public domain, what can be the grounds for confidence that they are acting responsibly about information that until now has been entirely internal and private?

The practice of tire maufacturers, if not as extensively documented as that of the motor industry, is not more reassuring.

There is, of course, another major "industry" concerned with traffic safety: the insurance industry. With the exception of some mild experimentation carried out by Liberty Mutual and a few other groups, the insurance industry has done nothing about traffic safety of any consequence, so far as I am aware. I do not know why this is so and have only the vaguest impressions. One impression is that the insurance industry has not wished to get into a public row with the automobile industry: a kind of class solidarity that forbids washing dirty corporate linen in public. A second impression is that the executives of the insurance industry are not innovative men and do not have the initiative to undertake any serious efforts to change a system that is working well enough from their limited vantage point. (This seems true of the industry as a whole. The automobile is a nineteenth-century machine that has not been much changed for at least a generation now. General Motors does not seem to be a place where a genuinely creative engineer would want to spend much time—

certainly not in the age of the Moon Shot. Part of the task of the management of public affairs in the modern world must be to take into account the fact that large segments of life will be in the hands of men of modest endowment.) A third possibility would be that, despite denials, the insurance industry does in fact profit from automobile insurance to an extent that it finds satisfactory. The issue is not clear, nor have the companies sought to make it so.

As with the harassment of the driver in the first era of traffic safety, it seems we are now entering a period of indicting the businessmen involved. The need to impose guilt in this field is obviously deep-seated, and we may very well be overcorrecting. The more important question is, why have the very large number of persons in business, industry, and the law who have made large profits out of automobiles been impervious to the pleas to be rational about automobile safety? Has is got to do with the nature of corporate organization, or is it simply a matter that our society is easily corrupted in areas where individuals are asked to assume a personal relation to a collective responsibility, a matter Reinhold Niebuhr has insisted we attend to? Or alternately, is this simply more evidence of the trivialization of American business: the fact that the central concerns of American society are no longer in the hands of free enterprise, and that free enterprise is no longer in the hands of men who expect to lead society?

SECOND: THE PSYCHOLOGICAL ROLE OF THE AUTOMOBILE

It is surely clear that the largest reason we have not done anything to tame the automobile is that we have not much wanted to. That the automobile has a powerful symbolic, emotional role in American life is a proposition few would doubt. It is a central symbol of potency and power: the equivalent of the sword, the horse, the spear of earlier ages. It is both a symbol of aggression and a vehicle thereof. It is a sanctioned form of violence. In American society one can injure and kill another person with an automobile at virtually no risk of *physical* reprisal. It is also a prime agent of risk-taking in a society that still values risk-taking, but does not provide many outlets.

Anatol Rapoport has suggested that the most careful approach to accident prevention may in the end lead us nowhere if it turns out that "accidents are manifestations . . . of global cultural factors—that is, of social analogues of destructive drives."

> For example, if we should find that in spite of clear determination of the marginal effectiveness of certain measures and the actual implementation of these measures with the resulting reduction of accident mortality and morbidity in one area, the *overall* accident incidence of morbidity or mortality remains unaffected—i.e., if stopping up one wound we only help to open another, as sometimes happens in superficial cures of conversion hysterias—then we will know that something more basic is wrong with us.

Whatever the truth of this kind of speculation, at very least it can be said that the attitude of the public is ambivalent on the question of traffic safety. Too much attention to safety must necessarily call attention to the dangers of driving, which is not agreeable. At the same time, the dangers of driving *are* agreeable and *are* sought. By the almost total emphasis on the responsibility of drivers to drive safely, it becomes possible for the individual driver to assume he is safe when he wishes to be and to have the satisfaction of taking risks when he desires that experience. In this context, the otherwise absurd business of counting the death toll over the holiday weekends assumes a certain cultural consistency: it is rather like keeping score on Russian roulette—those who have successfully avoided disaster are pleased to be reminded of it; those who have not are beyond all reminding.

THIRD: THE FAILURE OF GOVERNMENT

The power of the automobile industry and the ambivalence of the public have combined to prevent effective governmental action. We have opted for an arrangement which is, I suspect, not unusual in such circumstances: working at the problem in ways fairly certain not to succeed. One of the most effective ways in which a government cannot do something is to assign the task to the kinds of people who never get anything done.

Since the nineteen-fifties there has existed in Washington an organization known as the President's Committee for Traffic

Safety, which uses the Presidential seal with abandon. I served as a departmental representative on the body for a year before learning that the executive director was neither chosen nor paid by the Federal government, but rather by the industry! This man presided over the expenditure of public funds allocated to the Department of Commerce and generally disported himself as the head traffic-safety man in government, although he was in fact a paid agent of the interests he ought at least to have been keeping an eye on. In 1963 I attended a meeting in the White House called by the Secretary to the Cabinet to consider whether the integrity of the Presidential seal was not being abused: it was, and it was so agreed; but what to do about it remained a puzzle.

Similarly, the public will have largely been paralyzed by the seeming incompatibility of safe driving and mass driving. In the course of the past half-century we have designed our cities and generally arranged our lives so as to make the use of the automobile indispensable to most persons. This makes it politically impossible to withdraw the right to drive from anything but a small fraction of adults, and then only for short periods. Hence any strategy based upon punishment of the driver for inadequate performance must tend to fail. Even drinking drivers, who are unquestionably dangerous persons who by and large must be said to be responsible for their dangerous condition, will nonetheless by and large continue to drive: the social life of the American middle class now primarily takes the form of getting into an automobile and driving to a place where alcohol is consumed—a friend's home, a tavern, or whatever. This is too deep a social pattern to be broken. Hence, at very least, massive ambiguity.

There is, however, another source of the failure of government: it is the striking absence of any of those conditions of self-generating reform which would enable government to take initiatives on its own—such conditions as money to carry out programs, social statistics and related data on which to base programs, and professional persons to devise them. To a surprising degree, none of these exist in the world of traffic safety.

The amount of money allocated to research in traffic safety has been minuscule. (The one exception—a major one—to this rule concerns highway construction. The nation has constructed a fabulously elaborate highway system designed with steadily improving safety features. In this instance, however, the interests of the industry and the public were harmonious with those of safety.) The automobile companies spend money designing their products so that they operate properly in traditional terms; but so far as is known, they do almost no research in crash injury prevention, nor do they seem to have done any work in the larger area of developing scientific data about the man-machine relationship in the highway complex. Recently a number of universities have begun to study the problem, but in general it is fair to estimate that at no one time over the past half-century have there been as many as a dozen senior scientists working in this field.

It is not to be supposed that there has been a deliberate strategy on the part of the automobile industry behind all this, but the outcome could not have been more effective if there had been. Because there has been so little money devoted to safety research, there are almost no facts. There being no facts, there is very little in the way of argument. Amateur efforts to produce "crashproof" cars have by and large been more ludicrous than not.

Directly related to the absence of facts about safety design is the absence of facts about the whole subject. This is central. Despite the inundations of putative data about death rates and the like, there are in fact no standard national statistics about traffic safety. The United States government does not collect them.

The only moderately reliable statistic that exists is the number of persons killed. We have this information in consequence of the established practice of coroners of reporting the probable cause of death of bodies found on public highways. Combining death and taxes, the death rate is obtained by a simple formula that derives total miles driven from gasoline taxes paid and then divides miles by the number of cadavers. The result of this not very complex calculation is the death rate, a dependable but meaningless number, in the sense that it provides no guide to action of any sort—and, more seriously, is probably misleading. (One would think the number of persons who actually die in motor vehicle accidents responds more to advances in medical practice than anything else.)

It is hardly a complicated matter to conceive what basic national data ought to be collected: rates for deaths, injuries, and accidents; geographical and temporal distribution of such; types of vehicles involved; types of driver failure; types of vehicle failure; types of drivers involved; types of roadway and environmental failures. That would be a beginning. Most of the data could be gathered by standard sampling techniques.

To repeat: *none* of these data now exists, save the death rate. (A few states also gather injury and accident rates.) Thus, so far as is known, the automobile manufacturers do not keep any systematic records of the injuries that occur to automobile occupants when they are thrown against the vehicle's interior in the course of the accident. There are, of course, millions of such events each year, and it may be said that it would be a rare layman whose self-composure would survive fifteen minutes of color photographs of the results.

In 1963, testifying before the Subcommittee on Public Health and Safety of the House Committee on Interstate and Foreign Commerce, I dwelt at some length on this subject. In the course of my remarks I made the following statement:

> In an effort to keep up with the problem [of traffic safety] for little more than a generation agencies of local, State, and Federal Governments have been compiling statistics about accidents, injuries, and deaths with a diligence and industry that seems to grow as the years go by.
>
> But that has been an almost wholly uncritical effort. As a result, it has been almost wholly useless. It is my impression, and it is the firm opinion of research workers for whom I have the greatest regard, that with perhaps one or two exceptions all the vast accumulation of data about automobile accidents over the past half century has contributed almost nothing to our understanding of the cause and prevention of accidents.

The hearing room in which I made this statement was filled with persons representing the major institutions concerned with traffic safety. I appeared, not as an interested amateur, but as a member of the subcabinet supporting a bill to establish a National Accident Prevention Center which had been introduced by the chairman of the subcommittee. This was a serious level of government. Thus the reaction to the statement is a good illustration of the atmosphere that has pervaded this subject. There was no reaction. So far as I am aware, the statement never appeared in any of the myriad traffic-safety publications. No one commented on it. No one attempted to refute it. No one attempted to do anything about it.

What is true of accident statistics is similarly true of accident investigations: there are none. Save for an aborted experiment at the Harvard Medical School, there has been almost no effort over the past half-century to unravel the etiology of actual automobile accidents in the way that is routine for airplane accidents. The concept of "grounding" a particular model of vehicle that appears to have safety problems does not exist with respect to automobiles.

A final aspect of the failure of government, and the crucial one, has come from the fact that, despite its long history, the problem of traffic safety has never yet associated itself with a professional group that would apply to it standards of evidence, evaluation, and self-criticism that the solution of problems of this kind requires.

Government regulation of the automobile began as a form of tax collection, upon which a layer of law enforcement was superimposed. In time the automobile helped create a new institution of law enforcement: the State Police. Probably because they are characteristically not corrupt, very little attention has been paid to them. However, they have been a dominant institution in traffic-law enforcement (and, by a feedback process, probably to traffic law enactment as well), and little notice has been given to what a very poor job they have made of it, despite their high standards of personal conduct.

The entire pattern of State Police management of the automobile complex is derived directly from the model of the prevention, detection, and punishment of—crime. From the cowboy hats to the six-gun to the chase scene, the entire phenomenon is a paradigm of the imposition of law on an unruly and rebellious population. This involves intense concentration on the guilt of individuals, as measured by conformance to statutes, and belief in the efficacy of punishment, either threatened or carried out, as a means of social regulation. There is not much evidence that this works. More to the point, the police have almost no tradition of controlled enquiry that would find out. Thus, in 1955 the Connecticut State Police began a crackdown on speeders that soon brought nationwide attention. In a curious way the efficacy of such an effort is somehow presumed. Yet by any measurable standards the Connecticut program has been a distinct failure. Nonetheless it is clear that the Connecticut State Police do not, in any meaningful sense, know this and do not intend to find it out. Their response to the gentlest criticism is pure Hibernian apoplexy. (It happens there is a Bureau of Public Roads study which shows the rate of accidents decreases as speed increases between 35 and about 68 miles per hour. Most probably this is because both speed and accidents are functions of density. But it could be hoped that even the most dense Police Commissioner might wonder if there were not some relation between this study and results that seem to bear it out, even if on further reflection they might not.)

Similarly, there is no evidence that drivers who are arrested for speeding, or similar offenses, are in fact any different from other drivers, or that they act differently thereafter. Since most drivers, according to Bureau of Public Roads studies, exceed posted speed limits much of the time, it is likely that to be arrested for speeding is in the nature of a random event. Again it must be emphasized that such drivers may in fact be different—and worse, or whatever—but the management of traffic safety has largely been in the hands of institutions and groups that do not routinely ask such questions, much less tease out the answers. And we must live for the moment with the probability that most "convicted speeders" are little more than innocent victims of the Poisson distribution.

The highway engineers, whose research I have cited, are the major and the most revealing exception to this rule. They are a profession; they have standards; they pursue them. When a bridge falls down, they try to find out why. When a new road is to be designed, they try to calculate how many cars will be using it and at what speeds, and design accordingly. By and large they have been predictably, sometimes brilliantly, successful.

III

By the mid-nineteen-fifties it was becoming evident that this overall situation could not persist. A matter of considerable public interest was in the hands of incompetents or worse. *Some* protest was inevitable, and it arose, in a natural course of events, among a small group of professional persons—lawyers, doctors, engineers, and public officials. Articles began to appear. Intellectuals were doing their work.

Up to this point the automobile industry had options. There were two courses open. The industry could recognize that the automobile system was working badly from the point of view of safety and could seek to organize a mixed public and private effort to introduce rational and effective measures, including much greater attention to automobile design, but by no means limited to that. This would have involved considerable shaking up of the corporate staffs, the disestablishment of flunky organizations such as the National Safety Council, and the creation of a Federal automobile agency modeled on the FAA, which has presided over a highly creative relationship between the Federal government and the aviation industry. Alternately, they could go the route of the railroads in the nineteenth century, which also sought to brazen out a safety problem and ended up with a particularly dreary form of Federal statutory regulation. There was no third way.

The sequence of events is important. The medical doctors were the first on the scene. The enormous medical problem created by accident trauma led in a quite natural way to the question of whether these could not somehow be reduced. The American Medical Association and the American College of Surgeons set up committees on the subject. By this point, techniques of crash injury protection (padded dashboards, seat belts, and so on) had become quite sophisticated in aviation. The orderly instinct of the doctors was to transfer these techniques to automobile design. In the nineteen-fifties the Public Health Service began making small grants with these possibilities in mind. Inevitably there arose a body of opinion, to which some information was attached, to the effect that the automobiles were not as safe as they might be. *This was the crucial moment for the industry;* had they joined in this enquiry with a modicum of zeal, they would be a free enterprise to this day. Instead, they chose to resist.

Students of American business ought really to try to learn what decision-making processes went on at this point. The largest and most profitable industry in the world faced the relatively simple problem of responding to criticism couched in terms of the public interest, and it could not do so. The industry gave almost no sign that it was aware of criticism: it was not so much a matter of responding badly as not responding at all. Presumably this has mostly to do with the nature of the organizations involved and of the men who were running them. The physical isolation of Detroit is probably another significant factor. It is also true that the business schools and their various journals, which might have given some guidance, gave none (as far as I am aware). Some of these journals are notable for their interest in the Christian Responsibilities of the American Business Executive, but somehow the question of the responsibilities of the nation's largest industry for the safety of its products never came to mind. Nor, when others drew attention to the subject, did the business schools and journals comment.

In 1961, in a paper given at one of the very few meetings at which the manufacturers and their critics came together, I wrote:

> It would not appear that the industry is particularly conscious of the fact, but the belief is well established among intellectually influential circles in the United States that the automotive manufacturers are essentially indifferent, and sometimes even opposed, to traffic-safety measures. This is a scandalous position, but it is nonetheless held, and before long it will begin to damage the manufacturers more than they may imagine.

There was no response to this conciliatory gesture any more than to the defiant ones. The industry became more and more a caricature of an overmuscled, underbrained organism heading for disaster.

Disaster came from an unlooked-for source: the legal profession. Not from the Bar Association, or the Wall Street firms, or the great law schools, which are said to maintain a watching brief of sorts on such matters, but rather from the *déclassé* claimants' attorneys, organized as the American Trial Lawyers Association. Out of a combination of self-interest and genuine, hot indignation at the indifference of the manufacturers, this professional association decided the time had come to stop "Murder by Motor" by the direct and lethal process of suing the manufacturers in whose automobiles their clients are killed and injured in such wholesale numbers.

This process has begun, aided by judicial rulings concerning the nature of the automobile manufacturer's warranty. Just as importantly, the reactions of the industry to criticism have steadily eroded the presumptions of good faith and diligence on its part: juries are more and more disposed to find the manufacturers guilty. A certain political edge has also appeared. The ATA is known as the "Democratic Bar Association": its members are instinctual Democrats, much as the ABA members are Republicans. At recent meetings of the Trial Lawyers, elected and appointed government officials have competed with one another in denouncing Detroit.

It may also be noted that the failure of the executive branch of the government (until the recent and perhaps determinant initiative taken by the Johnson administration) has given an unusual opening to legislators, which by and large they have exploited. At the Federal level, for example, it has been men such as former Congressman Kenneth Roberts and Senator Abraham Ribicoff who have prodded the government into action. Somehow there were legislators who retained their freedom of action when all else was paralysis.

The industry has now announced that it will not only accept but actually request government regulation. This is a normal, predictable outcome. *For its own protection the industry has to get itself regulated by the Federal government.* What only a decade ago was unthinkable has now become all but inevitable. The companies must get their products formally certified as safe in order to protect themselves from massive litigation. If everything continues according to form, the next step will be for the industry to seek to dominate the government agency charged with regulating it, and so we commence another chapter of exposure leading to legislation imposing regulation that ends up more like collusion than anything else.

This process has, of course, begun. The Federal government now specifies safety features that must be incorporated in vehicles it purchases. The administration proposes to extend this technique to all vehicles sold in interstate commerce. Federal tire-safety specifications are on their way. State regulations of this or that feature of vehicle design are starting up again (there was an earlier period when such items as windshield wipers were ordained) and may be expected to multiply. A Federal law controlling automobile exhausts was signed in October 1965, and Federal standards will take effect in the fall of 1967.

Because of the failure of leadership in the automobile industry, the issue is coming more and more to be defined as one of regulating the conduct of that one industry. But this would deal at best with only part of the problem. From the outset, the principal question of traffic safety has been: *What kind of problem is it?* It is not fundamentally a problem of lawbreaking or of profit-making, although it involves both those things. The closest one can come to an adequate conception is reflected in the statement of John F. Kennedy during the presidential campaign of 1960: "Traffic accidents constitute one of the greatest, perhaps the greatest, of the nation's public health problems." I wrote the statement; I rather doubt the President ever saw it. Certainly nothing much was done about it in his administration. But the idea has gained increasing acceptance. Senator Robert F. Kennedy, for one, clearly grasps the concept and cites his brother's statement.

The point is that traffic accidents are part of the general phenomenon of accidents, which have become the largest single cause of death between ages one and thirty-five for most of the industrial nations of the world. They are a particular aspect of our culture. Moreover, the social response to them has been characterized by a peculiar cultural lag. Just as classical forms of disease were in general treated by magic until perhaps two centuries ago, accidents have until this moment been thought of as somehow "wild" occurrences which do not conform to the sequential chain of causal events that define the way things in general take place.

This happens not to be so. In a series of *aperçus* that began hardly two decades ago, a tiny number of American and British researchers, primarily medical men, have unraveled the etiology of the accident to show that it is, in fact, fundamentally similar to disease—to the initiation of infectious and other insults to the body, which have long been the concern of preventive medicine. This began with the perception that accidents do in fact fit the classic public health pattern of host-agent-environment. Perhaps the most important refinement came with the conception that the agent—for example, the bacillus—was not all the various instruments by which one can get knocked on the head, but rather the abnormal energy exchange produced thereby. (In an instance of scientific serendipity, this occurred almost simultaneously to two men: William Haddon, Jr., and James J. Gibson working un-awares within miles of each other in upstate New York.) As the forms of energy exchange can for practical purposes be reduced to five categories—mechanical, thermal, electrical, ionizing, and chemical—the conception of accidents as disease suddenly emerges in a manageable form. Significantly, it was in puzzling over traffic safety that much of this theory was formulated.

The issue, then, is whether the national commitment to the problem of traffic safety will occur at this level of understanding, or whether it will proceed in the honorable but outdated tradition of muckraking, exposure, legislation, and regulation by bureaucracy. Traffic safety is a problem for scientists, including social scientists. The object should be not merely to produce adequately designed vehicles but to produce a traffic system that is as efficient as can be attained, given competing values, and that will as much as possible put an end to the present idiocies of armed police arresting and often imprisoning hordes of citizens who are then haled before courts incompetent to judge a problem that in any event is almost impossible to define in legal terms. Federal concern with automobile transportation, properly conceived, could in the end produce less bureaucracy, less harassment, less regulation, less intimidation, insult, and coercion. That should be the national object, rather than simply the punishment of motor magnates. The Highway Safety Act of 1966, which President Johnson has sent to Congress, having announced it in his State of the Union Message, has this potential. The issue now is whether the forthcoming legislation will evoke the sustained and responsible concern of those who have so neglected the subject in the past.

The nation's largest industry is about to come under Federal regulation. The reaction of the automobile industry has been to try to discredit the character of one of its most responsible critics. The professors of business administration are silent. The regulatory economists are elsewhere engaged. The press is mostly interested in the humbling of General Motors. Somewhere in all this there must be persons who will try to sort out the public interest. The outcome will test the vitality of the American system. In the meantime, the failure of the business and government bureaucracies is a fact to be noted with little pleasure.

The Automobile
and the Courts

4

In a decade during which considerably more in the way of purposeful social change has been promised than has been delivered, it may well turn out that one of the most important developments was one not at all intended, scarcely noticed, and even now barely appreciated. Somehow, during this time, America began to be sensible about the automobile.

Given the other problems that face the nation, this may seem a modest event. But in the aftermath of a half century during which those problems were all but systematically neglected in the face of any demand, howsoever irrational, made in the name of the automobile, it suggests a change in attitudes of fairly large consequence.

By the end of the nineteen-fifties the automobile was causing four distinct sets of problems, all of which were getting out of control, and none of which was seriously being attended to.

First, the cars were not always carefully built, and in terms of crash-injury protection often hideously designed. Driver training and licensing verged on the superstitious. The result was a mas-

"The Automobile and the Courts" was first published in *The New York Times Magazine*, August 27, 1967, under the title "Next: A New Auto Insurance Policy."

sive public-health problem; something like one vehicle in three was ending up with blood on it.

Second, automobile exhaust fumes had become a major source of air pollution, a matter then approaching the point of crisis.

Third, Federal highway construction was radically altering the design and function of American cities, usually to the sharp disadvantage of the inner-city poor, but with no means for taking such effects into account.

Fourth, the system of accident insurance and claims litigation was steadily paralyzing the American legal system, and at immense cost to everyone involved.

In a series of swift and decisive moves, Congress imposed Federal controls over each of the first three sets of problems. (In the case of highways it was essentially a matter of redirection.) Only the last remains untouched, and clearly this issue also is now being joined. Congressional hearings are about to begin; automobile insurance is about to become a national issue.

The new era in traffic safety, in air pollution, and in highway construction came quietly, almost stealthily. Starting in 1964, Congress began enacting legislation having to do with safety features for Government-purchased vehicles, tire standards, automotive exhaust controls, and the like.

No great notice was taken until President Johnson in the 1966 State of the Union message proposed a general measure providing for safe cars. Then in a rush of events ending in a Rose Garden ceremony nine months later on September 9, 1966, the decisive battle was fought and won. The largest manufacturing complex on earth, which into the sixth decade of the twentieth century had persisted as an utterly unregulated private enterprise, was of a sudden subjected to detailed and permanent government regulation.

Next, a Department of Transportation was established, making highway design a matter of Cabinet-level responsibility, with a clear mandate to end the mindless obsession of the Bureau of Public Roads with pouring concrete regardless of the consequences to the urban environment.

Nothing comparable has occurred since the establishment of railroad regulation in the late nineteenth century. But the process was essentially different. The establishment of the Interstate Commerce Commission in 1887 was the result of basic changes in the political attitudes of the nation, preceded by decades of controversy. The National Traffic and Motor Vehicle Safety Act of 1966, by contrast, was preceded at best by a few dozen articles in small magazines and professional journals, and perhaps three books written almost simultaneously with the legislation.

Probably not fifty men in the United States were even aware that President Johnson was going to send up a highway-safety proposal. (And not one of them would have predicted it would pass the House of Representatives unanimously!) These were essentially apolitical events.

Thus, not one but two traffic-safety bills were passed in 1966. The second of these, the Highway Safety Act of 1966, established pervasive Federal regulation of the traffic-safety activities of state governments. Driver licensing, traffic laws, emergency medical services, driver training, all these previously exclusive state concerns fell under Federal control. It was surely the largest single transfer of authority from the state to the Federal level of this generation, indeed one of the largest in American history, but it passed almost without comment.

Similarly, official attitudes toward highway construction have profoundly, but almost silently, changed. "Half the people in this building," an Assistant Secretary of Transportation remarked recently, "will die happy if we never again build a foot of urban highway." The construction of urban highways will continue, but the era when government viewed them as an unquestionable good is over.

What happened was that people changed their minds about the automobile. Or rather the people who have the power to direct such matters in America did so. The scientist Michael Polanyi has called attention to how much more common this process is than is generally recognized. One day a society appears to be operating within a well-established and untroubled system of belief, the next day it turns out to have abandoned its old convictions in favor of entirely new ones. (Walter Lippmann suggests something of the same process in his "law of accumulated grievances.")

The point is that the private automobile, as authors Alan K. Campbell and Jesse Burkhead say, "is undoubtedly the greatest generator of externalities that civilization has ever known." Its only possible rival, they add, would appear to be warfare among nations. One day the country woke up and found it had decided many of those externalities simply did not have to be tolerated indefinitely.

Something just like this is now happening with respect to the automobile insurance system. The problem is precisely parallel to that of automobile safety. The system is not working well as such, and its secondary effects are wasteful and expensive. On either ground change is in order, and, given both, change is as near to urgent as a world of competing sorrows will permit.

The presumption that the automotive companies knew more about their business than did their critics went on for a prolonged period of time, and then suddenly was reversed. That same onset of disbelief is now happening to the insurance companies. Change is upon us.

What is involved, however, is not just the insurance system, but the business system. The automobile industry let free enterprise down pretty badly: it did nothing serious whatever about the problem of vehicle safety until its freedom to do so on its own was taken away.

If the insurance industry does no better, we shall doubtless end up with improved liability arrangements, but in the process we are likely to have discredited the integrity and competence of American business management to a point that liberals and conservatives alike must view with dismay.

There are two senses in which the automobile insurance system is not working well. First, it is an extremely *costly* system. Twice as much is paid out in insurance premiums as is received back in insurance benefits. Moreover, the cost of the system would appear to be especially heavy for the poor, and others who can least afford it. Second, it is a grievously *incomplete* system, which fails to cover many of the most serious accidents.

The present system is, for the most part, based on the concepts of tort liability that developed a century ago. In essence, an individual buys protection against the risk that he will *negligently* cause an accident that will injure another person, or damage another person's property. If that should occur, his insurance company is responsible for compensating the victim, up to the amount of insurance coverage. The company, as it were, goes to court and argues the case.

The problem with the system starts right there, at the beginning. It has to do with the nature of traffic accidents. If they were orderly, discrete events, in which cause and effect could be clearly discerned and ascribed to this person or that, then the present insurance system would work well enough. But accidents are nothing of the sort. In the present stage of motor-vehicle transportation, accidents, perhaps minor ones specially, typically involve a whole range of contributory factors for which the concept of a single "cause" or "negligent party" is very near to absurd.

There are something like 13,600,000 automobile accidents per year in the United States. Given the present driving population, automobile stock, and road system, it is unlikely that any but a fraction of these accidents could be prevented, and impossible in the case of a great number to state with any certainty who is responsible. Moreover, as the number of automobiles inceases, it can be stated with confidence that the number of automobile accidents will also increase.

The result is an insurance system that is inherently unstable. The number of accidents goes up and up, and so does the number of claims and counterclaims. No one involved has any incentive to moderation or reasonableness. The victim has every reason to exaggerate his losses. It is some other person's insurance company that must pay. The company has every reason to resist. It is somebody else's customer who is making the claim. Delay, fraud, contentiousness are maximized, and in the process the system becomes grossly inefficient and expensive.

A study of traffic accidents in Michigan has shown that "for every $1 actually paid into the hands of the injury victim, $2.20 must be contributed by insurance policyholders and taxpayers." By contrast, group health programs such as Blue Cross and Blue Shield can deliver a dollar of benefits for only $1.07, and the Social Security Administration can do so for $1.02 (not counting, it is true, employers' costs in collecting social-security taxes.)

Moreover, scholars such as Alfred F. Conard have shown that while settlements of small claims are if anything overly generous, just the opposite is the case where serious injuries and losses are involved: "The plain fact," he writes, "is that if one suffers large economic losses from lost wages and extended medical treatment, he cannot expect to recoup these losses from tort law." Just as certainly, the system is biased against the poor, who are least able to wait out the years of litigation which insurance companies are free and able—and all too often anxious—to use as a bargaining weapon.

In their monumental study, *Automobile Accident Costs and Payments,* Professors Conard and James Morgan quote persons who have found themselves caught up in the personal injury automobile accident claim process.

"They were trying to humiliate me for a quick settlement."

"If I had been financially able, I would have held out longer."

"It was too long to wait for a settlement. It seems like insurance companies prolong cases too long."

"It was pretty miserable—justice isn't for the little man. I've had enough of courts. If you have [a] sharp lawyer, you're all set."

"It just dragged and dragged. It threw me from being a self-supporting woman, so that I'm dependent on others."

"The settlement was unfair, but the lawyer said take it or you might get nothing."

"[My lawyer] wanted me to say something that wasn't true. I wouldn't tell a lie for money."

Automobile accident litigation has become a twentieth-century equivalent of Dickens's Court of Chancery, eating up the pittance of widows and orphans, a vale from which few return with their respect for justice undiminished.

If the system is stacked somewhat against the traffic victim who is poor and cannot wait out litigation, or who is stigmatized in some way that will deprive him of sympathy before a jury (e.g., a teen-age "hot rodder"), it is also true that the insurance companies are in an equally difficult position. Given the present system, they are by definition the enemy of the victim: it is the role of the company to argue that the victim's injuries, no matter how hideous, are not as serious as he claims, etc., etc. Not exactly a lovable role, nor necessarily a persuasive one, given the disparity in resources between the giant corporation and the lone individual.

Moreover, given the system as it is, other than by beating down claims, *the only way the companies can compete with one another is by seeking out "preferred" clients who presumably will have fewer accidents than average.* There appears to be some basis in fact for the notion that certain classes of drivers will have a lower rate of accidents than others. People appear to drive as they live, and some live more dangerously, less responsibly than others. The problem, however, is that it is rarely possible to identify such persons individually; it is absurd to think of denying them insurance en masse. In any event, it is socially necessary that automobile insurance be as near universal as possible. Nonetheless, insurance companies—some more than others —seek to "cream" the market, with results that verge on outrage.

For a decade now, students of the subject have been convinced that groups such as Negroes, teen-agers, divorced women, and others are significantly discriminated against in the writing of automobile insurance. Perhaps more significantly, many companies writing automobile insurance appear to make it a practice to cancel policies of drivers who have accidents or otherwise get involved with the law. The *New Republic* writer James Ridgeway reports the experience of a North Carolina man whose policy was canceled.

Asked why, the company said, "Investigation reveals that your automobile coverage was terminated due to circumstances surrounding a parking ticket which your wife received recently." The woman had protested the ticket to the police, because, she said, the meter was broken. Nonetheless she paid the fine. (In this case, the best guess is that by protesting the ticket, she gave the company an opportunity to define her as an unsuitable customer.)

A sociological phenomenon of sorts appears to be at work. Insurance agents are for the most part careful middle-class persons who are suspicious equally of working-class (not to mention lower-class) types who might tend to get into trouble, and educated types who might cause it. Occasionally the categories overlap. A University of California professor on his way back from a world tour stopped in Cambridge last spring to give a series of lectures. He and his wife took a small furnished apartment, and bought a car, thinking to drive back to Berkeley. He applied for insurance at a nearby Sears, Roebuck branch, but unaccountably was turned down. Several days later, a stranger mailed the professor the rejected application form. It apparently had been thrown away by the insurance agent, who had written across it in ballpoint pen, "Lives on Wrong Side of Massachusetts Avenue."

For some time evidence has been mounting that a very large proportion of persons whose licenses are revoked or suspended continue nonetheless to drive. And there is hardly any question that this is the case with a great number of those who merely lose, or do not obtain, insurance. This is the beginning of the incompleteness of the present system: the large number of drivers who have no liability insurance, either because their state does not require it, or because it has been canceled. The uncompensated accident victim had become a social problem as early as the nineteen-thirties, when probably fewer than half the cars on the road were insured and when, as one student put it, "Accident insurance [was] the privilege of those with some surplus income."

Some of the most appalling cases of incomplete coverage, however, arise not from the failure of drivers to insure themselves, but from the concept of negligence as the operative principle behind liability. As applied to traffic accidents, the concept is obviously flawed. For example, in a line of 20 cars, car No. 1 suddenly brakes. A disturbance is generated in the line of cars behind it. The disturbance grows more instable. Finally, car 14 rams into the rear of car 13. Which driver is responsible? Nonetheless, the system manages through various conventions and fictions to point to some guilty party in most cases. But there are many instances in which clearly neither party is at fault, *and as a result neither party is liable.* A California bar report, soon to be published, recounts a number of such cases:

¶ Two cars, properly driven, collide on a skiddy road without the fault of either. One driver loses his eyesight and the other has to have both legs amputated. Each carries heavy bodily-injury liability insurance. Neither can recover. Reason: No recovery unless the plaintiff can prove the defendant to have caused the injury by his negligence. Here neither was negligent.

¶ One party is traveling down a freeway in excess of the speed limit; the other at the moment decides to change lanes and does so without signaling. The resulting smashup demolishes both cars and sends one man to the hospital with a broken pelvis and the other is killed. Each carried full bodily-injury and property-damage insurance. Neither can recover for personal injury or damage to the car. Reason: Each party was guilty of contributory negligence.

¶ Defendant runs his car across a sidewalk and smashes into

the front room of a simple cottage, killing the grandmother and crippling for life the little children. The cause of the accident was that the driver was hit in the eye with a bullet from a BB gun shot by someone unknown. The driver carried public liability insurance, but the injured persons cannot recover. Reason: The injuries were purely accidental; the driver wasn't to blame.

Finally, there is an increasing problem of insurance companies that go bankrupt. There is no reason to doubt the general validity of the industry claim that over the past decades they have lost something like $1 billion. One result is that, of the 3,000-odd companies that sell some form of property and liability insurance, 73 have failed during the past five years, leaving the policy-holders without protection. In consequence there is now a growing number of cases in which accident victims are left helpless. The plight of the victims, if never standard, has none-theless a consistency to it: the promising high-school athlete, the smashed school bus, the endless operations and deformed limbs, the mortgaged farm and ruined parents. The firm that had in-sured the truck had gone bankrupt.

As stated earlier, the secondary effects of the present insurance system are wasteful and onerous. The most ironic—and absurd—of these secondary effects is that the liability system has worked in such a way that the influence of the insurance industry in the field of traffic safety has been almost entirely negative. The central myth of the prescientific stage in this field was that drivers are responsible for accidents *and can be made not to have them.*

This view harmonizes so well with the tort system of adjudicat-ing traffic accidents on the basis of who was at fault that over the decade preceding the imposition of Federal safety regulation, the insurance industry was steadfastly indifferent to or even opposed to all serious proposals made in the field. In logic, those in the insurance industry should have been at the forefront of traffic-safety research and development. In fact, with the honorable exception of the Liberty Mutual Company, their voice was in-distinguishable from the chorus of Yahoos in Detroit bellowing about the "nut behind the wheel." They set up the usual trade associations, staffed with the usual incompetents, and spent much of their time conferring citations on one another.

. . .

The most serious secondary effect of the existing insurance system, however, lies in its impact on the courts. This process begins with the use of the police to enforce the traffic laws, as a result of which the incidence of arrest by armed police in the United States is the highest of any society in history. The jam starts there, and is followed by a flood of accident litigation cases that derive, in part at least, from the original criminal case. We have now reached the point where accident litigation accounts for an estimated 65 to 80 percent of the total civil court cases tried in the United States. This in turn has brought us to the point where delays in justice here are the longest of any democracy on earth. It now takes an average of 30.1 months to obtain a jury trial in the metropolitan areas of the nation. In Westchester and Kings counties, it is 50 months plus. In Chicago it is 69 months plus.

A legal expert in the field, James Marshall, has argued that persons involved in or witnessing an automobile accident are not really capable of reconstructing it in court. The event is too complex, and levels of perception too low. (How would a witness to a shooting respond to a question as to which way the bullet was traveling?) *A fortiori* the attempt to reconstruct such an episode three, four, or five years afterward is nigh impossible. Thus the question must be asked whether a social concern of the highest order—the administration of justice—is not being sacrificed to one of a much lower priority, the reenactment of traffic accidents. (As indeed the whole cops-and-robbers, shoot-'em-up paradigm for managing the road system must be questioned. It was not just chance that the riots in Watts and Newark began with police arresting a motorist.)

There is little likelihood, however, that greater efforts toward the administration of justice—more judges, or whatever—would change matters. A New York survey has shown that of 220,000 annual claims of victims seeking to recover damages caused by another's fault, only 7,000 reach trial, and 2,500 reach verdict. Given the number and rate of accidents in the existing transport system, a kind of Malthusian principle governs the courts: the number of litigated cases will automatically increase to use up all the available judicial facilities and maintain a permanent backlog. At a time when issues of justice, violence, and civic peace are of immediate and pressing concern, to devote the better part of the judicial (and an enormous portion of the legal) resources of the nation to managing the road system is the kind of incompetence that societies end up paying for.

Only one adult response is possible: the present automobile insurance system has to change.

Two courses are open. Given the profit-and-loss record (which doubtless is more complicated than we know), it would on present appearances be a favor to the insurance industry to get it out of the traffic-accident business altogether. A simple means of doing this would be for the Federal Government to begin automatically providing all licensed drivers with a minimum amount of insurance against injuries and property loss that they might suffer. Claims could be adjusted in much the same manner as the workmen's compensation system that has been operating for a half century in most states. Awards would be made on the basis of loss rather than fault, and much of the vast, clumsy apparatus of claim, counterclaim, litigation, delay, and evasion might be done away with.

Financing such a system might be the easiest part of all. The Federal Highway Trust Fund obligated $3.4 billion in highway-user taxes in 1966 solely for the construction of the Interstate Highway System, which is scheduled for completion in 1973. We are therefore approaching the point when we must decide to go on pouring concrete at the enormous pace of the past decade even after the Interstate System is finished, or whether to taper off somewhat.

One alternative use for the taxes that were imposed to build the Interstate System would be to finance an insurance system. Automobile liability premiums came to $8.3 billion in 1965; given the egregious wastefulness of the present system, the sums are not disparate. For an extra penny or so in gasoline tax, an efficient national system of accident compensation could be established, modeled perhaps on the existing accident compensation system for Federal employees. This would involve considerable dislocation for those now employed by or involved with the private insurance industry, but these are, generally speaking, valuable workers for whom an orderly transition could be arranged.

By this all too familiar process, government would reform

industry. The alternative is for industry to reform itself. A proposal to do just this was put forth last year by Robert E. Keeton of the Harvard Law School, and Jeffrey O'Connell of the University of Illinois College of Law in their book, *Basic Protection for the Traffic Victim: A Blueprint for Reforming Automobile Insurance*. After a definitive exposition of the ways in which, and the reasons why, the present system does not work, they propose a substitute that is simplicity itself.

As Keeton and O'Connell see it, the basic flaw in the present system has to do first with the concept of liability in traffic accidents, and, second, with the relationship between the insurance company and the driver. As stated, for most accidents liability is an elusive and unproductive question. With 103,000,-000 licensed drivers, there is going to be an enormous number of accidents regardless. The larger social need is to compensate those who are injured, or whose property is damaged, in such a way as not to bankrupt those who are putatively responsible. Hence they propose a system which would suspend the issue of liability for the first $10,000. The insurance companies would routinely pay up to $10,000 per victim for out-of-pocket losses, which consist principally of medical expenses and wage losses. Much of the time it is impossible to determine who, if anyone, was to blame for an accident, but it is always possible to find out who gets hurt.

The key difference between the Basic Protection plan and the old workman's compensation system is that the new plan eliminates the need to make the often very difficult judgment as to what a sprained back, etc., is worth. The victim is simply paid, by his insurance company, whatever his actual losses in wages and medical expenses and property damage are.

Under this system, persons would still go to court when the injury is permanent and serious—i.e., costing more than $10,000 and, it is hoped, involving someone else's responsibility. But the overwhelming number of small cases would be handled quickly and efficiently out of court. In that way the danger is avoided that in the effort to make settlements prompt, but moderate, some victims with large and legitimate claims will be forced to settle for less than a jury would award.

The second and crucial element in the Keeton and O'Connell Basic Protection plan has to do with the relationship between the insurance company and the driver. As they see it, much of the present misery derives from the fact that this relationship is, with but rare exceptions, an adversary one. The company wants to pay as little as it can; the victim wants to get as much as possible.

Keeton and O'Connell argue that this is inevitable given that the company insures the other fellow. They propose to solve it by the simple process of having the company insure the victim. This is exactly what happens, for example, with fire insurance. Householders buy their own insurance. If their house catches fire, regardless of who is responsible (barring fraud), their company compensates them. The settlement process involves a relationship between a business firm and one of its clients. Thus, the many hundreds of thousands of fire insurance claims are settled each year with nothing like the turmoil accompanying automobile claims.

It is hard to fault the Basic Protection scheme. The authors are right in their facts, and right in the all-important perception as to what it is Americans are good at. We are good at maintaining business relationships once a basis for mutual self-interest is established. The Basic Protection plan would establish one. Moreover, they are right in seeing the insurance issue as part of the general issue of Taming the Automobile, to use the title of a long law review article by O'Connell which proposed many of the present Federal safety programs. (His book *Safety Last,* written with Arthur Myers, was judged by Lewis Mumford to be the best of its kind, in competition even with Ralph Nader's redoubtable *Unsafe at Any Speed.*)

Professor Conard has written of *Basic Protection* that is is "surely one of the most important law books of the current decade. . . . To find legal effort on a similar scale, one would have to go back over thirty years to the famous study by Frankfurter and Green of the labor injunction." Variations on the Keeton-O'Connell proposal are certainly possible. Thus the Massachusetts Democratic Advisory Council has proposed a mixed system, with Basic Protection for personal injuries and liability insurance for property damage. But in all its essentials, it is hard to deny the fundamental rightness of the Basic Protection plan.

Nor is it difficult to see that it provides the private insurance industry with a means for insuring that their business stays private. What then has been their reaction?

The ominous and manifest fact is that the reaction so far has been not very different from—has been very near identical to—that of the automobile industry to the criticism of vehicle design that began in the mid-nineteen-fifties and ended a decade later with Federal regulation. Let it be clear that the rather small group of persons who formulated what are now the general outlines of public policy in traffic safety did not at first assume that Government regulation was inevitable or even desirable. Almost to the last moment it was fully within the powers of the industry to take on the task itself.

Detroit is now routinely ascribing higher prices to safety regulations, and industry spokesmen recurrently offer dark forecasts of their future under socialism. The conservative economist Milton Friedman has deplored the whole development, stating, "Time and again, laws passed to protect the consumer have ended up by restricting competition and so doing the consumer far more harm than good. Is it too much to hope that one of these days we shall learn this lesson before we enact a new law rather than after?"

A fair point. (Although how much competition there is in an oligopoly such as automobile manufacturing and just how much profits can be hurt in consequence, remains to be seen.) But it is also fair to ask if private industry will ever learn to listen to responsible criticism before it is too late.

Anyone who went through the battle of automobile design will have doubts. Somehow, with the giants such as Ford, Kettering, and Sloan gone, the industry fell into the hands of hired managers with a deficient sense of personal responsibility, and possibly also of personal influence. Interestingly, the one company that did take some chances in the name of traffic safety was Ford, which had remained under family direction. But in general the executives in Detroit had little but disdain for their critics, dismissing them as busybodies, Democrats, or worse. (Actually, some were solid Republicans, motivated more by a sense of professional ethic than of social reform, but if anything more effective for that reason.) The industry listened instead to those who assured it nothing was the matter, and paid fortunes to public-relations advisers who merrily marched them off the cliff.

Some insurance industry executives have given Keeton and O'Connell a hearing. Once again the place of honor goes to

Liberty Mutual, with the Aetna and the Kemper companies also playing a role. But by and large the reaction of the industry has been rather like that of the *ancien régime,* hoping to live out their own careers and resigned to the deluge that follows.

This may be good enough for executives in Hartford getting on toward retirement. It is not good enough for the nation. We are paying a great cost for our present mental slovenliness in this area, which we certainly should not and probably cannot afford.*

What is to be done? The first and obvious step is the opening of Congressional hearings, a matter under preliminary study by Representative Emanuel Celler of New York, and others. The role of the Congress in enacting the safety legislation was superb: there is probably not another democratic legislature in the world that could have taken on a private interest the size of the automobile industry and legislated as calmly and effectively in the public interest. It is to be noted that Congressional involvement in this area began with the Interstate Commerce Committee hearings of Representative Kenneth Roberts of Alabama in 1956. Congress was far ahead of both the public and the executive branch, and when the time came to legislate did so with immense competence and style.

As a second step, it is altogether reasonable to ask that the professional business schools of the nation involve themselves with this issue. In the decade that preceded the imposition of Federal regulation on the automobile industry they remained silent. It was a time of moral crisis, but the great complex of business-oriented academics, with their unparalleled access to the business world, maintained their neutrality. The views of Dante and President Kennedy on such persons are well known. But America, as David Riesman reminds us, is a land of the second chance. The business schools have such a second chance: to take on the issue of automobile insurance and develop a community of opinion as to what can and should be done.

Similarly, the American bar has a responsibility here. Apart from the American Trial Lawyers Association, the legal profession contributed almost nothing to the effort to obtain safer

---

* On balance, the response of the insurance industry to this issue was considerably more adept and sensible than that of the automobile manufacturers. People learn; institutions learn.

automobiles. With respect to automobile insurance, not just the responsibility of the legal profession is at stake, but also its integrity. As much as half the income of American lawyers is earned in accident litigation. For the bar to remain silent about, or actively oppose, reform of the insurance system would have implications that scarcely need elaborating.

But the essential step is for the leaders of the insurance industry itself to take on the issue—directly, openly, willingly. Is this out of the question? Some small part of the future of American private enterprise will be determined by the response to that possibility.

Nirvana Now

5

One of the defining qualities of the period of current history that began, roughly, with the assassination of President Kennedy has been the emergence of widespread, radical protest on the part of American youth. As it happens, this development has been congruent, and in some measure associated, with even wider protest against the current course of American foreign policy, but there is a distinction between those who differ with decisions made by the existing system, and those who reject the system itself. There is at this moment a high level of both kinds of protest, but the latter is the more singular, and almost certainly the more significant.

Following a period when college youth in particular were repeatedly accused of quiescent conformism, this development has taken the World War II generation rather by surprise. More than one college president given to deploring "the silent generation" appears in retrospect not half so bold, and considerably less prescient than he would have had his charges suppose. Never to trust anyone under thirty has become almost a first principle of prudence for academic administrators, and not a bad rule for politicians. It is yet to be seen, however, what if anything we shall learn from this surprising and unexpected development.

"Nirvana Now" was delivered as the Phi Beta Kappa Oration at Harvard University, June 1967. It was first published in *The American Scholar*, Autumn 1967.

Of necessity, we tend to interpret present events in terms of past experience, there being as yet, despite the efforts of the American Academy of Arts and Sciences, but little future experience to guide us. I would, however, argue that we have so far been looking to misleading analogues. We have been seeing in the flamboyance of the hippies, the bitterness of the alienated college youth, the outrageousness of the New Left, little more than mutants of the old bohemianism, the never-ending conflict of generations, and perhaps the persistence of neo-Marxist radicalism. We may be wrong. Just possibly, something more important is abroad. We may be witnessing the first heresies of liberalism.

In its familiar setting heresy refers to religious views contrary to the established dogma of a church. It will seem odd to use it to describe such assertively nonreligious phenomena as the Students for a Democratic Society. Some also will object that inasmuch as the doctrines of liberalism are derived from experience, rather than right reason, there can be no final liberal view about anything, and therefore no finally heretical dissent from such views. I suggest, however, that the phenomenon of protest we observe today is more psychological than doctrinal in origin, and that to the youth of this time secular liberalism presents itself as every bit as much a system of "established and commonly received doctrine" as did Christianity, for example, when it was the legally prescribed belief of the Holy Roman Empire, or the Massachusetts Bay Colony. To be sure, the doctrines of liberalism can be elusive. It is a conviction, Learned Hand might say, that is not too sure of itself—save on the point that it is vastly to be preferred to any creed that is. Liberals are not without tracts—hardly—but tend more to look to institutions as repositories of their beliefs, liberalism being in every sense as much a *way* of doing things as it is a set of propositions as to what is to be done. It is not without its schisms and assuredly not without its confusions. But in all its essentials of an optimistic belief in progress, in toleration, in equality, in the rule of law, and in the possibility of attaining a high and sustained measure of human happiness here on earth, liberalism is the nigh universally accepted creed of the ruling elites of the Western world. Religious faith persists, even grows. But it does so as a private matter: supernatural beliefs have almost no influence on the course of events. Secular liberalism is triumphant. Not surprisingly, then, given especially the great value liberalism places on skepticism and inquiry, liberalism itself is beginning to be questioned.

It is notorious, of course, that among the most eminent of the literary men of this century the liberal values of the larger society have been viewed with a detachment ranging from indifference to detestation. But these were men born in the nineteenth century, and raised in a world that still had, or thought it had, some options with respect to forsaking the traditionalist, hierarchical, Christian past and embracing the new creed. To these writers it had been a mistake to do so; they withheld their own assent. Thus it may have been incongruous, even perhaps unpatriotic, for a St. Louis boy such as Mr. Eliot to show such enthusiasm for the Church of England and the Royal Family, but it was not absurd. American youth today have no such option. The liberal present is the only world they know, and if it is not to their liking, as for many it is not, their only alternative is to consider how it might evolve into something new, there being no possibility of reverting to something old. What follows is very like a spiritual crisis, and in the manner of individuals and communities that have confronted such in the past, some lapse into indifference and quietism, others escape into varied forms of stabilized hysteria, while still others turn to confront doctrine itself, and in a mood of intensely felt revelation reject the very foundations of orthodoxy.

What indeed is most striking about the current surge of protest is the degree to which it reenacts in matters of style and structure the great heresies that have assailed the religious establishments of other ages. "The sun shone," Samuel Beckett writes in the opening passage of *Murphy*, "having no alternative, on the nothing new."

The forms of youthful protest at this time are many, and not all, of course, visible. But there are three clusters of behavior that are coherent enough to suggest a central tendency in each, and to offer the possibility of analogies with earlier phenomena.

The most familiar-seeming, and for that reason possibly the most deceptive, of the new tendencies, is that of the New Left itself. It is familiar because it has taken a familiar form: the organization of a group defined by political objectives. Yet in truth something profoundly new may be present here, for the object of the New Left is not to capture the system but to transform it. The older radicalisms were inextricably involved with things-as-they-are, and, owing especially to Marx's view of economic determinism, they largely deprived the radical challenge to liberal capitalism of any *moral* basis: the system had a destiny that was working itself out regardless of any intentions, good or evil, on the part of mortals so innocent of the laws of economics as to suppose they, rather than things, were in the saddle. The Old Left was so utterly "materialistic" and "realistic" as to use those very terms to describe one of its defining dogmas. As Richard Blumenthal, of the Harvard Class of 1967, recently observed in the *Nation*, it is precisely this "crass materialism" that the Students for a Democratic Society reject. It is precisely the "dehumanizing" of modern society that they resent. Society's "main and transcending" concern, Tom Hayden writes, "must be the unfolding and refinement of the moral, aesthetic and logical capacities of men in a manner that creates genuine independence." However that is to be achieved, Blumenthal adds, it is not likely to be by way of "a house in the country and a two-car garage." The movement is purposely "anti-ideological, even anti-intellectual." It is precisely that rational commitment to logic and consistency—of the kind that can lead from game theory at the RAND Corporation to the use of napalm in Vietnam—that these young persons abhor.

Of late they have set about building things called "independent power bases" among the poor (a concept one fears may have been borrowed from the Strategic Air Command), but the striking fact about the famous Port Huron Statement adopted by SDS in 1962 is that it barely, and then only indirectly, touches on problems such as poverty. It is addressed exclusively to middle-class intellectuals and college students: the "people of this generation, bred in at least modest comfort, housed now in universities, looking uncomfortably to the world we inherit." The world about them was so content with material affluence as to suppose it had attained stability, where in truth there was only stagnation. The theme of the Port Huron Statement is that men must *live*, not simply exist. "Some would have us believe that Americans feel contentment amidst prosperity—but might it not better be called a glaze above deeply felt anxieties about their role in the new world?" Man, they declared, had acquired a role of consumer rather than creator. His capacity for love, for creativity, for meaningful relations with others was being lost amidst the machinery of government. SDS proclaimed a social system in which men would not only share one another's fate, but participate, each one, in shaping that destiny: "We believe in generosity of a kind that imprints one's unique individual qualities in the relation to other men, and to all human activity." For such a goal the Gross National Product is indeed a crude indicator of success.

Who are these outrageous young people? I suggest to you they are Christians arrived on the scene of second-century Rome. The quality of life of that time remains difficult to assess, not least because triumphant Christianity did so much to put an end to it. James Anthony Froude, however, in his great Victorian essay "Origen and Celsus," gives us a glimpse of that world in his reconstruction of the mind of the Epicurean Celsus, a contemporary of Marcus Aurelius, who composed a tract concerning the illogicalities and misstatements of fact in Christian doctrine of such apparent force that Origen himself undertook to refute him. The second century was not unlike the twentieth, and, leaving aside the somewhat gratuitous assumptions of Europeans that they are the Greeks of this age, let there be no doubt that we are the Romans. It was a world, Froude writes, in which "Moral good and moral evil were played with as fancies in the lecture-rooms; but they were fancies merely, with no bearing on life. The one practical belief was that pleasure was pleasant. The very memory disappeared that there was any evil except bodily pain. . . ." It was a tolerant world that knew too much about itself to expect words and deeds invariably to conform. "Into the midst of this strange scene of imposture, profligacy, enthusiasm, and craving for light," Froude continues, "Christianity emerged out of Palestine with its message of lofty humility."

Who were these Christians? They were first of all outrageous. They were "bad citizens, refusing public employment and avoiding service in the army; and while . . . they claimed toleration for their own creed, they had no toleration for others; every god but their own they openly called a devil. . . ." They had no temples, no altars, no images, and boasted just that. "Fathers and tutors, they say, are mad or blind, unable to understand or do any good thing, given over to vain imaginations. The weavers and cobblers only are wise, they only have the secret of life, they only can show the way to peace and happiness." Of learning they had little and cared less. Nor had they any great interest in respectable people who observed the rules of society and tried to keep it running; they cared only for the outcast and miserable. To be a sinner, they seemed to say, was the one sure way to be saved. They were altogether of a seditious and revolutionary character.

Such people were a bafflement to Celsus. If he spoke bitterly about them, he observed, it was because he was bitter. One can imagine him thinking, if not quite putting to paper, "Do they not see how precarious is the balance of things; how readily it might all be brought down?" He was every bit an admirable, reasonable man. "He considered," Froude writes, "that human affairs could be best ordered by attention and obedience to the teaching of observed facts, and that superstition, however accredited by honorable objects or apparent good effects, could only be mischievous in the long run. Sorcerers, charlatans, enthusiasts, were rising thick on all sides, pretending a mission from the invisible world. Of such men and such messages Celsus and his friends were inexorable antagonists." His is the tone of the sensitive, and in ways holy, Inquisitor speaking before the trial of the Maid in Shaw's *Saint Joan:* "If you had seen what I have seen of heresy, you would not think it a light thing even in the most apparently harmless and even lovable and pious origins. Heresy begins with people who are to all appearances better than their neighbors. A gentle and pious girl, or a young man who has obeyed the command of our Lord by giving all his riches to the poor, and putting on the garb of poverty, the life of austerity, and the rule of humility and charity, may be the founder of a heresy that will wreck both Church and Empire if not ruthlessly stamped out in time." The Christians, Celsus declared, were welcome to stay and become part of the commonwealth, but if that was to be their choice, they must live by its rules. Otherwise, be gone. Nothing was required that a reasonable man need find objectionable: to salute the sun, or to sing a hymn to Athene did no harm to anyone. Whatever private views one might have on the subject were one's own affair. But society had a right to allegiance.

Point by point Celsus took on Christianity. Point by point he won the intellectual argument, and lost the moral and spiritual one. For he was thinking about the world, and Christians were thinking about the soul. "Most persons," Froude notes, "would now admit that Celsus spoke with wise diffidence when he hesitated at the assumption that the universe and all that it contained was created solely for the sake of man. Origen is perfectly certain that God had no other object. Sun, moon, and stars, and earth and everything living upon it were subordinated to man. In man alone, or in reference to man, the creation had its purpose and meaning." God commanded that the world provide that which is needed by man: as he is weak there must be compassion; as he is sinful there must be the forgiveness of sins; and above all, as he is Godlike, his life must be seen as sacred. If that condition has never been achieved, neither has the Western world ever been the same since first embracing the belief that it should be. Can there be any mistaking that the New Left speaks to the rational, tolerant, reasonable society of the present with the same irrationality, intolerance, and unreasonableness, but possibly also the same truth with which the absurd Christians spoke to Imperial Rome? Even Froude, professed and militant Christian, was not less a product of Imperial Britain, and in his grasp of Celsus' arguments, a certain affinity shows through. One recalls the curious moral judgments on display in his own essay, "The English in Ireland in the Eighteenth Century."

> Among reasonable beings right is forever tending to make might. Inferiority of numbers is compensated by superior cohesiveness, intelligence, and daring. The better sort of men submit willingly to be governed by those who are nobler and wiser than themselves; organisation creates superiority of force; and the ignorant and the selfish may be and are justly compelled for their own advantage to obey a rule which rescues them from their natural weakness. . . . And the right of a people to self-government consists and can consist in nothing but their power to defend themselves. No other definition is possible. . . . When resistance has been tried and failed—when the inequality has been proved beyond dispute by long and painful experience— the wisdom, and ultimately the duty, of the weaker party is to accept the benefits which are offered in exchange for submission.

In truth, is there not a touch of this in the liberal doctrines of the American Empire, with its panoply of technical assistance, constitutional conventions, mutual assistance treaties and development loans, accompanied as it seems to be by the untroubled, or at least willing, use of astonishing degrees of violence to help others perceive the value of going along?

The young people of the New Left know what they want; a larger, more diffuse group can best be described as knowing what they do not want, which is what they have. These are so-called alienated students of the present generation. The psychiatrist Seymour L. Halleck recently described them as "existing in a state of chronic identity crisis. . . . [their] constant cries of 'Who am I, I don't know what I believe, I have no self' are accompanied by anxiety which while subdued is nevertheless pervasive and relentless." Affluence means nothing and the increase in personal freedom that comes with growing up is as much as anything a threat to which the individual responds with "a peculiar kind of apathy and withdrawal. . . . Having failed to develop an internalized value system which allows him to determine his direction in life, he is paralyzed when the external world removes its guidelines and restraints." Such a person, Dr. Halleck reports, will occasionally involve himself in campus protest movements and sustain the interest for a short while, but not long, which is perhaps just as well, as, "When he does become involved with the activist groups, he can be characterized as the most angry and irrational member of that group." Sex and drugs are outlets, but joyless ones. They have everything, but nothing works.

Have we not seen this person through history, turning away from a religion that was failing him, rejecting its laws and opting instead for standards of conduct derived wholly from internal personal resources? The object of a liberal secular society being to induce human happiness, it more or less follows that those who reject it will choose to be unhappy and evoke their spirituality in despair more than ecstasy, but *mutatis mutandis,* are we not witnessing the emergence of secular antinomianism?

Not a precise, but an interesting parallel is to be seen in Sabbataianism, the mystical Jewish heresy that sprang up in the Holy Land in the seventeenth century and spread through large sections of Sephardic and then Ashkenazic Jewry. Gershom G.

Scholem described this heresy in the Hilda Stich Stroock Lectures delivered in New York in 1938. Judaism faced a series of crises at this time: persecution, apostasy and, for some reason, a sudden impatience with the Lord: how long were the Jews to wander in exile? Scholem writes: "Doctrines arose which had one thing in common: That they tried to bridge the gap between the inner experience and the external reality which had ceased to function as its symbol." In the seventeenth century Sabbatai Zevi, a Cabalistic ascetic, and almost certainly a manic depressive, proclaimed himself the Messiah and eventually won a great following even though—and seemingly because—he went on to become an apostate! A singular quality of the man was that under the influence of his manic enthusiasms he would commit acts counter to religious law. Harmless enough at first, this practice developed among his radical followers into full-fledged antinomianism. "The Torah," the radical Sabbataians were fond of declaring, "is the seed-corn of Salvation, and just as the seed-corn must rot in the earth in order to sprout and bear fruit, the Torah must be subverted in order to appear in its true Messianic glory." This developed in time into a doctrine of the holiness of sin when committed by an elect who are fundamentally different from the crowd. It was of course a profound affront to Rabbinical Judaism, and in its extreme forms acquired a sinister cast indeed, but Scholem writes, "The religious . . . and moral nihilism of the radicals is after all only the confused and mistaken expression of their urge towards a fundamental regeneration of Jewish life, which under the historic conditions of those times could not find a normal expression." The heresy plagued Jewry for a century or more, and seems to have had some influence in the rise of the openly antireligious doctrines of the French Revolution. Nathan M. Pusey has voiced his own serious doubts about "the idea that the way to advance civilization is to start over," but one cannot deny the attraction of just this view for persons who find themselves inexplicably not getting from society exactly those satisfactions society most confidently promises them.

Of course, far the most visible of the new protestants are those who do not protest at all, who simply smile, wave daffodils, cover the walls of their *quartiers* with graffiti suggesting we "Legalize Living," and wear their own variety of campaign buttons the quintessential of which demands with purest obstinacy, "Nirvana

Now." These are the hippies. Lilies of the field. Bearded and sandaled, they live on air, and love, and, alas, drugs. They seek not to change our society, but simply to have nothing to do with it. They are in quest of experiences wholly mystical and internal on the one hand, and tribal on the other. The modern American style of the effective individual functioning in a coherent but competitive society is not for them. Hunter S. Thompson in the *New York Times Sunday Magazine* recently reported an interview with such a young woman living in the Haight-Ashbury section of San Francisco: "I love the whole world," she said, "I am the divine mother, part of Buddha, part of God, part of everything." How did she live? "From meal to meal. I have no money, no possessions, money is beautiful only when it's flowing; when it piles up it's a hang-up. We take care of each other." Did she use drugs? Yes: "When I find myself becoming confused I drop out and take a dose of acid. It's a shortcut to reality; it throws you right into it." Did she pray? "Oh yes, I pray in the morning sun. It nourishes me with its energy so I can spread love and beauty and nourish others. I never pray *for* anything; I don't need anything. Whatever turns me on is a sacrament: LSD, sex, my bells, my colors . . . that is the holy communion, you dig?"

Perhaps not. Yet those assertions would have seemed perfectly clear and altogether admirable to a member of the Brethren of the Free Spirit (or the Spiritual Libertines), a mystical Christian heresy that permeated vast areas of medieval Europe, notably the teeming cities of Flanders and the Lowlands, from the twelfth century onward almost to our time. Perhaps because its adepts lived in communities within larger polities, and never took over regions for themselves, and also, being clearly heretical, tended at most times to be more or less underground, little attention has been given the Brethren. But they appear to have significantly influenced the political, if not the religious, development of Europe.

In their mystical craving for an immediate experience of God, their antinomianism, and emphasis on ecstasy, the Brethren of the Free Spirit were not unlike the Jewish Sabbataians, or for that matter the early Christians. Indeed a certain correspondence obtains among all these movements. When they took matters to an extreme of public display, the Brethren, like those before and after them, both fascinated and horrified the orthodox. "The core of the heresy," Norman Cohn writes in *The Pursuit of the Millen-*

nium, ". . . lay in the adept's attitude towards himself: he believed that he had attained a perfection so absolute that he was incapable of sin." Sexual promiscuity became a matter of principle, and marriage was denounced as an impure state. Eroticism and ecstasy were valued beyond all things as symbols of having achieved what was in truth a state of self-deification. In an age when wealth suddenly appeared in Europe, these heretics characteristically preached a communism of property, and chose to be utterly penniless: in Cohn's words, an elite of amoral supermen.

As with Celsus, we are forced to learn most about the views of the Brethren from denunciations by their enemies. Documents from Cromwell's England, a time when the Brethren, known as Ranters, were flourishing, leave no doubt, again in Cohn's words, that the " 'Free Spirit' really was exactly what it was said to be: a system of self-exaltation often amounting to self-deification; a pursuit of total emancipation which in practice could result in antinomianism and particularly in anarchic eroticism; often also a revolutionary social doctrine which denounced the institution of private property; and aimed at its abolition." The Quakers at first saw them as kindred spirits—and the two were often lumped together by others—but efforts at rapprochement were unavailing. The saintly George Fox came upon a group of them as fellow prisoners at Charing Cross. He proposed, we cannot doubt, that they meditate together on the love of God. They called instead for beer and tobacco. A comedy of 1651 by Samuel Sheppard describes the "Character of the roaring Ranters of these Times" in terms that are familiar to say the least:

> . . . our women are all in common.
> We drink quite drunk together, share our Oaths,
> If one man's cloak be rent, all their Cloaths.

A chorus goes:

> Come away, make no delay, of mirth we are no scanters,
> Dance and sing all in a Ring, for we are Jovial Ranters.

And the verses fearfully so:

> All lie down, as in a swown,
> To have a pleasing vision.

And then arise with bared thighs,
Who'd fear such sweet incision?

About, about, ye Joviall rout,
Dance antick like Hob-goblins;
Drink and roar, and swear and whore,
But yet no brawls or squoblings.

It is said the youth of Haight-Ashbury are not much addicted
to scholarship, and they may be pardoned for giving to their
service corps the name of "Diggers," after the primitivist community established near Cobham in Surrey in 1649–50. (Such
folk have an instinct for agreeable settings.) But they are nonetheless mistaken. Hippies are Ranters.

Supposing all this to be so, does it matter? I believe it does. In
the first place these persons matter: they number some of the fine
spirits of the age. A liberal must regret the loss of belief in another
as much as a decent churchman would. In the second place, these
youths are trying to tell us something. It was Chesterton, surely,
who described heresy as truth gone astray.

Seen in large terms, it is clear that these protests have been
generated by at least three problems facing our society, each one
of which can be said to arise from tendencies that are distinctively
those of secular liberalism.

The first tendency is that our optimism, belief in progress, and
the possibility of achieving human happiness on earth, combined
with our considerable achievement in this respect at home, have
led us to an increasingly dangerous and costly effort to extend
our system abroad. We are in the grip of what Reinhold
Niebuhr has called "The Myth of Democratic Universality,"
the idea that democracy is a "universal option for all nations."
The irony, of course, is that it is just because our own history
has been unique that we are led to suppose that the system that
has emerged from it can be made worldwide. It is an effort
doomed to fail.

No civilization has ever succeeded in doing anything of the
kind, and surely none whose qualities are as historically conditioned as ours should even try. But it is not just that we shall
fail: something more serious is involved. In his inaugural lecture
at the London School of Economics and Political Science, Michael Oakeshott, succeeding Harold Laski, made a remark of

some significance here. ". . . To try to do something which is inherently impossible," he said, "is always a corrupting enterprise." That, in a word, is what I believe has happened to us overseas. As our efforts repeatedly fall short of their pronounced goals, we begin covering up, taking shortcuts, and in desperation end up doing things we would never conceivably start out to do. Princes of the Church, modest sons of small-town grocers, begin proclaiming holy wars in Asia, while the man in the street acquires an appallingly troubled vision of those who protest. In the words of a Columbia student, describing the mood of a crowd watching a peace march: "War is virility; love of peace is bohemianism and quite probably a sexual perversion."

Liberals have simply got to restrain their enthusiasm for civilizing others. It is their greatest weakness and ultimate arrogance. Bertrand Russell suggests that the great Albigensian heresy, with its quest for personal holiness and cult of poverty, was due at least in part to "disappointment of the failure of the crusades." Very likely it will be the success rather than the failure of *our* crusades that will most repel youth. Nathan Glazer has suggested that this generation is already marked by the belief that its government is capable of performing abhorrent deeds.

Not the least reason the American commitment to the diffusion of liberal democracy abroad has become a corrupting enterprise is that those values are not yet genuinely secure at home. This is an ugly fact we somehow never finally confront. At just those moments when we seem about to do so, something, somehow, comes along to distract us. Yet there persists in American opinion a powerful component that is illiberal, irrational, intolerant, anti-intellectual, and capable if unleashed of doing the most grievous damage to the fabric of our own society. A century of universal education has not destroyed this tendency, it has only made it more articulate. And it can drive the liberal elite to astonishing distortions. During this past year we have had to begin admitting that during the height of the cold war the United States government began secretly using intelligence funds to support organizations of liberal and even left-leaning students and intellectuals. This was done out of a sincere and almost certainly sound conviction that the activities of these groups would aid in the struggle against totalitarianism. Observe the irony: the liberals running American foreign policy were forced to resort, in effect, to corrupt practices—totalitarian practices if you will—in order to advance liberal causes—*because the popularly elected Congress would never dream of doing so*. The man most commonly blamed, of course, is a decent enough Irish Democrat from Brooklyn: his voting record is impeccably progressive, but neither he nor his constituents share the elite enthusiasm for intellectuals. In the explanations of it all a note even of poignancy enters: can you imagine, writes one former member of the intelligence establishment, trying to get the FBI to grant security clearances to the Boston Symphony Orchestra? The problem goes beyond an affinity for Culture. We have not been able to get rid of racism, or to secure an equal place for Negroes in our society. (An effort in which liberals themselves have not been unfailingly helpful: Woodrow Wilson restored segregation to Federal employment policies.) And we begin to perceive that Negroes are not immune to some of the less attractive qualities of their persecutors. We have not been able to get rid of poverty, and begin to perceive that some of our more treasured liberal reforms may have had unanticipated consequences that may even make it more difficult to do so. (Thus, having destroyed the power of the working-class political party organization in our cities, we now pour millions of dollars of Federal funds into projects designed to overcome the psychic effects of "powerlessness" among the poor.) And we have not rid ourselves of a brutal streak of violence. If the Administration has escalated the conflict in Vietnam, remember that the largest body of opinion in the United States would bomb the yellow bastards into the Stone Age, and a solid quarter specifically favors using the atom bomb. Cohn reports that the Ranters really began to flourish after the execution of Charles I.

A third problem that has contributed to the rise of youthful protest is, I would suggest, that as the life of the educated elite in America becomes more rational, more dogged of inquiry and fearless of result, the wellsprings of emotion *do* dry up, and in particular the primal sense of community begins to fade. As much for the successful as for the failed, society becomes, in Durkheim's phrase, "a dust of individuals." But to the rational liberal, the tribal attachments of blood and soil appear somehow unseemly and primitive. They repress or conceal them, much as others might a particularly lurid sexual interest. It is for this reason, I would suggest, that the nation has had such difficulties accepting the persistence of ethnicity and group cohesion as a fact both of domestic and of world politics.

Thus it is possible not only to sympathize with the new protest, but to see much that is valid in it. At the same time we are required to note that which is dangerous. The protest movement is likely to grow rather than otherwise, for the educated middle class from which it draws its strength is growing, and will soon be the dominant American social group. Moreover, the forms of protest are likely to have a striking impact for the very reason that their object is not to redirect the system, but to disrupt it, and this is never a difficult thing to do. It is entirely possible that this disruption could bring to power the forces of the right, and this is indeed an avowed strategy. *Nach Hitler uns.* As the traditional radical Tom Kahn wrote recently in *Partisan Review*, it would be silly to blame the 1966 liberal defeat in California on the New Left and the advocates of Black Power, but "it is enough to say that what they could do, they did." In some forms the rejection of existing society is merely confused, and essentially sophomoric. This winter at Harvard, for example, a document was distributed by a left group that brought to light the fact that in certain regions of Alaska community affairs are under the control of "local politicians, a control that in practice has often been responsive to local interests." At another level, it is anything but. This year, also at Harvard, when a member of the Cabinet came as an invited guest, but under arrangements that did not suit them, the students of the New Left took possession of his person. Such tactics in the early days of Fascist Italy appalled civilization. They are not less objectionable on the Harvard campus. Kahn has described the New Left as "panic disguised as moral superiority" and others have noted how that panic subtly induces a fascination with violence—the most grievous of all possible liberal heresies.

To see history as an earnest evolution from the peat bogs to John Stuart Mill, or to the 1964 Democratic platform, is a simplicity that will not much commend itself to anyone any longer. Having read Mill and having helped draft that platform, I am for one aware of greater shortcomings than, say, the former's need to read Wordsworth at the onset of middle age. But neither would I reject the theme of J. H. Plumb's new series, *The History of Human Society,* "that the condition of man now is superior to what it was." Things are better, and where they are best is in the liberal industrial democracies of the North Atlantic world. I hold these regimes to be the best accommodation to the human condition yet devised, and will demand to know of those who reject it, just what they have in mind as a replacement. By and large the central religious and philosophical traditions of the West have led us to where we are now. Some of the heresies against that tradition have helped, and some indeed have been incorporated into it. But just as many have evidenced ugly and dangerous tendencies, of which a terrible certainty about things is surely the foremost.

The ancient Gnostics were a charming people, and there is much to be learned from their contrast between the hidden, benevolent God, and the Old Testament, law-giving one. But as Scholem writes, "The term *Jewish God,* or *God of Israel,* is abusive and meant to be so. The Gnostics regarded the confusion between the two Gods, the higher, loving one, and the lower who is merely just, as a misfortune for religion. It is metaphysical antisemitism in its profoundest and most effective form which has found expression in these ideas and continues to do so." The Brethren of the Free Spirit are nothing if not a lovable folk, but Cohn notes, "They were in fact gnostics intent upon their own individual salvation; but the gnosis at which they arrived was a quasi-mystical anarchism—an affirmation of freedom so reckless and unqualified that it amounted to a total denial of every kind of restraint and limitation." They were in fact the "remote precursors" of Bakunin and of Nietzsche: "Nietzsche's Superman, in however vulgarised a form, certainly obsessed the imagination of many of the 'armed bohemians' who made the National-Socialist revolution; and many a Communist intellectual, whether he knows it or not, owes more to Bakunin than to Marx."

To protect dissent, no matter how noxious, is one thing. To be indifferent to its growth is another. Men who would undo the system may speak: but they must be answered. The less than soul-stirring belief of the liberal in due process, in restraint, in the rule of law is something more than a bourgeois *apparat:* it involves, I argue, the most profound perception of the nature of human society that has yet been achieved, and, precisely in its acknowledgment of the frailty of man and the persistence of sin and failure, it is in the deepest harmony with the central tradition of Judeo-Christian theology. It is not a belief to be frittered away in deference to a mystique of youth.

What we must do first of all is listen. Young people are trying to tell us something. They are probably right in much of what they say, however wrong their prescriptions for righting matters. Then we must respond. American liberalism needs to bring its commitments in balance with its resources—overseas and at home. Some years ago Robert Warshow noted that "So much of 'official' American culture has been cheaply optimistic that we are likely almost by reflex to take pessimism as a measure of serious- ness." It is just this unthinking encouragement of bloated ex- pectation that leads young persons to compare forecast with outcome and to conclude that hypocrisy and duplicity are at work. What is asked of us is honesty: and what that requires is a great deal more rigor in matching our performance to our standards. It is now the only way to maintain the credibility of those standards.

If we do this we shall find, of course, that there is altogether too much that is shoddy and derivative, and in a final sense dis- honest, about American life. I suspect we will also find that the awareness of this fact is more diffused within the American electorate than it will have suited the mildly dissenting liberal *cognoscenti* to imagine. It is one thing to read in Richard Rovere's "Letter from Washington" in *The New Yorker* that "This city is awash with lies and deceptions. . . ." It is another to learn, as Rovere with his unmatched toughness of mind would insist, that two-thirds of the American people believe the assassination of President Kennedy to have been part of a broader conspiracy. The Catholic philosopher Michael Novak, commenting in *Com- monweal* on the growing rejection of the American system by the New Left, has suggested:

> Perhaps the rumors that wealthy businessmen hired former CIA agents to assassinate Kennedy are the mythical expression of a growing perception of reality: a majority of Americans, and certainly a very wealthy and politically powerful minority, do not wish to see a further social, or political, revolution in America.

These are signs of danger, as much as are the rioting cities and turbulent campuses. The foundations of popular confidence in the American system are proving to be nothing like so solid and enduring as the confident liberal establishment has supposed. The ability to respond to signs of danger is the essential condition of the ability to survive. It is not too much to declare that our ability is now being tested: it is always being tested. If we respond well to these signs of danger—and if we find a meaningful role in helping to transform the system for those who now attack it—we are likely to evolve a society of considerable nobility. But the first requirement is to acknowledge that what we have so far made of our opportunity is very much less than we should have.

The story is told of the building of the great Catholic Shrine of the Immaculate Conception in Washington: generations of truck drivers, coal miners, and cleaning women contributed their pittances to the coffers of the American hierarchy which slowly amassed the fortune required to construct this most fabulous edifice. It was a building that had everything. Nothing was spared of precious metal and lustrous stone. Nothing was spared by way of design: elements of every architectural tradition in the world were skillfully incorporated in the soaring façade and billowing dome. At last it was finished, and there followed a triumphant week of procession and ceremony, chorus and sermon. Then silence fell. The next morning a child was praying in the crypt when a vision of Our Lady appeared. Smiling that most beatific of all smiles, She looked down and said, "Build a beautiful church on this site."

The Crises in Welfare

6

In the course of the Second Session of the Ninetieth Congress, the House of Representatives by near-unanimous action approved what must surely be the first purposively punitive welfare legislation in the history of the American national government. On the initiative of the Ways and Means Committee, the House inserted provisions in the Social Security amendments of 1967 which deny Federal funds for any further proportionate rise in the number of children being supported by the Aid to Families of Dependent Children program, thus placing enormous pressure on the mothers of such children to go to work, and which also institute formal investigations to determine who and where are the fathers. Inasmuch as no effort was made to conceal the fact that these provisions were designed to halt the rise in *Negro* dependence on the AFDC program, the House action might also be considered the first deliberate anti-civil-rights measure of the present era.

The targets of the legislation—weak and abandoned women, helpless and surely innocent children—are equally without precedent. Dickens would have been hard put to invent a credible sponsor. The Mayor of New York declared that, if enacted, the

"The Crises in Welfare" was read before the Arden House Conference on Public Welfare in March 1967. It was first published in *The Public Interest*, Winter 1968.

legislation would cause a "thundering crisis" in his city. The same would be true of a dozen cities, half of them even now going through the shudders of near insurrection. But there was no flinching in the House, and in Washington little more than embarrassed silence accompanied by hurried moves to set things right in the Senate and hope for the best in the conference. But for all this, on balance, the House move was probably a useful one, since it brought into the open the mounting crises in the American welfare system, all of which were worsening as a result of the general disinclination to acknowledge that they even existed.

The arithmetic of the present situation is clear enough. The 1960s have seen an economic expansion in the United States of all but unimagined proportions. The *increase* in the Gross National Product each year now routinely matches the *total* GNP of the early 1930s. Yet with each year of growing affluence the number of persons dependent on public charity also grows. In many cities the growth has been quite startling. New York is now at the point where 10 percent of its population and 20 percent of its children live on welfare. The relationship of mounting dependency to escalating violence demands further explanation, while the prospect that both will lead to a massive withdrawal of support for programs to eliminate poverty and break down racial barriers is rapidly becoming a reality. After a generation of something less than "benign neglect," the time is at hand for a thorough reassessment of public welfare.

The *first* of five general points this paper will make about the welfare situation is that the rising incidence of dependency in the United States has not been distributed evenly across the full spectrum of welfare categories.

Anything but. Old-age assistance, for example, once the central activity of the Federal welfare program, has shown a steady relative decline, in direct response to increasing national wealth and the widening coverage of social-security insurance programs. In this case forecasts have been perfectly sound. In 1940, 2,066,000 persons were receiving old-age assistance, a rate of 288 per 1,000 of population aged sixty-five and over. By the end of 1966, more than a quarter century later, the number of OAA recipients, in a much larger population, was still only 2,073,000, and the rate had dropped to 113. In 1940, 3,618,000 persons were receiving general assistance, such as Home Relief. At the end of 1966, this number had dropped to 663,000. That year was a particularly strong one for the economy, and there were declines in the number of recipients for almost all welfare programs, with one conspicuous exception—Aid to Families of Dependent Children.

In 1940, there had been 891,000 children supported by this Federal program. By the end of 1966 there were 3,526,000. With parents and caretakers the total came to 4,666,000. (It has now passed 5 million.) The recipient rate for children had risen from 22 per 1,000 population under eighteen years of age to 48. During 1966 the number of such children increased 6.3 percent, and the cost of the program, 17.4 percent. At a monthly cost of $184.6 million, the AFDC program had now passed Old-Age Assistance as the most expensive Federal welfare program, and had become perhaps the leading conundrum of American domestic policy.

THE VIEW FROM NEW YORK

In New York State this uneven development has been even more accentuated. By the mid 1960s, most public-assistance programs in New York were either steady or declining in terms of numbers (excepting, of course, the newly established Medicare and Medicaid programs). The number of persons on AFDC, however, was rapidly and unaccountably rising. By January 1967, the total number of AFDC recipients was, at 653,144, almost ten times that of 1945. In 1964, before the medical assistance programs came into effect, AFDC accounted for more than 70 percent of welfare recipients in the state, and more than half of welfare expenditures. From 1953, the end of the Korean War, to the beginning of 1967, the number of children supported by the program increased 407 percent and approached the half-million mark. There had been an increase in the total number of children under eighteen, but the number of children on welfare had increased at a rate ten times greater during this period.

The costs of welfare, shared in roughly equal portions at the Federal, state, and local levels, rose accordingly. During the decade 1955–1965, state and local expenditures more than doubled, from under $300 million to over $600 million, and in the latter year the total cost nudged the billion-dollar level for the first time. In his annual message to the legislature of that year, Governor Rockefeller described this phenomenon of rising prosperity and rising welfare dependency as "the most serious economic paradox of our times."

During this period many suburban counties began for the first time to feel the effects of serious welfare problems. In 1966 the budgets of Nassau, Suffolk, and Westchester counties reached record highs, and, as *The New York Times* reported, "The increases are primarily the result of growing welfare costs."

But it was in New York City itself that something like a crisis arose.

Once again, the number of persons in the "adult programs," such as Old-Age Assistance and Aid to the Disabled remained steady or grew slowly. It was dependent children whose numbers were swelling. In October 1966, as the numbers continued to rise, *The New York Times* noted that the number of dependent children in the city exceeded the entire population of Omaha or Akron. At the outset of 1967, in his annual budget request, Commissioner of Welfare Mitchell I. Ginsberg reported that toward the end of 1966 there had been 600,000 persons receiving public assistance, of whom "about 80 percent were mothers and their children in families without a male member of the household to bring home a weekly paycheck." The anticipated caseload for 1967–1968 was 709,000, indicating that by the end of the period the number of welfare recipients would be approaching three-quarters of a million, and the annual rate of expenditure would be nearing $1 billion.* Already more than 400,000 New York City children were on welfare. At the outset of 1968 the total had reached 800,000 and the number of children, 500,000.

At this point it was also becoming clear that the "at risk" population was even larger than the welfare rolls recorded. During the fiscal year 1966–1967, 128,000 new cases were opened in New York City, but *100,000 cases were closed,* which would suggest that welfare had become an on-and-off experience for an even larger proportion of the city's children. Not, of course, for all children. In 1965, when there were 288,624 children in all welfare cases in the city, the New York City Youth Board calculated that the average welfare rate per 1,000 population under eighteen

* By 1972 the AFDC rolls in New York City passed 1.2 million.

years in Brooklyn was 170.0. This rate, however, ranged from 1.8 per 1,000 in one health area to 781.1 per 1,000 (sic) in another. Of the 113 health areas with recorded rates, 51 had fifty or fewer children per thousand on welfare, whereas 42 had two hundred or more. Probably never had the city known such contrasts: not between extreme wealth and extreme poverty, for the welfare population was living at a decent level by any historical standard, but rather between mass security on the one hand and mass dependency on the other.

On May 10, 1967, Welfare Commissioner Ginsberg went before a Senate subcommittee and declared that the nation's welfare system was "bankrupt" as a social institution.

II

Just so. What then are the prospects for reorganizing the system? This raises the *second* general point about the existing welfare system, namely that the nation is not likely to do anything much to change it.

What we can do is to improve it somewhat. It is an American fault to insist on extravagant goals—as if to set out to achieve anything less than everything suggests a lack of sincerity, manliness, or both—and to be exceedingly busy with other matters when it subsequently develops that little or nothing has happened. The social history of the 1960s is already littered with the wreckage of crash programs that were going to change everything and in fact changed nothing, save possibly to diminish ever so slightly the credibility of those who claimed credit in advance for the achievements that never, somehow, came to pass.

The idea that the welfare system is not working is gaining currency among the elite groups in business, politics, labor, churches, and universities that in normal circumstances legitimatize and direct government-managed social change in the United States. This means there is an opportunity to make a number of important, incremental advances. The danger, and probably also the likelihood, is that those who wish—and with good reason— for radical change will dominate the discussion and set an agenda so extreme that in the end little if anything will happen. This is a recurring dilemma in American life, and it is rarely resolved.

A word of further explanation is perhaps in order. The problem with changing the welfare system is not that the present system does not work, but rather that it does. It maximizes the advantages and conveniences of almost all the parties involved. It would be difficult, nigh impossible, to point to another government program of comparable importance—and equivalent potential for conflict and controversy—that works as smoothly as does welfare, or that makes as few difficult or dangerous demands on those who run the society. The present welfare system is the social equivalent of an automated factory: the input goes in and the output comes out untouched by human hands. If anything goes wrong, it is the machinery that is to blame. Moreover, the system is not costly. As a percentage of Gross National Product, social welfare expenditures are quite low in the United States as compared with other Western nations, and public assistance has consistently used up only about 1 percent of the national income. In New York State, in the decade 1956–1965, the amounts budgeted for public assistance and work relief more than doubled, but, as a proportion of the state budget, welfare expenditures actually declined from 10.01 percent to 8.98 percent. It may very well be, as Senator Kennedy argues, that the present system of welfare destroys family life. But it does not endanger the public fisc. One of the paradoxes of affluence is that it permits a society, as it does an individual, to indulge in practices that are both expensive and ultimately harmful, but that appear pleasant or convenient in the short run. The United States economy has reached the point where it can sustain a full-scale land war in Asia with no significant cutback in domestic spending, and, yet, no increase in taxes. To such a behemoth, the cost of an annual increment in the number of welfare mothers is insignificant.

THE COSTS OF TRANSFORMATION

By comparison, the cost of transforming the system would disrupt a vast array of entrenched social arrangements, changing not only the distribution of wealth, but probably also the distribution of power. Perhaps the clearest idea as to how unlikely an occurrence this would be can be gained from our experience with the closely related—and every bit as serious problem—of unemployment. For almost four decades now, the United States has experienced high and sustained levels of unemployment. In general, since 1945 American unemployment rates have been sharply higher than those of any other industrial democracy. The only occasions when the unemployment rate has gotten even *near* to levels which other Western nations have come to regard as socially indispensable have been when we have gone to war. And even then, for Negro Americans unemployment rates have persisted at levels which any other industrial democracy would regard as obscene. Throughout this period there has never ceased to be a high level of informed and responsible comment as to how serious a problem unemployment is, and as to what may be done to eliminate it. This goal has not been an evanescent one of intellectuals: in election after election, it has proved one of the decisive forces of American politics. The fact that the Republican party became associated with unemployment in the mind of the electorate has more than any other single thing kept it almost continually out of office at the national level throughout this period. And yet the nation never got rid of unemployment during peacetime, and we may be confident that with the end of the war in Vietnam we shall have it back with us again, while in the meantime it persists as ever for the minority poor.

To repeat: Most industrial democracies would consider our national behavior in this respect to be profoundly short-sighted and potentially disastrous. Nonetheless it has proved more convenient for us to accept these short-run costs than to undergo the reforms in economic organization that a solution would entail.

The problem of unemployment is not only analogous to that of welfare, but is actually related to its recent social and intellectual history. Both the present unemployment insurance system and the welfare system (in its major components) were provisions of the Social Security Act of 1935. Both were products of the depression, and both were accompanied by the assumption that, once the economy had recovered, the need for both programs would recede as social insurance provided for the needs of the aged, of survivors, and of the temporarily unemployed. Gilbert Y. Steiner has termed this "the withering-away fallacy." Unemployment compensation would both smooth out the business cycle and enable those laid off at low points to get by in tolerable comfort—and without the onus of the dole, since it was, after all, paid-up insurance that they were getting. Similarly, once the social-security coverage had settled in, the need for such non-contributory programs as Old-Age Assistance and Aid to Families of Dependent Children would drop off. In each instance the assumptions have proved just correct enough to dissipate any effective social pressure for reforms that would make them correct altogether. Vast numbers of workers came to be covered by unemployment insurance, but somehow coverage eluded another group within which unemployment became chronic. Similarly, the nation is approaching universal social-security coverage. In December 1966, Old-Age, Survivors, and Disability Insurance benefits were paid to 22,767,252 persons, more than one person in ten in the population. Yet a large and growing number of *other* persons are dependent on AFDC. Again it is a matter of a minority group that somehow misses out on benefits enjoyed by the great majority.

STRUCTURAL REFORMS

Economists speak of structural unemployment, and the concept is similarly useful with respect to welfare dependency. For some time the national government has acknowledged the former and has taken, not total, but tentative steps to deal with the problem in terms of manpower retraining and the like. It is reasonable to think similar measures are in the offing with respect to structural problems in the field of welfare. But it is necessary to insist that we are no more likely to make a total effort with regard to welfare than with regard to unemployment. It may be useful here as well to draw a list of what such a total commitment would involve in order to understand, if not to accept, this point.

Much, much less is known about the sources of welfare dependency than those of structural unemployment, so that any list must be tentative to the point of speculation; but, for the very reason that dependable knowledge is lacking, any serious total effort would have to take the unavoidably inefficient form of testing all probable approaches. A total effort to put an end to mass welfare dependency, then, would require something as follows:

1. An end to structural unemployment and the achievement of consistently low levels of cyclical unemployment.

2. Universal coverage for all social-insurance programs, universal application of minimum-wage standards, and the adoption of a nationwide system of disability insurance such as now exists in New York and three other states. The length of unemployment compensation should be permanently extended and should provide, far better than is now the case, for workers with large families.

3. Systematic and rigid enforcement of national minimum standards of social and educational services throughout the nation, and especially in the rural South, Puerto Rico, Appalachia, Indian reservations, and the Alaskan interior.

4. A system of income supplements for workers with families, such as now exist in most parts of the world.

5. A massive dissemination of birth-control knowledge and practice among low-income groups.

6. Greatly increased levels of social service, directed particularly at the needs of female-headed households, combined with a greater willingness on the part of the state to remove children from homes deemed improper, and on the part of the community to encourage interracial adoption of children.

7. Significant diminishment in racial discrimination against Negroes, especially in the area of private housing.

8. A sharp curtailment of the freedom now by and large enjoyed by low-income groups to produce children they cannot support and, in the case of family heads, to abandon women and children they are no longer willing to live with.

GROUP VALUES AND GROUP POWER

In the context of such a list, it is possible better to appreciate the implications of the thought that welfare dependency is a structural problem in American society. This means it is a problem with markedly different impact on different ethnic, racial, and religious groups. To resolve it will require the imposition of uniformities of behavior in a society that has vigorously resisted anything of the sort, and has done so in the name of values a great deal more important to it than the size of the welfare rolls.

These issues, moreover, involve not just group values, but group power as well. The resistance of Southern whites to improvements in social services that would benefit Negroes is commonly understood as resistance to changes that might potentially threaten white dominance of Southern society. But not dissimilar considerations exist outside the South. Thus the United States is the only industrial democracy in the world that does not have a family allowance, a system of flat grants to all parents of dependent children. This program, which might be expected to have great support among white liberals, has so far had little—and for the openly (if mistakenly) declared reason that it would encourage the poor to have children; that it would be, in common usage, a baby bonus. White liberals are in favor of birth control, which will enable the poor to have not more but fewer children. Now at one level these are entirely benevolent attitudes. But at another they amount to nothing more or less than the view that a family allowance will increase the number of Negro votes, or Puerto Rican, or whatever, while a birth-control program will decrease the number of such votes. And minority group leaders are beginning to suspect as much.

Similarly, while minority group spokesmen are increasingly protesting the oppressive features of the welfare system, and liberal scholars are actively developing the concept of the constitutional rights of welfare recipients with respect to such matters as man-in-the-house searches, it is nonetheless the fact that the poor of the United States today enjoy a quite unprecedented *de facto* freedom to abandon their children in the certain knowledge that society will care for them, and, what is more, in a state such as New York, to care for them by quite decent standards. Through most of history, a man who deserted his children pretty much ensured that they would starve, or near to it, if he was not brought back and that he would be horsewhipped if he were. Much attention is paid the fact that the number of able-bodied men receiving benefits under the ADFC program is so small. In February 1966 Robert H. Mugge, of the Bureau of Family Services of HEW, reported that of 1,081,000 AFDC parents, there were but 56,000 "unemployed but employable fathers." But in addition to 110,000 incapacitated fathers, there were some 900,-000 mothers, of whom far the greatest number had been divorced or deserted by their presumably able-bodied mates. A working-class or middle-class American who chooses to leave his family is normally required first to go through elaborate legal proceedings and thereafter to devote much of his income to supporting them. Normally speaking, society gives him nothing. The fathers of AFDC families, however, simply disappear. Only a person invincibly prejudiced on behalf of the poor will deny that there are attractions in such freedom of movement.

It will thus be seen that welfare involves issues which American society does not readily grapple with. In Gilbert Y. Steiner's words, "public assistance introduces problems of race, of sex, of religion, and of family relationships. It is hard to think of four areas most American politicians would rather avoid."

III

The *third* general point about the welfare situation is that the political leaders of the nation have done just that: they have more or less consistently avoided any serious involvement with the problems of welfare. Which is not to say that welfare has been kept out of politics: on the contrary, it has become increasingly involved, but normally at the instance of minor figures seeking to make an impact on the public by charges of abuse and fraud, or by extremely conservative leaders who see in the rising welfare rolls a symbol of developments they generally disapprove of. But since the establishment of the present welfare system under the New Deal, the major national political leaders, sensing perhaps that their freedom of action was quite limited here, have only rarely allowed themselves to become involved with the subject, and in no case has any stayed with it long enough to make an impact. What they have done is to leave the matter to the professionals, and in so doing have given rise to an extraordinary chapter in the history of American professionalism.

For roughly a quarter century, from the end of the legislative period of the New Deal in the late 1930s to the enactment of the Economic Opportunity Act in 1964, the care of the poor in the United States, to the extent at least that it involved the management and direction of the welfare system, was almost entirely in the hands of social workers, or persons whose professional careers were wholly confined to this area. Welfare was kept "out of politics." This was possible largely because of a technicality in the

Social Security Act that was little noticed at the time, but which was decisive later on. *Welfare costs are a charge on the Treasury which are automatically disbursed.* Neither the President nor the Congress has any but a *pro forma* say in the matter—which made it not only possible but almost necessary to leave matters to the administrators, and this is what happened.

So, after a moment in the sun under the New Deal, the administrative direction of the Federal end of the welfare system settled fairly low down in the Federal hierarchy, with a minimum of visibility, while the principal administrative activity remained in any event with the states. On the whole, Congressional interest in the program has been confined to sweetening the Federal contribution to the state programs and letting matters rest at that. Presidents have pretty much gone along. At the state and local level the welfare program has been much more frequently the subject of political controversy, but these have normally turned on issues of administration. Few persons have questioned the existence of the system as such. The only near analogy would be that of the Federal highway program, the funds for which are also automatically disbursed, in this case from a trust fund, and which states and municipalities accept with few arguments save as to the precise location of this or that highway. It is not mere chance that the two largest items of Federal expenditure on domestic programs are highways and wefare.

Matters might have gone on peaceably enough, save that about halfway through this period the character of the welfare program began to change in somewhat inexplicable ways. There was nothing unusual about this. Such turnings are a law of life for all systems. Some are able to respond creatively; some are not. Welfare was not. That is why the present crises exist.

THE AFDC EXPLOSION

What happened, of course, was that the nature of the AFDC program changed profoundly, and it commenced growing at a wholly unexpected rate. The major thrust behind the Social Security Act had been the mounting Congressional support for an old-age assistance program. Little attention was paid to the ADC provision, which was modeled directly on the widow's laws that had been enacted by the states. It was to be a sensible, low-key program, in the oldest, indeed Biblical, tradition of community responsibility. What no one thought about, because at that time Americans did not much think of such things, was that the program was perfectly adapted to providing support for the female-headed, lower-class family.

In his classic study, *The Negro Family in the United States,* published in 1939, E. Franklin Frazier of Howard University forecast that, as the bankrupt system of Southern agriculture forced more and more of the rural Negro proletariat into the cities, the problem of welfare dependency of Negro families would become increasingly acute. But World War II followed and few listened. As it turned out, Frazier was perfectly correct in his forecast, and the AFDC program responded by changing, almost abruptly, from a widow's program to what in certain important respects became a Negro program.

Because this is an extremely sensitive subject, it is necessary to be explicit and somewhat detailed. Until the present moment, at least, the majority of families receiving AFDC support have been white. However, the Negro proportions have been rising steadily. A special HEW study in 1948 showed that only 29 percent of ADC families were Negro. By 1961 the proportion had increased to 44 percent, and accounted for *60 percent* of the increase in the total number of AFDC families from 449,154 to 921,102. Because Negro families were larger, 1,112,106 or almost half the children supported by the program in 1961 were Negro, as against 1,165,308 whites. Moreover, 72 percent of white children receiving AFDC support in 1961 were living in rural nonfarm areas, whereas 75 percent of the Negro children were living in central cities.

It must be insisted that these proportions are functions of class far more than of race. In 1964, for example, in New York State, Puerto Ricans, who comprised an estimated 4.53 percent of the population, accounted for an average of 26.5 percent of AFDC recipients—rather more than five times their proportion. Negroes, on the other hand, with an estimated 10.19 percent of the population, accounted for 46.1 percent of AFDC recipients—rather less than five times their proportion. However, Americans are accustomed to thinking in categories of race, rather than class, and the AFDC program began to acquire this cast. Just as importantly, the nature of the families changed. In 1940, in the nation as a whole, 42 percent of the fathers of AFDC children were dead. By 1963 this proportion had declined to 6 percent. A good two-thirds of the children were, for practical purposes, simply abandoned. Again, this was a characteristic of lower-class *urban* families, with perhaps some reinforcement from Negro family patterns that had developed in the South. Moreover, the growth in Negro population in Northern states occurred at a period when, despite strong popular convictions to the contrary, the "stability" of white families in the nation was if anything improving, as can be seen from Table 1.

Thus, between 1953 and 1961 the number of white AFDC families in which the father was not married to the mother

Table 1. *New York State Status of Father with Respect to ADC Families, November 1953 and November 1961*

	NOVEMBER 1953	NOVEMBER 1961
Status of Father, White Families		
Total	23,000	25,000
Dead	3,358	1,325
Incapacitated	4,071	4,825
Legally separated or divorced	1,840	2,075
Deserting or separated w/o court decree	6,808	6,825
Not married to mother	4,945	2,875
Unemployed	—	5,275
Other status	1,978	1,800
Status of Father, Nonwhite Families		
Total	21,600	58,200
Dead	1,123	2,328
Incapacitated	1,145	5,413
Legally separated or divorced	518	2,503
Deserting or separated w/o court decree	7,001	15,947
Not married to mother	10,798	22,465
Unemployed	—	5,354
Other status	1,015	4,190

Source: Trends in the AID to Department Children Program, New York State Department of Social Welfare, Office of Social Research and Statistics, Special Research and Statistical Reports, No. 28, January 1964, mimeographed.

Note: "White" families do not include Puerto Rican families.

dropped sharply, and the slight increase in the total number of AFDC white families was more than accounted for by the addition (in 1961) of the AFDC-U category, which made families with unemployed parents eligible for assistance. During this period the number of nonwhite families on AFDC more than doubled and much of the increase came from the fatherless family segment, which itself more than doubled, whereas the nonwhite AFDC-U group was just level with the white counterpart.

As of January 1967, a full third of the West Virginia families receiving AFDC support were involved with the unemployed partner segment (AFDC-U) in which both parents are normally at home. But in New York State at that time, only 8.4 percent of the families were AFDC-U. In 1964 in New York, Negro recipients made up 46.1 percent of the regular AFDC program, but only 26.5 percent of the AFDC-U segment. The proportions for whites were almost exactly reversed: 27.4 percent of the AFDC and 47 percent of the AFDC-U. Puerto Ricans were 26 percent of each.

Probably this development was at least in part due to a rise in illegitimacy. Between 1940 and 1965 the estimated *rate* of illegitimate births (per 1,000 unmarried women aged 15–44) rose from 7.1 to 23.4 for the nation as a whole. For whites the increase was from 3.6 to 11.6. For nonwhites it was from 35.6 to 97.7. The estimated illegitimacy *ratio* (per 1,000 births) rose from 19.5 to 39.6 for whites, and from 168.3 to 263.2 for nonwhites. In the Central Harlem district the ratio in 1965 was 465, an increase from 324 in 1955. Only a minority of illegitimate children receive public assistance, and they are a distinct minority of AFDC children. (In 1965 the Department of Social Welfare reported that "an estimated 35 percent of the children on ADC in New York State have been born out-of-wedlock.") However, there was an increasing number of such children, and they must have had an impact on the welfare program.

In short: from being a program designed to aid unfortunate *individuals,* AFDC gradually turned into a subsistence program for both individuals and for a *class.* Robert Mugge has calculated that for youths reaching eighteen in 1963 approximately one white child in ten, and *six* nonwhite children in ten, had at some point in their life been supported by AFDC.

THE GREAT SILENCE

This silent transformation is the essential fact behind the present crises in welfare. The public is beginning to see it as a crisis in public expenditure. Social scientists are beginning to see it as a crisis in social structure: the development of a permanently dependent class. And the members of that class are beginning to see in the inadequacies of the system the source of their dependency, to the point that an even greater crisis must be created in order to force the larger society to change the system.

A principal reason that these crises have crept into being is that somewhere along the line the social-welfare professionals decided, in effect, to say nothing about them. In effect, to cover up. This was in some respects a consequence of the political climate of the times. The period 1946–1960, when this transformation occurred, was one of conservatism and worse in American domestic politics. ("Worse" in the sense of an unwillingness to experiment with social programs on behalf of the poor.) But it has also to do with the nature of the role of nonpolitical professionals in government.

The ADC program began with the least controversial of objectives: to aid the children of widows. In the compassionate 1930s an especially appealing gloss was added: one learns that the administrators liked to think of the typical recipient as a West Virginia mother whose husband had died in a mine accident. Honest, hardworking, God-fearing white Protestant folk. Rural. Gradually the typical recipient became an urban Negro or a member of some other minority group, the source of whose dependency the larger society not infrequently classified as grossly immoral conduct. It was unlikely in the extreme that the Congress would ever have enacted a program *de novo* to serve such a clientele, and even less likely that it would be moved to improve the program if greater attention were drawn to its new dimension. Lee Rainwater has suggested that, finding they could do little to improve the conditions of the welfare population, the social-welfare professionals opted instead to protect its good name. In the abstract this was a generous enough decision, but in practice it developed habits of mind and patterns of conduct that were—and are—ominously close to dishonest. There were honorable exceptions. The American Public Welfare Association sponsored the powerful study of the AFDC program by M. Elaine Burgess and Daniel O. Price, "An American Dependency Challenge," published in 1963, and various individuals sought to communicate the horror of welfare reality. But, in general, the decision to protect the good name of the clients tended to strengthen the very forces opposed to social change. A circular process took effect: despairing of the public being willing to improve matters if it were told the truth, the professionals opted more or less to conceal the truth, which left the public with the impression that matters were not particularly in need of improvement.*

* A personal note may be in order. In the early 1960s, while in the United States Department of Labor, I became interested in the impact of employment conditions on welfare. By comparatively simple calculations, I was able to show that, during the 1950s, there were quite astonishingly strong correlations between nonwhite male unemployment rates and such phenomena as the number of new AFDC cases opened and the number of nonwhite married women separated from their husbands, *but* that with the onset of the 1960s, these relations seemed to disappear, so that, for example, the unemployment rate would decline but the number of new AFDC cases would rise. These were no more than correlations, but they had not, to my knowledge, been done before and the implications of the apparent weakening influence of aggregate economic movements on social conditions are surely interesting and possibly of considerable importance. I included portions of these data in a policy paper prepared for internal government use, and in signed articles that appeared in *Daedalus*, the journal of the American Academy of Arts and Sciences, and *The Annals* of the American Academy of Political and Social Science. One would imagine that a hypothesis of this kind would arouse interest and bring about serious efforts either to confirm or disprove it. Nothing of the sort occurred. A storm of controversy arose over the government report, but I have seen but one citation, by a sociologist, of the changing employment-welfare relationship hypothesis, and have had no comment whatever from the social-welfare profession.

Lee Rainwater and William L. Yancey have noted that "the welfare establishment's policy of trying to be 'color-blind' " required that there be no regular breakdown of AFDC rates by race. "What kind of 'good public relations' logic justifies such a policy?" they ask. None does, but the policy persists because the persons who established it are still running the programs, and will continue to do so. This was why, for example, the poverty program could not possibly have been entrusted to

The heart of the matter is as follows: Developments in the 1950s would have made it apparent to anyone closely involved that, despite burgeoning prosperity, patterns of income, employment, housing, discrimination, and social services—*very possibly including the welfare system itself*—were somehow undermining stability of family life among the poor, particularly the urban Negro poor. There was, moreover, growing evidence that the more prestigious forms of casework and counseling had relatively little effect on the clients, however much they enhanced the status of the counselors.

The social-work professionals, the inner circle of whom had continued access to the political leaders of the nation, could have developed and presented this information and pleaded for consideration of its implications. They did not. That is all there is to say: they didn't do it. Their clearest opportunity came at the outset of the Kennedy years, when the national enthusiasm for new ideas and new challenges was once again at a peak, but they made little of their opportunity. It was a period of task forces galore, and a variety were assembled to develop what became the Public Welfare Amendments of 1962, the first comprehensive change in the Federal system since it had been established. But the key conception of the amendments was the need to provide increased professional services to the poor in order to restore their ability to support themselves: *ergo*, first train more social workers. It is a system known as feeding the sparrows by feeding the horses. Hailed at the time as historical changes, in retrospect the 1962 amendments simply confirmed all the major tendencies in a system which, five years later, the Commissioner of Welfare in New York City, former Associate Dean of the New York School of Social Work at Columbia University, was to declare "bankrupt."

IV

The *fourth* general point about the welfare situation is that the period of nonpolitical professional direction appears to be coming

---

the Welfare Administration (much less the Children's Bureau!). An entirely new organization had to be established. This is a familiar situation in American government: one of the unanticipated complications of civil-service reform.

to an end. Welfare is becoming politicized. The events of 1967 in the House of Representatives settled that.

The reasons for this are various, although convergent. A principal one is that the transformation of the program and its increasing size is becoming a matter of wider public knowledge and concern. Here and there in the nation more conservative political leaders have been able to exploit the issue with some success. Terms such as "welfare mothers" and demands for residency requirements have emerged as effective forms in which to exploit anti-Negro sentiment among voters to whom raw racism would appear vulgar, even immoral. Newburgh, New York, has become a symbol for such efforts, dating from the events of 1961, when the city manager, Joseph Mitchell, undertook to remove able-bodied males from the relief rolls and generally to impose strict moral sanctions on all the recipients of welfare.

Negro and other minority groups have found it difficult to respond to these attacks. The dilemma of the Negro groups is clear enough, and would perhaps be less painful and paralyzing if it were better understood and more readily acknowledged. It is this:

From one point of view the conditions of family life among the Negro lower class constitute the strongest possible indictment of the social conditions that have been imposed upon that class by the larger American society. The fact that a large group of persons is reduced to such conditions declares that the system under which they live is unjust. Period.

But from another point of view the conditions of family life among the lower-class poor constitute ammunition for the charge that the people involved are worthless, are responsible for their own plight, and should expect nothing from society save ostracism and perhaps punishment. When directed against Negroes, this attitude may be based on nothing more than race prejudice. But it would be greatly mistaken to suppose that it is derived solely or even largely from racial considerations. Ironically it is every bit as likely to be associated with religious or moral convictions as is the very opposite view. In the United States, a conspicuous streak of this kind of thinking is to be found among a certain type of Catholic, preoccupied with problems of contraception and dirty magazines to a point perhaps injurious to spiritual life. But the central tradition is that of Protestant fundamentalism, and most especially *Southern* Protestant fundamentalism. It is necessary to consider whether Negro Americans, being themselves permeated with this tradition, find it particularly excruciating to deal with the subject of disorganized family life for the very reason that their own religious inheritance is so remorselessly unforgiving of it. In truth, the inheritance of slavery—certainly a hateful thing for Negro Americans to consider—may be a relatively minor consideration in this matter when compared with the inheritance of Bible Belt fundamentalism. This inheritance is, of course, especially marked among the Negro leadership groups, who by and large come from long-established Southern families whose domestic standards appear to have been as rigid as anything a Hard-Shell Baptist could hope for, and indeed a rebuke to their neighbors, white and black.

Yet another convolution must be explored. Family morality or, specifically, sexual morality is such an obsession among religious conservatives in the United States that those who are in rebellion against religious conservatism tend to lump the two together. As it happens, it is just such persons, notably liberal white ministers, who have provided much leadership and support for civil-rights activities. These activists and militants have been especially active in national church organizations, and by and large have resisted any examination of family problems among the poor as both an insult to a class of persons already sufficiently stigmatized and as a concession to the very forces of conservative religiosity which, in truth, in the South, are very much part of the racist coalition.

In general, many persons active in the civil-rights movements, as in most social-reform efforts in recent American history, bring to the undertaking a considerable disenchantment with the traditional "middle-class" values of the society. Although they are likely to be—or because they are—the products of quite successful families, ideas of family stability and morality tend to be seen by such persons as part of the bourgeois *apparat*. And they say to hell with it. Thus, a recent article on Harlem in *The Urban Review*, published by the Center for Urban Education in New York City, spoke with scorn of "Victorian notions about broken homes." Somehow or other, the idea that sexual repression is bad has gotten mixed up with the idea that illegitimacy, or whatever, is good. In a curious way the more liberated youth of the present seem to be affected by a culture lag of sorts: The newest and best thinking about such matters is considerably more respectful of the "nuclear family" than they seem to know. Or care to know.

THE MILITANTS

Minority-group spokesmen, when the subject is raised, tend to respond with arguments about their group values being different from those of the larger society, which is a way of saying "Let's not talk about it." Which in effect declares "Let's not do anything about it." The response is perfectly human, but not much help save to a policy of *laissez-faire*. Nevertheless, despite an occasional reference in NAACP literature to the fact that in the South welfare laws require families to break up in order to receive assistance, in the main the established Negro organizations, and the only now emerging organizations of Puerto Ricans and Mexican Americans, have been silent and essentially obstructionist about the subject. This of course can change, but to the present moment welfare has been a subject that civil-rights leaders have chosen to ignore for the essential fact that to confront it would seem to give ammunition to their worst enemies.

Not surprisingly then, the issue has been raised by militant civil-rights activists who (regardless of their own color) are in revolt, not only against white American society, but also against the established Negro leaders whom they regard as mere appendixes of the larger system. Greatly stimulated by the Federal government's poverty program, with its emphasis on organizing the poor and its frequently avowed contempt for "social workers," these militants are seeking to transform welfare recipients into a powerful interest group that will no longer be forced to accept whatever bargain the welfare establishment could strike with the larger society, but rather will themselves become a party to the negotiations. A Poverty/Rights Action Center has been established in Washington headed by a former Assistant National Director of CORE. Demonstrations have become frequent, and have sometimes gotten out of hand. The welfare office sit-in by Mothers for Adequate Welfare in Boston led to four days of rioting in a city that had hitherto been without racial violence. As is not uncommonly the case, the rhetoric of such organizations is combative, and the principal target for abuse is the welfare department, personified by the welfare worker herself. Three generations of professional work on behalf of the poor have ended with the professional worker being labeled the enemy—by the poor.

The aims of these groups are as yet indeterminate and not without a measure of inconsistency. Many of those involved seek nothing more than to improve the situation of welfare recipients, responding to the conviction that the existing system inculcates and perpetuates precisely the dependency that it nominally seeks to overcome. This is an essentially conservative goal, comparable in many ways to that of traditional trade unionism. (And, of course, as likely as not to be seen as radical and threatening by more comfortable parties.) Notable among the intellectual progenitors of the movement is Professor Richard A. Cloward of the Columbia School of Social Work, the prominent social theorist who contributed much to the conception of the Mobilization for Youth program on the Lower East Side of New York. Cloward proposes a "strategy for crisis" based on the proposition that twice as many persons are eligible for welfare benefits as those who actually receive them and that by organizing the poor to demand their rightful benefits a crisis can be induced in state and local government revenues of such magnitude as to force the national government to guarantee an annual income. It should be noted, however, that while Cloward's objective—the inclusion of the poor in the larger, affluent society—is conservative, his strategy is readily adapted to the desires of many in the penumbra of the welfare movement who would wish such a crisis to bring down the whole system in that apocalyptic and purifying ruin so beloved of radical eschatology,

Dr. Cloward is a professor. Dr. Wiley, the head of the Poverty/ Rights Action Center, is a former professor. The New Left students who helped found the MAW are, in considerable number, future professors.* There is as yet no great evidence that the welfare population has accepted their message. But the very notion that there is a welfare population—and the spectacle of the riot-torn streets of the American cities where, by and large, it lives—suggests that welfare will become an increasingly prom-

* The writer is a professor.

inent political issue in the years ahead. And an ugly one. A most powerful member of the United States Senate, the man in charge of the legislation involved, openly refers to the Poverty/Rights mothers as "Black Brood Mares, Inc.," and in truth their tactics have invited such racial slurs.

V

The *fifth* and final general point is that, by and large, the proposals now being made for improving the welfare system would, in the first instance at the very least, have the effect of enlarging it rather than utterly transforming it.

The features of the existing system that are most objected to (and indeed are most objectionable) arise from what is almost a conflict of interest on the part of welfare agencies: they want to help their clients, but they must also strive to keep costs down. There is the added internal conflict that, within the human species, dependency evokes disdain. "Cold as charity" is the old and accurate description. Nowhere more than in New York State has social welfare been more imbued with compassion and understanding derived from religious and professional convictions. That the New York welfare system is under attack from militants probably reflects in large part the common-sense judgment that friends are easier targets than enemies. However, the mutual tension and dislike between those who give and those who receive exists even in New York, and there is probably no complete cure for it.

Two general approaches to this dilemma have been suggested, and deserve close attention. The first is an administrative approach, which seeks to eliminate the complexities and built-in tensions of the present system, involving as it does cost sharing by three levels of government in a literal maze of programs defined by category, i.e., blindness, disability, and widowhood. The Advisory Council on Public Welfare, in its June 1966 report to the Secretary of Health, Education, and Welfare, proposed that these be scrapped and replaced by "A Nationwide Comprehensive Program of Public Assistance Based upon a Single Criterion: Need." Government would ask not *why*, but simply *whether* a person needed assistance, and then provide it in a context of national minimum levels. This would eliminate much confusion, and dickering—but also, the Council makes clear, it would increase the number of persons receiving public assistance. The Council estimated that only one-fifth of those families with annual incomes under $3,000 were being helped by public assistance and that many more would be if a single-criterion system took effect.

In another vein, a number of legal scholars and social scientists have proposed that the harassment and humiliation of welfare recipients will never end until welfare is established as a *right*, a new form of property that entitles the individual to receive benefits quite apart from his meekness, moral worth, or lack thereof. In order to achieve this, there should be a guarantee of counsel in relations between the recipient and the welfare agency, and a heightened concern by all involved for the constitutional rights of recipients in such matters as unannounced visits, without benefit of search warrant, to determine if welfare mothers are cohabiting without benefit of clergy. Again it may be noted that these are proposals that in the instance will tend to increase the number of persons on welfare. It should also be noted that they may also serve to lower the public's acceptance of the program. Social-work professionals and bureaucrats assuredly have their limitations, but it is as near to certain as social science can be that they are considerably more permissive, broad-minded, and tolerant than the public at large. The strategy of politicizing the welfare issue is risky, indeed. It could easily serve to divide rather than unify American society, and would do so along just those lines of race and ethnicity that it has been the genius of politics in New York to keep blurred.

On the other hand, in a state such as New York welfare has every reason, as it were, to become a political issue in that it profoundly affects the distribution of power and wealth among groups in the society. *The true issue about welfare is not what it costs the taxpayers, but what it costs the recipients.* Evidence—as usual—is practically nonexistent, but the probability is strong that the present welfare system is serving to maintain the poorest groups in society in a position of impotent fury. Impotent because the system destroys the potential of individuals and families to improve themselves. Fury because it claims to do otherwise.

VI

The new militancy is likely to have some effect, and the number of welfare recipients will be affected accordingly. It is at least possible that part of the recent rise in AFDC rates has reflected not so much a change in the size of the eligible population—no one has the foggiest idea what that size might be—but rather an increased willingness and ability on the part of eligible persons to claim what are indeed their rights. It may be assumed that this process will continue. But the larger question for public policy is, of course, how to set in motion forces that will gradually diminish the size of the population that *needs* public assistance. For some special groups—the blind, the aged, the disabled—there is likely always to be a measure of need, and this will no doubt grow somewhat with the population. But these groups are not now, and are never likely to be, either a threat to social stability or a serious charge on public resources. Indeed, in the case of the blind and the disabled it is reasonably clear that investment of public resources brings ample returns, with benefits all around. *The heart of the problem is dependent children from broken families.* The swelling number of such children must be reversed if we are not to create out of our very affluence the "under class" of which Gunnar Myrdal has warned.

And the first point to be made is that we do not know how. This is in part the price of progress: knowledge has not kept pace with change for the simple reason that change has been so rapid and in many respects radical. But it is also the legacy of the generation of professionalism during which the changing nature of the problems faced, and the apparent inefficacy of earlier solutions, was by and large kept secret. We simply do not know the answers to most of the basic questions as to what forces people into dependency and what liberates them from it. All that can be said is that, in a short period of time, we have at least brought that all-important fact out into the open.

One further point has also become clear. A high level of welfare dependency appears to have become a *normal* function of American society. What is more, if normal social functioning will not solve the problem, then it is required that the notion of what is normal be redefined. In a word, what is required is social change. Unhappily, this brings on the question of theory. What works?

In the main, efforts to bring about social change on behalf of the American poor, and especially the Negro poor, have been dominated by two theories, that of legal action and that of services. The former obviously is a theory widely held by lawyers. "In this theory," James S. Coleman writes, "the arena of social action is the court, and any advocate of social change implements his advocacy by obtaining court rulings." The movement to establish the rights of welfare recipients and to provide them legal counsel is derived from this theory. Coleman argues that the evidence on the theory is quite mixed, and from his analysis it would appear particularly difficult to apply to a highly decentralized system such as those under which education and welfare are administered.

The second theory is that of services—providing advice, counsel, and assistance to needy persons to enable them to function better. This has been a dominant theme in social-welfare practice and, as Lee Rainwater argues, the "principal thrust" of the community-action programs of the Federal antipoverty program, designed as they are "toward restructuring communities to make life more tolerable for poor people."

Clearly neither of these theories is without value, and efforts to implement them must continue, but by themselves they appear to be inadequate to the present task. What is needed now is a strategy of *income equalization*. The point Rainwater and others continually make, and which events continue to confirm, is that the problem of the poor is that they are excluded from the larger society because they do not have the income needed to sustain an "average" life. As a result we have built up a dual system under which the goods and services—from foodstuffs to marriage counseling—which most persons purchase in the marketplace are provided to the welfare population by the government. The poor get their victuals from a massive company store, and it may be doubted how much the essence of things will be changed by transforming it into a supermarket. There will be no end of this until the incomes of the poor are brought up to average levels. American income distribution for the past several decades has resembled an elongated diamond—widest in the middle ranges, but reaching both far above and below the average. Rainwater proposes a triangle-shaped distribution in which great heights may be reached, but with no one below the base. He is right.

THE FAMILY ALLOWANCE

It might be imagined that the goal of full employment would be much more politically feasible than that of income redistribution, but it may prove just the opposite. The reason for this is that full employment requires structural changes in the economy—in the society—that impinge on a whole range of great and petty sovereignties, and in truth it may prove easier to redistribute money than power. In any event discussion of the problem of income maintenance is at a new high in the nation, with the not unimportant byproduct that the rigors of economics have been brought to bear on the sometimes all-too-fuzzy world of social welfare. Proposals abound, most of them associated with the idea of providing a national minimum income for all. The attractions of such programs are considerable, but it must be said that so also is their cost. If they have one crucial failing, however, it relates to the present political climate of the nation, rather than to any intrinsic defect. The Negative Income Tax, and similar arrangements, would divide the nation between those who receive the benefit and those who pay for it. In the present state of race relations, and the mounting radicalism of both the left and the right, it may be argued that what is needed is a program that will benefit everyone, rather than just a few, thereby asserting the unities of the nation, rather than emphasizing those qualities that divide it. For this purpose the family allowance would seem an ideal solution, and particularly so for those concerned with problems of social welfare.

The United Sates is the only industrial democracy in the world that does not have a family allowance. We are also the only one with anything like the welfare population in our cities today. The relationship is not a direct one, surely, but neither is it for certain nonexistent. As encountered throughout the world, family allowances are, as James V. Vadakin explains, a system for redistributing income in such a way as to benefit the child-rearing portion of a nation's population. They respond to an essential fact of an industrial society which Sir William Beveridge described in his famous report to wartime Britain:

> Social insurance should be part of a policy of a national minimum. But a national minimum for families of every size cannot

in practice be secured by a wage system, which must be based on the product of a man's labour and not on the size of his family.

The advantages of a family allowance are many. It is paid automatically, requiring no means test, nor a great bureaucracy. (The cost of delivery could probably be kept within one cent and two cents on the dollar.) It is provided not for adults, but for children, in response to the one fact that any group can be brought to agree on, namely that kids cost money. The principal disadvantage of the family allowance is that a large portion of the payments would go to families that are not now defined as poor. But this is also an advantage! The greatest number of these families are working-class or lower-middle-class people, earning incomes in the $5,000 to $8,000 range. This is the group that by and large has been left out of the recent spate of government programs: if not forgotten, it is at least ignored. We have established a Job Corps for the drop-out, and a Peace Corps for the college graduate, but the plain fellow with a high school diploma, and his parents, have little to show from either the New Frontier or the Great Society. This—majority—group of Americans cannot but wonder what it is getting out of all the activity, and in particular has to be asking whether the government is playing favorites, or greasing squeaky wheels, or whatever. This is especially so because this group is anything but affluent. These are families that know where every half dollar goes. In March 1967 the spendable average weekly earnings of workers *with no dependents* on private nonagricultural payrolls were $81.37. The spendable earnings for workers *with three dependents* were $88.75. On a fifty-two-week basis this would mean spendable incomes of $4,231 and $4,615 respectively. In other words, a man with a wife and two children will on average bring home only $7.38 a week more than the bachelor working alongside him. Just as importantly, the average industrial wage in the United States today does not provide even half the income necessary to meet the City Worker's Family Budget as calculated by the Bureau of Labor Statistics. In fall 1966 this budget, providing a moderate standard of living for an urban family of four, came to $9,200, in the nation generally, and was over $10,000 in such cities as New York and Boston.

Obviously, the worker with a large family is at a special disadvantage, and in the United States today this tends to mean the workers at the lower end of the wage scale. Dependency ratios, defined as the number of children under age eighteen per 1,000 adult males aged twenty-one to sixty-four, are significantly higher for Negroes than for whites, and *are becoming more so.*

Table 2.

	DEPENDENCY RATIO (CHILDREN UNDER 18 PER 1,000 ADULT MALES)	
	1960	1966
White	1,365	1,406
Negroes	1,922	2,216

Between 1960 and 1966 the white ratio rose only 3 percent, while the Negro ratio increased 11 percent. Over the six-year period, the adult males increased by 5.4 percent among both whites and Negroes, but the child population under eighteen expanded two and a half times as rapidly among Negroes (21.6 percent) as among whites (8.6 percent).

The family allowance system in Canada currently provides $6 a month for each child under age ten, and $8 for those aged ten through fifteen. An American equivalent might be the payment of $8 for those under six and $12 for those between six and seventeen. For an average worker in private industry with two teenage children, it would increase the "family increment" in his annual take-home pay from $384 to $672, and for one with four such children, to $960 (there being no reason to believe workers with larger families have any larger incomes, and indeed clear evidence that they tend to have less). Families with much larger incomes would, of course, receive a family allowance, but they would pay much of it back in income taxes. Such a system in the United States would cost in the neighborhood of $9 billion a year. In this context, let it be noted that as of 1964 the United States devoted the lowest percentage of Gross National Product to social-welfare measures of any of the Western democracies: 7.0 percent as contrasted with 17.0 percent in West Germany, which has the highest proportion.

A SEQUENCE OF ASSUMPTIONS

With respect to welfare problems, a family allowance would involve a sequence of assumptions. First, that a small increase in income would be accompanied by an important increase in the financial "solvency" of low-income families of the kind that now break up in large numbers, and would do so especially at the point where children are beginning to make serious demands on family budgets. This is no more than a bet, but it is not a foolish one. It must be remembered that the United States now has a family allowance for *broken families* and that it is widely argued (although typically there are not five cents' worth of research findings on the subject) that the availability of AFDC payments does lead to family breakup.

Moreover, a careful economic analysis might very well demonstrate that the present welfare system is indeed, as Duncan M. MacIntyre has argued, a kind of latter-day Speenhamland system under which society supplements the wages of a particularly depressed group doing the dirty work that the rest of the population would as soon avoid. This is a matter of particular concern to New York City, where average weekly earnings in manufacturing have been dropping further and further behind the national average, and, where, perhaps significantly, the increase in the number of persons on Home Relief, i.e., intact families with an employed father whose income supply does not meet family needs, appears to have been rising faster than that of the AFDC program. Among some groups in New York City, it is fairly clear that these wage levels have forced married women into the work force, with resultant strains on family life. In a study of delinquency and narcotic use among Puerto Ricans in the city, Edward Preble observes that "Probably the most significant social factor affecting the Puerto Rican family in New York is the down-grading of the Puerto Rican male." This comes about in the first instance through the changed position of the working wife, with, among other things, a sharp drop-off in the supervision of children.

The second bet would be that a family allowance would not increase the birth rates of the poorer section of the population. There is no evidence that it would. During the past two decades, for example, the Canadian and the American birth rates have risen and fallen together, with apparently no "family allowance" effect whatsoever. On the other hand, there might be—and among middle-class persons there is, a fixed conviction that there would be. This conviction is probably the single most serious obstacle to achieving a family allowance, and is itself a commentary of sorts on our existing social dilemmas: persons who would never dream of having another baby in order to get hold of an additional $8 or $12 a month instantly conclude that, out of depravity, cupidity, ignorance, or whatever, the poor would automatically do so.

At all events, it may be said that, accompanied in particular by serious efforts to attain higher levels of employment for male family heads, a family allowance has the makings of sane social policy in a world where nothing ever is certain. Excepting, as James M. Tobin argues, that the continuation of the present AFDC program by itself is social *in*sanity.

Two other significant measures appear to be in the realm of practicable possibility for the near future: the establishment of national standards for welfare payments under the Social Security Act, and the beginning of serious research efforts to try to find out what is going on.

The case for national standards in welfare assistance is in ways a close one, although given the recent trends in welfare dependency it is at least possible that the Congressional delegations of the industrial states outside the South will organize themselves to bring about some change. The essential facts are two. First, that a large proportion of the poorest people in the nation are located in states whose welfare payments are miserable to the point of being punitive, with the result that the children dependent on them certainly suffer and very possibly are hurt in lasting ways. Second, the differential in payments between jurisdictions, however, *has* to encourage *some* migration toward urban centers in the North. Thus, as of December 1966 New York State paid AFDC families an average of $226.85 a month. South Carolina paid $62.10. Between 1961 and 1965, the number of AFDC recipients in New York State increased 104 percent to a rate of 69 per 1,000 children under eighteen. In South Carolina the number of recipients *decreased* by 26 percent, to a rate of 22 per 1,000 children under eighteen. There is no solid evidence that migration had anything to do with these changes, but the possibility is surely strong, and it is absurd to suppose that a one-year residence restriction would discourage such obviously rational moves. From the point of view of the migrants, the move from South Carolina to New York is bound to be a good thing, and it would be wrong, from that point of view, to improve matters in South Carolina to the point that more persons would stay there. On the other hand, not to do so is to leave those who do remain to the mercies of an indifferent or hostile majority. It is a dilemma not easily resolved.

Puerto Rican migrants are in a fundamentally different situation from that of Southern Negroes: it is only when they leave their homeland and come to New York that they encounter discrimination and a dominant majority made up of persons of different ethnic origin. Thus, there would be no reason save economic ones to encourage migration, and good reasons to raise Puerto Rican standards even if that should have the effect of discouraging it. In any event, welfare standards appear to have little influence on events. In a recent study of Puerto Rican families in Greater San Juan and New York, Oscar Lewis found that "Higher welfare payments in New York did not appear to be an important factor in migration," and noted that while both in New York and Puerto Rico 20 percent of the families in his sample received some form of relief payments, "Most of the families that had been on welfare in Puerto Rico were self-supporting in New York."

In the matter of research, two general areas cry out for support. In the first instance there is a need for sustained, longitudinal studies of poverty populations to try to determine which factors lead into welfare dependency, and which lead out. The need, as Paul Appleby would say, is for someone to make a mesh of things: to find just what are the interconnections of employment, family budgets, children, sex, housing, education, and all the myriad of forces impinging on life that sustain some persons and fail others. (An elemental question: is it a good or bad thing for AFDC mothers to go to work? In what circumstances? No one knows. Many prescribe.)

In the second instance, after three generations of professional casework, it is time we learned how genuinely to give help to those deepest in poverty. It is the judgment of such researchers as Oscar Lewis and Jane C. Kronick that there are vast numbers of families caught up in poverty who *cannot* get out by themselves and need intensive help. Oscar Lewis talks in terms of providing one caseworker for every two such (extended) families and carrying on for a decade each. In New York City, which has a turnover of caseworkers of 40 percent a year, the implications of Lewis's judgments are unnerving, but the source commands attention and respect. In any case, the argument for research is compelling. Our existing social science cannot explain what is going on. We must learn more. It is as obvious as that, but as this paper has tried to suggest, it is not to be supposed that we will do what is obvious. More today, perhaps, than ever, the truth about the welfare problem is likely to be envisioned as threatening by those who are in a position to block any serious efforts to find it out. This need not be a crude affair: indeed, probably the very best way to ensure that no significant research is done is to pound millions of dollars of research funds down the various holes into which appropriations have been disappearing for years. This is so elemental a fact that nothing more can be said about it save this: the welfare profession cannot at this point be relied on to ensure the quality of intellect brought to bear on this issue. It is a matter that must become the direct concern of elected officials and the more central academic disciplines.*

* In *The Politics of A Guaranteed Income* (Random House, 1973) I describe the events that led to the proposal of a negative income tax by the Nixon administration. This was put forward as "welfare reform" but for reasons set forth in "The Crises in Welfare" it was well enough understood that there was no way to reform welfare as such. Change would come slowly, if at all, from changes effected elsewhere, in this case in the amount and stability of the income of the working poor. At one point both Republicans and Democrats seemed committed to a negative income tax. By now, however, both parties have seemingly abandoned the idea. As I reread "The Crises in Welfare" I wonder why we went to such effort—and with such high hopes! There are things that cannot be done. In the period just passed, providing income by right to the poor could not be done. The poor would not help in bringing it about, and their nominal spokesman would be as obstructive as their nominal enemies. *I knew this.* As I hope the foregoing article suggests. And yet I spent two years in a Republican administration pretending otherwise. So much for right reason.

The Education of the
Urban Poor

7

Half a year and more has passed since the publication of James S. Coleman's epic study of *Equality of Educational Opportunity*. From the first it was clear that this study would have profound import for the education of the urban poor. The brief period of scrutiny that has intervened since its appearance has confirmed this beyond even the expectations of those of us who expected most.

The Office of Education, not without a tinge of anxiety, had released the report early in July to a nation that had not known it was coming and that was in any event preoccupied with the Fourth of July weekend. It would be difficult to describe the reaction to the report, for in truth there was none. Some of the newspaper accounts were better than we had reason to expect—John Herbers of *The New York Times*, for example, got close to the heart of the matter—but the overall impression was simply that another government study had confirmed what everyone had known all along.

If you happen to share my considerable respect for the open-

"The Education of the Urban Poor" was read before a meeting of the Harvard Club of New York City and the M.I.T. Alumni Center of New York on March 1, 1967. It was first published in the *Alumni Bulletin* of the Harvard Graduate School of Education, Fall 1967.

ness of American society to new information, you would none-theless have expected, even then, that before the year was out the study would become a matter of profound interest to American educators, and beyond them to a whole range of persons concerned with the nature of American society, and the education of the urban poor, most especially that very great portion of the urban poor composed of Negro Americans.

The information produced by the study—perhaps the second largest in the history of social science—was too powerful, and too profoundly at odds with the conventional wisdom, to remain unnoticed. Moreover the analysis, thanks to the initiative of the U.S. Office of Education, was the work of distinguished American scholars—Coleman and associates such as Ernest Q. Campbell—in collaboration with no less distinguished civil servants such as Alexander M. Mood. Further, it came at just the moment when the technology and the theory of mathematical sociology were able to undertake an enterprise of near Promethean daring.

Let there be no mistake as to the drama of the study. The early assumption that it had merely proved what everyone had known all along was at least partially due to the fact that this was what was expected of it. The study was called for by Section 402 of the Civil Rights Act of 1964. The initial Congressional intent seems to have been that the study should become a tool for legal actions designed to put an end to deliberate discrimination against minority groups. The final intent, however, seemed more in the direction of showing the kind and degree of differences in available educational facilities as between minority group children and majority group children in American life.

No one questioned that these differences existed, nor yet that they were deeply consequential. In an interview in *Southern Education Report* of November–December 1965, published more than midway through the project, Coleman himself put it:

> . . . the study will show the difference in the quality of schools that the average Negro child and the average white child are exposed to. You know yourself that the difference is going to be striking. And even though everybody knows there is a lot of difference between suburban and inner-city schools, once the statistics are there in black and white, they will have a lot more impact.

As is increasingly well known, the study found nothing of the sort. At this point lesser men would have gone back to recheck their data. Coleman and his band chose instead to push on into the unknown, whence they returned with the proposition that Robert C. Nichols in *Science* has described as being of "literally revolutionary significance . . . [standing] like a spear pointed at the heart of the cherished American belief that equality of educational opportunity will increase the equality of educational achievement." What emerged was a study which, in Robert A. Dentler's words (in *The Urban Review*), "makes a contribution to the study of American intergroup relations second only to Myrdal's *American Dilemma*."

What are the findings? This is not as clear as might be hoped. Persons will differ as to what has been proved, or, more importantly, disproved, and there will be considerable variance in the priorities different persons will assign even to those findings they can agree upon, the great quality of the study being that it raises so many more questions than it answers. I shall, then, offer you my list; others will have their own.

I believe the first finding is that the educational achievement of "racial" minority groups in the United States is grievously below that of the white majority, with the immensely significant exception of Chinese-Americans. It is fairly clear that in the course of going to school, the children of these groups fall further behind the majority rather than being helped to catch up. This is most pronounced for Indian Americans, who in the first grade score 53.0 on the nonverbal test, 50 being average, but by the twelfth grade drop to 47.1. But inequality of educational achievement is greatest with respect to Negro Americans who, for example, in the metropolitan Northeast, wind up in the twelfth grade 3.3 years behind whites in verbal achievement, and 5.2 years behind in mathematics. Twelfth-grade Negroes do sixth-grade arithmetic—not in Mississippi, but in New York.

I believe this must be the starting place for any consideration of Coleman's findings. The American educational system as it now operates is turning out seriously unequal citizens. We learned this within months, as it were, of having enshrined in law the principle of equality of opportunity. One does not have to share my view that the Civil Rights Act of 1964 marked the highwater mark of Social Darwinism in the United States in order to perceive that given unequal educational achievement, equal opportunity thereafter will produce unequal results. I do not see how this can be questioned. Coleman, or rather the Educational Testing Service of Princeton, has established that the problem of racial inequality is imprinted in the very nerve system of American society. Anyone who supposes it is going to fade gently away like the Vietnam war* or the Soviet state is out of his mind.

It is, I should think, more than likely that a study of this kind done, say, in a country of Northern Europe would find similar gaps in the educational achievement of different groups defined in terms of occupation or class, but the essential fact in the United States is the additional category of race. I do not wish to underestimate the bitterness and antagonism that class difference can bring about, but surely the history of the twentieth century must persuade us that they are as nothing compared with the cleavages created by racial and ethnic differences. That is a plain fact and one we must live with in America.

The second finding of the Coleman study, and here I must mildly differ from the view put forth by Robert Dentler, is that there does not appear to be any significant degree of discrimination in the quality of the school facilities provided minority children. This is not the same as saying that the school facilities are equal. They are not. But one has the distinct impression that where there do exist inequalities, they are more to be explained by the nature of the urban and rural environment than by any internal functioning of the school system itself. Thus if Negroes live in the rural slums of the South and the urban slums of the North, then they are likely to attend older, more run-down schools characteristic of slums everywhere. The Negro children of the Roxbury section of Boston (who have almost no elected political leaders) attend old, run-down schools—as also do the white children of South Boston (who are represented in Congress, for example, by the Speaker of the House of Representatives). If

---

* The record will show, I believe, that at this time (March 1967) there was not a little talk in high places that the war in Vietnam might quietly subside and finally disappear altogether.

anything, in the nation as a whole, schools attended by whites appear to be somewhat older than those for Negroes.

This must be taken as a general impression gained from reading a complex set of tables from which particulars can be had that would support quite different, even opposed, points of view. My impression is that the American education system is performing in the classic manner of all bureaucracies, that is to say, it is imposing conformity in those realms subject to the bureaucratic writ. This writ does not extend, of course, to the huge wrong of racial segregation of neighborhoods, which if anything grows more pronounced, and is producing in effect two school systems: one occupied by whites, the other by Negroes.

A third finding is that despite our convictions to the contrary, it does not appear that the quality of school facilities, as we now conceive of the subject, has any very powerful differential effect on student achievement. Coleman's analysis revealed the school-to-school variance in pupil achievement in proportions of 10 to 20 percent:

> School to school variations in achievement from whatever source (community differences, variations in the average home background of the student body, or variations in school factors), are much smaller than individual variations within the school, at all grade levels, for all racial and ethnic groups. This means that most of the variation in achievement could not possibly be accounted for by school differences, since most of it lies within the school.

In point of fact, as a number of persons have noted, if one wished to press the matter, it would be possible to argue that the Coleman data suggest there is in truth almost no "school effect" whatever, inasmuch as the school-to-school variances exist in the first grade as well as the twelfth, and therefore must reflect the community rather than the institution as such.

I believe it is necessary here to fight against our own strong contrary perceptions, as well as, perhaps, our ideological convictions. Persons who are very much interested in a given subject—be it race horses, French wines, corn whiskey, or public schools —will frequently develop extraordinary acuteness in perceiving the most subtle—and to them crucial—differences between ob-

jects that would appear more alike than otherwise to the untrained observer. Thus Mencken suggests that romance is the
illusion that one woman is different from another. They are, and
they aren't, and that is about all there is to say.

This, I believe, is what Coleman says: not that schools have
no effect—a preposterous notion—but rather that, by and large,
given the vast educational system of the United States, they
appear to have surprisingly similar effects. This proposition
emerges from what is in truth an important methodological innovation (innovation on such a scale, at all events). Coleman
measured the *output* of the schools, rather than their input, and
found the differences in output to be considerably smaller than
was assumed.

It must be stressed that the data are complex, open to many
issues of interpretation, and subject possibly to considerable
reinterpretation in the light of different techniques of analysis.
But for the moment this is the proposition we have before us, and
it is not, after all, such an extraordinary one. Indeed it is in ways
a profoundly heartening proposition: the most important in-
gredients in a school, says Coleman, are not the grown-ups, and
certainly not the fixtures, but the young people themselves.

Thus the recent report of the U.S. Civil Rights Commission
on *Racial Isolation in the Public Schools*, on further analysis of
the Coleman data, finds that "There are noticeable differences
in the quality of the schools which Negroes attend and those
which whites attend." The Commission then adds: "There is
some relationship between such disparities and the achievement
of Negro students." (Emphasis added.)

It is essential that we at least acknowledge this proposition,
even if we continue to disbelieve it and to test it. There is no
need for final, ultimate knowledge here: all that can be expected
of us is that we keep inquiring and be candid about what inquiries disclose.

One of the more unsettling statements in the study, for example, concerns the effect of the revered pupil/teacher ratio.
Coleman found none: not even enough to make up a table.
"Some facilities measures," the report states, "such as the pupil/
teacher ratio are not included because they showed a consistent
lack of relation to achievement among all groups under all conditions." This is no doubt the case. But it is also the case that

Coleman was measuring the effects of variations that cluster around the current 23-to-1 average. What if, as Alan K. Campbell and Philip Meranto have suggested, the ratio were reduced to that of the Job Corps Center at Camp Kilmer, which has one professional instructor for every four and one half students?

Similarly, Coleman found that variance in per-pupil instructional expenditures could account for almost none of the differences in pupil achievement when the more significant background variables were controlled. For Negroes in the North this variance reached virtually nonexistent proportions measured in hundredths of one percent (e.g., .02 percent in the ninth grade). But again this concerns variations clustered around an average of about $500. What if per-pupil expenditure on instruction were something like the $4,350 that Campbell and Meranto estimate for the Camp Kilmer Job Corps? And what, for that matter, if the pupil/teacher ratio achieved the ultimate nineteenth-century formulation of Mark Hopkins on one end of a log and a student on the other?

A fourth finding—really it should be termed a reminder, for this is something we have always known, but somehow in the United States try to forget—is the all-powerful fact of social class, or if you prefer the term, social stratification. In specific terms, this means the family background of the individual student, and the family backgrounds of his fellow students. Writing in *The Public Interest,* Coleman put it thus:

> Altogether, the sources of inequality of educational opportunity appear to lie first in the home itself and the cultural influences immediately surrounding the home; then they lie in the school's ineffectiveness to free achievement from the impact of the home, and in the school's cultural homogeneity which perpetuates the social influences of the home and its environs.

The issue can be put fairly bluntly as follows: Can a middle-class school be created without a middle-class student body? I believe Coleman's answer would have to be at most a highly tentative "maybe." I believe our assumptions here have been far more optimistic, and that we have in this respect been at fault.

Because race is the single most inclusive (although not, of

course, complete) determinant of class in the United States, I shall argue that Coleman's data represent the most important demonstration of the absolute necessity of racial integration in education that has ever been assembled. He has shown that the achievement of lower-class students is raised when they are included in a predominantly middle-class school, and that the corresponding achievement of the middle-class students is not thereby lowered. Again, we may resist the finding but we must acknowledge it.*

Quality education in segregated schools is what is not happening. Now it may be that it can be made to happen. Certainly there are instances where things seem to go right despite the probabilities to the contrary, and we must dig into those exceptions. But the evidence of the moment is against it. The evidence is that if we are going to produce equality of educational opportunity in the United States in this generation, we must do so by sending Negro students, and other minority students as well, to majority white schools. We cannot do this given the present system of school administration. And even given changes in that system, the all-powerful facts of demography—soon now almost one child in five entering public schools in the nation will be Negro, and in central cities the proportion will be far higher— make clear that we cannot do it without great expenditure. But I believe Coleman has taken us pretty much to the point where there can be no fuzzing the decision: either we are willing or we are not.

In this connection, let me also note that because the issue is class not race, there is perhaps more to be done by way of integrating lower-class Negro youth in middle-class Negro schools than we have so far managed. Evidence that the Negro community is splitting as between an increasingly well-to-do middle-class group and an increasingly worse off lower-class continues to come in. Recent census studies in Cleveland suggest this phenomenon in striking detail. Middle-class Negroes have much more to contribute here than they may have realized.

. . .

* It must be acknowledged that subsequent analyses have shown a much weaker "integration effect" than we originally supposed. To my mind this merely raises the issue of integration back up to the level of moral concern from which it ought never to have been allowed to descend.

A fifth finding concerns the elusive question of motivation. Let there be no doubt that American children have learned to like school, and to expect it to be a primary source, even *the* primary source, of their own social mobility. This is most especially true of Negro children, who report the utmost attachment to all the approved attitudes toward education, and clearly set themselves very high standards of performance. Just as clearly, the greatest number of these children do not achieve these standards. Coleman cannot explain this but his data demand that someone try.

The question comes to something like this: What are the correlates of realism among students from deprived backgrounds? What is it that will translate great expectations into great achievement? What, on the other hand, suggests nothing more than pathetic and doomed fantasy? One thinks of the nine-year-old Puerto Rican girl Catín in Oscar Lewis's brilliant book *La Vida*. Catín loves her desperately disorganized family, loves her mother, is determined to help earn money for them. "That's why," she says, "when I grow up, I want to be a doctor or a chambermaid."

I believe it is now well known that in this area Coleman found that a sense of control of one's own destiny was far the best predictor of performance. He writes:

> Despite the very large achievement differences between whites and Negroes at the 9th and 12th grades, those Negroes who gave responses indicating a sense of control of their own fate achieved higher on the tests than those whites who gave the opposite responses. This attitude was more highly related to achievement than any other factor in the student's background or school.

But we do not know how this attitude comes about, and in particular we do not know how much it is simply a mirror of success that has its origins elsewhere. Nonetheless, it is likely that Coleman has isolated a highly significant variable.*

How then is the intelligent and concerned person to respond to all this? One thing may be said with certainty: it is no use

---

* I fear we were all being less than candid here in the hope of sounding positive. As time passed, what impressed me most was the extraordinarily high proportion of young persons of all groups that *had* a "sense of control of their own fate."

hoping the Coleman study will go away. It does not at all follow that the future course of American education will be shaped by it, but it is near to inevitable that it will profoundly influence both the study of education and the public discussion of educational policy.

The first large instance of this is the report of the United States Commission on Civil Rights, *Racial Isolation in the Public Schools,* in the preparation of which Professor Thomas F. Pettigrew was chief consultant. The report is based in considerable measure on further refinement of the Coleman study data, and on evaluation of educational experiments that bear upon it. Its "Findings" represent the first effort to spell out the policy implications of the Coleman study and these elaborations.

Not surprisingly, the Civil Rights Commission reached conclusions significantly at odds with many present assumptions, and proposed a course of action that runs almost directly contrary to the current drift of events. The Commission found that racial isolation in the public schools is both "intense" and "increasing"; that there are "marked disparities in the outcomes of education for Negro and white Americans"; that programs of compensatory education do not have lasting effects in improving the achievement of Negro children; and that programs on the present scale are not likely to do so as long as the children remain isolated "by race and social class." The Commission concluded that the only solution to a mounting crisis will be for Congress to mandate by law the *de facto* integration of Negro and white students in the United States, and provide "substantial financial assistance" in the construction of the vast new facilities that would be required to do so. Although not quite spelled out, the Commission fairly clearly sees *de facto* integration as a condition in which the overwhelming majority of Negro students attend schools in which they are a minority.

Now it should be clear enough that these are not proposals likely to bring on an outpouring of public support. The report on *Racial Isolation in the Public Schools,* like the report on *Equality of Educational Opportunity,* was filled, in effect, with bad news. It is certain to be seen almost as a racial slur by some of the more militant members of the Negro community, and resisted for equal but opposite reasons by many whites. The Commission declares in effect that this is a white country and that to succeed in it one must grow up with whites: exceptions only prove the rule. One Negro member of the Commission, understandably sensitive to this point, appended a Supplementary Statement to the report. In it she indicates her sympathy for those who, seeing segregation as inevitable, wish to concentrate on providing a superior education for the Negro poor, but adds:

> However, there is little that is healthy and much that is potentially self-defeating in the emotionalism and racial bias that seem to motivate a small but vocal minority among those who now argue for "separate-but-equal" school systems. (Supplementary Statement of Commissioner Freeman)

With respect to the white majority, the Commission report declares that the social directions that have resulted from the sum of individual decisions of the past generation have led the nation to the brink of social disaster, and must be reversed. The Commission in effect proposed a level of deliberate and voluntary social change that may be possible, but that certainly has rarely if ever before occurred.

The Civil Rights Commission has already aroused a certain amount of dismay, and one can anticipate more. Similarly, the Coleman study itself has sent a tremor of anxiety through the educational establishment. One can sympathize with the harassed school superintendent or commissioner of education just waiting for the moment when some member of the local school board or state legislature comes forth with the news that an Office of Education study has "proved" that teachers' salaries, classroom ratios, library books, laboratory facilities, or whatever, don't make any difference in educational achievement.

With this prospect in mind, some elements of the educational bureaucracy have made tentative efforts to discredit Coleman. For example, one of the nation's most influential Washington columnists recently declared that "The Coleman Report . . . has already done profound though still invisible harm." Typically the charge is not that the facts are wrong, but that they will be misused by persons whose motives are wrong, which by implication raises doubts about the motives of the person who was so ill-advised as to present the facts in the first instance. I can testify that this can be a lethal polemical device. Moreover it points to several problems concerning the profound but troubled impact of the social sciences on public policy in the United States at this time that bear comment.

The first such problem is one with which the history of the natural sciences has made us familiar if not comfortable. It concerns the simple fact that the methodology of educational research is now reaching a degree of complexity such that the results of inquiry are no longer directly accessible to the policy-maker. He does not understand the language. He cannot judge the validity of the results, or perhaps it should be said that he cannot counter a "scientific" argument with his own interpretation of the "scientific" data. If Coleman had concluded that it is fluorescent lights that make all the difference, one must fear that there are few educational policy-makers who could have demanded to see the equations and disproved him on the spot. Thus does science reintroduce the necessity of faith. Data such as those of the Coleman study are immensely difficult to interpret. This past year at Harvard, thanks to the generosity of the Carnegie Corporation and the unfailing cooperation of the Office of Education, we have been conducting a faculty seminar on the Study. Each fortnight a group that grew to some 75 assorted professors and scholars, among them some of the commanding intellects of their particular specialties, has been assembling to see what is to be made of it all, and I can assure you that our progress has been modest. It would be unreasonable to ask persons with almost no advanced training in the fields involved to do better. It is not a matter of experts always being right: surely they are more often wrong when it comes to the large movements of history. But it is very much a matter of command of the language of expertise, which increasingly is limited to the experts themselves.

That being the case, it would then seem clear that there is a need for the development in the field of education policy, and of social policy generally, of that rare and wondrous quality of intellect that is to be seen in men such as George Kistiakowsky and Jerome Wiesner who can serve as conduits between the world of the natural sciences and that of public policy, speaking the language of both worlds, and holding the respect and confidence of the leaders of both. It may be hoped that the private philanthropic foundations that have so greatly contributed to the development of the social sciences might now give some thought to this problem of translating and communicating their products. Otherwise we must expect more, not less, of the vulgarization and distortion which often do accompany such findings, and further, for that reason, even greater resistance to the conduct of such studies and the release of their findings.

A second problem concerning the relation of social science to public policy in this and related fields is one for which there are perhaps fewer precedents (although, as in the case of Herman Kahn, these have been most powerful ones). It has to do with the differences between the politics of social scientists and the social science of politics.

I would very much share the judgment of Kenneth Boulding that mankind is entering a profound new era in which man is becoming widely conscious of his own societies and of the larger "sociosphere" of which they are a part. In *The Impact of the Social Sciences* he writes:

> This movement of the social system into self-consciousness is perhaps one of the most significant phenomena in our time, and it represents a very fundamental break with the past, as did the development of personal self-consciousness many millennia earlier.

Increasingly, moreover, this self-consciousness is being shaped by social-science findings that are apt to be significantly at odds with the ideology-based assumptions of the past. This process is begun, just barely so, largely because the social sciences have as yet received relatively little support, and that has been concentrated in relatively narrow specialties. (Note what Boulding has to say on the subjects we have been discussing: "Research in race relations virtually ceased with the Supreme Court decision of 1954." "The sociology of the family has been shockingly neglected in recent years after some very exciting work a generation ago." "I am struck . . . with the relatively meager resource which is devoted to the problem of human learning, in spite of the fact that this is the core of virtually all developmental processes."

In recent years, however, it has also been true that social scientists have been playing rather an active role in seeking to shape public attitudes on social issues with proposals based not so much on their professional findings as on personal proclivities. Social scientists have been liberals, even radicals, about a wide range of public issues. They have been deeply committed to the need for and possibility of social change. They have been often as not at odds with the forces of personal wealth and political power, as any reader of the advertisements in the Sunday *Times* "News of the Week in Review" will attest. As a result, many minority groups, of which schoolteachers and Negro Americans are prominent examples of the moment (trade unions would be a good example from the preceding generation), have come to assume that social scientists will always be on their side, and this in turn has led to the assumption that social *science* will be as well. This is not necessarily so, the more so if being on the "side" of a given group involves attesting to the efficacy of whatever social program that group is favoring at the moment. Social scientists worthy of the name will call 'em as they see 'em, and this can produce no end of outrage at the plate, or in the stands.

There is no cure for this, but neither is there any reason to expect that the embattled partisans of this cause are in the future going to be any more understanding of the problem than they have been in the recent past. Whoever is not with them will be judged against them, and whoever produces "facts" that are against them will be doubly damned. What we can hope for, however, is a larger sensitivity to this matter from the information media and within the social sciences themselves. This form of rejection will never become a pleasant experience for anyone, but to understand, even to anticipate, it is, one hopes, to be better able to ride out the storm.

Howsoever anticipated, the prospect that a considerable body of opinion might come to feel duped or betrayed by those in intellectual or political "authority" would be a matter of some concern at any moment in history, but it would seem to be especially so at this moment. It is not necessary to look for trouble in order to find it in American life. The fact of the matter is that this decade, which began with such great expectations, is taking on an ominous and threatening quality. "The center will not hold." We murdered our President. Then murdered the man we say murdered him. And from that moment on the confidence in the institutions of American life has been slipping away. I do not wish to sound apocalyptic. As with most of us, I share the senior Holmes's skepticism about instant doom. But one would be blind not to see that the extremes of distrust and alienation are acquiring a position in American life that is unusual and very possibly dangerous.

In the early 1960s we saw the emergence of the radical right, and saw it profoundly influence one of our two great national parties. In the past two elections we have seen the forces of unregenerate racism assert themselves here and there throughout the nation, and in portions of the Old South we have seen the politics of moderation very near to annihilated. Now, as in no time since the 1930s, we see the arguments of the radical left gaining increasing strength and credibility among the youth of the nation. The antics of these young persons in turn produces a reaction in other segments of the society, and we see in a state such as California events not very different from those of Alabama; in the clash of extremes, the center is destroyed.

And now, as if fate were taking an active role, we find that, one by one, organizations of the widest variety—the United States Senate, the Department of Justice, General Motors, and, thanks to the Central Intelligence Agency, many of the most respected and valued institutions of American life—find themselves in situations of profound embarrassment. This country begins to look corrupt: not more so than other countries, but we have not thought of ourselves in terms of other countries. Let me not conjure visions merely of increased numbers of young men in sandals or old ladies in tennis shoes. Let me cite to you a statement made on Lincoln's birthday by Mr. Gregory B. Craig, Chairman of the Harvard Undergraduate Council, to Ambassador Arthur J. Goldberg on the occasion of his recent visit to Cambridge, as an honorary associate of the Institute of Politics:

> Mr. Ambassador, we've tried everything; we've written letters signed by student leaders, we have signed petititons, we have written to our Congressmen and to our Senators, and we are frustrated. . . . Our friends to the left have made their complete alienation from United States policy absolutely clear. What you should be concerned about is the more moderate group of

students who on this campus and in universities and colleges throughout the country are becoming increasingly disaffected. Six years ago, the American government captured the imagination of a whole new generation of young people. Today, these same people, some of our country's most talented and thoughtful citizens, regard the notion of national purpose with cynicism, and in some cases, outright hostility. The sad thing is that our own leaders have destroyed our idealism. To me this is one of the great sorrows of the war in Vietnam. . . . Until our government returns to a certain elemental faith in its people, our disaffection will increase and some of America's most loyal and idealistic youth will be left with little loyalty and even less idealism.

The plain fact is that the United States had best look to its standards of conduct, or face the prospect of being discharged from the decade of the 1960s under conditions less than honorable.

And here is the point with respect to the dilemmas we now face concerning the education of the urban poor. At the outset of this decade we began to make promises such as have never been made, and to raise expectations to a level that might never have been envisioned. Part—just part—of the reason we did this was that we genuinely believed it to be in our power to do fairly directly what it is we said needed to be done. "This nation can afford whatever is required to . . ." Now, however, we begin to see that it will not be that easy. We cannot buy our way out of that commitment. But—and this is the point—neither can we go back on the commitment. In any circumstances it would be an outrage to do so. In our present circumstances it would be, as the French say, worse than a crime: a blunder. Given the mounting extremism of American politics, to fail to deliver on the promises made to the Negro Americans in the first half of this decade will be to trifle with the stability of the American republic. There is no other way to state it save bluntly thus.

But what to do if it turns out that those measures in which we have had so much confidence may have let us down? It seems to me that once this question is asked it answers itself readily enough. If old techniques don't work, devise new ones. Of all institutions, American education ought to be open to experimentation and innovation and to the evaluation of results. It would seem this has not been necessarily so. We may, as Robert Nichols writes, "find it hard to believe that the $28-billion-a-year public education industry has not produced abundant evidence to show the differential effects of different kinds of schools, but it has not." One can sympathize with the executive committee of the American Association of School Administrators in its recent statement that "No public institution in the world is assessed more frequently and critically than American education," while at the same time agreeing with the statement of a group of my colleagues, headed by Dean Sizer, that there is a difference between frequent assessment and meaningful assessment, that "the improvement of the quality of education has always been hampered by our remarkable ignorance of what happens to young people as a result of the time and money expended on them in schools."

The only useful response, it would seem to me, is to begin with the premise that the American people look to their school system not only to educate children to the always more demanding skills of modern society, but also to keep America an open society. Education in the United States has had this deep social, and if you will political, purpose for well over a century now, and there is no sign of any diminishment in that intent. It is not enough for us that the school system should simply replicate and legitimatize the existing social order from one generation to the next. That being the case, it is up to educators to find out how to achieve change. Here as elsewhere, as nineteenth-century Americans used to say, the great problem is not ignorance so much as knowing all those things that ain't so. Coleman suggests to us in the most powerful terms that a lot of things we have taken for granted just are not so.

Thus one could argue from the Coleman data that the provisions of Title 1 of the great Elementary and Secondary Education Act of 1965 are misconceived, and improving the education facilities provided to poor children will not of itself do the job. (I don't personally share this view; I merely assert the possibility of such an argument.) Very well, the question then should be, What *will* carry out the intent of Congress, which was to improve the educational achievement of poor children? That intent does not change, simply because we find one method may not work as well as another.

I believe that these and other questions being raised in other fields are all heading us in the same direction: toward concern with the fundamental issues of social class and family welfare, and in particular to a realization that education is the product of the total environment of the child, of which the school as such is only one, and probably not the most powerful, of multiple factors.

This can do us nothing but good. After perhaps too long a period of being infatuated with education, it appears we may at last be getting serious about it. The summons to do just that was put powerfully and well by Theodore R. Sizer in his 1967 annual report of the Harvard Graduate School of Education:

> There are hopeful signs in the country that American education may be moving into a period of realism and candor. If this eventuates, it will be historically unique. Schooling since the nation's founding has been shrouded with optimism, even utopianism. Jefferson never questioned the merit of the institutions he proposed or, as in the case of the University at Charlottesville, created. Jacksonian reformers had equally little question of the power of formal schooling. More recent theorists have compounded the issues: the schools were to carry the load not only of instructing children in the rudiments and in the rules of moral behavior but also to civilize them in the broadest sense. Schools were to be society's microcosms; and within them children could learn to grow. The rhetoric of American Education Week annually repeats this hopeful assurance of the power of the school. Education's claims are vast and in their repetition a peculiarly American cliché. They are also education's worst enemy.

The Politics of Stability

8

President Johnson is said to be fond of relating the experience of an out-of-work schoolteacher who applied for a position in a small town on the Texas plains at the very depths of the depression. After a series of questions, one puckered old rancher on the school board looked at the applicant and asked, "Do you teach that the world is round or that the world is flat?" Finding no clues in the faces of the other board members, the teacher swallowed hard and allowed he could teach it either way.

That is the position of just about anyone who would assay the state of the American republic at this moment from the middling vantage point known generally as liberalism. Two views are possible: On the one hand, it may be argued that the nation is entering a period of political instability from which it will not emerge intact; or the other, that we have entered a troubled time and will not only survive, but will emerge from it wiser and having demonstrated anew the deep sources of stability in American life.

I cannot imagine what would constitute irrefutable evidence for either stand, and I assume that persons adopt one or the other according to their personal taste and condition. The apocalyptic view has many supporters, of course, most notably those of the newly emergent Left who foresee a period of Right-wing oppres-

"The Politics of Stability" was delivered as an address to the National Board of Americans for Democratic Action, September 23, 1967. It was first published in *The New Leader*, October 9, 1967.

sion and excess, followed by the triumph of a new ideology—a conviction that will seem absurb to anyone who has never visited East Berlin. The more sanguine view commends itself to those who would like to believe it true. This includes, almost without exception, any liberal who has shared considerably in the "rewards" of American life, and who can look forward to continued sharing on, if anything, more favorable terms.

The alternatives, then, are to agree with Andrew Kopkind that in the summer of 1967 the war abroad and the revolution at home contrived to "murder liberalism in its official robes" (with few mourners), or to conclude that although we are in a lot of trouble, we can think and work (and pray) our way out of it. It is worth stressing that no one whose views we have learned to trust over the years would offer us a happier option than the latter, which means that if we do not think well enough, or work hard enough, or if our prayers are not answered, we can bring this republic to ruin.

Certainly things have not turned out as we had every reason to think they would. Walter Lippmann, with merciless clarity, has argued that the unexampled mandate of the 1964 election was "to be quiet and uninvolved abroad and to repair, reform, and reconstruct at home." Fate took another direction, and has exacted a double price: not only troubles abroad, but disasters at home because of—or seemingly because of—the troubles abroad. Tom Wicker has stated the matter plainly, as is his failing. "The war," he wrote in late August 1967, "has blunted and all but destroyed the hopeful beginnings of the Great Society. It has produced the gravest American political disunity in a century, and it has aggravated the profound discontent with America of the postwar generations."

The violence abroad and the violence at home—regardless of political persuasion, all agree that these are the problems, that they are somehow interconnected, and that in combination they have the potential for polarizing, then fracturing, American society. But the situation is especially embarrassing for American liberals, because it is largely they who have been in office and presided over the onset both of the war in Vietnam and the violence in American cities. Neither may be our fault, yet in a world not overmuch given to nice distinctions in such matters, they most surely must be judged our doing.

The Vietnam war was thought up and is being managed by the men John F. Kennedy brought to Washington to conduct American foreign and defense policy. They are persons of immutable conviction on almost all matters we would consider central to liberal belief, as well as men of personal honor and the highest intellectual attainment. Other liberals also helped to persuade the American public that it was entirely right to be setting out on the course which has led us to the present point of being waist deep in the big muddy. It is this knowledge, this complicity if you will, that requires many of us to practice restraint where others may exercise all their powers of invective and contempt. The plain fact is that if these men got us into the current predicament, who are *we* to say we would have done better?

This is more the case with respect to the violence at home. The summer of 1967 came in the aftermath of one of the most extraordinary periods of liberal legislation, liberal electoral victories, and the liberal dominance of the media of public opinion that we have ever experienced. The period was, moreover, accompanied by the greatest economic expansion in human history. And to top it all, some of the worst violence occurred in Detroit, a city with one of the most liberal and successful administrations in the nation; a city in which the social and economic position of the Negro was generally agreed to be far and away the best in the nation. Who are we, then, to be pointing fingers?

The question is addressed as much to the future as to the past, for the probabilities are that the present situation will persist for some time. By this I mean that President Johnson will almost certainly be reelected in 1968 and that, with some modifications, the national government will remain in the hands of the same kinds of liberals who have been much in evidence for the last seven years. The war is Asia is likely to go on many years, too, although possibly in different forms. Most importantly, the violence in our cities, tensions between racial and ethnic groups, is just as likely to continue and if anything get worse (as indeed the war could get worse).* But our responses will have to be suf-

* A cloudy crystal ball. President Johnson did not run for reelection. (Although, had he done so, I expect he would have won.) The war in Asia, in different forms, continues. Urban violence has receded to interpersonal forms, although it could always break out again.

ficiently different from those of the immediate past to suggest that we are aware of some of our apparent shortcomings.

What, as someone once said, is to be done? I offer three propositions.

1. *Liberals must see more clearly that their essential interest is in the stability of the social order; and given the present threats to that stability, they must seek out and make much more effective alliances with political conservatives who share their interest and recognize that unyielding rigidity is just as great a threat to continuity of the social order as an anarchic desire for change.*

For too long we have been prisoners of the rhetoric that Republicans do not know or care about the social problems of the nation. This is not only a falsehood, but as any New York Democrat can testify, it is seen by the electorate to be a falsehood. In New York City two years ago, Mayor Lindsay was elected because he was the most liberal of the three candidates. Last year, Governor Rockefeller was reelected for precisely the same reason. The hooting at the callous indifference of Republicans toward human needs recently reached considerable levels in the rumpus over the rat bill. I don't doubt they deserved what they got in that uproar. The argument can nonetheless be made that we would have more to show for it all if somewhere along the line the Democrats had taken at face value the statement of Congressman Melvin R. Laird (R.-Wis.) that he was in favor of "massive" Federal aid to city governments, but not through the techniques of proliferating grant-in-aid programs which he and many like him thought to be an ineffective form of administration.

Interestingly, in the area of foreign affairs the idea that Republican Congressmen and Senators are supporters of a moderate course is more readily accepted. It is time the idea became familiar in domestic matters. It is pleasant to hear the New Left declare that the white liberal is the true enemy because he keeps the present system going by limiting its excesses, yet the truth is that the informed conservatives deserve the greatest credit for performing this function—the Robert Tafts of the nation—and at the present juncture they are needed.

1. *Liberals must divest themselves of the notion that the nation —and especially the cities of the nation—can be run from agencies in Washington.*

Potomac fever became a liberal disease under the New Deal

and it has turned out not only to be catching but congenital, having somehow worked into the gene structure itself. The syndrome derives from one correct fact that is irrelevant, and two theories that are wrong.

It is certainly a fact that strolling across Lafayette Park to endorse or to veto a public works program is much more agreeable than having to go through the misery of persuading fifty state legislatures. But this has to do with the personal comfort of middle-aged liberals, not with the quality of government action, and in a time of some trouble comfort cannot be the sole consideration.

The first theory is that the national government and national politics are the primary sources of liberal social innovation, particularly with respect to problems of urbanization and industrialization. I do not believe history will support this notion, for the cities and to a lesser extent the state governments have been the source of the preponderance of social programs in the twentieth century—mostly the cities and states in the North, of course. Probably the most important reason for this is that until recently these were the areas where such problems first appeared, and where the wealth and intellect—and political will—existed to experiment with solutions.

There is another reason which we tend to be reluctant to talk about, but the discussion of which is perhaps admissible in a time of trouble. In the spectrum of regional politics, the South has for a century been the most socially and politically conservative part of the nation. In the spectrum of American religious groups, American Protestants have fairly consistently been more conservative than American Catholics, and Catholics in turn more so than American Jews. It happens that Washington is, for practical purposes, a Southern Protestant city which combines both these pervasive conservative tendencies—or at least has done so in the past. In an odd combination of historical events, the cities of the North have been dominated by Catholic votes and Jewish intellect, and the result very simply has been a much greater level of liberal political innovation. If this potential has not been much in evidence of late, it is mostly, I believe, because we have allowed state and local governments to get into such fiscal straits that they have no resources left for innovation. But the impulse and potential remain there rather than in Washington.

The second theory I have labeled false is that you can run the nation from Washington. I don't believe you can, at least not with respect to the kind of social change liberals generally seek to bring about. In the field of legislating social attitudes and practices, it is pretty clear that the old-time Tories had a point when they said you can't change human nature—for good or for ill—with a bill-signing ceremony in the Rose Garden. I would note that twenty years ago the Taft-Hartley Act outlawed the closed shop, and that today the closed shop is probably more completely in effect in our building trade unions than ever in history.

The record of social innovation through various public programs is equally unreassuring, largely because the American system of public administration has turned out not to be very good at that sort of thing. Richard Rovere recently noted that "the new Federal agencies set up to deal with the distress of the cities—the Office of Economic Opportunity, the Department of Housing and Urban Development, and the Department of Transportation—have turned in generally disappointing performances." Not because of their leadership, which has often been brilliant, but because of the resources available, and particularly the bureaucracy available. Rovere continues: "In the new agencies, for example, almost everyone feels that there is no greater hindrance to the war on poverty and no greater force for the perpetuation of slums than the public-welfare system administered by, and providing a *raison d'être* for, a huge, entrenched, and complacent sub-bureaucracy in H.E.W." Think of the dreams that had to die before that sentence could be written! But it happens to be true.

"How one wishes," Nathan Glazer writes, "for the open field of the New Deal, which was not littered with the carcasses of half successful and hardly successful programs, each in the hands of a hardening bureaucracy." But the pattern persists: the bright idea, the new agency, the White House swearing in of the first agency head, the shaky beginning, the departure eighteen months later of the first head, replacement by his deputy, the gradual slipping out of sight, a Budget Bureau reorganization, a name change, a new head, this time from the civil service, and slowly obscurity covers all. Who among us in 1967 could state with certainty exactly what did become of the Area Redevelopment Administration, that early, shining creation of the New Frontier?

But the biggest problem of running the nation from Washington is that the real business of Washington in our age is pretty much to run the world. That thought may not give any of us great pleasure, but my impression is that it is a fact and we had better learn to live with it. Martin Luther King, Jr., and many other liberals, are no doubt correct in holding that the war in Vietnam has stalemated government efforts on behalf of Negroes at home, but they are wrong, I think, in their proposed solution: The government should get out of Vietnam. As far as I can see, an American national government in this age will always give priority to foreign affairs. A system has to be developed, therefore, under which domestic programs go forward regardless of what international crisis is preoccupying Washington at a given moment. This, in effect, means decentralizing the initiative and the resources for such programs.

3. *Liberals must somehow overcome the curious condescension that takes the form of defending and explaining away anything, however outrageous, which Negroes, individually or collectively, might do.*

In the course of the summer of 1967 it became clear that with respect to this question there are two significant groups—related, but distinct—within the black community. One is the vast Negro underclass that has somehow grown up in our Northern cities; a disorganized, angry, hurt group of persons easily given to self-destructive violence. Alongside it is a group of radical, nihilistic youth, not themselves members of this underclass, but identifying with it, able to communicate with it, and determined to use it as an instrument of violent, apocalyptic confrontation with a white society they have decided is irredeemably militaristic and racist. I do not believe we have yet realized the depth and intensity of this second group's feelings, nor the extent to which it has succeeded in politicizing the always existing torment of the urban masses—persuading them both of the inevitability and the desirability of a nihilistic solution. All the signs declare that the violence is not ended. Worse still, a new set of signs tells us something that is painful, even hateful to have to hear: We must prepare for the onset of terrorism. Indeed, it may already have begun. How widespread and how successful remains to be seen, but the probability is so great that ignoring it would be an act of irresponsibility or of cowardice.

For liberals, this poses a special problem that derives in a sense from our own decencies. Trying to be kind, trying to be helpful, we somehow have got into the habit of denying the realities of the life-circumstances of the lower class, and this has curiously paralyzed our ability to do anything to change these realities. Typically, we have blamed ourselves for the shortcomings of the poor—and left it at that. A terrifying example was the response in ultra-liberal quarters to the findings of James S. Coleman in his massive report on *Equality of Educational Opportunity*. Coleman, a distinguished social scientist, concluded that the disastrously low level of educational achievement on the part of most Negro youth was the result not nearly so much of the quality of their schools, as of their own family background and that of their classmates at school. With the hand of the Federal bureaucracy barely concealed, Coleman was labeled a racist by people who went on their way deploring conditions in slum schools and blaming Lyndon Johnson or John Lindsay; they were not disturbed by the thought that they might be wrong, or that the politics of stability might involve something more hardheaded than the untroubled indulgence of sado-masochistic fantasy.

The point is a simple one: There is nothing whatever to be done to change the minds of the black nihilists and their white associates, who have been so much in evidence of late. Their course is set. The only option for the nation is to deprive them of the Negro underclass which is the source of their present strength. This means facing up to some of the realities of life in that class that liberals have been notoriously unwilling to acknowledge, so much so that I would not be surprised if it developed that this fact itself was an element in the rage that roared through the streets of America this past summer.

The situation of the Negro masses today is startlingly like that of Yank, the quintessential, apolitical proletarian stoker in one of Eugene O'Neill's plays. Determined to make the world of the first-class passengers recognize his existence, he makes his way to Fifth Avenue and the Fifties and begins jostling top-hatted gentlemen and insulting bejeweled, befurred ladies. He elicits only politeness, which actually is a refusal to acknowledge that he is what he knows himself to be. He is driven mad by "I beg your pardons," finally turns violent, and in the end is destroyed.

The time for confronting the realities of black and white has come in America. It will not be pretty. More is the reason that liberals, rather than avoiding or explaining away that reality, should be the ones to work hardest at moving the nation in sane directions. Such words come easy; the effort itself will go against most of our tendencies. But we would do well to remember similar times of crisis in the past when our failure to lead gave the direction of events to others whose purpose was more to destroy than to build. If the politics of stability are to come to anything, they must be translated into programs.

In foreign affairs, surely, this involves the recognition that getting out of Vietnam is not just a matter of summoning the will, but also of finding a way. It is time to acknowledge that the prestige and the credibility of the Armed Forces is involved and is entitled to consideration, as is the self-regard of the tens of thousands of American youths who perform honorably and well in those jungles because they were asked or told to do so by their government. The task of liberals is to make it politically worthwhile and possible for the administration to disengage. This requires that we continue to work within the party system, and to make clear that we do in fact love peace more than we love the Vietcong. It also requires us to be unrelenting in our exposure of what the war really is doing to the Vietnamese people, and of the future obligations which we incur with every day of its prolongation. In this respect, it seems to me that Senator Edward Kennedy's inquiry into civilian casualties is a model of informed and effective liberal action.

In domestic affairs, we have got to become a great deal more rigorous in the assessment not only of the reality of problems, but of the nature of proposed solutions. We have to pay attention to what it is we are good at, and to work from strength. In particular, we must attend to what the Federal government is good at. On examination, this becomes fairly clear. The Federal government is good at collecting revenues, and rather bad at disbursing services. Therefore, we should use the Federal fisc as an instrument for redistributing income between different levels of government, different regions and different classes. If state and local governments are to assume effective roles as innovative and creative agents, they simply must begin to receive a share of Federal revenues on a permanent, ongoing basis. Let us be frank: The original, determining opposition to this proposition in Washington has come from liberals, not conservatives, and we should be ashamed of ourselves.*

At stake is not just the viability of municipal governments, but also the sense of urban populations controlling their own destinies. Fifty years of social reform have pretty well destroyed the bases of working-class politics in this country. It is not at all funny to note that having broken the power of the bosses, destroyed their control over city jobs and cleaned up the police force to boot, we find the Federal government pouring millions into what Bayard Rustin has termed a "bedlam" of community action programs to overcome the sense of powerlessness among the urban poor, while private donations are sought to enable mayors to hire proletarians who could never pass civil-service examinations, and the Justice Department laments the fact that organized crime rather than the police seems to control the streets. The next irony in the history of the Negro in America will be that having acquired a majority of the votes in a number of major American cities, he will find direction of city affairs has been transferred to Washington. Unless we start now to reverse that trend.

Finally, it is also reasonably clear that we must begin getting private business involved in domestic programs in a much more systematic, purposeful manner. Making money is one thing Americans are good at, and the corporation is their favorite device for doing so. What aerospace corporations have done for getting us to the moon urban housing corporations can do for the slums. All that is necessary, one fears, is to let enough men make enough money out of doing so. It is encouraging to note how much ferment there seems to be in this direction at this time; hopefully, the liberal community will support the effort to involve private business rather than oppose it.

The politics of stability are not at first exciting. It is only when we come to see how very probably our national life is tied to them that they acquire a sudden interest.

---

* Revenue sharing was enacted in 1972, having been proposed by the Republican administration in 1969.

The New Racialism

9

The great enterprise on which the American nation was embarked when the Vietnam storm arose was the final inclusion of the Negro American in the larger American society. That the Negro was, and still in a measure is, excluded none will doubt; it seems not less clear that this fact of exclusion has been the lot of a very considerable portion of the American people over the generations, and the process of inclusion, of "national integration," in Samuel H. Beer's term, a process "in which the community is being made more of a community," has been going on almost from the moment the fortunes of war and empire defined this hopelessly heterogeneous people as made up exclusively of General de Gaulle's "Anglo-Saxons." In fact, at mid-century only 35 percent of the American people were descendants of migrants from Great Britain and Northern Ireland.*

"The New Racialism" was delivered as a commencement address at the New School for Social Research, June 4, 1968. It was first published in *The Atlantic Monthly*, August 1968.

* A Census survey of March 1972 found 14.4 percent of the American population stating that by "origin or descent" they were "English, Scot or Welsh." Another 8 percent designated themselves "Irish." These are "pure" as against "mixed" bloodlines. Persons of "mixed" descent—as, say, "English-French"—could designate themselves "Other." Half the population identified themselves as belonging to eight ethnic categories of European origin. Another two-fifths described themselves as "Other," with most, presumedly, being European mixtures. Even so, it would be fair to state that at most one tenth of the American population is anything approaching "pure" Anglo-Saxon, even allowing a lashing of Norman ancestry.

Most of the rest have known greater or lesser degrees of exclusion —and into the present. But none quite like that of the Negro, and final, palpable equality for him became the essential demand of our time, just as it became the demand of the American presidency; only to arouse among some elements of the society—in greater or lesser degree in all elements—a pervasive fear and deep resistance. Laws in the hundreds were passed, but changes were few. As the black masses for whatever reasons became increasingly violent, white resistance became more stubborn, even as it assumed more respectable forms: "Law and order."

This resistance has produced something of a stalemate, and in consequence a crisis. The essential symbol, and in ways the central fact, of black exclusion in white America is that the Negro is not permitted to move about freely and live where he will. Increasingly he is confined to the slums of the central cities, with consequences at once appalling to him and disastrous to the cities. The laws do not require this exclusion; in fact, they forbid it. Now also does the Supreme Court. But it prevails because of a process of private nullification by whites.

More and more one hears that this situation is likely to persist so long as to require that it be treated as a permanent condition. And largely as a result of this conclusion, a marked reversal appears to be taking place in what are generally seen as liberal circles on the subject of decentralized government and racial quotas. For a good half-century now—longer than that, in truth—liberal opinion has held quite strong views on these issues, and they are almost wholly negative. Nor have these views been in any sense marginal. Quite near to the core of the liberal agenda in the reform period that began at the turn of the century and continued almost to this moment we find two propositions.

The first is that local government is conservative or even reactionary. Such nostalgia as might have persisted about New England town meetings was seen as historically obsolete and ethnically inapplicable. Local government in New York, for example, was known to be run by Irishmen, who were bosses wielding vast but illegitimate power, placing unqualified men on public payrolls, consorting with criminals, and lowering the standards of public life. In the South, local government was in the hands of racists, who systematically excluded Negroes from participation in public affairs, and much else as well. The West was far away. Hence the great thrust of liberal/intellectual political effort, and central to liberal/intellectual political opinion, was the effort to *raise* the level at which governmental decisions were made above that of state and local government, to that of the federal government. The great and confirming successes of that effort were, of course, the Administrations of Woodrow Wilson and Franklin D. Roosevelt. "States' rights" became a symbol of reaction. Distinguished public servants such as Paul Appleby developed the doctrine that those who insisted that this or that governmental activity was best carried out at the local level were in fact opposed to such activity, and confident that in actuality the local government would do nothing. E. E. Schattschneider explained the whole thrust of liberal politics in terms of the effort to raise the level at which the decisions were made. These views had consequence. Three years ago, for example, when the Johnson Administration was about to come forth with a proposal for revenue sharing with state governments—the well-known Heller-Pechman plan—the proposal was vetoed by the labor movement on grounds that giving more resources to local powers could only strengthen the forces of conservatism and reaction.

The second general theme has to do with the whole issue of ethnic, racial (if one wishes to make a distinction between those two), and religious heterogeneity. These were matters which liberal opinion firmly held ought not to be subjects of public moment or acknowledgment. Rather as politics and women are proscribed as matters of conversation in a naval officers' mess, it was accepted that such categories existed, and, given the doctrine of freedom of conscience, it was also accepted that religious diversity would persist, but in general, opinion looked forward to a time when such distinctions would make as little difference as possible. Opinion certainly aspired to the complete disappearance of ethnic characteristics, which were felt to have little, if any, validity. Increasingly, the identification of persons by race or religion, especially in application forms of various sorts, was seen as a manifestation of racism, of unavoidably malign intent.

It is hard to judge which is the more extraordinary: that Americans could have thought they could eliminate such identities, or that so little comment was made about the effort. (Resistance, then as now, was largely silent and ashamed.) Andrew Greeley has recently speculated that the historians of, say, the twenty-third or twenty-fourth century looking back to this time will find that, apart from the great population increase in the world, and its Westernization and industrialization, quite the most extraordinary event was the fusing of cultures in the American republic.

> The historians of the future will find it hard to believe that it could have happened that English, Scotch, and Welsh, Irish, Germans, Italians, and Poles, Africans, Indians, both Eastern and Western, Frenchmen, Spaniards, Finns, Swedes, Lebanese, Danes, Armenians, Croatians, Slovenians, Greeks, and Luxembourgers, Chinese, Japanese, Filipinos, and Puerto Ricans would come together to form a nation that not only would survive but, all things considered, survive reasonably well. I further suggest that the historians of the future will be astonished that American sociologists, the product of this gathering in of the nations, could stand in the midst of such an astonishing social phenomenon and take it so for granted that they would not bother to study it.

I agree, largely as I feel that future historians, relieved of our nineteenth-century preoccupation with the appearance of industrialization and the issue of who would control the artifacts thereof, a preoccupation, in other words, with issues such as capitalism, socialism, and Communism, will also see that the turbulence of these times here and abroad has had far more to do with ethnic, racial, and religious affiliation than with these other issues. Nonetheless, beginning with the New Deal, federal legislation began prohibiting discrimination based on race and religion, and this movement increasingly took the form of forbidding acknowledgment even of the existence of such categories. In New York, for example, a prospective employer simply may not ask to know the religious or ethnic identity of an employee. A dean of admissions may not ask for a photograph of an applicant. The culmination of this movement, and, given its insistence on absolute equality in competition, the high-water mark of social Darwinism in the United States was, of course, the Civil Rights Act of 1964.

Now, of a sudden, all this has changed. The demand for decentralization of government and local participation in decision-making about even the most global issues has become almost a leading issue with liberal thinkers and politicians. Distrust of Washington, once the sure giveaway of a conservative or reactionary mind, has become a characteristic stance of forward-looking young men. And now ethnic quotas have reappeared, although primarily in terms of racial quotas. That which was specifically forbidden by the Civil Rights Act is now explicitly (albeit covertly) required by the federal government. Employers are given quotas of the black employees they will hire, records of minority-group employment are diligently maintained, and censuses repeatedly taken. In universities in particular the cry has arisen for racial quotas, roughly representative of population proportions, in both university faculties and student bodies, and the proposal is most ardently supported by those who would have themselves considered most advanced in their social thinking. It would seem altogether to be expected that this process will continue, and come to be applied to all the most visible institutions of the land, starting, of course, with those most sympathetic to social change, and therefore most vulnerable to such pressure, and gradually, grown more legitimate, extended to the more resistant centers.

What on earth happened? Taking these developments in the order that I listed them, one can perceive at least two sources of the thrust toward decentralization, both related to the racial stalemate and both of which can properly be described as the result of a learning process, and on that ground welcomed. The first is the discovery by liberal middle-class America that many of the institutions of urban working-class politics served important and legitimate purposes, and that the destruction of these institutions created a vacuum in which by and large Negroes now have to live. Having destroyed the power of the local bosses, we learn that the people feel powerless. Having put an end to patronage and established merit systems in civil service, we find that the poor and unqualified are without jobs. Having banished felons from public employment, we find that enormous numbers of men who need jobs have criminal records. Having cleaned up law enforcement, we find that crime is run by the Mafia (or whatever is the current term for slandering Italians), instead of the police, as was the case in the idyllic days of Lincoln Steffens' youth. Hence liberals now are urged to return to local organization with an enthusiasm ever so slightly tinged with the elitism of the middle-class liberal/radical who now as always is confident that he is capable of running anything better than anyone else, even a slum neighborhood. Middle-class radicals continue to insist the blacks in Harlem are powerless, not least, one fears, because the one type who is rarely elected is the middle-class radical. (But to my knowledge there is hardly a single significant elected or appointed political, judicial, or administrative office in Harlem that is not held by a Negro.) Hence an ever-increasing enthusiasm of liberal foundations and reform mayors for creating new "indigenous" community organizations and giving to them a measure of real or pretend power. Whether in fact outsiders can create an "indigenous" organization is problematic. (Would it not be good sport for the Landmarks Commission to assign to Mayor Lindsay's Little City Halls their traditional Tammany designations of Tuscarora Club, Iroquois Club, Onondaga Club?) But the effort is sincere, if withal tinged with a certain elitist impulse to manage the lives of the less fortunate.

On a different level, a movement toward decentralization has arisen largely from the emergence of what James Q. Wilson has called the bureaucracy problem, the fact that "there are inherent limits to what can be accomplished by large, hierarchical organizations." Although Max Weber explained to us why large bureaucracies, once established, would work for themselves rather than the putative objects of their concern, it was not until the bureaucracies were established, and someone tried to do something with them, that any great number of persons came to see the point. Interestingly enough, this seems to have happened in the Soviet Union at about the same time as in the United States. For certain it is an endemic mood among men who went to Washington with John F. Kennedy. The problem involves not just the dynamics of large organizations, but also the ambitiousness of our society. As Wilson continues: "The supply of able, experienced executives is not increasing nearly as fast as the number of problems being addressed."

This is all to the good. It responds to reality; it reflects an openness to experience. Irving Kristol has remarked, echoing Sir William Harcourt at the turn of the century on the subject of socialism, "We are all decentralists now." The acknowledgment that race and ethnicity are persisting and consequential facts about individuals that ought in certain circumstances to be taken into consideration is long overdue. (Several years ago, to my ultimate grief, I tried to get the welfare establishment in Washington to abandon its "color-blind" policy which refused to record anything about the race of welfare recipients. Last year Southern committee chairmen brought about the enactment of vicious anti-Negro welfare legislation, which no one could effectively oppose because no one is supposed to "know" about such things.) But before lurching from one set of overstatements to another, is it not possible to hope that a measure of thought will intervene, and that the truth will be found, alas, somewhere in the middle?

The issues are intertwined, and tend to work against one another. Thus the fundamental source of equal rights for Negro Americans, for all Americans, is the Constitution. Where the federal writ runs, all men are given equal treatment. But this process is not directed by some invisible hand; it is the result of political decisions made year to year in Washington. "Local control" means a very different thing in Mississippi than it does in New York, and let us for God's sake summon the wit to see this before we enshrine the political principles of George C. Wallace in the temple of liberal rationalism. Paul Appleby knew what he was talking about. An aggressive federal insistence on equal treatment for all races is indispensable to the successful inclusion of the Negro American into the large society.

Further, to assert that government in Washington can't run everything is not to argue the impotence of government generally. Unfortunately, a good deal of decentralization talk is fundamentally antigovernment in spirit, and this can be a calamity in areas such as race relations. Giving a mayor enough untied federal funds to enable him to govern his city could release immensely creative energies. Forcing him to break up his administration into endlessly fractionating units will bring on anarchy at best and chaos at worst. Given the heterogeneous political community of most large cities, this potential for ethnic and racial chaos, Kristol remarks, is especially great.

School decentralization in New York seems to be encouraging just this. The problem is that now, as ever in the past, the lower classes of the city are ethnically quite distinct from what might be termed the bureaucratic classes, and neighborhoods tend to conform to those distinctions. The result is that conflict induced between the two groups gets ugly fast. Thus *The New York Times* reported that the militant picketing of I.S. 201 in east Harlem in 1967 was "flagrantly anti-Semitic." Similar tendencies have appeared in the Ocean Hill–Brownsville area where decentralization is being experimented with. A leaflet recently distributed there reads:

> If African-American History and Culture is to be taught to our Black Children it Must Be Done By African-Americans Who Identify With And Who Understand The Problem. It Is Impossible For The Middle East Murderers of Colored People to Possibly Bring To This Important Task The Insight, The Concern, The Exposing Of the Truth That is a *Must* If The Years of Brainwashing And Self-Hatred That Has Been Taught To Our Black Children By Those Blood-sucking Exploiters and Murderers Is To Be Overcome.

A pretty sentiment, to which, not surprisingly, there are Jews capable of responding in kind. Charles E. Silberman, the distinguished author of *Crisis in Black and White*, recently demanded of an American Jewish Committee meeting that it

> face up to the raw, rank, anti-Negro prejudice that is within our own midst. We talk—endlessly—about Negro Anti-Semitism; we rarely talk about—let alone try to deal with—the Jewish Anti-Negroism that is in our midst and that is growing very rapidly.

All too familiar. And as Archbishop John F. Dearden of Detroit, president of the National Conference of Catholic Bishops, observed last year, in other cities of the nation the Negro-white confrontation is becoming a Negro-Catholic (Protestant-Catholic) encounter. *Plus ça change . . .*

The danger is that we shall see the emergence of a new racialism. Not racism, a term—dreadfully misused by the Kerner Commission—that has as its indispensable central intent "the assumption that psychocultural traits and capacities are determined by biological race and that races differ decisively from one another" (Webster's *Third New International Dictionary*). There is a streak of the racist virus in the American bloodstream, and has been since the first "white" encounter with the "red"

Indians. But it is now a distinctly minority position, and mainly that of old or marginal persons, with an occasional politician seeking to make use of what is left. Yet there is a strong, and persisting, phenomenon of racialism, defined as "racial prejudice or discrimination: race hatred." This is in no sense confined to "whites," much less "Wasps." (I use quotation marks. The geneticist Joshua Lederberg notes that it is scientifically absurd to call anyone in this country "black," and probably not accurate to speak of "whites" either.) Writing in a 1935 issue of *Race*, E. Franklin Frazier, for example, referred to W. E. B. DuBois's then current proposal that the Negro build a cooperative industrial system in America as "racialism." There is nothing mystical about racialism; it is simply a matter of one group not liking another group of evidently antagonistic interests. It is a profoundly different position from that of racism, with its logic of genocide and subordination. And it does no service whatever to this polity to identify as racist attitudes that are merely racialist and which will usually, on examination, be found to have essentially a social-class basis. But our potential for this type of dissension is large and very likely growing. In the hands of ideologues (who often as not enjoy the chaos) or charlatans (who stand to benefit) or plain simpletons, many forms of decentralization in the modern city will give rise to racialism. Responsible persons should examine that prospect beforehand.

The question of quotas raises the same issue. As I am almost certain to be misunderstood—that appears to be an occupational hazard in this field (and I would seriously suggest that the training of social scientists in years to come should include something equivalent to the processes by which psychiatrists are taught to anticipate and accept hostility)—let me offer a word or two by way of credentials. I believe it fair to say that I have been one of a smallish band of sociologists and political scientists who have insisted that race, ethnicity, and religion were and are relevant and functional categories in American life. I accept fully, as does Greeley, the Weberian analysis of E. K. Francis that the ethnic collectivity represents an attempt on the part of men to keep alive during their pilgrimage from *Gemeinschaft* to *Gesellschaft*, or as Greeley puts it, "from peasant commune to industrial metropolis," some of the diffuse, ascriptive, particularistic modes of behavior that were common to their past. I have argued in favor of the balanced political ticket; I have even been a member of one. I see the emergence of "black pride" as wholly a good thing. And so on. But at the same time, I would hope as we rush toward an ethnically, racially, and religiously conscious society that we try to keep our thinking just a bit ahead of events.

My concerns are twofold and come to this. First, I am worried that having so far been unable to assemble the political majority that would enable the nation to provide a free and equal place for the Negro in the larger society by what are essentially market strategies (full employment, income supplementation, housing construction, and such-like), we will be driven to institutional strategies involving government-dictated outcomes directed against those institutions most vulnerable to government pressure. I don't like this mostly because I don't like that kind of government pressure. But I oppose it also because I fear the kind of rigidities that it can build into a society that obviously is most effective when it is most flexible.

Remember, the Negro middle class is on the move. A recent study at Columbia found that the proportion of Negroes with professional or technical occupations in New York City is distinctly higher than that of Irish or Italians.

If there is an ethnic balance "against" Negroes in many municipal bureaucracies today, there is likely to be one "for" them in the not distant future. These are for the most part truly integrated groups, which, much as do the Armed Forces, provide major opportunities for Negro advancement on purely equal terms involving neither discrimination nor preference. (When the Jewish principal at I.S. 201 resigned, his Negro deputy refused the job on grounds that she would not be appointed *as a Negro*. She had no need to be. Inspired or lethargic, brilliant or bright, she was on her way to a principalship on her own. That is what bureaucracy is like.)

My second concern is, to my mind, the greater. Once this process gets legitimated there is no stopping it, and without intending anything of the sort, I fear it will be contributing significantly to the already well-developed tendency to politicize (and racialize) more and more aspects of modern life. Thirty years ago Orwell wrote, "In our age there is no such thing as 'keeping out of politics.' All issues are political issues. . . ." I resist that. Not all issues. Not yet. Note that he added "and politics

itself is a mass of lies, evasions, folly, hatred, and schizophrenia."
Not all American politics. Not yet. But enough is, and we must
therefore struggle against the effort of government, in some
large general interest, to dictate more and more of the small
details. It is necessary to be more alert to Robert A. Nisbet's observation that democracy is, fundamentally, "a theory and structure of *political power*," but that liberalism is "historically a
theory of *immunity* from power."

This, to my mind, is something more than a generalized concern. For centuries it has been obvious that property is not always
evenly distributed, and it has been more or less legitimate to talk
about it. In America, however, in the modern world generally,
there have grown up new forms of property and influence, not
so readily perceived, and the people who possess them have been
wisely content to leave it at that. Success, as Norman Podhoretz
wrote, and as he learned, is a dirty little secret in America, which
those who are successful very much dislike to see discussed in
public. A quality which makes for social stability at this time
is that different groups in the population value different kinds of
success, and tend to be best at those they most value. But government knows little of such variegations, and I very much fear that
if we begin to become formal about quotas *for* this or that group,
we will very quickly come to realize that these are instantly
translated into quotas *against*. This is painfully true in the field of
education and culture, which to a very considerable degree at this
particular moment in our history is exceptionally influenced by
American Jews. It was in a certain sense in an effort to resist the
processes that brought about this partial hegemony that the
"older American" institutions imposed quotas in the first place,
and it was to abet the process that the quotas were abolished.
Those were in fact quotas on success, imposed against a disproportionately successful group.

Let me be blunt. If ethnic quotas are to be imposed on American universities and similarly quasipublic institutions, it is Jews
who will be almost driven out. They are not 3 percent of the
population. This would be a misfortune to them, but a disaster to
the nation. And I very much fear that there is a whiff of anti-
Semitism in many of these demands. I was interested that when
demands for quotas were made at Harvard, the *Crimson* endorsed
with some enthusiasm the idea of ethnic representation, if not

exactly quotas, on the faculty, but the editors were not at all impressed with the advantages of extending the principle to the student body. I do not know what was on their mind, but I do know that if ethnic quotas ever should come to Harvard (surely they won't!), something like seven out of eight Jewish undergraduates would have to leave, and I would imagine it to be a higher proportion in the graduate schools. This, I repeat, would be a misfortune for them, but a disaster for a place like Harvard. And much the same exodus would be required of Japanese and Chinese Americans, especially in the graduate schools.*

One assumes that America has known enough of anti-Semitism and anti-Oriental feeling to be wary of opening that box again. Especially now. Given the prominence of Jews in current American radical movements—the *Times* describes the student activists at Columbia as "typically very bright and predominantly Jewish" —and the hostage of Israel, Jews are at this moment perhaps especially exposed to conservative or reactionary pressures which could easily make an issue of "overrepresentation." Recalling what we did to Japanese Americans in World War II, we surely should be careful about exposing Chinese Americans today to reactionary pressures simply on the basis that mainland China is our enemy.†

It comes down to a matter of prudence: of recognizing our potential for racialism, and guarding against it, while responding to real and legitimate racial needs. Thus Negroes need preferential treatment in some areas, and deserve it. The good sense of the country in the past has been to do this kind of thing by informal arrangements—the balanced ticket. At the present time Israel, for example, seems to be having success with similar arrangements for its Eastern Jewish immigrants. Can we not do as much?

I hope I will not be interpreted as resisting a more open acknowledgment of these factors. To the contrary, I feel they should be more in our minds, but at a private and informal level of concern. I am acutely aware, for example, of the debilitating

* The *Harvard University Gazette* of September 29, 1972, reported that HEW had "accepted Harvard's Affirmative Action Plan with some modifications." Among the latter, the federal government asked the university to draw up immediately what the *Gazette* described as "a statement indicating there is no anti-nepotism policy." Thus passeth away, presumedly, a once proud symbol of probity!

† One peril past!

imbalance in the ethnic origins of American social scientists. I say debilitating because it is the nature of heterogeneous societies such as ours that analysis that could in any way be taken as criticism is routinely rejected when the analyst is of a distinctly different group. That is the plain truth of it. And it is a truth much in evidence with respect to Negro studies at this time. Thirty years ago in this country anyone seeking to learn more *about* Negroes would have had to read books written *by* Negroes: Frazier, Drake, Cayton, Johnson, and others. Somehow that tradition, nobly begun by DuBois, faltered. There was not, for example, a single Negro social scientist on the research staff of the President's Advisory Commission on Civil Disorders. Now, with only a few exceptions, social-science studies of Negroes are carried out by whites, and we are not to wonder that more and more the cry goes out from the slums that they are tired of that white magic and will listen no more. But Negroes are only one case, and not a particularly special one. American social science desperately needs to expand its ethnic, racial, and religious base, just as it has got to expand its interests in those areas.

Let me conclude with the words with which Nathan Glazer and I closed our own study of the city:

> Religion and race define the next phase in the evolution of the American peoples. But the American nationality is still forming: its processes are mysterious, and the final form, if there is ever to be a final form, is as yet unknown.*

* This paper was first given as a commencement address at the New School for Social Research. I had just returned from campaigning for Robert F. Kennedy in the California primary election. (He was shot the night of the commencement.) By then the divisive potential of this issue for liberal forces was evident. Even so, it did not surface during the 1968 presidential campaign. Four years later, however, it had become a major issue, and one working almost wholly to the disadvantage of liberals. In general, events had followed the pattern evident in 1968. Specifically, Jewish organizations, reflecting at least portions of Jewish opinion, had become considerably and actively concerned that the federal government, in the name of equal opportunity, was imposing de facto quotas on Jews. Anyone familiar with the near-preeminent role of American Jews in contemporary liberalism will not be surprised that many Jews protested and resisted this interpretation. But this only emphasized the strength of concern that made this one of the identifying political controversies of that year. On August 4, 1972, the president of the American Jewish Committee sent identical letters to President Nixon and Senator McGovern expressing the AJC's "grave concern over a trend which is in sharp conflict with our longstanding commitment to the principle of equal oppor-

tunity for all Americans . . . the current widespread efforts and promises to achieve 'proportional representation' in our society by providing opportunities in employment, in education, in governmental appointments and civil service and in other areas of American life on the basis of race, sex or ethnic affiliation." The AJC related its support for "open enrollment" in universities and other such programs, but continued:

> Such affirmative action programs designed to seek out, encourage, assist and accept those previously excluded, must not however be permitted to lead to the acceptance by government or the private sector of the concept of "proportional representation" which we believe is but a euphemism for quotas. For this concept substitutes new forms of discrimination for old, creates new breeding grounds for intergroup anger and hostility and greatly downgrades the importance of merit.

On August 4, Senator McGovern replied: ". . . I share the concerns you have expressed and reject the quota system as detrimental to American society." On August 11, President Nixon wrote: "I share the views of the American Jewish Committee in opposing the concepts of quotas and proportional representation." These statements were made public August 16. On August 30, as reported by *The New York Times,* Representative Louis Stokes, Democrat of Ohio and chairman of the Congressional Black Caucus, "issued a denunciation of the Jewish group's action, describing its statement on quotas as 'high-handed at best and racist at worst.' " Yet both candidates for President had agreed to that statement! On September 1 the *Times* reported that "During Senator McGovern's campaign appearance . . . before the New York Board of Rabbis, the sole question asked of him concerned his stand on quotas."

The end of campaign scarcely put an end to the controversy. In November, HEW's Office of Civil Rights announced that "it is investigating some 15 complaints by the Anti-Defamation League of B'nai B'rith of discrimination against white males in hirings and promotions at colleges and universities." (American Council on Education, *Higher Education and National Affairs,* December 1, 1972.) The following spring Albert Shanker, president of the United Federation of Teachers, declared that the basic issue of the 1973 mayoral campaign in New York would be the triumph or defeat of the extremist wing of the Democratic party "which antagonizes, polarizes and divides" the "traditional majority coalition of labor unions, minority groups, the ethnics and liberals" through such devices as "ethnic quota systems."

Liberal purposes have suffered in this squabble, and so have liberal institutions. Indeed, sophisticates in Cambridge and New York could be heard to argue that the sustained pressure on behalf of affirmative action programs by the Office of Civil Rights during the first Nixon Administration was in fact a reactionary scheme devised to divide and destroy the majority liberal coalition. Would that politics were as interesting! Still, even as President Nixon was assuring the AJC of his abhorrence of quotas, his Office of Civil Rights at HEW was preparing "guidelines" for "Affirmative Action" programs for colleges and universities which by most earlier understanding imposed quotas. Each "contractor"—which is to say just about every college and university in the land—was "first to establish a basic data file on its employees including name or identification number, sex, ethnic identification. . . ." "Goal" were then to be set "so as to overcome deficiencies in the utilization of minorities and women. . . ." Five years was about the right time in which to comply. "Goals may be set in numbers or percentages." To achieve compliance, "professional associations, including committees and caucus groups, should be contacted. . . ." (*The Chronicle of Higher Education,* "Excerpts from U.S. 'Affirmative-Action' Guidelines," October 10, 1972.)

I should like to state once more what I tried to state in 1968: if we are serious about achieving such goals, we must make some effort to anticipate consequences as we move toward them. This has not generally been the case—as Trilling agrees— and there have been losses and setbacks which could have been avoided. No one is without fault. Note how little I anticipated that the major impact (or as it would now seem) of federal "goals" would be to increase employment opportunities for women, a group with much the same "ethnic" profile as the previously entrenched males. Hence a countervailing effect. Still, one would like an hour with the clod who devised the "Survey of Doctoral Scientists and Engineers" which reaches me here in New Delhi courtesy of the National Research Council and the National Science Foundation. After inquiring of my date and place of birth, citizenship, and Social Security number, the survey launches directly into detailed inquiries concerning those preeminently scientific categories "Race" and "Ethnic Group." That, evidently, is what the National Science Foundation wants first of all to know about American physicists.

The City in Chassis

10

There is to be encountered in one of the Disraeli novels a gentleman described as a person "distinguished for ignorance" as he had but one idea and that was wrong. It is by now clear that future generations will perforce reach something of the same judgment about contemporary Americans in relation to their cities, for what we do and what we say reflect such opposite poles of judgment that we shall inevitably be seen to have misjudged most extraordinarily either in what we are saying about cities, or in what we are doing about them.

We are, of course, doing very little, or rather, doing just about what we have been doing for the past half century or so, which can reflect a very great deal of activity, but no very considerable change. Simultaneously, and far more conspicuously, we are talking of crisis. The word is everywhere: on every tongue; in every pronouncement. The President has now taken to sending an annual message to Congress on urban subjects. In 1968 it was bluntly titled, *The Crisis of the Cities*. And indeed, not many weeks later, on Friday, April 5, at 4:02 P.M., to be exact, he was issuing a confirming proclamation of sorts:

> Whereas I have informed that conditions of domestic violence and disorder exist in the District of Columbia and threaten the

"The City in Chassis" was read before the Massachusetts Historical Society, April 1968. It was first published in *American Heritage*, February 1969.

Washington metropolitan area, endangering life and property and obstructing the execution of the laws, and that local police forces are unable to bring about the prompt cessation of such acts of violence and restoration of law and order . . .

The excitement is nothing if not infectious. In its most recent publication, "Crisis: The Condition of the American City," Urban America, Inc., and the League of Women Voters noted that during 1967 even the Secretary of Agriculture devoted most of his speeches to urban problems. In mid-1968, the President of the University of California issued a major statement entitled, "What We Must Do: The University and the Urban Crisis." The Bishops of the United States Catholic Conference came forth with their own program, entitled "The Church's Response to the Urban Crisis." At its 1968 convention, the Republican Party, not theretofore known for an obsession with the subject, adopted a platform plank entitled "Crisis of the Cities," while in an issue featuring a stunning black coed on the cover, *Glamour* magazine, ever alert to changing fashion, asks editorially the question many have posed themselves in private—"The Urban Crisis: What Can One Girl Do?"

Academics who have been involved with this subject might be expected to take some satisfaction that the alarums and jeremiads of the past decades seem at last to have been heard by the populace, and yet even those of us most seized with what Norman Mailer has termed the "middle-class lust for apocalypse" are likely to have some reservations about the current enthusiasm for the subject of urban ills. It is not just a matter of the continued disparity between what we say and what we do: it is also, I suspect, a matter of *what* we are saying, and the manner of our saying it. A certain bathos comes through. One thinks of Captain Boyle and Joxer in that far-off Dublin tenement of Sean O'Casey's *Juno and the Paycock*; no doubt the whole world was even then in a "state of chassis" but precious little those two could or would do about it, save use it as an excuse to sustain their own weakness, incompetence, and submission to the death wishes of the society about them. One wonders if something similar is going on in this nation, at this time. Having persistently failed to do what it was necessary and possible to do for urban life on grounds that conditions surely were not so bad as to warrant such exertion, the nation seems suddenly to have lurched to the opposite position of declaring that things are indeed so very bad that probably nothing will work anyway. The result either way is paralysis and failure. It is time for a measure of perspective.

I take it Lewis Mumford intended to convey something of this message in his recent book *The Urban Prospect* which he begins with a short preface cataloguing the ills of the modern city with a vigor and specificity that command instant assent from the reader. "Exactly!" one responds. "That is precisely the way things are! Mumford is really 'telling it like it is.'" (A measure of *négritude* having of late become the mark of an authentic urban crisis watcher.) One reads on with increasing recognition, mounting umbrage, only to find at the end that this foreword was in fact written for the July 1925 edition of *Survey Graphic*. Things have changed, but not that much, and in directions that were, in a sense, fully visible to the sensitive eye nearly a half century ago. To be sure, at a certain point, a matter of imbalance becomes one of pathology, a tendency becomes a condition, and, for societies as for individuals, there comes a point when mistakes are no longer to be undone, transgressions no longer to be forgiven. But it is nowhere clear that we have reached such a point in our cities.

Continuity and change: these are the themes of all life, and not less that of cities. However, as in so many aspects of our national experience, Americans seem more aware of and more sensitive to modes of change than to those of continuity. This is surely a survival from the frontier experience. There has not, I believe, ever been anything to match the rapidity, nay fury, with which Americans set about founding cities in the course of the seventeenth, eighteenth, and nineteenth centuries. Only just now is the historical profession beginning to catch up with that breathless undertaking. Before long we are likely to have a much clearer idea than we now do as to how it all began. But it is nonetheless possible at this early state, as it were, to identify a half dozen or so persistent themes in the American urban experience, which nonetheless seem to evolve from earlier to later stages in a process that some would call growth and others decay, but in a manner that nonetheless constitutes change.

THEMES IN URBAN EXPERIENCE

Violence

Through history—the history, that is, of Europe and Asia and that great bridge area in between—cities have been, nominally, at least, places of refuge, while the countryside has been the scene of insecurity and exposure to misfortune and wrongdoing. Obviously the facts permit no generalization, but there is at least a conceptual validity, a persistence over time, of the association of the city with security. In the classical and feudal world, to be outside the gates was to be in trouble. Writing of the destruction of Hiroshima and Nagasaki, George Steiner evokes the ancient certainty of this point, and suggests the ways in which it lives on.

> In those two cities, the consequences have been more drastic and more specialized. Therein lies the singularity of the two Japanese communities, but also their symbolic link with a number of other cities in history and with the role such cities have played in man's consciousness of his own vulnerable condition—with Sodom and Gomorrah, visited by such fiery ruin that their very location is in doubt; with Nineveh, raked from the earth; with Rotterdam and Coventry; with Dresden, where, in 1944, air raids deliberately kindled the largest, hottest pyre known to man. Already, in the *Iliad*, the destruction of a city was felt to be an act of peculiar finality, a misfortune that threatens the roots of man. His city smashed, man reverts to the unhoused, wandering circumstance of the beast from which he has so uncertainly emerged. Hence the necessary presence of the gods when a city is built, the mysterious music and ceremony that often attend the elevation of its walls. When Jerusalem was laid waste, says the Haggada, God Himself wept with her.

Little of this dread is to be encountered in the United States, a society marked by the near absence of internal warfare once the Indian conflicts were over. Warfare, that is to say, between armies. We have, on the other hand, been replete with conflict between different groups within the population, classified in terms of race, class, ethnicity, or whatever, and this conflict has occurred in our cities, which in consequence have been violent places.

An account of the draft riots in New York City in 1863 strikes a surpassingly contemporary note:

> Nothing that we could say, could add to the impressiveness of the lesson furnished by the events of the past year, as to the needs and dangerous condition of the neglected classes in our city. Those terrible days in July—the sudden appearance, as if from the bosom of the earth, of a most infuriated and degraded mob; the helplessness of property-holders and the better classes; the boom of cannon and rattle of musketry in our streets; the skies lurid with conflagrations; the inconceivable barbarity and ferocity of the crowd toward an unfortunate and helpless race; the immense destruction of property—were the first dreadful revelations to many of our people of the existence among us of a great, ignorant, irresponsible class, who were growing up here without any permanent interest in the welfare of the community or the success of the Government—the *proletaires* of the European capitals. Of the gradual formation of this class, and the dangers to be feared from it, the agents of this Society have incessantly warned the public for the past eleven years.
>
> —*Eleventh Annual Report*
> *Children's Aid Society, New York*

In some degree this violence—or the perception of it—seems to have diminished in the course of the 1930s and 1940s. James Q. Wilson has noted the stages by which, for example, the treatment of violence as an element in American politics steadily decreased in successive editions of *Politics, Parties, and Pressure Groups,* V. O. Key's textbook on American politics that first appeared during the latter part of this period. It may be that depression at home and then war abroad combined to restrict opportunity or impulse. But in any event, there was something of a lull, and in consequence all the more alarm when violence reappeared in the mid-1960s. But it was only that: a reappearance, not a beginning.

Yet with all this it is necessary to acknowledge a transformation, however subtle and tentative. The tempo of violence seems to have speeded up, the result more or less direct of change in the technology of communications, which now communicate not simply the fact but also the spirit of violent events, and do so instantaneously. More ominously, there appears to have been a legitimation of violence, and a spread of its ethos to levels of society that have traditionally seen themselves, and have been, the repositories of stability and respect for, insistence upon, due process. It is one thing to loot clothing stores—Brooks Brothers was hit in 1863—to seize sections of the city, to fight with the police, and hold out against them. It is another thing to seize university libraries, and that is very much part of the violence of our time, a violence that not only arises among the poor and disinherited, but also among the well-to-do and privileged, with the special fact that those elements in society which normally set standards of conduct for the society as a whole have been peculiarly unwilling, even unable, to protest the massive disorders of recent times.

Migration

The American urban experience has been singular in the degree to which our cities, especially those of the North and East, have been inundated by successive waves of what might be called rural proletariats, a dispossessed peasantry moving—driven from other people's land in the country—to other people's tenements in the city. American cities have ever been filled with unfamiliar people, acting in unfamiliar ways, at once terrified and threatening. The great waves of Catholic Irish of the early nineteenth century began the modern phase of this process, and it has never entirely stopped, not so much culminating as manifesting itself at this time in the immense folk migration of the landless Southern Negro to the Northern slum. In small doses such migrations would probably have been easily enough absorbed, but the sheer mass of the successive migrations has been such as to have dominated the life of the cities in their immediate aftermath. The most dramatic consequence was that popular government became immigrant government: in the course of the nineteenth century, great cities in America came to be ruled by men of the people, an event essentially without precedent in world history. And one typically deplored by those displaced from power in the course of the transformation. Let me cite to you, for example, a schoolboy exercise written in 1925 by a young Brahmin, the bearer of one of Boston's great names, on the theme "That there is no more sordid profession in the world than *Politics*."

> The United States is one of the sad examples of the present form of government called democracy. We must first remember that America is made up of ignorant, uninterested, masses, of foreign people who follow the saying, "that the sheep are many but the shepards are few." And the shepards of our government are wolves in sheep's clothing. From Lincoln's Gettysburg address let me quote the familiar lines "a government of the people, for the people, and by the people." In the following lines I shall try and show you how much this is carried out in modern times.
>
> Let us take for example the position of our mayors. They are elected by majority vote from the population in which they live. Let us take for a case Mayor Curley of Boston. He tells the Irish who make up the people of Boston that he will lower their taxes, he will make Boston the greatest city in Amercia. He is elected by the Irish mainly because he is an Irishman. He is a remarkable politician, he surrounds himself by Irishmen, he bribes the Chief Justice of the court, and although we know that the taxes that we pay all find a way into his own pocket we cannot prove by justice that he is not a just and good mayor.

But such distaste was not wholly groundless. The migrant peasants did and do misbehave: as much by the standards of the countryside they leave behind, as by those of the urban world to which they come. The process of adapting to the city has involved great dislocations in personality and manners as well as in abode. From the first, the process we call urbanization, with no greater specificity than the ancient medical diagnosis of "bellyache" or "back pain," has involved a fairly high order of personal and social disorganization, almost always manifesting itself most visibly in breakdown of social controls, beginning with the most fundamental of controls, those of family life. The Children's Aid Society of New York was founded in response to the appearance of this phenomenon among the immigrant Irish. Let me quote from their *first* Annual Report, written a decade before the draft riots:

> It should be remembered that there are no dangers to the value of property, or to the permanency of our institutions, so

great as those from the existence of such a class of vagabond, ignorant, and ungoverned children. This "dangerous class" has not begun to show itself as it will in eight or ten years, when these boys and girls are matured. Those who were too negligent or too selfish to notice them as children, will be fully aware of them as men. They will vote. They will have the same rights as we ourselves, though they have grown up ignorant of moral principle, as any savage or Indian. They will poison society They will perhaps be embittered at the wealth and the luxuries they never share. *Then let society beware, when the outcast, vicious, reckless multitude of New York boys, swarming now in every foul alley and low street, come to know their power and use it!*

Lewis Mumford speaks of precisely the same phenomenon:

> One of the most sinister features of the recent urban riots has been the presence of roaming bands of children, armed with bottles and stones, taunting and defying the police, smashing windows and looting stores. But this was only an intensification of the window-breakings, knifings, and murders that have for the past twenty years characterized "the spirit of youth in the city streets."

And note the continuity of his last phrase, which alludes, of course, to Jane Addams' book, *The Spirit of Youth and the City Streets*, in which she describes just those conditions at the turn of the century in terms that William James declared "immortal" and which, we must allow, were hardly ephemeral.

Yet here too technology seems to have been playing us tricks, accentuating and exacerbating our recent experience. The newest migrants come upon an urban world that seems somehow to need them less, to find them even more disturbing and threatening, and to provide them even less secure a place in the scheme of things than was ever quite the case with those who preceded them. I take this to be almost wholly a function of changing employment patterns consequent upon changing technology. But this very technology has also provided an abundance of material resources—and a measure of social conscience—so that people who are not especially needed are nonetheless provided for, so that for example, after seven years of unbroken economic expansion, by 1968 there were 800,000 persons living on welfare in New York City, with the number expected to exceed one million in 1969. In part this is a phenomenon of birth rates. One person in ten, but one baby in six, today is Negro. The poor continue to get children, but those children no longer succumb to cholera, influenza, and tuberculosis. Thus progress more and more forces us to live with the consequences of social injustice. In a more brutal age the evidence soon disappeared!*

Wealth

Those who have moved to cities have almost invariably improved their standard of life in the not-very-long run. Nor has this been wholly a matter of the consumption of goods and services. "City air makes men free," goes the medieval saying, and this has not been less true for industrial America. The matter was settled, really, in an exchange between Hennessy and Dooley at the turn of the century. The country, said that faithful if not always perceptive patron, is where the good things in life come from. To which the master responded, "Yes, but it is the city that they go to." Technology is at the base of this process. The standard of life in American cities rises steadily, and there are few persons who do not somehow benefit. And yet this same technology—wealth—takes its toll. More and more we are conscious of the price paid for affluence in the form of manmade disease, uglification, and the second and third order effects of innovations which seem to cancel out the initial benefits.

Nathan Keyfitz has nicely evoked the paradox implicit in many of the benefits of technology. Plenty encourages freedom. It also encourages density. Density can only be managed by regulation. Regulation discourages freedom. The experienced, conditioned city dweller learns, of course, to live with density by maintaining, as Keyfitz puts it, "those standards of reserve, discretion, and respect for the rights of others" that keep the nervous system from exhausting itself through the overstimulus available on any city street. The traditional assertion of Manhattan apartment dwellers

* Seymour Spilerman has shown that outside the South the most potent variable relating to the location of urban disturbances during the 1960s was simply the size of the minority community, by definition made up mostly of relatively recent migrants. (Seymour Spilerman, "The Causes of Racial Disturbances: Tests of an Explanation," *American Sociological Review*, June 1971.)

that they have never met their neighbors across the hall is not a sign of social pathology: to the contrary, it is the exercise of exemplary habits of social hygiene. Borrowing a meter from Canning's account of the failings of the Dutch, the rule for the modern cliff dweller might be put as follows:

> In the matter of neighbors, the sound thing to do,
> Is nodding to many but speaking to few.

It may be speculated, for example, that a clue to the transformation of the roistering, brawling, merrie England of tradition into that somber land where strangers dare not speak to one another in trains lies *in the fact of the trains*. Technology— in this case the steam engine, which created the vast nineteenth-century complexes of London and Manchester—brought about urban densities which required new forms of behavior for those who would take advantage of, or at very least survive, them. The British, having been first to create the densities, were first to exhibit the telltale *sangfroid* of the modern urban dweller.

It may also be speculated that the "disorganized" life of rural immigrants arises in some measure at least from an inability to control the level of stimulus: to turn down the radio, turn off the television, come in off the streets, stay out of the saloons, worry less about changing styles of clothes, music, dance, whatever. Lee Rainwater has provided us with painful accounts of the feeling of helplessness of the mothers of poor urban families in the face of the incursions from the street: the feeling, literally, that one could not simply close one's door in the housing project, and refuse to allow family, friends, neighbors, and God knows whom else to come and go at will. This makes for lively neighborhoods, which from a distance seem almost enviable, but also for very disturbed people.

When such groups become large enough, when densities become ominous, government regulation becomes necessary or, at least, all but invariably makes its appearance, so that even for the disciplined urbanite, technology at some point begins to diminish freedom. Keyfitz writes:

> George Orwell's *1984* is inconceivable without high population density, supplemented by closed circuit television and other

devices to eliminate privacy. It exhibits in extreme form an historical process by which the State has been extending its power at the expense of the Church, the Family, and the Local Community, a process extending over 150 years.

There are but few bargains in life, especially in city life.

Mobility

Cities are not only places where the standards of life improve, but also very much—and as much now as ever—they are places where men rise in social standing. Otis Dudley Duncan and Peter Blau in their powerful study, *The American Occupational Structure,* have made this abundantly clear. American cities are places where men improve their position, as well as their condition or, at least, have every expectation that their sons will do so. The rigidities of caste and class dissolve, and opportunity opens. Yet this has never been quite so universally agreeable an experience as one could be led to suppose from the accounts of those for whom it has worked. If in the city men first, perhaps, come to know success, it is there also that often, especially those from the most caste-ridden rural societies, they first come to know failure. It seems to me that this is a neglected aspect of the urban experience. I would argue that the rural peasant life of, let us say, the Irish, the Poles, the Slavs, the Italians, and the Negro Americans who have migrated over the past century and a half was characterized by a near total absence of opportunity to improve one's position in the social strata, but also it was characterized by the near impossibility of observing others improve theirs. Rarely, in either absolute or relative terms, did individuals or families of the lowest peasant classes experience decline and failure: that in a sense is the law of a noncontingent society. Only with arrival in the city does that happen, and I would argue that for those who lose out in that competition, the experience can be far more embittering than that brought on by the drab constancy of country life.

Again technology—again television, for that matter—plays its part. Stephan Thernstrom has noted that the immigrant workers of ninteenth-century New England, earning $1.50 a day when they had work, nonetheless managed in surprising numbers to

put aside some money and to buy a piece of property and re-
spectability before their lives were out, despite the fact that their
incomes rarely permitted them to maintain the minimum standard
of living calculated by the social workers of the time. The difference, Thernstrom notes, was that for the migrants a minimum
standard of living was potatoes—period. So long as they did
not share the expectations of those about them—even the small
expectations of social workers—they were not deprived. But
advertising and television, and a dozen similar phenomena, have
long since broken down that isolation, and the poor and newly
arrived of the American city today appear to be caught up in a
near frenzy of consumer emotions: untouched by the disenchantment with consumption of those very well off, and unrestrained by
the discipline of household budgets imposed on those in between.
The result, as best such matters can be measured, is a mounting
level of discontent, which seems to slide over from the area of
consumption as such to discontent with levels of social status
that do not provide for maximum levels of consumption, so that
even those who might be thought to be succeeding in the new
urban world appear to feel they are not succeeding enough,
while others are suffused with a sense of failure.

Intellectual Disdain

". . . Enthusiasm," Morton and Lucia White write, "for the
American city has not been typical or predominant in our intellectual history. Fear has been the more common reaction."
Fear, distaste, animosity, ambivalence. "In the beginning was
the farm," or so the Jeffersonian creed asserts. And the great
symbol—or perhaps consummation would be the better term—
of this belief was the agreement whereby in return for the
Jeffersonian willingness to have the federal government accept
the debts acquired by states during the Revolutionary War, the
capital of the new nation would be transferred from the City
of New York to a swamp on the banks of the Potomac. Do not
suppose that that agreement has not affected American history.
New York remains the capital of the nation, as that term is
usually understood, in the sense of the first city of the land. It is
the capital of finance, art, theater, publishing, fashion, intellect,
industry . . . name any serious human endeavor other than

politics, and its center in the United States will be found in New York City. In years of hard-fought presidential primaries, it is even for many purposes the political capital of the nation. But the seat of goverment is in Washington, which is only just beginning to respond to the fact that for half a century now ours has been a predominantly urban society.

Once again technology seems to be interacting with a pre-existing tendency. As the American city came more and more to be the abode of the machine, the alarm of American intellectuals, if anything, was enhanced. And to a very considerable degree legitimated, for surely machines have given a measure of reality to alarums that were previously more fantasy than otherwise. To this has been added an ever more persistent concern for social justice, so that American intellectuals now conclude their expanding catalogues of the horrors of urban life with ringing assertions that the cities must be saved. But it is to be noted that this comes almost as an afterthought: the conviction that in the cities will be found the paramount threat to the life of the Republic has changed hardly at all. What has perhaps changed is that at long last what they have been saying may be beginning to be true.

Ugliness

The ugliness of American cities is singular. That there are great and stunning exceptions is as much a matter of accident as anything. The essential fact is that for all the efforts to sustain and assert a measure of elite concern for urban aesthetics—of the kind one associates with historical preservation societies—and for all the occasional bursts of energy within the urban planning profession, the American city remains an ugly place to live, pretty much because we like it that way. A measure, no doubt, of this persisting condition can be attributed to the business and propertied interests of the nation that have resisted municipal expenditure, notably when it passed through the hands of egalitarian city halls. But it is more than that. Somehow, somewhere, in the course of the development of democratic or demagogic tradition in this nation, the idea arose that concern for physical beauty of the public buildings and spaces of the city was the mark of—what?—cryptodeviationist anti-people monumentalism—and in any event an augury of defeat at the polls. The result has been a steady deterioration in the quality of public buildings and spaces, and with it a decline in the symbols of public unity and common purpose with which the citizen can identify, of which he can be proud, and by which he can know what he shares with his fellow citizens. Since 1961, I have been involved with efforts to reconstruct the center of the city of Washington, an attempt that begins with the assertion of the validity and viability of L'Enfant's plan of the late eighteenth century. In this effort we have had the tolerant to grudging cooperation of a fairly wide range of public and private persons, but let me say that we have had at no time the enthusiasm of any. And now I fear we may have even less, since of late there has arisen the further belief that to expend resources on public amenities is in effect to divert them from needed areas of public welfare. The very persons who will be the first to demand increased expenditures for one or another form of social welfare will be the last to concede that the common good requires an uncommon standard of taste and expenditure for the physical appointments of government and the public places of the city.*

This attitude was perhaps unintentionally evoked by the respected Episcopal Bishop of New York who in 1967 announced that, in view of the circumstances of the poor of the city, he would not proceed with the completion of the Cathedral of St. John the Divine, the largest such building ever begun, situated on a magnificent site overlooking the flat expanse of Harlem. Why? Meaning no disrespect, is it the plan of the church to liquidate its assets and turn them over to the poor? How much would that come to per head? But even so, would not the completed cathedral be an asset? If men need work, could they not be given jobs in its construction? The French—*toujours gai*, as Mehitabel would have it—built Sacré-Cœur as an act of penance for the excesses of the Commune. Could not the Episcopalians build St. John the Divine—a perfect symbol of rebirth—as a gesture of penance for all that Brahmin disdain which, in one form or another, to use Max Way's phrase, taught us to despise our cities until they become despicable.

* In 1972, after eleven years of efforts by three Presidents, Congress at last enacted a statute providing for the redevelopement of Pennsylvania Avenue. This probably marked a *receding* sense of urban crisis!

If the phenomenon of ugliness, the last of my urban themes, can be thought to have arisen from more or less abstract qualities of American society, in the present and foreseeable future its principal cause is visible, concrete, and ubiquitous, which is to say it is the automobile. More than any other single factor it is the automobile that has wrecked the twentieth-century American city; dissipating its strength, destroying its form, fragmenting its life. So utterly pervasive is the influence of the automobile that it is possible almost not to notice it at all. Indeed, it is almost out of fashion to do so: the men who first sought to warn us have almost ceased trying, while those who might have followed have sought instead formulations of their own, and in that manner diverted attention from the essential fact in the age of the automobile; namely, that cities, which had been places for coming together, have increasingly become machines for moving apart, devices whereby men are increasingly insulated and isolated one from the other.

TECHNOLOGY AND THE CITY

The Automobile

A coda of sorts that has persisted through the elaboration of the successive themes of this chapter has been the recent role of technology in accentuating and in a sense exacerbating long-established tendencies. The impact of technology on human society—on all forms of life—is the preeminent experience of the modern age, and obviously of the city as well. But only of late, one feels, has any very considerable appreciation developed that, after a point, change in quantity becomes change in quality, so that a society that begins by using technology can end by being used by it, and in the process, somehow, loses such control of its destiny as past human societies can be said to have done. The sheer rationality of technology has argued against any such assumption which has seemed more allied to a lack of comprehension than otherwise. People fear what they do not understand, and the command of technological skills among critics of technology has tended to be minimal, hence the presumption that warnings of disaster, while interesting, were at the same time self-serving.

One begins to think that this may not be so. Take the family automobile. A simple, easily enough comprehended (or seemingly so), unthreatening, and convenient product, if anything, of folk technology rather than of modern science. Who would imagine any great harm coming from the automobile? Yet consider a moment. With the advent of the automobile everyday citizens, for the first time in human history, came into possession of unexampled physical energy: the powers of the gods themselves became commonplace. And from the very outset violence ensued. In 1895, for example, when there were only four gasoline-powered vehicles in the United States, two were in St. Louis, Missouri, and managed to collide with such impact as to injure both drivers, one seriously. Thus was introduced a form of pathology that was to grow steadily from that year to this. Today, somewhere between one-quarter and two-thirds of the automobiles manufactured in the United States end up with blood on them. Indeed so commonplace and predictable have collisions become that the U.S. Court of Appeals for the Eighth Circuit recently ruled in *Larsen v. General Motors* that a crash must be considered among the "intended uses" of a motor vehicle, and the manufacturers accordingly responsible to provide for such contingency in their design.*

It becomes increasingly clear that the major environment, or, if you will, vehicle, in which incidents of uncontrolled episodic violence occur within the population is that of the automobile. Whether access and exposure to this environment has increased the incidence of such episodes, or whether the urban environment now largely created and shaped by the automobile has generally increased the violence level is an uncertain question at best—there has, of course, been a great decline in violence

---

* *Erling David Larsen v. General Motors.* U.S. Court of Appeals, 8th Circuit 18, 853 (March 11, 1968.) A not unrelated form of technological style is involved in this decision. The concept of the probability of crash per vehicle was developed by Haddon and me in lectures at the Maxwell Graduate School of Public Administration of Syracuse University in 1959 and 1960. It was refined and presented as a paper by Haddon and Goddard in 1961 and published in 1962. Within six years it had made its way, by specific reference, into a federal judicial decision. The near volatile degree to which new ideas, good and bad, are put into practice in a technologically advanced society is very likely a source of the common complaint about unsettledness.

directed toward animals—but with the number of deaths and injuries at the present ongoing rates, and the number of vehicles in use approaching the 100 million mark, it is a matter worth pondering.

Crashes are but one form of pathology. Each year in the United States, automobiles pour 86 million tons of carbon monoxide, oxides of nitrogen, hydrocarbons, sulfur oxides, lead compounds, and particulates into the air we breathe. So much that recently my youngest son came home with a button that announced "Clean air smells funny." Dr. Clare C. Patterson of the California Institute of Technology put it another way in testimony before a Congressional committee: "The average resident of the United States is being subject to severe chronic lead insult," originating in lead tetraethyl. Such poisoning can lead to severe intellectual disability in children, so much that Patterson feels it is dangerous for youth to live for long periods of time near freeways.

But that is only the beginning, hardly the end, of the impact of this particular form of technology on the society at this time. In consequence of the management of the automobile traffic system by means of traditional rules of the road, the incidence of armed arrest of American citizens is the highest of any civilization in recorded history. In 1965, for example, the California Highway Patrol alone made one million arrests. Indeed so commonplace has the experience become that a misdemeanor or felony committed in a motor vehicle is no longer considered a transgression of any particular consequence, and to be arrested by an armed police officer is regarded as a commonplace. That is precisely what Orwell told us would happen, is it not?

There are some 13.6 million accidents a year, with some 30 million citations for violations issued each twelve months. And at this point, ineluctably, technology begins to have impact on the most fundamental of civil institutions, the legal system itself. Largely in consequence of the impact of traffic crash litigation, it now takes an average of 32.4 months to obtain a civil jury trial for a personal injury case in the metropolitan areas of the nation. In Suffolk County, New York, it is 50 months. In the Circuit Court of Cook County, serving Chicago, it is 64 months. This past winter in Bronx County, New York, the Presiding Judge of the Appellate Division announced he was suspending civil trials altogether while he tried to catch up with criminal cases. The courts are inundated, the bar is caught up, implicated, and confused, the public knows simply that somehow justice is delayed and delayed. All of which is a consequence of this simplest form of technology, working its way on the institutions of an essentially pretechnological society.

Technology as Art

It sometimes happens that a work of art appears at a particular moment in time and somehow simultaneously epitomizes and reveals the essential truths of the time. In a most astonishing and compelling way this has happened for the American city, and it has done so, most appropriately, on Forty-second Street in Manhattan, in the persona, if you will, of Kevin Roche's Ford Foundation headquarters. So much comes together here. A great firm of architects, successor to Eero Saarinen Associates whose first large commission was, of course, the General Motors Technical Center outside Detroit, Saarinen, and now Roche, have gathered a group of artist-technicians whose work, from the Dulles Airport at Chantilly, Virginia, to the Trans World Airlines Terminal at Kennedy Airport and the Columbia Broadcasting headquarters in New York City, has evoked the power and purpose of the age of technology as perhaps no other organization has. Aline B. Louchheim once wrote of her future husband Eero Saarinen that his contribution lay in "giving form or visual order to the industrial civilization to which he belongs, designing imaginatively and soundly within the new esthetics which the machine age demands and allows." Allan Temko describes the General Motors center as a "fusion of serious design and technological power." *Architectural Forum* called them "exalted industrial products."

Here in the Ford Foundation headquarters is expressed the very highest purposes of that technological power: compassionate and potent concern for the betterment of man's lot. The building is everything a building could be: a splendid workplace, a gift to the city in the form of a public park, a gift to the world simply as a work of imagination and daring. If it be a reproach of sorts to the public and private builders of the nation who by and large show little of either, it is a gentle reproach, more show than tell. In that favored form of foundation giving, it is a demonstration project: an example of what can, and what therefore, in the formulation of Jacques Ellul, in an age of technology must be done.

The exterior of the building is quiet and unassertive: it is not a big building, and seeks rather to understate both its size and importance. Shafts of Corton steel rise from the ground, here and there sheathed with a blue-brown granite, and interspersed with large rectangular glass panels. Rather in the mode of a cathedral, the portals do not so much impart as suggest the experience to come. It is only on entering—Chartres, say, or Vézelay —and encountering the incomparable space, shaped and reserved for a single purpose only, that one leaves off observing the building and begins to be shaped by it: the eye rises, the mind turns to last things. So with the Ford Foundation headquarters. One passes through revolving doors to enter a garden. Truly, a garden, a small park, like nothing anywhere else to be encountered, a third of an acre, lush and generous, climbing a small hill that follows the terrain of Manhattan at this point, illuminated by the now vast windows that climb nine stories towards heaven itself, and there only to be met by a glass roof. Water moves slightly in a pool—a font? Attendants move quietly, and are helpful. One notices that vegetation sprouts from beams and ledges on the third and fourth and even the fifth floors. One is awestruck by the wealth and power of the Foundation, and the sheer authority of its intent to do good. Only the gray-white light is not quite what it should be: as in those French and German cathedrals whose stained glass was lost to war, or revolution, or Protestantism.

But this is only the entering light. As in any such edifice, there is a light within. In this case a very monstrancelike golden brown glow that shines forth from the offices of the Foundation executives, who from the floor of the park are to be seen at their work behind glass panels formed and reticulated by the same rusted beams that frame the colorless glass of two sides of the building. (Corton steel seals itself by rusting and need not be painted.) At this point one perceives readily enough that the building has been built as a factory. Not precisely as a factory—any more than the Gothic revival built office buildings precisely as medieval monasteries—but rather to evoke the style and somehow the spirit of a great plant. The huge, heavy lateral beams, from which elsewhere would be suspended the giant hoists that roam back and forth amidst the clatter and roar, the sawtooth roof, the plant managers' eyrie hung from the ceiling, keeping an eye on everything, the perfectly standardized, interchangeable fixtures in each office, the seriousness and competence of it all, even the blue-black, somehow oily granite of the cheerless rest rooms ("No Loitering in the Can") magically, stunningly, triumphantly, evoke the style and spirit of the primeval capitalist factory. Corton. Red. Rouge. River Rouge. Of course! And why not for $16 million of Henry Ford's money? He was that kind of man. Knew how to make automobiles and obviously liked to. Else he could hardly have done it so well. All black, just as the Ford Foundation headquarters is all brown. Same principle. So also the Panopticon effect of the exposed offices wherein the presumptively interchangeable officers at their perfectly interchangeable desks labor at their good works in full view of management and public alike. (The public serving perhaps as the visitors to Bentham's prospective model prison: a "promiscuous assemblage of unknown and therefore unpaid, ungarbled and incorruptible inspectors"?) Critics, at least in the first reviews, seem to have missed most of this, but no matter: the architecture needs no guide book: the intellectual and aesthetic effect is not to be avoided, even when the intent is least perceived. All in all it is just as McGeorge Bundy proclaimed it in the 1968 annual report of the Foundation: "Kevin Roche's triumph."

But it is more than that. Or rather there is more than is to be perceived at one time. A great work of art has levels of meaning at once various and varying. Standing in the park, gazing upwards, following the factory motif, the mind is suddenly troubled. Something is missing. Noise. Factories are places of noise. Of life. Clatter. Roar. There is no noise here. Only quiet. The quiet of the . . . ? The mind oscillates. It is a factory, all right. *But a ruined factory!* The holocaust has come and gone: hence the silence. The windows have blown out, and only the gray light of the burnt-out world enters. The weather has got in, and with it nature now reclaiming the ravaged union of fire and earth. The factory floor has already begun to turn to forest. Vegetation has made its way to ledges halfway up the interior. (Trust Dan Kiley to understand.) The machine tools are gone. Reparations? Vandalism? Who knows? But the big machines will no longer be making little machines. Gone too is the rational, reforming, not altogether disinterested purpose of the Panopticon. One is alone in the ominous gloom of a Piranesi prison, noting the small bushes taking hold in the crevices of the vast ruined arches.

Is it the past or the future that has taken hold of the mind? Certainly the ruined steel frame is a good enough symbol of the twentieth century so far. (Where had one last seen that color? Of course. Pingree Street in Detroit after the riot. A year later there it was again on Fourteenth Street in Washington: the fiery orange-red of the twisted steel shopping centers' framing after the looting and arson has passed.) Or is it the future? There is *surréel* quality that comes of standing in the ruined half of the building, watching the life going on behind the glass walls of the intact half, seemingly oblivious to the devastation without. Can ruin advance slowly like rot? No. Yes. Did the automobile start all this? No. Surely it is all this that started automobiles. One-quarter to two-thirds of which end up with blood on them. Blood. Red. Rouge. River Rouge.

Enough.

But then why has Stein built the Ford Foundation headquarters in New Delhi immediately adjacent to the Lodi Tombs, symbols of death and sensual to the point of necrophilia? Did not Bentham remark that he could legislate wisely for all India from the recesses of his study? There's a Panopticon in your future.

No. Enough.

Architecture and "Community"

And yet it comes together in a way. *"Le siècle de la machine,"* Le Corbusier wrote in 1924, *"a réveillé l'architecte."* Not least because the machine destroys so much of that experience of community that the architect seeks to create. Allan Temko in his study of Eero Saarinen describes Saarinen's purpose in these terms. "What . . . [he] wished to renew, maintain, and improve was the organic expression of the *civitas* which he found weakened or destroyed virtually everywhere in modern civilization, with one significant exception—the university campus." And so

Roche built a ruined machine-for-making-machines as the headquarters of a great philanthropic foundation whose principal
concerns have been to support the universites of the nation,
and to seek to strengthen the community life of its cities.

The research of James Q. Wilson and Edward C. Banfield at
Harvard University is now beginning to produce results surprisingly similar to the visions of the architect-artist. A thousand
Boston homeowners were asked what they thought to be the
biggest problem facing the city. As Wilson puts it, "After a
decade or more of being told by various leaders that what's
wrong with our large cities is inadequate transportation, or declining retail sales, or poor housing, the resident of the big city
is beginning to assert his own definition of that problem—and
this definition has very little to do with the conventional wisdom
on the urban crisis." Wilson and his colleague asked one thousand
Boston homeowners what they thought to be the biggest urban
problem of this time.

> The "conventional" urban problems—housing, transportation,
> pollution, urban renewal, and the like—were a major concern of
> only 18 percent of those questioned, and these were expressed
> disproportionally by the wealthier, better-educated respondents.
> Only 9 percent mentioned jobs and employment, even though
> many of those interviewed had incomes at or even below what
> is often regarded as the poverty level. *The issue which concerned
> more respondents than any other was variously stated—crime,
> violence, rebellious youth, racial tension, public immorality,
> delinquency. However stated, the common theme seemed to be a
> concern for improper behavior in public places.*
>
> What these concerns have in common, and thus what con-
> stitutes the "urban" problem for a large percentage (perhaps a
> majority) of urban citizens, is *a sense of the failure of com-
> munity.*

And yet cities, by definition, destroy community. Or is it only
when they are too big, too unsettled, that they do this? Is it
only when social conditions are allowed to arise which lead inevitably to assaults on the private communities which experienced city dwellers create for themselves, which in turn lead
to more collective regulation, and in consequence less of the
self-imposed decision to behave properly and as expected, which
is the essence of community?

We do not know. "Them what gets the apple, gets the worm," goes the Southern saying. Is that what the Ford Foundation building represents: a shining exterior, rotting from within? A civilization whose cancerous growth has already devoured half its offspring, and is moving towards the unthinking, untroubled other half? We shall see. It is to be hoped that in the meantime we shall also think about it a bit. Mumford, unfailingly, has sorted out the levels of immediacy and difficulty of the current crisis.

> To go deeper into this immediate situation we must, I suggest, distinguish between three aspects, only one of which is open to immediate rectification. We must first separate out the problems that are soluble with the means we have at hand: this includes such immediate measures as vermin control, improved garbage collection, cheap public transportation, new schools and hospitals and health clinics. Second, those that require a new approach, new agencies, new methods, whose assemblage will require time, even though the earliest possible action is urgent. And finally there are those that require a reorientation in the purposes and ultimate ideals of our whole civilization—solutions that hinge on a change of mind, as far-reaching as that which characterized the changes from the medieval religious mind to the modern scientific mind. Ultimately, the success of the first two changes will hinge upon this larger—and, necessarily, later—transformation. So, far from looking to a scientifically oriented technology to solve our problems, we must realize that this highly sophisticated dehumanized technology itself now produces some of our most vexatious problems, including the unemployment of the unskilled.

But something more than thinking will be required. A certain giving of ourselves with no certainty what will come of it. It is the only known way, and imperfectly known at that.

Attend to Mrs. Boyle at the end of *Juno and the Paycock,* pleading for the return of a simpler life, a life before all things had become political, before all men were committed, before all cities somehow seemed in flames:

> Sacred Heart o' Jesus take away our hearts o' stone, and give us hearts o' flesh. Take away this murdherin' hate, and give us Thine own eternal love!

Architecture in a Time
of Trouble

11

Ours is a society that stands accused; or, rather, has become self-accusatory. If one recalls only a few years ago, at the outset of this decade, how singularly self-congratulatory we were, the transformation is indeed striking.

An astonishingly radical critique of the society has acquired immense authority among the elite youth of the nation, and this world view—for it is nothing less—is rapidly diffusing. In particular, one notes a backward diffusion from this new generation to its parents. This explains the curious topography of radical criticism of this time: It is not only to be found among those assaulting the establishment but is singularly well entrenched within the establishment itself.

There are, of course, large groups that are not at all affected, indeed rather otherwise. The disturbances that accompanied the 1968 Democratic Convention brought forth from what is loosely termed the Eastern Establishment a nigh universal exclamation that "Those are our children!" and a not inconsiderable outpouring of class solidarity with same. It remained for Pete

"Architecture in a Time of Trouble" was read before the annual convention of the American Institute of Architects in June 1969. It was first published in the *Journal of the American Institute of Architects,* September 1969.

Hamill to remark that you'd think no cop ever had a mother, but that is sort of beside the point. Self-condemnation by nominally successful and virtuous persons is as much a quality of the moment as is accusation by the young and untried.

From the time of the Moscow trials this has been a recurrent theme of twentieth-century experience. Most recently, for example, one of China's foremost mathematicians and computer experts, director of the Institute of Mathematics of the Chinese Academy of Science, confessed that his forty years of academic work had been profoundly in error, reflecting the personal aggrandizement of the self-certifying cadres of the privileged. "In the ranks of intellectuals," the scholar declared, "I became a living example of 'achievement of fame and academic standing' and 'a self-made man,' a living instrument who has been deeply poisoned by revisionism, in turn poisoning others just as deeply."

Now, if the computer experts are driven to recant their passion for notoriety, for the achievement of individual fame and the erection of personal monuments, there is surely little hope that architects will remain unscathed. Of all the professions, architecture stands today as the one most vulnerable to the criticism that its curriculum is irrelevant, its standards hypocritical, and its achievements deplorable. No one could finally say that such criticism is justified, but the profession is vulnerable to it, not the least because it half shares this view, or so it would seem to an observer.

This is nothing special; to the contrary, it is a quite common state of mind and spirit among men who have hoped much for their society and themselves in the years since the triumph of the Second World War raised the possibility of an aroused society, truly engaged with the issues of the time and formidable both in its anger and its compassion. Enough time has gone by now, and something so much less than that has come to pass, that we are all required to change our expectations, if not indeed to question our capacities. We have aged—with respect to morale and confidence as much as with regard to the slipping away of time. It is not then to be wondered that resistance to challenge is less spirited than it might be.

For individuals as for epochs the process of aging is normally a quiet and gradual affair, but the realization of youth having passed comes often as not with a suddenness, even a shock. Most of us mark that moment well, and often thereafter in idle passages find ourselves touching the wound it left. My moment, and that of many like me, came with the death of John F. Kennedy, and, along with the others, I know it. About the third day of that long, terrible time, Mary McGrory said to me, "We'll never laugh again." And I answered, "Heavens, Mary, we'll laugh again. It's just that we'll never be young again." And I really knew that.

I would like to argue that something of this kind is happening to the nation generally. For all the extraordinary prominence of young persons in the politics and passions of the moment, a certain kind of youthfulness has passed from us. Whether it be SDS delegates hurling the dread charge of "counterrevolutionary" at one another, or high school students stupefying themselves with chemicals, or well-bred college girls flinging obscenities at police officers, we all seem older than we had supposed.

We have become so in a time frame surprisingly human. What has been called, and properly, the American epoch began—what?—say thirty years ago when it developed that Europe had lost control over events and would descend into destruction, impotence, and ruin. Thereafter, America would dominate and, for a time, command events. And this was so whether we would have it such or not. The fact of American might resided in its weapons and its wealth: matters to some degree under our control, the results more or less of deliberate decision.

But in a far more fundamental way, our power was ideological. We were what the world wanted to be like, and never more so than when denouncing the cultural imperialism that jammed the shops and bazaars of the world with American products, filled the air with American music, packed the theaters for American films, the libraries with American books and, increasingly and not least importantly, the cities with American buildings, surrounded, to be sure, with American automobiles.

This is not over. To the contrary, I would think it has only begun in terms of how much further it is likely to go and how much longer it is likely to go on. It is America, not the world, that has changed. Of a sudden the American epoch is no longer young. The ease and assurance of youth is gone: the certainty that there will always be another girl, a new opportunity, plenty of energy, plenty of time, and, most of all, the careless—even at times cruel—confidence that it will all work out.

Well, of course, it hasn't. Life has caught up with us, as it will with all men and all peoples. We collide with the realization that things do not always work out, that time is short, energies limited and overextended, options so much more restricted than we had supposed. We have entered a time of trouble and are young no more.

What hurts so, what is resisted, is the idea that it has come too soon, that our time has been cut short, that *our* revels, too, are ended. But only that argues more convincingly the case that indeed a period has come to a close. There is no pleasure to be had in reciting the specifics, and no need either as they are all too manifest.

The idea of a society confidently directed to ever higher levels of social justice and equality has been shaken by the obstinacy of things. The civil-rights revolution, once the very embodiment of our dignity and pride, has somehow faltered, weakened by internal dissension and external opposition. Worst of all, the great ideal of internationalism, the splendid succession of noble deeds and magnanimous gestures that marked American foreign policy, has been grievously depleted—not by theory but by events.

What is to be done, as another man asked in a not too different time at the beginning of this century? The failure of nerve among many elements in American society is already evident enough: a retreat into privatism or, worse, a surrender to nihilism, a turning to the politics of the impossible. And it is not good enough. The end of youth is not the end of life, much less the end of the world. It is, or ought to mark, the onset of a period of less fun but far more satisfaction and much greater consequence.

Poets do their best work young, philosophers late. Nations, I would argue, do it in the middle years, and these are now upon us in America, and it should be with a sense of expectation rather than dread that we greet them. I will argue further that, properly used, this should be a time of great expectation. Some years ago the French Dominican, Father Bruckberger, declared, "Either America is the hope of the world or it is nothing." I believe that still to be so, and further that hope is better grounded today than ever before for the very reason that we are being forced to see what threatens us; and, being so, forces are vastly more likely to preserve those qualities and strengths which are indeed the hope of mankind.

Thus the thing we see more clearly now is that the great strength of the American nation lies not in its national wealth, nor its physical isolation, nor its social ease. Our strength lies in our capacity to govern ourselves. Of all the 126 members of the United Nations, there are not more than eight or nine which both existed in 1914 and have not had their form of government changed by force since that time. We are one of that fortunate few.

And more than luck is involved. In nation after nation that has been rent by insurrection, subverted by conspiracy, or defeated by enemies, it is not luck that has run out but judgment, and the capacity to live with one another, the ability of the people to pick wise rulers and of those picked to rule wisely.

Clearly, it is the task of those concerned with the health of American society to retain the large and still preponderant trust that remains and to regain that which has been lost. It will not be easy, if only for the reason that the very success of American society so far is producing an even larger proportion of persons who are trained to be skeptical, inquiring, and demanding of a great deal of information before they give their assent to any individual or policy.

It is because we have always had such persons in sufficient numbers that we have governed ourselves successfully in the past, and they are not less the occasion for confidence on that score in the future. Our students today are not raising hell because they are mindless but precisely because they are thoughtful —which is a different thing from being wise but surely a precondition of wisdom. All in all, it is a good state of affairs for a society that can respond to it. The question is what that response is to be and how it is to be mounted.

The presumption that this response must consist primarily of policies and programs in the traditional areas of politics is sound enough and in any event inevitable. But it is also inadequate and, left at that, will very likely fail. With no very great evidence, to be sure, but with much conviction, I will argue that the American policy—the experience as well as the sense of community and shared convictions—has been impaired, has atrophied, in our time because of the retreat from architecture and public buildings as a conscious element of public policy and a purposeful instrument for the expression of public purposes.

The concept of private affluence and public squalor in the United States is a familiar one, and correct as far as it goes. But save for a rare person such as John Kenneth Galbraith it rarely extends to the notion that public squalor includes the penury and squalor of public buildings and city planning.* Indeed, the very persons who will be the first to demand their increased expenditures for one or another form of social welfare will be the last to concede that the common good requires an uncommon standard of taste and expenditure for the physical appointments of government and of the public places of the city. Even those most vocal in support of government support for the arts will resist, even reject, the manifest fact that architecture and urban planning are the two arts which government by definition must be involved with, for better or worse.

This is not a matter of oversight but of conviction, and it has never been more manifest than in recent months when, in response to what is generally known as the urban crisis, some of the best and most generous minds in public life appear to have concluded that the first "luxury" to be sacrificed is that of elegance and—yes, face the word!—display in communal development and urban design.

Somehow, somewhere, in the course of the development of democratic or demagogic tradition in this nation, the idea arose

* I should acknowledge that of late I have argued that Galbraith succeeded too well, and that American society was beginning to show signs of private squalor and public affluence. A good portion of these essays were written in an upstate New York county in which the population is very nearly divided between those who gain their living in the private sector (milk farming, logging, gathering ginseng —and a squalid living it is for the most part) and those who earn good to very good incomes and live splendid secure lives as workers and contractors on interstate highways, county agents for the U.S. Department of Agriculture, or professors in the burgeoning state colleges in the region. Even so, save for the design of the highways, architecture has all but vanished. Indeed, to visit our county seat, Delhi, and compare the nineteenth-century Court House Square with the twentieth-century college campus is to encounter the near-disappearance of the impulse to art.

that concern with the physical beauty of the public buildings and spaces of the city and nation was the mark of mistaken priorities. From generation to generation the "approved" priorities change, often wildly, but somehow an urban aesthetic is never among them. The result has been a steady deterioration in the quality of public buildings and spaces, and with it a decline in the symbols of public unity and common purpose with which the citizen can identify, of which he can be proud, and by which he can know what he shares with his fellow citizens.

In our time the fear of taxpayer resentment of the costs of excellence in public buildings has been compounded with an almost ideological alarm at the implications of modern design. When President Kennedy took office in Washington, for example, it had been very near to half a century since the federal government had constructed in the nation's capital a building that was contemporary to its time, and the House of Representatives was soon to begin the Rayburn Building, perhaps the most alarming and unavoidable sign of the declining vitality of American government that we have yet witnessed. And this is the point: Good or bad architecture is not an option. It is as fundamental a sign of the competence of government as will be found. Men who build bad buildings are bad governors. A people that persists in electing such men is opting for bad government.

I believe this is beginning to be seen. It is a matter of significance that mayors such as Richard J. Daley, John Lindsay, and John Collins, governors such as Nelson Rockefeller, Presidents Kennedy and Johnson, and now Mr. Nixon, have been actively concerned with the quality of the public buildings by which—like it or not—posterity is likely to recall their administrations.

This concern has begun to show results. We are not really that distant from the time that it fell to me as a young member of the New Frontier to draw up the "Guiding Principles for Federal Architecture," which President Kennedy proclaimed on June 1, 1962. This was the first time a national policy has been stated (although why a country whose third President was Thomas Jefferson should ever come to the point of needing one is surely a puzzlement!), and it does seem to have had an effect. So much so that *Architectural Record* recently referred to its "now-famous words." It may be useful to recall them. Three points of policy were stated:

> 1. The policy shall be to provide requisite and adequate facilities in an architectural style and form which is distinguished and which will reflect the dignity, enterprise, vigor, and stability of the American National Government. Major emphasis should be placed on the choice of designs that embody the finest contemporary American architectural thought.
> 2. The development of an official style must be avoided. Design must flow from the architectural profession to the government, and not vice versa.
> 3. The choice and development of the building site must be considered the first step of the design process.

It is the common opinion that those guiding principles have had consequences, both in Washington and elsewhere, and we may hope for the continued exercise of such influence under the often vigorous and enlightened leadership of the General Services Administration.

We can look, moreover, to involved and active Presidential leadership. *Architectural Record* recently let go with "three cheers" for the most recent Presidential statement on the development of Pennsylvania Avenue. The President's words are perhaps particularly to be cited in this connection:

"Carved out of swampland at our country's birth, the nation's Capital City now sets a new test of national purpose. This was a city that men dared to plan—and build by plan—laying out avenues and monuments and housing in accordance with a common rational scheme. Now we are challenged once again to shape our environment; to renew our city by rational foresight and planning. . . ."

And he added: "This noble aim—this planning of a Capital City—encompasses a drive which must apply to areas of rebuilding beyond a single avenue. It infuses our knowledge of human want with a new urgency. It tests our vision of man and the future of cities."

But let us not wax too eloquent. Architectural policy was at best a marginal interest of the Kennedy Administration and even less that of its successor. The redevelopment of Pennsylvania Avenue has been faithfully supported by the American Institute of Architects, but neither of the two previous administrations was ever willing to expend five cents' worth of political popularity to advance it. (Kennedy might have. Almost his last instruction before leaving for Texas was that arrangements should be made for him to show the Pennsylvania Avenue model to the Congressional leaders immediately upon his return. William Walton, Charles Horsky, and I were at lunch making just such arrangements when the White House switchboard got through to say, as it turned out, that he would not return.)

The present administration would be the first to insist that it is by performance rather than words that we must be judged. But it is the fact that this issue has been moved ever so slightly up the national agenda; and were it more fully understood, I hold it would move even higher.

This is a matter for the architectural profession to concern itself with, and returns us to the subject of the integrity of the present social order. If the architectural/design profession is under great and growing attack from within, may I say as an outsider that I feel it deserves to be. I have been in the business of trying to improve the level of public design on and off for twenty years now, and the one thing I have been repeatedly struck by is the effective indifference—save for rare men such as Nathaniel Owings, Philip Johnson, or Archibald Rogers—of architects generally to the success or failure of those of us who as political executives have sought to further the presumed higher aspirations of their profession. The plain fact is that architects are, with respect to the quality of public building, much in the position of stockbrokers. Whether the market rises or falls, you still get your commissions. And the present American city is the result.

This result is something to be ashamed of—and we know it. All I would plead is that in the rush to make psychological amends—a paroxysmic convulsion which will become increasingly common throughout the professions—architects hold on to the conviction that the only purpose of changing ideals or standards is to change outcomes. The risk of self-induced paralysis is far greater than is supposed, not least by those who now advocate changes in the style and processes of urban planning.

Similarly, the risk of a withdrawal from politics is far greater than would be presumed, and just at that moment when the political system is showing some capacity to respond to the demand for better urban design; indeed, at just the moment when the political system itself is generating that demand.

This subject is still far too little insisted upon by those who realize its import. If we are to save our cities and restore to American public life the sense of shared experience, trust, and common purpose that seems to be draining out of it, the quality of public design has got to be made a public issue because it *is* a political fact. The retreat from magnificence, to use a phrase of Evelyn Waugh's, has gone on long enough: too long. An era of great public works is as much needed in America as any other single element in our public life.

Magnificence does not mean monumentality. That seems to be a point to be stressed. I have heard Saul Steinberg quoted as saying that the government buildings of Washington seem designed to make private citizens realize how unimportant they are, and there is much to what he says. But that seems to me simply to define the special requirements of this age of enormity: to create a public architecture of intimacy, one that brings people together in an experience of confidence and trust.

The City Beautiful is as valid a concept today as it was when George Washington and Thomas Jefferson established it as an American principle almost two centuries ago. It is not a concept to be traded in for anyone's notion of private or social welfare. It is not an efflorescence of elite aestheticism; it is the bone and muscle of democracy, and I repeat that it is time those who see this begin insisting on it.

At a time when there is so much that is brutal, we risk nothing less than our humanity if we fail to do so. The task of this less than all-powerful nation is to show to the world and to ourselves that, sensing our limitations, we know also our strengths and that we will husband and develop those strengths. The surest sign of whether we have done this will reside in the buildings and public places which we shall build in our time and for which we will be remembered or forgotten.

Maria Regina Martyrum

12

I am not, I think, different from some others in this respect: what I bring back from Europe is impressions, for the most part, of restaurants and churches—a habit acquired from guidebooks, but by now a matter also of taste. It is possible to like that sort of thing, and over the years to get better at it, or at least more complex. We have little by way of either restaurants or churches in America, and those we do have are, in the main, imitations: capable of telling much, but pleasing little; at best "worth seeing, but not worth going to see."

The north of Germany is, I think, more like America in this respect than any part of Europe I have come to know. The food is plentiful and plain. And the women. And the churches. Especially the churches. Built like factories before factories: gray light seeping through gray windows, cold, unadorned, repetitive: places to get out of.

This can hardly ever have been more so than in the avenging winter of 1950–1951, when I was first there. The old war was scarcely over and a new one seemingly determined to begin. I had been called back into the Navy, part of an abortive effort to set up, as we later gathered, some kind of united North Sea command. Complications arose, and Bremerhaven sent us on

"Maria Regina Martyrum" was first published in *The Atlantic Monthly*, May 1967.

tour: to Hamburg to stay at the Vier Jahreszeiten and prowl the Reeperbahn, to Berlin to drink at the Kempinski and to wander about gazing at the emptiness of the Eastern sector. (One recalls an Englishman summing up: "Nothing here but the handwriting on the wall.")

This must be the route for Americans on tour. It is just the one we followed this time. That, and the times being somehow alike, made the differences come through more insistently than they might.

Mankind counts heavily on the permanence of things, and is rewarded for doing so. In North Germany in 1950, however, it was hard. Impermanence was everywhere. The churches were empty and the restaurants filled. After dark both Hamburg and Berlin lurched into a kind of frenzied Brechtian caricature: the drinking brutal, the human beings damaged, spoiled, the mass dancing a form of immolation. And in the midst of it all at three thirty in the morning, heavy men and their heavy wives and small children sat around in nightclubs watching with sad intent the juggling and the striptease. As dawn came on, the fighting and vomiting began in streets too cold for it.

This is over. Life is in working order again. People stay home, save their money, and take vacations. The restaurants and cafés are busy, but in an unanxious way. Dutch oysters and French cheese have improved the menus, but rather as they do at the Hilton Wherever: without rousing the least sense of wonder, much less gratitude.

And so one's mind kept insistently going back to the question that is always there, What do they think about what happened?

Not what do they say? And certainly not what do they say to an American? But what do they themselves think?

There are no clues in Hamburg. They aren't in that business, really, and perhaps shouldn't be asked to be. But then Berlin, and the first indication; a deeply troubling one.

Somehow, from the outset, the symbol of Berlin in ruins was not the Reichstag, or the bunker, or the Brandenburg Gate, but the wreckage of the Kaiser Wilhelm Gedächtniskirche on the Kurfürstendamm at the center of the life of the free city. Everything came together here. "High Hohenzollern"—a great stuffed building, belted, sabred, and bemedaled. Built as a memorial to the great King of Prussia, Caesar of Germany. *The* place for a Prussian officer to be married, surrounded by Junkerdom and gazed upon by golden mosaics of decent grenadiers killing Frenchmen, and ironclad knights exalted in a mystic union of violence and virtue. At the end of the war only the tower and a few ruined walls were still standing. It was perfect.

They have spoiled it. All but the tower has been cleared away, and on the one side they have placed a campanile about two thirds the remaining height of the older steeple, and on the other a flat pentagonal building that serves as the missing nave. In the ruin of the old church a statue of Christ (apparently salvaged from the statuary of the original edifice) has been set up at street level in a kind of grotto-shrine arrangement. Spotlighted at night, with a few flowers at the base, and with one arm missing, it is infinitely sad and helpless. In any event religious. The new buildings are neither. They are merely pretty: international airport style, a pleasant, undemanding gathering point for persons on a long journey, that will be equally undemanding and painless. Soft blue light inside. On a Saturday afternoon, immensely fashionable young persons are joined in matrimony, with coach-and-four awaiting. Too eager by half, Berliners tell you the new structures are known as "the lipstick and the compact," but it is not at all clear how far they have thought through that image.

All the more then the shock to find that several miles away, in a surpassingly ordinary housing development named for a local politician, the Catholics have built what may well be the great church of this age, Maria Regina Martyrum.

The banality of evil. There is little to note about the Paul Hertz *Siedlung* (settlement project) save that it is a few blocks from the similarly unprepossessing Plötzensee prison where the victims of the Nazi regime were executed, and the leaders of the 1944 plot were hung with piano wire from meat hooks while moving pictures were taken for the Führer. At a meeting of German Catholics in 1952, the Bishop of Berlin proposed that a church be built there in witness to those who perished "for the rights of God and of conscience."

The church, finished in 1961, evokes a concentration camp in the presence of grace. One enters, through a single iron gate, onto a large prison yard. The bell tower is a guard tower. There is no possibility of intimacy within the enclosure; the yard is large and empty; one is alone. Across the expanse, huddled against the dark wall like prisoners awaiting roll call, are the Stations of the Cross, gathered into seven groups, cast of fiercely striated, encrusted black bronze from which somehow faces and gestures emerge. Golgotha appears as a slight rise in the stone floor of the yard. Nearby there is an outdoor altar, with a crown of thorns for a base.

The church proper is a large rectangular box set down on a pair of upright slabs within the yard. This rectangle is at right angles to that of the prison yard itself, and at one end rests on and extends slightly beyond the wall against which the Stations of the Cross are located. Above the entrance formed by the two slabs is a great golden abstraction, *The Woman of the Apocalypse*. One passes through a plain foyer and directly up a stairway to the empty nave. Le Corbusier wrote of his chapel at Ronchamp that "the key is light and light illuminates shapes and shapes have an emotional power." Just so here, save that there are no shapes, no emotions. Only concrete walls, thrown up hurriedly, the lines of the rough board forms very much present: a place for persons of little consequence and less permanence. The dim gray light seeps in with neither interest nor comprehension. Behind the altar is a vast, brilliantly colored painting from which the eye of heaven peers out. "I wouldn't," a friend said, "want to get married here."

Below, in the crypt, there is no light at all, seemingly, only the glow given off the dull gold walls and the all but unbearable *Pietà*. Done in the manner of Henry Moore, it is all the more rending for just that reason: something the age has learned to do well is here brought to the point of timelessness. Mary utterly alone; Christ broken and failed.

In the crypt are three graves, representing those in whose memory the church is built. Prelate Bernard Lichtenberg, who, in St. Hedwig's Cathedral in Berlin, publicly prayed for the Jews and other prisoners of the regime, and who died on the way to Dachau; a layman, Erich Klausener, who was murdered early in the regime; and a Jesuit, Alfred Delp, who died with Von Moltke at Plötzensee. Only Klausener's remains are present. With their unfailing talent for the contemptible, the authorities in the Eastern sector refuse to release Lichtenberg's body; Delp's ashes were scattered by the Nazis. Banality will not be stayed; in a setting of ineffable simplicity, a French pilgrimage has placed one of those hideous black and gold plaques: *"A nos camarades . . ."*

Perhaps the final triumph is that of the individual in this setting of annihilation. The church and all its embellishments are unmistakably the work of individual and very different human beings. The building is by the architects Hans Schädel and Friedrich Ebert; the Stations of the Cross by Herbert Hajek; *The Woman of the Apocalypse* and the *Pietà* by Fritz Koenig, and so through a series of triumphant artifacts. Only two things are not new. In a confessional chapel at the back of the nave there is a small wooden statue, *The Suffering Lord*, of the fifteenth century, and on the main altar a carved *Madonna and Child* from the fourteenth century, south of France. To see either is to know that we have lost something.

It is a place of implacable understanding, but also of hope. The church is a memorial to martyrs. But surely also it is an act of atonement by the Church itself, which did not fail them, but failed the great masses it ought to have led, and failed itself. And Him. This thought is not to be found in the guidebook, but it is there, inscribed on the Ambrose bell, "Yet I have to act and to prefer God to the Emperor."

As I write, one learns that by mistake yet another village has been destroyed in Vietnam.

Politics as the Art of the Impossible

13

I take for my theme a sentence from Georges Bernanos: "The worst, the most corrupting of lies are problems poorly stated."

My charge is similar. It is that much of the intense difficulty of our time is in nature conceptual, and that it arises from a massive misstatement of our problems. Intellectuals, if this view is correct, have done their work badly and there is little prospect that their mistakes will soon be undone. As ours was perhaps the first society consistently to expect the future to be better than the past, the apprehension that we may have profoundly mistaken the nature of our difficulties, so that we must expect years of effort to resolve the wrong problems and in presumedly unavailing ways, strikes with special force. A certain nostalgia arises for a future that now appears lost. It becomes necessary to live much more in the present than has been the American mode.

If this be no great pleasure, it can, nonetheless, be stimulating. Here a subtheme can be taken from another alert Frenchman— when asked what he had done during The Terror, the Abbé Sieyès answered, *"J'ai vécu."* "I survived." This must now be a

"Politics as the Art of the Impossible" was delivered as the Commencement Address at Notre Dame University, June 1969. It was first published in *The American Scholar*, Autumn 1969.

very great concern of those Americans whose lives, in Midge Decter's formulation, are devoted to the direction of their thought. Anyone old enough to have had any intellectual contact with the 1930s will take my meaning. The men of both the Left and the Right who dominated, even terrorized, *that* time lived intense but brief lives. Their intellectual corpses are still stacked in the odd corners of universities, government departments, and the like where they do whatever it is that they do. No one much cares, for they were subsequently judged to have been appallingly wrong about American society and, worse, were seen to have been unforgivably intolerant of any who hesitated to embrace their all-encompassing credos. Archibald MacLeish has remarked of his fellow poets that "there is nothing worse for our trade than to be in style." The equivalent, for those whose concern is governance, is submission to the noisiest problems of the moment to the exclusion of the most important ones.

What then are the "problems poorly stated" of our time? They are various but have, it seems to me, a unifying characteristic; namely, the rejection by those seeking a more just, more equal society of any indications that our society is in fact becoming more just and more equal. Society is seen in ahistorical terms: what is not altogether acceptable is altogether unacceptable; gradations are ignored and incremental movements are scorned. Those who by disposition are incrementalists, or for whom the contemplation of society has led to a conviction that incremental change is a necessity, not a choice, in human affairs, are baffled by this attitude and resentful of it. The exchanges that follow are bitter and unproductive. It is at all events my view that this is so because the problems at issue have so far been defined in fairly traditional *political* terms when what in fact is at issue is an immense stirring, little understood, if indeed understandable, of cultural dimensions. Fundamental ethical and moral issues— religious issues—are involved: issues that politics, especially the politics of a liberal democracy, are uniquely unable to resolve.

In 1967, in the Phi Beta Kappa oration at Harvard, I argued that in fact we were witnessing the onset of the first heresies of liberalism. Heresy is an unloved term, especially in a liberal society, but it has real meaning: the rejection of beliefs fundamental to the dominant, pervasive world view of the society involved. Of necessity, the heresies of liberalism would be procedural in nature, for it is in process that a liberal society defines itself. In thinking about the subject, I have not been able to get much further than this, but neither have events moved so as to cast greater doubt on the thesis than that which must attend any such large assertion. To the contrary, the rejection of the *authority* of liberal processes, the code that holds that it is bad form to club the dean, that civic statutes must be abided by, that rules of order and civility will be followed at meetings—all that —continues apace, and the pace if anything quickens. As Robert A. Nisbet continues to remind us, when authority relations collapse, power relations take their place; and this process, too, has advanced. Violence, which is the means by which power relations are maintained, is considerably more widespread now than it was two years ago, and surely vastly more common at the end of the decade of the 1960s than it was at the beginning of it.*

Nothing suggests that the pattern of former times will quickly reassert itself. To the contrary, the indications are that we rose to a new plateau of internal violence in the mid-1960s and that the most we can hope for is to keep from yet another escalation.

Such violence has, of course, made its way onto university campuses and this has led to great apprehension for the future of academic freedom. There are analogues, indeed precedents, for the violence of the streets, the poor, the police, and such-like. But nothing like the present pattern of threats to and actual assault on university institutions and university members has ever before occurred. Here, in particular, it would seem a future has been lost to us.

This has led to great despair among academic intellectuals: far greater than the news media have yet let on. From one's personal knowledge, on one campus after another there are men of intellectual distinction who are now very close to Joyce's resolve: "silence, exile, cunning." Nor is the alarm simply that of Bourbons. A Marxist historian such as Eugene Genovese speaks with not a little alarm of the "pseudo-revolutionary middle-class totalitarians . . . of the left-wing student movement," and one learns that even Professor Marcuse has suggested that professors ought to be treated differently from the oink-ish common swine.

---

* One of the uses of the Watergate revelations has been to demonstrate anew that persons toward the right as well as persons toward the left in the American polity are capable of contempt for the processes of American government.

Indeed it does seem hard, after all the struggles, bare victories, and bitter disappointments of the past quarter century, to be called out in middle age to defend the Rockefeller banks against the onslaught of the boys from Milton Academy. More depressing yet is to find how all too willing a frightened patriciate can be to sacrifice the freedom of the university—or the liberal intellectuals thereof—in the apparent hope that the *furor scholasticus* will go no further.

The strongest such view, from a notably unhysterical pen, is the recent assertion by Arnold Beichman, writing in *Encounter,* to the effect that university faculties

> have quietly decided that for the foreseeable future the university is no longer a place where truth is to be pursued. What has been tacitly ratified is a decision that the American university is primarily (not secondarily) the springboard for upward social mobility as the ascriptive right for ethnic minorities.

This can be overdone. Beichman accurately (but almost alone in the current flood of commentary) notes that ethnic mobility has always been a prominent component of higher education—certainly so from the time Catholics began to establish competitive institutions with Protestants. One recalls Yeats's letter of 1904 to Lady Gregory:

> I have been entirely delighted [he writes] with the big, merry priests of Notre Dame, all Irish and proud as Lucifer of their success in getting Jews and nonconformists to come to their college and of the fact that they have no endowments.

One recalls far more vividly growing up in New York City in the poverty-ridden 1930s, and yet possessing in that Notre Dame football team a symbol of tribal might and valor that can stir the blood atingle to this day. O, the golden Saturday afternoons when, in the name of every Irish kid caught in the social wreckage of the Eastern slums, thunder indeed shook down from the skies, and those mighty Polish tackles swamped the Navy. . . !

If the demands of newer groups come as a shock to some, it is at least in part because this group function of higher education has tended to be ignored by those groups for which it has been functioning. Yet the role was obvious enough; and it was not less clear that it would become, if anything, more pronounced to the degree that universities became more central institutions of the society. In the concluding paragraph of *Beyond the Melting Pot,* Nathan Glazer and I wrote: "Religion and race define the next stage of the American peoples." We were not wrong, and one is mystified still that the proposition was viewed at the time with such skepticism on the part of so many. (Not a few of them, it may be added, having become committed to ethnic studies, pursue the matter with the single-minded zeal that is notoriously the accompaniment of sudden religious conversion.)

Simultaneously, if somewhat incompatibly, universities have been mini-bastions of class privilege. This phenomenon has been evident enough in the insistence by almost all parties to intra-mural disputes that those involved are exempt from punishment for deeds that would send lesser persons—without the walls—to court, at the very least, and prison in all likelihood. But again, this is nothing new.

Indeed, some good could come of this if the excesses of the moment were to serve to restore some perspective on just what universities are and what they can do. They are institutions inhabited by younger and older persons often of very great abilities, but usually of very limited experience. With respect to their individual specialties, the judgment of the professors is singularly valuable. But their collective judgment is no better—could, indeed, be worse—than that of the common lot of men. This is not an incidental, random fact; it is a fundamental condition of human society, and the very basis of democratic government.

When William F. Buckley, Jr., wrote that he would far rather entrust his governance—in which he would include the preservation of his civil liberties and his intellectual freedom—to the first hundred persons listed in the Cambridge telephone directory than to the faculty of Harvard College, he was saying no more than what Thomas Jefferson or Henry Adams would have thought self-evident. The remark was greeted at the time with some derision by said faculty, but it may be stated with certainty that more than one tenured professor of that ancient institution has come of late to see its soundness with sad clarity.

All this is to the good. What is bad is that the diffusion of violence to the intellectual life of our society is likely to lead to even greater failure to state our problems correctly than has been the case to date. This is so for the most elemental of reasons. Intellectual freedom in the American university has now been seriously diminished. It is past time for talking about what might happen; it has happened. We would do well to clear our minds of cant on that subject. Especially in the social sciences, there is today considerably less freedom than there was a decade ago; and we should expect that it will surely be ten to twenty years before what we would hope to be a normal state will be restored.

I deem it essential that this almost suddenly changed situation be more widely understood; otherwise, the sickness of the time will gradually come to be taken for a normal condition of health —and that would be a blow not merely to the age, but to the culture. But if we do perceive our circumstance for what it is, if we do come to accept that for reasons of prudence, or cowardice, or incompetence, or whatever, faculties have been everywhere allowing principles and men to be sacrificed, we will at least retain the understanding that something has gone wrong, something that it may be possible someday to right.

It is important then to survive, with our faculties, as it were, as little diminished as possible, and to seek to understand the times—which is to say to state the problems of the time correctly.

Few individuals can hope to contribute more than a small increment to this effort; greater, then, is the reason that as many as possible should seek to do so. Hence, with less hesitance than might otherwise attend the effort to make a simple abstraction about a hopelessly complex reality, I would offer, from the world of politics, the thought that the principal issues of the moment are not political. *They are seen as such:* that is the essential clue to their nature. But the crisis of the time is not political, it is in essence religious. It is a religious crisis of large numbers of intensely moral, even godly, people who no longer hope for God. Hence, the quest for divinity assumes a secular form, but with an intensity of conviction that is genuinely new to our politics. Central to the quest for secular grace is the detestation of secular sin incarnate, namely, the United States of America, "the most repressive, inhumane capitalistic-imperialistic nation," as the student paper of a Middle Western state university recently put it, "the world has ever seen."

It is important to be clear whence this peculiar moral passion arises. It is from the very eighteenth-century Enlightenment from which arose the American civilization that has so far followed so different a course. The rejection of Christian religion by the Enlightenment has obscured the fact, especially to Christians, that it did not constitute a rejection of Christian morality. To the contrary, it was more often in the name of that morality that the creed was attacked. It was Rousseau, as Michael Polanyi argues (although others would disagree), whose work widened the channels of Enlightenment thought so that in fact "they could be fraught eventually with all the supreme hopes of Christianity, the hopes which rationalism had released from their dogmatic framework." Wherewith, supreme of ironies, was loosed upon the world a moral fury that has wrought as much evil, in contrast with the mere brutality of the past, as mankind has ever known, an evil that may yet destroy us. The process arises from a sequence of premises that is logically unassailable, yet that in practice produce a society that is inherently unstable. Polanyi states the argument, which, he correctly observes, no one has yet answered.

> If society is not a divine institution, it is made by man, and man is free to do with society what he likes. There is then no excuse for having a bad society, and we must make a good one without delay. For this purpose you must take power and you can take power over a bad society only by revolution; so you must go ahead and make a revolution. Moreover, to achieve a comprehensive improvement of society, you need comprehensive powers so you must regard all resistance to yourself as high treason and must put it down mercilessly.

Repeatedly, as this fervor becomes pathological, a kind of inversion takes place that transforms violence from a means to an end to an end in itself. There are surprises but few mysteries to this process: the nineteenth century was able to read it in Russian novels; the twentieth to watch it on film. It has been the great disease of the committed intellectual of our time. Thirty years ago, Orwell wrote: "The common man is still living in the mental world of Dickens, but nearly every modern intellectual has gone over to some or other form of totalitarianism." For that is the correct term. The total state; the politicization of all things. It seems that Britain and America managed in the nineteenth century to escape any deep infestation of this view mostly by not thinking too closely about politics. But one result of this is that in political theory there is no serious counterargument: all one can say is that one does not like doing good by sending men "up against the wall" to use the apparent term of Che Guevara and the battle cry of the Barnard girls. For the disease is amongst us, and will spread. Incongruously, it appears to have taken roots within organized religion itself. The course of the coming generation is all but fixed: it will include a strong and possibly growing echelon that will challenge the authority of American institutions across the board, and will not be especially scrupulous as to how it does so. In this the extreme Left is very likely to be joined by the extreme Right, for to each the values and process of the present American democracy are the enemy to be destroyed.

All in all, there is cause enough for despair. As Midge Decter has put it: "When you are caught between left and right, the only way to go is down." But we are not yet down. We are a strong and competent people, increasingly, I think, aware of our troubles and dangers and shortcomings. The challenge to authority that is now upon us can strengthen and renew institutions as much as it can weaken them. And it can be fun. There is always room, as Orwell wrote, "for one more custard pie." We are not especially well equipped in conceptual terms to ride out the storm ahead, but there are things we know without fully understanding, and one of these is the ultimate value of privacy, and the final ruin when all things have become political.

Having through all my adult life worked to make the American national government larger, stronger, more active, I nonetheless plead that there are limits to what it may be asked to do. In the last weeks of his life, President Kennedy journeyed to Amherst to dedicate a library to Robert Frost and to speak to this point. "The powers of the Presidency," he remarked, "are often described. Its limitations should occasionally be remembered."

The matter comes to this. The stability of a democracy depends very much on the people making a careful distinction between what government can do and what it cannot do. To demand what can be done is altogether in order: some may wish such things accomplished, some may not, and the majority may decide. But to seek that which cannot be provided, especially to do so with the passionate but misinformed conviction that it *can* be, is to create the conditions of frustration and ruin.

What is it that government cannot provide? It cannot provide values to persons who have none, or who have lost those they had. It cannot provide a meaning to life. It cannot provide inner peace. It can provide outlets for moral energies, but it cannot create those energies. In particular, government cannot cope with the crisis in values that is sweeping the Western world. It cannot respond to the fact that so many of our young people do not believe what those before them have believed, do not accept the authority of institutions and customs whose authority has heretofore been accepted, do not embrace or even very much like the culture that they inherit.

The twentieth century is strewn with the wreckage of societies that did not understand or accept this fact of the human condition. Ours is not the first culture to encounter such a crisis in values. Others have done so, have given in to the seemingly sensible solution of politicizing the crisis, have created the total state, and have destroyed themselves in the process. Irving Kristol has warned against it in terms at once cogent and urgent:

> The one way not to cope with this crisis in values is through organized political-ideological action. Most of the hysteria, much of the stupidity, and a good part of the bestiality of the twentieth century have arisen from efforts to do precisely this. Not only do such efforts fail; they fail in the costliest fashion. And if modern history can be said to teach anything, it is that, intolerable as a crisis in values may be, it invariably turns out to be far less intolerable than any kind of "final solution" imposed by direct political action.

This is only to insist that neither the new Left nor the new Right, if that should come along, nor any such movement should be allowed to impose its particular moral imperatives upon the institutions and processes of the democracy. Without exception these movements are repressive, and almost without exception they are elitist. Their purpose is to impose the superior values of a minority on the inferior lives of the mass. (As illustrated by Nathan Glazer's point that the SDS will typically denounce voting and majority rule in campus matters as "counterrevolutionary." By which read that in a referendum students typically vote to *keep* ROTC. That is, no process is morally acceptable that produces a morally *un*acceptable outcome.) But this is a very different thing from saying there is no moral content to politics. To the contrary, politics is an expression of morality: a form of morality. But it cannot create moral values any more than a steel mill can create iron ore. The problem of the moment is that the ore is running thin. The governments of the Western world have not been notable in their zeal for putting in practice the social morality of religion—charity, compassion, love of neighbor, *et cetera*—most commonly identified as the Christian social ethic, but obviously also Judaic, and for that matter Islamic. But formal attachment to that morality rarely wavered, simply because it was the belief of the mass, and generally speaking still is. Now this belief has eroded if not vanished in the leadership echelons of most nations, with the result that increasingly nations are governed, or at least cultures are directed, by men who *know* that they don't know what to do. Even where they delude themselves, the Niebuhrian dilemma remains: man may be moral, but increasingly his will is manifested in the acts of complex organizations that not infrequently are amoral to the point of being positively immoral. (For example, Vietnam: the war of liberal anti-Communism. The primary moral passion of "good" men of one generation, leading to acts that evoke the primary moral revulsion of "good" men of the following one.) The result, necessarily, is a certain faltering of leadership, and increasingly also of followership. The Captain Veres are rare now, and soon we shall be running low on Billy Budds.

But all this is obvious. What was Eliot, what was anybody, writing about for the first half of the twentieth century? In retrospect, it was easy to be captain of the *Indomitable*, was it not? But what commands shall issue forth from the quarterdeck of the *Worried*, the *Uncertain*, the *Not Sure*.

It would seem—conditional tense always!—that what we have to do is to create a secular morality, acceptable to the nonreligious, that accommodates itself to what man will actually do, which is to say, persists in the face of imperfection. This cannot be an easy thing to accomplish, but it would seem the only reassuring course, and probably ought to be pursued with much more deliberation than is now the case.

I surely do not argue for a quietistic government acquiescing in whatever the tides of fortune or increments of miscalculation bring about—and in our time they have brought about hideous things. I do not prescribe for social scientists or government officials a future of contented apoplexy as they observe the mounting disaffection of the young. I certainly do not argue for iron resistance, as other societies have effectively resisted somewhat similar movements in the past.

I simply plead for the religious and ethical sensibility in the culture to see more clearly what is at issue, and to do its work.

Sympathy is not enough. *Tout pardonner, c'est tout comprendre* is not a maxim that would pass muster with Bernanos or any who have helped us through the recent or distant past. If politics in America is not to become the art of the impossible, the limits of politics must be perceived, and the province of moral philosophy greatly expanded.

Liberalism and Knowledge

14

A public official asked to comment on a subject as complex and allusive as the relationship between received social policy and recent social science ought to assume he is asked to do so in his public capacity. Which is to say, he is asked not to say much. This would be admissible, even prudent in most settings. The forum of the American Jewish Committee, however, summons a higher prudence: the acknowledgment that the unexamined life is not so much a lamentable loss as an intolerable risk. These, then, are the thoughts not of a Cabinet officer, but of a *Commentary* writer, for among those whose task it is to maintain a sustaining connection between the liberal tradition of respect for facts, and the disconcerting facts which so much of late descend upon us, the most significant work of the American Jewish Committee is that it sponsors that extraordinary journal—it may well be the "world's best magazine" as some of its advertisements suggest. It is an opportunity not to be let pass by one who has not only written for *Commentary* but who also regards himself as a member of that invisible university for which *Commentary* is written.

"Liberalism and Knowledge" was read before the annual meeting of the American Jewish Committee, May 1970. It was first published in *Psychology Today*, September 1970, under the title "Eliteland."

In a spirit not of apology, but merely of preface, let it be allowed that my thoughts will seem somewhat abstruse. I should like to discuss the subject of liberalism and knowledge, referring in the latter term not so much to the religious and humanist idea of truth as to that curious synthesis of statistics and opinion which has emerged from the breeding of truth with technology. In a word, to social science.

It is more than a sense of appropriateness that impels me. Fear moves me as well. Fear of all those things *Commentary* has stood against: untruth, distortion, suppression, credulity. I see these rising on every hand, and, more to the point, I see them increasingly dominant in precisely those institutions one was raised to understand are dedicated to the virtues that are the opposite of these vices.

The rise in this phenomenon has been precipitant of late, but the long-term secular trend has been upwards. And having now commenced the jargon of my subject, let me turn to the subject itself.

In the spirit of the age, let me begin with recantation. I have been prone to profound ideological error. A crypto-deviationist antipeople incrementalist, I have been guilty of optimism about the use of social-science knowledge in the management of public affairs. The time is at hand to acknowledge my wrongdoing, renounce my past, beg the forgiveness of my colleagues, and simultaneously warn them of the subtle and seductive deviations from truth which can lead them as well into such grievous error.

If I were to mark that moment when apostasy became public and until that moment presumably revocable, it would be the fall of 1965 when I published in *The Public Interest* an article entitled "The Professionalization of Reform." I plead, not in extenuation, but in explication only, that this was the first issue of a new and promising journal and that that somehow explains something. Whatever the etiology of error may have been, the fact is that I suggested the nation was entering—had entered— a period in which the econometric revolution, which assured a steadily rising Federal revenue surplus, the professionalization of the middle class, which brought more and more energetic persons to the calling of social change, and the exponential increase in knowledge, which gave method and direction to such change, would combine to produce a fairly steadily self-correcting and self-improving society. I warned, citing Harold Lasswell, of the dangers of a "monocracy of power" in which a combination of enlightenment, resources, and skill so overwhelms—or outperforms—the normal processes of democracy that there is a diminishment in the vitality of the larger culture. But the warning was brief, and the essential message was positive, taken directly from Wesley C. Mitchell.

> Our best hope for the future lies in the extension to social organization of the methods that we already employ in our most progressive fields of effort. In science and in industry . . . we do not wait for catastrophe to force new ways upon us. . . . We rely, and with success, upon quantitative analysis to point the way; and we advance because we are constantly improving and applying such analysis.

It is now some years since the article was written, and as I say, I think I was wrong. In all seriousness, hopelessly wrong. The three phenomena on which I based my argument have persisted. They may if anything have become somewhat more conspicuous. But ours has hardly become a self-correcting, self-improving society.

How so? How is it that so much went wrong in the 1960s?

Nathan Glazer and I have just finished a new edition of *Beyond the Melting Pot,* in which we conclude that, so far as racial and ethnic relations are concerned in the North, the decade was a near disaster. I tend to think history will see that as a near-term judgment. In other words, that the long-range consequences were good enough. In time it may come to be judged that the real disaster was in the area of the social sciences; that is to say, those studies that seek to enlighten and improve the public mind with respect to social phenomena such as race relations. And yet just the opposite would have seemed likely. I repeat. What happened?

There is an insight, I believe, to be had from the troubles which now beset the physical sciences. Of all the academic pursuits of this age, surely none was as little likely to produce large-scale protest, and even small-scale destructiveness. But that is precisely what has happened. Almost in an instant. The basis of such protest, confined until recently to the university communities themselves, although likely now to spread with the growing concern about ecological degradation, is that the consequences of science are unacceptable. People don't like what happens when science is applied, through technology, to the human environment. What is meant, of course, is that some people don't like *some* of the things that happen. But the whole enterprise is being tarred with the same brush, and it is difficult to imagine that this will not have some consequences, and not very attractive ones, for science as a whole. One reason *this* has happened is that a new and far more threatening objection has been raised to scientific progress. This objection has only indirect reference to the *results* of science. Rather it concentrates on its *methods*. These methods are, correctly, declared to be elitist in the extreme, and consequently capable of being manipulated only by elites, from which it is said to follow that they will also be manipulated only for the advantage of elites. An impressive, if somewhat fuzzy point. If there is something in the water supply that is changing my genes, it surely is not something I know anything about. Moreover, while the fellows who put it there are likely to know one another, I surely don't know them.

It would appear that somewhat similar events are abroad in the field of social science. The first of these concerns the matter of results. For a very long while American social science lived in a more or less satisfactory symbiotic harmony with political progressivism. This was a period of roughly the first half of the twentieth century. To a curious degree, or this at least is my impression, the great issues of that period in American life were normative, having to do with the assimilation into the society of various excluded, or at least external, groups, of the legitimate uses of power, and the fair distribution of power. Social science was asked, for example, to attest to the equality of the races, and did so with commanding evidence and great influence. It was asked to legitimate the demand of wage workers under capitalism to organize and bargain collectively. Again it did so, albeit with perhaps less cosmic assurance. It was asked to provide measures of intellectual worth so that applications for college admission and such-like might be judged by some objective criterion, and here it succeeded splendidly. Increasingly, also, it was asked to prescribe measures for a high-level functioning of the economy and, again, it did so with notable success.

It is one thing, however, to argue that workers ought to be allowed to organize and bargain collectively, and another to get involved in the bargaining process and ensure that the workers win. It is this latter process, the concern with actual outcomes, that seems to me to distinguish the demands being made on social science today from those of the recent past and it is here I fear that the old symbiotic relations with advocates of social change is breaking down.

The difficulty is easily explained. Advocates of social change, especially to the degree that they base their advocacy on normative grounds, are naturally disposed to be impatient, to ask that remedies be as near as possible immediate. So long as social science was essentially asked to certify that the normative grounds were justifiable, its task was relatively simple, and it could be sure to be invited back for the next round of certification. But once it is asked actually to implement—forthwith—the normative imperative, it is up against a very different matter indeed. By and large it knows that it cannot. The evidence is all to the contrary. Even the most rapid social change, as seen from the perspective of history, comes slowly, one step at a time, from the point of view of the individual demanding it. The dilemma of social science is exquisite and unavoidable. To assert that nothing can be done overnight is to be accused of supporting those who want nothing done ever. To assert the contrary is to debase the science. There are a few who will accept the former condition; more than a few, certainly more than enough, who will submit to the humiliations exacted by the latter course. In between, a silent near majority of social scientists looks about for a research topic no one seems too much interested in just at the moment.

I take it that this phenomenon accounts for a good deal of the current rhetoric from the left demanding that university courses be relevant, that universities themselves serve their communities. Theodore Lowi has nicely pointed out that this simply extends a long American tradition that knowledge, especially knowledge in a professor, is tolerable only so long as it is useful.

The demand that the Ivy League universities somehow save the slums, is no more than the nineteenth-century demand that cow colleges save the dirt farmer. The long-run outcome is just as likely to surprise the presumed clients. But in the short run the professors who go along with the fashion, in this case pretending to knowledge they just don't have, are likely to end up either despising themselves or being despised by their peers, while those who manage to keep out of sight are equally candidates for self-contempt or social obloquy.

But in the end the profession is likely to assert the limits of its knowledge. In any event, those limits will reveal themselves. The result will be a social science no longer quite so supportive of those groups that in the past could thoroughly depend on it. Increasingly then social science will be seen as threatening, even hostile.*

This process is likely to accelerate at times when the storm signals of social reaction are flying. If social progress is slow, social regression can be rapid indeed. Seemingly a point of tension and anxiety about too much change is reached, whereupon a quite punitive and defensive response occurs. The society regresses to a minimum responsiveness to change, save possibly change for the worse. In such circumstances, the warnings of the economists, be the subject inflation, or the caution of psychiatrists, be the subject pornography, or the frettings of political historians on the subject of excessive expansion of international commitments, can suddenly be seen as contributing to the trend toward social regression, or even of triggering it. Something like this, for example, has happened to the academics at Berkeley who warned that continuous disruption by students would lead to the rise in California of a particularly virulent political conservatism. It did. Or as best one can tell it did. And the reward of many of those who forecast it was judged to have desired and even contributed to it.

Here I would perhaps differ from some other members of the profession. It has been the fashion of social scientists to see

---

* The natural sciences face similar strains. A committee on scientific freedom and responsibility has been appointed by the American Association for the Advancement of Science. A 1972 progress report in the AAAS Bulletin took note of Alfred North Whitehead's definition: "Duty arises from our potential control over the course of events." Obviously, different perceptions of the extent of that control lead to different presumptions of duty. I see no useful generalization as to whether laymen overestimate or underestimate potential control, but clearly the former situation does arise. Philip Abelson writes, there is "great impatience with the failure of science to solve many social problems, and it is implied that the failure is due to lack of good-will and a proper sense of priorities."

themselves as a slightly beleaguered group, taking risks on the edge of social innovation. Actually, for the past generation they and their students have been anything but. To the contrary they have been part of an exceptionally secure elite community, earning high salaries and passing about privileges in the manner of elites anywhere. (I suppose for that matter nineteenth-century aristocratical society in Europe had a self-image of military valor, but alas their valor was evinced primarily in marrying one another's cousins.) This has produced a certain dichotomous view of American society. Two establishments are simultaneously seen to exist. One, that of which the social scientist is himself a member. The other, that against which he is presumably arrayed. Thus in their admirable study "Knowledge into Action: Improving the Nation's Use of the Social Sciences" the Special Commission on the Social Sciences of the National Science Board listed under the heading "Obstacles to the Use of the Social Sciences" the risk of coming forth with *implications that threaten the status quo.* This is indeed a danger, but it is to implications that threaten the status quo of the first rather than the second elite that the wise professor will be alert. Findings as to the difficulties of social change would come under the heading, and so incur the risk of disestablishment.

Similarly, while social scientists generally regard themselves as persons of pronounced egalitarian principle, they are anything but egalitarian in their processes of co-optation. I should like to see a study of the social origins of the various professions involved, but I would not hesitate to argue at this point that they would turn out to be very narrow indeed. From time to time this minority group or that is singled out for favor and brought into the circle, but the mass remain without. Thus my university, Harvard, is located in a city and a metropolitan area which is rather more than half Roman Catholic, and has been so for the whole of this century. Yet I should be surprised to learn that 5 percent of the Harvard faculty is Catholic, and even more surprised to learn that the remaining 95 percent has even noticed the fact. There is nothing the least unusual, or to my mind wicked, about such conditions. Let people do what they want to do. Surely there is little protest from the Irish of South Boston or the Italians of the North End. Still less is heard from the Canadians, who comprise the Boston area's largest immigrant group. But it does mean that the products of social science will tend to be seen by these large outside groups as somewhat alien contrivances, with no very great claim on anyone's credence or compliance. It is for this reason social science has always been seen as a bit threatening by large portions of the populace, and this condition will surely persist and may become more pronounced.

There is a second general set of circumstances that contribute to the emerging threatening quality of the social sciences, and that is that they are getting complicated. The methodology of most social science is now quite beyond the comprehension of non-social scientists. In particular, it is beyond the ken of the lawyer class that tends to wield the levers of power in American government. Thus a priestly role of interpreting the mysteries is gradually emerging. And with it the anticlericalism of priest-ridden societies.

The simple fact is that it is harder and harder to know what it is social science says about anything, and it is impossible to do so when social scientists fall out with one another, as they have done, for example, in interpreting the data of the Equal Educational Opportunity Survey entrusted to Professor Coleman and his associates. Coleman's data were at once devastatingly critical of received truths about the educational process, and at the same time almost impenetrable to the layman. As a result it was relatively easy for the educational establishment to act as if nothing had happened. This process was abetted by the commonplace coincidence that there were some social scientists who disagreed with Coleman's interpretation and did so in even less decipherable terms, so that the whole matter could be dismissed as a scholastic squabble.

The trouble is that it was not. Controversy there was, but the rudiments of the findings and the concepts of social equity that emerged from the study have utterly changed our understanding of a fundamental social process. Once again, a dilemma is encountered. Increasingly social science is saying things that a great many people ought to know, but increasingly also it says these things in a manner very few people can understand. This is almost a formula for incurring displeasure.

What then is to be made of all this? I will venture a very few conclusions, but possibly useful ones.

The first is that the professionalization of reform will continue, but in a form somewhat different from that which I earlier envisaged. It is likely that increasingly the role of the social scientist will be to assert the *absence* of knowledge with respect to many of the most urgent issues of the turbulent and ambitious society we have created for ourselves. This will make social scientists less popular but more useful.

This point was in a way acknowledged in the 1968–69 annual report of the Social Science Research Council.

> The difficulty we as a nation face in solving our problems is not will but knowledge. We want to eliminate poverty, crime, drug addiction, and abuse; we want to improve education and strengthen family life, but we do not know how. Traditional measures are no longer good enough. Very different ones must be sought, invented, tried on a small scale, evaluated, and brought closer to perfection. Many schemes will fail and the most profitable failures will be those which lead to the clarification of understanding of the problems. Many schemes will simply expose additional problems that social scientists will need to solve. Both design and evaluation are needed. . . . The overwhelming complexity of the nation's social problems and their immediacy, however, should not blind us to our ignorance of ways to solve them.

The uses of ignorance—acknowledged, understood ignorance —are many, and one can imagine in the decade ahead that social science proceeding from these premises can help to impose a desperately needed discipline on the way we discuss social issues, and the programs we devise to deal with them. If there is a danger that we shall come to think things are too hard, let us be alert for signs thereof. But surely, for the moment, we suffer most from having thought too many things too easy. The result, of course, is the much-heralded crisis in confidence. If you think you know all there is you need to know in order to establish democracy in Southeast Asia, or social stability in the South Bronx, you are likely to make considerably more serious mistakes than would occur if you accept the fact that you don't know very much and aren't going to.

A second conclusion derives somewhat from the first, or so I would hope to demonstrate. It has to do with the troublesome question of elites. As should be perfectly evident, social-science knowledge, like scientific knowledge, poses problems for democracy. (It being, for example, a particularly perverse quality of many social situations that solutions are what may be termed "counterintuitive." That is to say the operation of the system is such that the "common-sense" solution to a problem is exceedingly likely to be wrong. There are good reasons for this, and they can be demonstrated. But only to a small number of persons. What then to do with the popular will?) Concentrated knowledge is a form of concentrated power and creates, simply, the elite condition.

One way to look at American democracy is to see it as not so much a democracy, but rather a society with an unprecedentedly large and varied assortment of elites. The people are asked which elite will govern them for which purposes. Typically there's a fairly wide choice. To an extraordinary degree, or so it sometimes seems to me, political and social conflict in this nation typically involves a contest between such elites as to which shall be chosen. Such contests can become impressively complex and subtle. It took some time before any considerable number of members of the Eastern Establishment awoke to the fact that Senator Joseph McCarthy was after them, and not, as he purported to be, after immigrant revolutionaries, or Jewish dentists. It will be some time hence, or so I would imagine, before it is widely appreciated that a fair amount of the current alarums within that establishment on the subject of the Vietnam war are perhaps not unrelated to the fact a surely disproportionate influence of that establishment was to be encountered in the councils wherein that war was first dreamed up. One learns from the *New York Times* that "1,000 'Establishment' Lawyers Join War Protest," and that they have done so in some measure in response to "labor fascists" who have of late taken to beating up peace demonstrators on Wall Street. Very well. No body should be beat. But one would hope some members of that professedly august company—"decidedly members of the Establishment," as one spokesman assured the press—would consider that very few construction workers took part in those Harvard Seminars on counterinsurgency, or have penetrated the inner sanctum of the Council on Foreign Relations, much less having had their voice heard in the hushed recesses of the White House basement where for a decade Ivy League professors and Wall Street lawyers gathered in the Situation Room for purposes I would suppose at this point need no elaboration.

My purpose is to assert that social science can at least keep the process of competition between elites from being abused to the point of trifling with the stability of the society. I believe that something very like this is going on today. Elites in conflict have summoned up, or at very least been altogether willing to make use of, terribly destructive forces within our society. *The violence of the moment is being used almost in direct measure that it is deplored.* I cite John Gardner on the supposed victimization of the moderates of the moment, of whom the great majority are truly that, but in whose ranks will be found in approximately equal proportion persons of unbridled aggression which on the right takes the form of seeking out conspiracy by the left, and on the left consists of summoning up portents of the hastening repression from the right. Gardner is perhaps even more caustic than I would be.

> Lest this give the impression that moderates are victimized, it must be said at once that most of them have a secret complicity in the activities of the extremist. The moderate conservative does not explicitly approve of police brutality, but something in him is not unpleased when the billy club comes down on the head of a long-haired student. The liberal does not endorse violence by the extreme left; but he may take secret pleasure in such action when it discomfits those in authority.

But the point, as I say, is not to disdain such tactics, but to seek to understand and to display them. Here, to repeat, I feel social scientists have an extraordinary potential for ring-keeping, for maintaining, that is, certain standards of conflict, and for detecting derelictions from such standards. It seems to me a role urgently needed at this moment. Let us face it, no one else can afford to be honest about these things. Only a very special and dedicated cadre—itself an elite of sorts—can hope to keep the other elites of the country from tearing the country apart.

This will require an objectivity we have not always had, and a stomach for telling the truth about who wins what and how in America life that we had once, I think, when it was a fairly simple matter of property-holding, but which we have quite lost in the past generation when winning and losing became inextricably mixed up with ethnic and religious, as well as social, groupings. To do this well will require a fairly sustained effort to recruit to the social sciences persons from the nonintellectual classes of America, and also persons of conservative as well as liberal politics. (There are conservative economists, to be sure, but a conservative sociologist is a pretty rare man, and ought not to be.) We need more women, a majority group, and of course, members of minority groups.

As I have argued over the years, we need to break the Marxist spell which it seems to me has immobilized so much twentieth-century social thought, and which has now returned to our campus in a vulgarized but appallingly virulent form. Gary R. Orren has recently noted that social science originates, for the most part, in Germany, England, and France—countries that are almost uniquely homogeneous in their populations. These are of course the countries of Karl Marx, and generally of socialist thinkers, to whom the fact of being Polish could be regarded merely as a transient "national problem." But for the rest of the world—not least the United States, and surely the same issues will soon be appearing within the Soviet Union—ethnicity persists and is an extraordinarily important, if not central, problem. For the Marxist class is the ethnic group. Glazer and I have noted that in the past ethnicity and social class have been closely correlated. This very likely seemed to confirm the Marxian model of societies torn by class conflicts. And to be sure, there are class realities. But ethnic realities are there as well. Increasingly they are, for certain purposes, and in certain places, the dominant realities. Social science needs to become much more sensitive to them.*

But most of all we need a sense that our mission involves the maintenance of social stability as well as the facilitating of social change. We must be prepared to lose a few friends in that process, possibly to become somewhat less admiring of ourselves.

---

* In these terms the current preoccupation with "racism" is a net plus, and may turn into a permanent advance. Yet too much of the present concern seems to me to involve a kind of displaced Marxist model of exploitation of one group by another. Ethnic relationships are far more complex.

History I think will forgive us. The sunny rationalism of the past is past. The times are tragic and will be surmounted only, I should think, by men capable of accepting that fact. Our politicians have been better about this than have our professors. Lincoln was better. Kennedy was better. Deep in their beings they knew how close a thing it always is. Let me finish with a passage from Arthur Schlesinger's *A Thousand Days* in which he treats at last with the seeming caution of the young President, and the great impatience it provoked in his even younger aides.

> I believe today that its basic source may have been an acute and anguished sense of the fragility of the membranes of civilization, stretched so thin over a nation so disparate in its composition, so tense in its interior relationships, so cunningly enmeshed in underground fears and antagonisms, so entrapped by history in the ethos of violence. . . . His hope was that it might be possible to keep the country and the world moving fast enough to prevent unreason from rending the skin of civility. But he had peered into the abyss and knew the potentiality of chaos.

To speak of the "potentiality of chaos" seems dated now. Chaos is increasingly our condition. If we are to overcome it, the men whose profession is social knowledge will have to acquire somehow the realization that the abyss is real and is near at hand.

Policy vs. Program
in the 1970s

15

One of the anomalies of the 1960s is that a period of such extraordinary effort at social improvement should have concluded in
a miasma, some would say a maelstrom, of social dissatisfaction.

What went wrong?

Well, countless things went wrong. But I believe one of the
more important things is that the structure of American government, and the pragmatic tradition of American politics, too much
defined public policy in forms of *program*, and in consequence
has inhibited the development of true *policy*. In simpler times a
simple programmatic approach was an efficient way to go about
the public business. The problem comes with complexity. More
specifically, the problem comes when society becomes ambitious
and begins to seek to bring about significant changes in the operation of complex systems such as the society itself. There is
nothing the least wrong with such ambitions. What is wrong is
a pattern in which the ambitions are reputedly proclaimed, and
just as repeatedly frustrated—especially when the source of the
frustration lies not in the malfeasance of individuals but in the

"Policy vs. Program in the 1970s" was read before a centennial observance of Hendrix College, April 1970. It was first published in *The Public
Interest*, Summer 1970.

limitations of the *program* approach to issues which demand the disciplined formulations and elaborations of public *policy*.

These are terms that rightly call for definitions. Here I think the temptation is to be too clever. As increasingly we perceive and begin to understand the social system as just that, a system, it is possible, and for many purposes necessary, to be meticulous about classifying various forms of system intervention. But, my rough purpose is more readily served by a simple distinction. Programs relate to a single part of the system; policy seeks to respond to the system in its entirety.

The idea of policy is not new. We have for long been accustomed to the idea of foreign policy, including defense policy. Since 1946 Congress has mandated an employment and income policy more or less explicitly based on a "general theory" of the endlessly intricate interconnections of such matters. Yet our ways of behavior resist this: only great crises, great dangers, seem to evoke the effort. Or have seemed able to do so in the past. I believe, however, that a learning process of sorts has been going on. Increasingly the idea of system-wide policies commends itself to persons of responsibility in public affairs as an approach both desirable and necessary. We can expect it to be one of the formative ideas of the 1970s.

CONSTITUENCIES AND MASTERS

As in most times, it is the style, the approach, of the incumbent administration that has most to do with such matters. The first official act of President Nixon, taken his third day in office, was to establish the Urban Affairs Council, a cabinet level body. The first task assigned the council was to "advise and assist" the President in the formulation of a National Urban Policy. This was something new. It had not been done before; no one was certain it could be done. No one is as yet certain it can be done successfully. Certainly there did not exist anything like Keynes's General Theory which guided our development of national policy on employment and income. Nor were there any Admiral Mahans or George Kennans to provide a master theory of an urban policy comparable to previous formulations of foreign and defense policy. Even so, the process went forward with fair dispatch, so that for anyone caring to know the general outlines of the urban policy of the present administration there is at least a document. Not a definitive one, nor even perhaps a comprehensive one; but an existing one. (*I do not infer that this urban policy has had any great consequence. It has not. Only a small element in either the political or career bureaucracy of the federal government has grasped the policy concept, and where it has been understood it has on the whole been opposed. It will be years— if ever—before the Presidential initiative will have any real consequence.** Changing the federal system is immensely difficult. Thus, the PPBS system [Planning—Programming—Budgeting System] was introduced in the mid-1960s with great energy and visibility, and strong Presidential support. By the end of the decade it had all but disappeared as an element in decision-making, at least at the higher levels of government. For purpose of provoking a discussion, I would be prepared to assert that the McNamara colonization of the domestic departments of the federal government with the system of benefit-cost analysis developed in the Pentagon failed. A primary source of failure was the lack of talent to carry out the analyses involved. Other sources were the resistance of the program bureaucracies, and probably also the insensitivity of PPBS analysis to the actual complexities of social interventions, a point argued in this paper.)

It is not my purpose here to discuss urban policy, but rather to suggest some of the principles which distinguish policy formulation from program formulation. The rules of the latter are, I should think, fairly well laid out in the descriptive political science of our time. The defining characteristic of a program is that it is directed to a specific situation with the purpose of maintaining or changing that situation in some desired fashion. We have programs to build roads, subsidize the growing of cotton, cure

---

* The essentials of this policy were presented in an address I gave at Syracuse University in the spring of 1969, later published in an article, "Toward a National Urban Policy," in *The Public Interest* (Fall 1969). Note how quickly—by the spring of 1970—the failure of the policy to "take" was evident. I would cite two considerations not so clear at the time this paper appeared. First, with respect to urban affairs, the Nixon administration was made up mostly of good men incapable of complexity, or complex men incapable of goodness. Each type avoided the idea of policy. But so did critics of the administration, many of whom explicitly called for the formulation of a "national urban policy" without ever acknowledging that a first approximation has been attempted.

cancer, retrain the unemployed. To be sure, there are programs that are quite general in their outlook; but here, with respect to the federal government and indeed to all levels and forms of government within the United States with which I am familiar, any tendency toward universality is immediately constricted by the structure of government. Doubtless there are even programs that would wish to evolve into policies, but reality is quickly enough imposed on them by the fact that one bureau in one department is responsible for performing the function involved; one branch of one division in the Bureau of the Budget handles the appropriation request; one super-specific subcommittee of one special committee of the Congress handles the substantive legislation, and an equivalent subcommittee handles the provision of funds. These are the constituencies of the program, and also its masters. It is a wise program that knows its place, and does not aspire beyond its station.

It would be foolish to be disdainful of such enterprises. Burke's dictum that the law sharpens the mind by narrowing it may be usefully applied to the program approach to social problems. Social commitments are not easy to sustain, certainly not over the long span of time which most social problems require. The program approach is designed to enhance the capacity of the enterprise to survive by narrowing its range of activity and intensifying the support for it. Come hell or high water, come Republicans, Democrats, or Free Silverites, the Bureau of Disabled Appalachian Urban Agronomists gets its appropriation and does next year the job it did last year. A quality, I repeat, not to be disdained.

But for all the plain-as-a-stick practicality about such arrangements, in the end they are self-defeating. They are in their way "realistic," but they do not adequately reflect a large enough part of reality. In fact, they will usually end by distorting reality. This is the essence of the problem.

By contrast, a policy approach to government does at least begin by seeking to encompass the largest possible range of phenomena and concerns. This has its dangers, its difficulties. But I shall argue that increasingly there is no respectable alternative. Knowing what we do about the nature of society and of social interventions, we have no option but to seek to deal in terms of the entire society, and all the consequences of intervention. One might wish for a simpler time when such knowledge was not available, but the loss of innocence is an old experience to mankind, and not perhaps to be avoided. Certainly not to be reversed.

THE ASSUMPTIONS OF A POLICY APPROACH

Let me then propose three propositions—I shall call them master propositions—that relate to a concept of government by policy as distinguished from government by program.

First is the familiar proposition that everything relates to everything. This is the fact that defines a system. Taken too literally it can be a bit traumatizing, but fortunately some things relate more than others. And it usually is possible to identify those components that in fact have the greatest influence.

The second master proposition is that from the fact that everything relates to everything it follows that there are no social interests about which the national government does not have some policy or other, simply by virtue of the indirect influences of programs nominally directed to other areas. These are *the hidden policies* of government.

This is not such a familiar proposition. The interconnections of programs directed to one area with outcomes in another are sometimes seen. Most of us have by now got it fairly straight that, for example, agricultural research can lead to the migration of farm populations, which has consequences for cities. But by and large these connections need to be pretty evident for much note to be taken of them, and ability to detect them is much influenced by intellectual and political fashion. It is fashion that dictates that some activities are interesting; others not. And if a subject is not interesting, it can have consequences all over the place of which no one is likely to take much heed.

Permit me an example. One of the received truths of contemporary liberal history is that no domestic initiatives of any consequence occurred during the Eisenhower Presidency. I will not contest the general point that was a period of relatively "low governmental profile," as the phrase now goes, following twenty years of the alarums and exertions of the New Deal and Fair Deal. Even so, there was one program of truly transcendent, continental consequence. This was a program which the twenty-first century will almost certainly judge to have had more influence on the shape and development of American cities, the distribution of population within metropolitan areas and across the nation as a whole, the location of industry and various kinds of employment opportunities (and, through all these, immense influence on race relations and the welfare of black Americans) than any initiative of the middle third of the twentieth century. This was, of course, the Interstate and Defense Highway System. It has been, it is, the largest public-works program in history. Activities such as urban renewal, public housing, community development, and the like are reduced to mere digressions when compared to the extraordinary impact of the highway program.

Once approved and begun, one would imagine it would have become the object of extraordinary interest, comment, and critique. If nothing of the sort occurred, the explanation would seem evident. Highways have never been a subject of any very great interest among persons given to writing or speculating about government. Certainly they have rarely been associated with social-welfare issues, save in the early days of "getting the farmer out of the mud." Further, the politics of getting the Interstate Highway program enacted decreed, or at least indicated, the narrowest possible definition of its purpose and impact. This was altogether agreeable to the Bureau of Public Roads, the slightly obscure organization established in the 1930s as a unit of the Department of Agriculture and shifted by degrees to the shadowy recesses of the Department of Commerce. The permanent staff of the Bureau of Public Roads had neither the inclination nor training to assert that they were doing anything more than obeying the narrow terms of their project descriptions. As bureaucrats, their instinct was faultless. Had anyone realized what they were in fact doing, the sheer magnitude of the interests they were affecting, it is nigh impossible to imagine that they would have won acceptance. Indeed a bare fifteen years after the Interstate program commenced, it is just about impossible to get a major highway program approved in most large American cities. But it is too late: most systems have already been built. In the process —such at least would be my view—quite appalling mistakes were made, but they were mistakes having to do with issues nominally altogether unrelated to the highway program itself, and so no one was responsible for them.

Surely it is possible to hope for something more. Government must seek out its hidden policies, raising them to a level of consciousness and acceptance—or rejection—and acknowledge the extraordinary range of contradictions that are typically encountered. (To the frequent question "Why don't government programs work?" it is often a truthful answer that they do work. It is just that so frequently the effect of a "hidden" program cancels out the avowed one.) Surely also it is possible to hope for a career civil service that is not only encouraged but required to see its activities in the largest possible scope. There are few things that ought more to annoy us than the misuse we make of such splendidly competent organizations as the Bureau of Public Roads. It is fully capable of making the most complex calculations of the effects of its programs (and increasingly does just that) but for many a long decade the word from the political world on high was to stick to building roads and to see that not too much sand was used in the concrete.

The third master proposition is clearly the least familiar of all, the one least likely of acceptance. It is not a matter that can be confidently demonstrated, or so at least would be my impression. It is rather the best available explanation for recurrent phenomena which increasingly demand explanation. I refer to what Jay Forrester has termed the "counterintuitive" nature of social problems. We learn to think, Forrester assures us, in simple loop systems. But social problems arise out of complex systems. The two are not alike, or so it is asserted by men who ought to know. They have fundamentally different properties, such that good common-sense judgment about the one will lead with fair predictability to illusions about the other. Thus Forrester: "With a high degree of confidence we can say that the intuitive solution to the problems of complex social systems will be wrong most of the time."

GRASPING COMPLEX SYSTEMS

Whatever the absolute nature of a proposition such as that, one surely can agree with Forrester that social systems have internal regulatory mechanisms that are, in effect, incentives (or disincentives) to behave in various ways. Just as surely, changing those incentives is an extraordinarily complex job. Surely also, too many programs of social intervention in the 1960s went about this extraordinarily complex task in a fairly simpleminded manner, usually just adding a few counterincentives to the prevailing incentive system. Stated perhaps too simply: the federal government has typically entered a situation in which most actors manifestly had strong incentives to act in ways which were not thought good for the larger society, or for the individuals involved, or both; incentives were offered to reverse the undesired behavior; but too commonly these incentives proved weak and ineffective when compared to the original set.

We should be clear, I think, that if this third proposition proves to be unavoidably the case, there are contained within it rather serious implications for the democratic direction of society. It is the old—or new—question of the expert again. I have gone on record as having a certain suspicion of intellectuals myself, and I think we all should, whatever the shape of our heads. Still, we have grown accustomed to depending on experts in science, and have developed reasonably appropriate ways of translating scientific and technological knowledge into forms of public action by statesmen. The problem arises with regard to social knowledge because, while most everyone will accept that he or she doesn't know much about implosion, everyone thinks he knows a lot about what makes a good school. And now men of unquestioned competence and good will are coming along with the information that what everyone knows about schools is almost precisely what is *not* the case. What do we do about that? What confidence are the people to have in their own judgment if such events multiply, as almost certainly they will?

I believe there is an answer to this. We must develop a new journalism, and political leadership, capable of handling information and of translating it into valid terms of public debate. But this will not be easy. I cannot imagine it happening inside a generation.

In the meantime, the one thing most likely to help us through the period of transition is the practice of thinking in terms of policy rather than of program. The policy-frame-of-mind may not grasp all the interrelations and surprises implicit in social problems, but it does at least start out with the expectation that there are such, and so is not only more on the alert for signals of such problems, but also is least resistant, least unbelieving, in the face of the evidence. That is no small thing.

Neither is it any small thing that we should begin to try to take this large view of events. If there is a tendency in our land, as in any, to complacency about many of the conditions of our lives, there is also, I would submit, an almost equal and very nearly opposite tendency to alarm. If man is a problem-solving animal, *homo Americanus* is also a problem-discovering one. The fact is that in our eagerness to draw attention to problems, we do frequently tend to make them seem worse than they are. In particular we tend to depict things as worsening when in fact they are improving.

This tendency arises from any number of sources. Three at least come to mind. There is surely a Protestant tendency to be dissatisfied with what might be called normal human behavior. On top of this we have of late had to learn to live with the burden of affluence. (Robert Nisbet frequently reminds us that boredom is the most underrated force in history. Heaven protect the land whose privileged classes get bored with their privileges, as clearly ours has done!) And there is also the tyranny of fashion: a mysterious force but an open enough one. Fashions of thought get set, and for a period at least they prevail. Evidence to the contrary is treated not as information but as wrongdoing, and woe betide the bearer of such news. The more, then, should we welcome a policy approach to social issues, simply because it insists on setting all specifics in a general context.

THE TREND OF RACE RELATIONS

An example of surpassing importance—or so it would seem to me—concerns the state of race relations in the United States at this moment. Are things getting better as most of us would define that term—namely, are we moving away from a past of racism and caste exclusion—or are they getting worse? I would believe it fair to say that the fashion of late has been to believe things are getting worse, and I can attest that it is costly to argue otherwise. And yet the data, such as they are, argue that indeed things are *not* getting worse. To the contrary, the Newsletter of the University of Michigan Institute of Social Research recently summarized the findings to this effect by Angus Campbell and others of the University's Survey Research Center, which we would all, I think, acknowledge as one of the four or five leading institutions of its type in the world.

The white backlash and the deterioration of white and black attitudes toward integration which have been noted by many social observers do not show up in the findings of a recent Survey Research Center nationwide survey.

"There is evidence that, in some respects, blacks and whites are in closer contact and more friendly contact than they had been for years earlier," Angus Campbell, director of SRC, reports.

The SRC data, gathered during the 1964 and 1968 election studies, represented possibly the only carefully designed academic study of national attitudes before and after the 1967 riots. They stand in marked contrast to the conclusion drawn by the Kerner Commission appointed by President Lyndon Johnson to study the riots. The Commission reported in March of 1968 that, "Our nation is moving toward two societies, one black, one white—separate and unequal."

In comparing racial attitudes over the four-year period, the SRC survey notes that whites favoring desegregation in 1968 outnumbered strict segregationists by a ratio of nearly two to one (31 and 16 percent respectively). Four years earlier whites had been about evenly divided on the question of desegregation or strict segregation (27 to 24 percent).

Although the doctrine of black separatism has been increasingly voiced by some members of the black community, it still has only minority support; and there has been little change in black attitudes toward desegregation over the four-year period. For example, in 1964 some 72 percent of the blacks questioned said they were in favor of desegregation (with only 6 percent favoring strict segregation) and four years later 75 percent were favoring desegregation (with only 3 percent for strict segregation).

Campbell indicates that not only were the attitudes toward desegregation more positive, actual contacts between the races seem to have increased. Whites and blacks were less likely in 1968 than in 1964 to say their neighborhoods or their schools were completely segregated. And whites were less likely to work and shop in all-white areas.

The percent of whites who said they live in all-white neighborhoods dropped from 80 to 75 percent, while the number of blacks living in all-black neighborhoods went from 33 percent to 25 percent.

In 1964, 43 percent of whites reported that the high school nearest them was all white.

That figure had dropped to 27 percent by 1968. Similarly, blacks reporting their nearest high school as all black dropped from 36 percent to 21 percent over the four years.

Whites who reported working in an all-white environment totaled 54 percent in 1964, but that number had dropped to 42 percent by 1968.

One might account for the reported increases in contact between the races on the ground that they don't represent real shifts in neighborhood and school population—just more awareness of each other's presence. The increase in publicity surrounding racial issues might have changed people's perception.

Campbell doesn't think so: "People now are more sensitive than they were four years ago but it's highly unlikely that the figures represent purely imaginary increased contact."

POVERTY AND POLICY

Similarly, a policy approach to government has profound consequences on the kinds of programs which are supported and pursued. I would suggest to you that this has been the case with respect to the problem of poverty and racial isolation in the nation. During the 1960s a quite extraordinary commitment was made by the national government to put an end to poverty. Yet the effort to do so went forward in entirely too fragmented a manner. In effect, a collection of programs was put together and it was hoped these would somehow add up to a policy. I don't believe they did. Nor do I believe there was any way we were likely to have found this out save by the route we did in fact follow. But after a point this became evident enough, and it became possible for the government to respond in terms of large-scale policy, and to fit programs to that policy.

The two basic networks of a modern society are the family structure and the occupational structure. A stable society attends to each. The preeminent arbiter of family stability is income. If social science has taught us anything, it is that. Income typically derives from employment, but also typically there are individuals and on occasion groups in the society whose income is not sufficient, either because employment is spasmodic or their skills insufficient to earn an adequate wage. Whatever the case, an effective war on poverty requires a strategy that deals first of all with problems of jobs and income. Once that became clear, it was relatively easy for the national government to develop programs in response.

Let me offer you an almost absurdly simple example. The federal government commenced in 1965 a formal policy of abolishing poverty. The Office of Economic Opportunity was established with that purpose in mind. But until 1970 almost a third of the expenditures of OEO were provided, in effect, by income taxes collected from the poor! Since it has been in the nature of the "services strategy" so much in evidence in early OEO programs to hire middle-class persons to be of assistance to poor persons, the actual *income transfer effect* of many of these OEO programs was to take money from farm laborers and give it to college graduates. No one intended it that way, but that was the unintended consequence of programs being operated in the absence of policy. Almost the first measure President Nixon proposed in this area upon taking office was to abolish income taxes for the poor, and this was done with the completely willing cooperation of the Congress once the absurdity of the previous arrangement was pointed out.

In a similar vein is the Family Assistance Plan which has, properly I would think, been termed the most important piece of domestic legislation to come before the Congress in four decades. The principle of the program is simple and it derives from policy. Families must have an adequate income, and this should be provided them with a minimum effect on their status as stable, self-determining units in society, and with maximum incentive to earn by their own efforts as large a proportion of their needed income as they possibly can. The President accordingly proposed to place a floor under the income of every American family with children, to provide within that context a specific incentive to work, specific opportunities for work training and placement, and the absolutely crucial provision that this assistance will not be conditioned on dependency. A family does not have to be down and out, busted and broken to get help, when often as not all that was needed at a particular moment was a relatively small bit of help at the margin.

DEFINING SUCCESS

Could such a program succeed? None of us could say right now. But there is one essential aspect to such a question—a question directed to a program that derives from a policy. Namely, that the question can be answered. Such a program would be deemed successful if in the aftermath of its enactment the number of dependent families in the nation begins to level off and then to turn down, both in terms of actual numbers and overall proportions. It is as simple as that to define success for a policy. Yet such definition is the one thing that often defies all effort when applied to programs.

This is the final point I would make about the concept of national policy with respect to social programs. It is a concept most explicitly outlined in the 1970 Presidential message to the Congress on Elementary and Secondary Education. *The test of a program, when this program is part of a policy, is not input but output.* It is interesting, and at times important, to know how much money is spent on schools in a particular neighborhood or city. But the crucial question is how much do the children learn. Programs are for people, not for bureaucracies. This is the final, as I say, and probably also the most important lesson of the policy approach to government.

On Universal Higher Education

16

I shall forgo the ritual of asserting what a pleasure and honor it is to present a paper to the American Council on Education, the one organization that most fully and faithfully represents the views and interests of higher education in the United States. Honor it remains, but to describe it as a pleasure would be to invite disbelief at the very outset. Anyone who attempts a serious statement about higher education at this moment courts serious trouble. In 1967, writing in *The American Scholar* I invoked Joyce's formula: "silence, exile, cunning." Nothing in the interval has changed my mind. I respond not to any sense of opportunity, but merely to dull Duty, Virtue's residue, Reason's remnant.

Duty is a conception that is all the more elusive for being familiar. It denotes something more than obligation, but nonetheless begins there. One service performed in return for another. In this instance I have not the least difficulty in perceiving and in acknowledging just where my indebtedness lies. For two decades now I have had access on the most generous bases to the worlds of government, of social science, and of university ad-

"On Universal Higher Education" was read before the annual meeting of the American Council on Higher Education, October 1970. It was first published in the *Educational Record*, Winter 1971.

ministration. Something is owed in return for that experience. At very least it involves the obligation to offer in a time of trouble such advice as may be asked for. This will be my purpose—to consider from the point of view of government a subject of considerable concern to education, namely, the subject of "Higher Education for Everybody?"

That government must be a party to any such decision will not, I would hope, be disputed. Elite education can be paid for by elites. Universal education must be paid for by taxes. That is all there is to that, save to note that given this ineluctability political science ought to explore this relationship, and may even be of some use in facilitating it.

This ought to be especially so at the present moment. Few things are more depressing to a social scientist than crisis mongering—especially of the sort we have witnessed over the past decade or so, when social scientists themselves have been the principal culprits. But there *are* such things as genuine crises, and one has come along in higher education. The present situation was fairly described in the opening statement of the 1970 report of the President's Commission on Campus Unrest: "The crisis on American campuses has no parallel in the history of the nation."

Let me state forthwith that a crisis for the campus is by no means necessarily a crisis for the society at large. It is easy to confuse or to equate the two. But crisis there is, and this has considerable consequences for the question of whether and how we are to move from our present situation, of mass higher education, to a universal practice.

In 1964 Earl J. McGrath assembled a group of us to consider this subject, and I believe it fair to state that we began our consideration with the assumption that our society was working its way in the direction of universal higher education. This certainly was my assumption, and I began my contribution to the volume that subsequently appeared with the assertion that the time had come to get on with the detailed business of specifying exactly what we would need to do, because clearly we were going to do it.

A point is reached in the development of any major social standard when the ability to conceive must be succeeded by the capacity to measure. That point is clearly at hand with regard to the question of universal opportunity for higher education.

American society has been working toward this standard for some generations now; in a sense, from the outset. The average level of education has steadily advanced; we have in the past two decades reached the point where a very large number of persons go on from secondary to higher education. With the resulting advantage both to the nation and to the individuals firmly established in terms of productivity, life income expectations, and the like, the comparative disadvantage of those who do not go on has become equally evident, whereupon the dynamics of a democratic and to some degree egalitarian society take hold and produce the demand that these opportunities be available to all.

Earlier that year I had drafted the portions of the Democratic Party platform concerned with education. It was, I believe, accurate to state, as I did, that the 1964 platform marked, in the 124-year sequence,

> . . . the transition from merely encouraging higher education to, in effect, insisting on it. The preceding platform had declared the belief "that America can meet its educational obligations" but had not really defined what those obligations might be. Rather, the 1960 document called for a series of specific categories of Federal assistance, leaving it for the future to determine just how much money and how many people would be involved. The 1964 platform, in contrast, said little about forms of assistance, but was explicit as to the objectives to be attained thereby.

> > Our task is to make the national purpose serve the human purpose: *that every person shall have the opportunity to become all that he or she is capable of becoming.*

> > We believe that knowledge is essential to individual freedom and to the conduct of a free society. We believe that education is the surest and most profitable investment a nation can make.

> > *Regardless of family financial status, therefore, education should be open to every boy or girl in America up to the highest level which he or she is able to master.*

It would hardly be fair to declare that all this is behind us, but surely what seemed an untroubled trajectory, a rather straightforward logarithmic projection, seems somehow less certain now. The course of events—the data—continue thus far pretty much as projected. But it is the projections that now come into question. Is it really likely that we will continue as we have?

It is necessary to ask what happened to call this seeming certainty into question.

This is a subject that has been widely and, on occasion, intelligently discussed. I would hope not so much to add to the discussion as to stress two points, familiar enough in themselves, but which appear to be of special consequence to the subject of universal higher education. The first point is that great dissatisfaction with mass education has arisen within the world of education itself, thereby necessarily casting a cloud on the prospect of proceeding from where we are to a situation which by simple extrapolation would presumably be even worse. The second point is that the growing politicization of higher education creates problems concerning continued public support for an ever larger and presumably more influential higher-education community.

It is not necessary for the present purpose to consider in great detail the sources of discontent. It is enough that discontent exists, and that it has assumed forms that are immediately threatening to the life of the university as such.

Witnesses abound. In his annual report to the Harvard Board of Overseers, Nathan Pusey described 1968–69 as "a dismal year" which in time will appear "to have been very costly." Gardner Ackley described 1969–70 as "a tragic year in the life of the University of Michigan—a year that has begun the destruction of this university as a great center of learning—destroyed not so much by outside forces as by the actions of its own faculty and administration."

Prognoses for the near future are as bad, although not, of course, necessarily correct. What this comes to is that the system isn't working very well, and that a large number of persons in the system appear to want it profoundly changed. It is hardly then to be assumed that there will be untroubled expansion of the present system from the point where about half the relevant age groups obtains some post-secondary education to the point where all, or almost all do so. The most generally agreed point is that the proportion of young persons who really would want and would benefit from higher education carried forth at traditional levels of intellect and discipline is limited. There is a genetic limitation, perhaps also a cultural one. Judgments will differ on just how large, or small, that proportion may be, but just about everyone agrees it is something considerably less than the proportion of students in higher education at this moment. Nathan Glazer writes:

> Higher education is not suited to training or apprenticeship, except for training and apprenticeship in learning itself. As a result, the colleges and universities filled with people who had no particular interest in what the institution had to offer, but had to undergo some unpleasant rite to take up decent and satisfying work.

If this is the case, as it appears to be, it is hardly then to be assumed that there will be an untroubled expansion of the present system to the point where everyone receives some kind of post-secondary education.

These limits are not imposed merely by a generalized public perception that all is not well on campus. To some degree at least the self-destructiveness of the higher education community has proceeded to the point where its capacity for expansion is limited. A good man has always been hard to find, and to find one for a serious position in academic administration or leadership is becoming very hard indeed. Stephen K. Bailey has been, I believe, most forthright on this not especially pleasant matter.

> As I watch the melancholy list grow of friends who have resigned (voluntarily or under duress) from college presidencies and school superintendencies during the past few years (or, more tragically, have dropped dead of heart attacks or have committed suicide), I begin to wonder how many contemporary educational leaders will survive the current educational revolution.
>
> Revolutions are insatiable maws—with cavernous appetite for men's lives and fortunes. The most civilized are a peculiar delicacy of the revolutionary appetite, for, unconsumed, they stand in the way of the necessary oversimplifications of the revolutionary mind. And they are readily betrayed into revolu-

tionary hands by the old guard, who always find perceptive consciences a threat and an embarrassment to the status quo.

Bailey's concern goes to the second of the two points I have indicated seem most relevant to the question of universal higher education, namely the growing politicization of the academic world. He speaks of the revolutionary appetite, the revolutionary mind. He is speaking about the rise on campus of activities directed toward shaping not just the character of the university community itself, but of the society at large.

This is a relatively recent event, the result of what Glazer has termed "the Berkeley invention," that is to say the joining of general political issues with specific university issues.

It seems to me that this relates in at least two ways to the issue of universal higher education. It has resulted in considerable measure from the rapid and recent expansion of higher education, such that sheer size gave political consequence to the views of dominant university opinions, and secondly from the fact that these opinions are increasingly opposed to those of the larger society.

What is at issue is an adversary culture firmly entrenched in higher education. The nature of this culture, the extent of its strength and its grip on the universities, as well as other institutions of acculturation, have come as a surprise to many. The patrician tradition and leadership of the most prestigious universities seems to me to have been painfully vulnerable in its initial encounters with this new reality. It seems to me that the individuals involved by and large could not understand or could not believe what suddenly was before their eyes, and in varying degrees panicked, collaborated, or simply collapsed. In this they displayed what I fear has been a problem in higher education, namely that its leaders have not been especially well educated. For all the spectacular minds that from time to time have been put in charge of our great institutions, on balance the leadership has been social and administrative—the right family or the right work habits—rather than intellectual.

We have paid and are paying a price for this. For example, it has become increasingly clear that in the early postwar period the radical impulse in politics moved over into the culture where it prospered as almost never before. Students fell silent about politics, and university administrators concluded that some strange malady or profound discontinuity had occurred. When in the course of the 1960s the radical impulse returned to politics, this time greatly strengthened and legitimized by the culture, administrators again concluded they were being confronted with something utterly new, altogether without precedent. We began to hear about the "youth culture." I for one would disagree. It seems to me that the present state of campus politics and manners represents a clear continuity with earlier forms, allowing only for changes of scale. For years now Lionel Trilling has been describing, defining, and projecting what he first termed "the adversary culture." Surely there are persons in authority in academia capable of understanding that Trilling is a most serious man, that, unlike some others perhaps, he really is trying to tell us something. Surely there are those capable of perceiving the polemical advantage of depicting a minority movement as a generational transformation. There is no justification for having been taken so utterly unawares.

I do not deny that some things have changed. For some time—by which I mean for years, not months—it has been evident that an almost classic form of nihilism has been taking root in upper-class culture in the United States. I so argued in a paper given in 1967, citing the analysis by Michael Polanyi of the bases of nihilist belief, and his superbly important aside that the nihilist argument, given its premises, had not been answered. The paper was duly published, and I subsequently learned from Polanyi that this was the first time anyone had referred to his earlier analysis. So far as I am aware it was also the last time, for not a murmur arose in response to my effort. How many university youngsters will have to blow up how many buildings before anyone begins to take Polanyi seriously is a question I will accordingly not seek to answer. But in a serious sense it can be said this knowledge was available to us had we cared to use it. It is simply that that work was not really taken seriously.

Nor has anyone grounds for being surprised at the increasing political ambitions and activities of the campus community. Writing in *Foreign Affairs* over three years ago Irving Kristol explained why this would happen, and what it would most likely mean. It would happen because the higher-education community had become large and important enough to serve as a viable base for intellectuals seeking "that species of power we call moral authority." A new class seems to have emerged.

> The politics of this new class is novel in that its locus of struggle is the college campus. One is shocked at this—we are used to thinking that politics ought not to intrude on the campus. But we shall no doubt get accustomed to the idea. Meanwhile, there is going to be a great deal of unpleasant turbulence. The academic community in the United States today has evolved into a new political constituency. College students, like their teachers, are "new men" who find the traditional student role too restrictive. Students and faculty therefore find it easy to combine their numbers and their energies for the purpose of social and political action. The first objective—already accomplished in large measure—is to weaken control of the administration and to dispossess it of its authoritative powers over campus activities. From this point the movement into politics proper—including elections—is about as predictable as anything can be.

Kristol was less confident concerning the consequences of this emergence save that they were not likely to be especially helpful.

> Just what direction this movement into politics will follow it is too early to say with certainty. Presumably, it will be toward "the left," since this is the historical orientation of the intellectual class as a whole. It is even possible that the movement will not be calmed until the United States has witnessed the transformation of its two-party system to make room for a mass party of the ideological left, as in most European countries—except that its "grass roots" will be on the campus rather than in the factory. But what is certain is that the national prestige and the international position of the United States are being adversely affected by this *sécession des clercs*. Imperial powers need social equilibrium at home if they are to act effectively in the world. It was possible to think, in the years immediately after World War II, that the United States had indeed achieved this kind of equilibrium—that consensus and equipoise at home would permit our statesmen to formulate and pursue a coherent foreign policy. But the "academic revolution" of the 1950s and 1960s raises this issue again, in a most problematic and urgent way.

Our concern here is not with the consequences for foreign policy, but rather with the effect of this academic revolution on the disposition of the public to support a continued movement toward universal higher education. It is impossible to know, and hazardous to speculate as to the answer to this question, but surely the presumption would have to be that public support will diminish, especially to the degree that the "academic" position is seen as hostile to the course of the larger polity in ways that are both hard to follow and hard to explain.

This is perhaps especially true of the present situation, in which so much of what university intellectuals detest about American foreign policy is so indisputably the product of American intellectuals. A consultant to the Special Committee on Campus Tensions which was established last year by the American Council on Education put this point with a certain acerbity.

> It wasn't the Mississippi tenant farmer who ordered the troops to Vietnam. More likely, and more specifically, it was the Harvard Junior Fellows—those who had maximum chance to develop intellectually.

Robert Nisbet has ascribed this to a "special kind of hubris that attacked the social sciences in this country in the 1950s." I have shared this view and agree. What one could wish for is a period of mild repentance. Instead the experience seems to have produced in many circles a kind of frustrated outrage of the kind Lenin might have described as an "infantile disorder," but which increasingly we are told is a virtuous rage to off the pigs and generally to punish working-class groups which are doubtless guilty of much wrongdoing, but which surely cannot be accused of having taken game theory too far in the evolution of the doctrine of counterinsurgency. This raises a further, and to my thinking, fundamental point about the increasing politicization of the university community. It is not likely to raise the quality, in the sense of the generally perceived effectiveness, of our politics. Kristol writes that "No modern nation has ever constructed a foreign policy that was acceptable to its intellectuals." I wonder if there is not a corollary that no group of modern intellectuals, when they have managed to get hold of a nation's foreign policy, has produced one satisfactory to the people at large. I don't know why this should be so—if indeed it is so—but I suspect it has something to do with an exaggerated notion of the power of intellectual analysis to master the political process. For reasons that I do not wholly comprehend, this has been accompanied by an increasing tendency among intellectuals in the modern era to be intolerant of deviations from prevailing doctrine, even contemptuous of dissent. Norman Podhoretz describes this as "the barbaric hostility to freedom of thought which by the late 1960s had become one of the hallmarks of [the radical] ethos." It was the practice of the university radicals of that period to compare the America of the Johnson administration to Hitler's Germany. It seems to me that only a serious abandonment of standards of evidence could make any such comparison even remotely credible. This was absurd. What one fears is not absurd is the growing conviction among critics *of* the left that the present era *can* be compared to the Weimar era in Germany, when the same devaluation and detestation of everything the polity was able to achieve was also the mark of the high intellectuals. One is struck, for example, by the echoes in our own times of Walter Z. Laqueur's account of Kurt Tucholsky and his circle.

> These were not insensitive men but they had no real roots themselves and, therefore, they lacked the sensorium for the patriotic feeling of their fellow-citizens. They were incapable of understanding anyone who reacted differently from the way they did.

For surely the manner persists. Aaron Wildavsky writes: "In the relation of the white elite to public issues there is a desire to condemn. There is a will to believe the worst. There is a compulsion to make events speak to the necessity of revolutionary change." Is this not almost a formula for lowering the level of esteem in which the elite institutions of advanced thought are held by the great mass of citizenry whose ideological life tends toward the unadventurous?

It is exactly that, and it is necessary to stay a moment with this point. Higher education in America, for all its size, remains a privilege. It is to some extent a generational privilege, separating old from young. But it is also a privilege among the young. Half get it. Half do not. Of those who do, far the most attractive arrangements are made for the children of the well-to-do, or for another and not less lucky group of persons who happen to be very smart. Of those who do not, the disadvantage is all the greater because they are so conspicuously chosen to be excluded.

This elite quality is not likely to change. The social composition of "high quality" American university is to the American social structure as a masked ball is to a mass movement. To be sure, one of the very best covers for class privilege is a passionate public concern with the underprivileged. But the sheer minority status of students and persons with higher education, and the fact of their vastly better prospects when compared with the rest of society, make it difficult to suppose their political demands will ever in our time acquire the legitimacy which democracies associate with majority opinion. Those seeking to induce the public to pay for universal higher education might usefully remember that only 11 percent of the adult population of the United States graduated from a four-year college. And despite the recent growth in college attendance, in 1985 that figure will have risen only to 14 or 15 percent. Put differently, 89 percent of American voters may or may not share the values and political inclinations associated with a college degree, but at all events they do not have the degree.

What this comes to is that the more politicized the universities become, the less public support they can expect. At least I believe this to be so. David Riesman, Nathan Glazer, and others have usefully questioned the notion that the economy, or the government, or the society at large genuinely "needs" to have a large number of young persons receiving higher education. We tend to cloak our idealist actions in pragmatic guise. The society pays for education because it is thought to be to the advantage of those who get it. If it should ever be widely perceived that the society itself is threatened in the process, we would have to expect that genuinely pragmatic considerations will come into play.

The Scranton Commission said as much.

> As a practical matter, it would be naive for universities that frequently or intensely involve themselves institutionally in controversial political issues to expect to retain the full financial and attitudinal support of a society to which they seem to be laying political siege.

A general change in public attitude, should it come, is likely to make an extraordinarily unpleasant impression on higher education communities which continue to enjoy among themselves a slightly beleaguered aura when in fact they are exceptionally free of outside pressures. In a study made for the American Council on Education in 1968, Heinz Eulau found that "legislative oversight of higher education is characterized by a norm of passivity." Constituents made few demands, and it was, in any event, assumed that the educators knew best. This assumption is eroding. Just last month at Berkeley Paul Seabury spoke of the university's "ominous and progressive estrangement from the people of California."

There is a poignant quality to this growing estrangement, namely that the encounter is so unequal. The silent majority, if you will accept that term, is silent not least because it finds it so difficult to say things in terms that will win a respectful hearing among those who judge such matters. Like Orwell's working class, it lives in a world not far removed from Victorian virtues. I for one find those virtues—confidence in the nation, love of the nation, a willingness to sacrifice for it—priceless. But the symbols of those beliefs are tattered, even at times tawdry. It is not fair. But it is true. Daniel Bell has recently stated the facts with an understanding but painful candor.

> . . . While minority life-styles and cultures have often conflicted with those of the majority, what is striking today is that the *majority* has no intellectually respectable culture of its own— no major figures in literature (the best is James Gould Cozzens), painting (except, perhaps, Andrew Wyeth), or poetry—to counterpose to the adversary culture. In this sense, bourgeois culture has been shattered.

If all this is true, it follows that higher education will increasingly come to stand for the humiliation of traditional America. It would then seem to follow that there will be some faltering in our apparent progress toward universal higher education. I expect there will be. But I would argue that it need be no more than that if we will be a bit more rigorous and also perhaps a bit more honest about the situation we are in, and try to respond accordingly.

This was the intent, and one hopes also the outcome, of the Presidential message to the Congress on Higher Education, sent in 1970.

The issue of universal higher education is a matter—I believe our data are now firm on this point—of primary concern to two groups: young persons from poor families, and those whose natural endowment is not such as would likely benefit from traditional forms of higher education. The message began by addressing itself to both these groups.

> No qualified student who wants to go to college should be barred by lack of money. That has long been a great American goal; I propose that we achieve it now.
>
> Something is basically unequal about opportunity for higher education when a young person whose family earns more than $15,000 a year is nine times more likely to attend college than a young person whose family earns less than $3,000.
>
> Something is basically wrong with Federal policy toward higher education when it has failed to correct this inequity, and when Government programs spending $5.3 billion yearly have largely been disjointed, ill-directed, and without a coherent long-range plan.
>
> Something is wrong with our higher education policy when— on the threshold of a decade in which enrollments will increase almost 50 percent—not nearly enough attention is focused on the two-year community colleges so important to the careers of so many young people.

The President went on to propose the Higher Education Opportunity Act of 1970, a series of measures which would greatly expand loan funds available to students in higher education, but with the unprecedented provision that the overall Federal program would be administered so that there would be, in effect, no such thing as a student from a poor family. That is to say, Federal subsidies would be used in such a way that the resources available to poor students would be brought up to the level of middle-income students. Another way of stating this is that the economic disadvantage of the bottom half of the income distribution would be eliminated. (To the degree that a Federal subsidy program can do this.) There is, in effect, no bottom half.

At the same time, students from the upper half of the income distribution would be assured the availability of loan funds, not so heavily subsidized as in the past, but still carrying the important discount associated with a Federal guarantee. The President stated:

> With the passage of this legislation, every low-income student entering an accredited college would be eligible for a combination of Federal grants and subsidized loans sufficient to give him the same ability to pay as a student from a family earning $10,000.
>
> With the passage of this legislation, every qualified student would be able to augment his own resources with Federally guaranteed loans, but Federal subsidies would be directed to students who need them most.

I believe it is fair to say that this is a proposal without precedent in American history. It would establish the conditions of universal higher education, and leave the outcome to the free choice of the young persons involved.

(It is important to be firm on this point. Not everyone will want to continue his education beyond high school or even through high school. I would be most dubious of a society that did any more than point out the likely advantages, make it possible to continue, and leave it to the individual to decide.)

Passage of the Higher Education Opportunity Act of 1970 would in effect establish the national goal of universal higher education. It is time we did just that.

The President simultaneously proposed a Career Education Program, funded at $100 million in fiscal 1972 "to assist States and institutions in meeting the additional costs of starting new programs to teach critically needed skills in community colleges and technical institutes." This seems to be an indispensable adjunct to any large expansion of the numbers of persons receiving post-secondary education.

What then impedes the passage of this historic legislation? For, surely, nothing whatever has happened in the Congress, and, more importantly, the proposal has been greeted with near silence on the campuses. The Scranton Commission was specific and enthusiastic in its endorsement of the legislation. Clark Kerr, who heads the Carnegie Commission on Higher Education, has spoken warmly of the message, and has noted with justice how closely the proposals parallel some of the Commission's. But on balance the response would have to be described as indifference in the Congress and embarrassed silence or even suspicion in the world of higher education.

There are some who have said the university elite has been silent about this bill because it likes to talk about equal opportunity, but wants nothing to do with it. For my part I reject any such notion. The record of higher education in America is manifestly otherwise, in the sense of what it has done with the resources available to it.

I suggest another reason, namely that the universities are so preoccupied with internal problems—the difficulty of managing what now exists—that they cannot for the moment give much thought to the larger problem of expansion.

The essential issue of higher education at this moment—the issue, that is, which is central to those responsible for it—is not that of expansion, but rather of maintaining what now exists. There is hardly a major educational institution in the nation— and this is likely soon to be true of many of our smaller and more specialized institutions—that does not now face a crisis of governance and a crisis of finance.

The latter is a situation in which the Federal government is inevitably involved. It seems to me that the task of statesmanship in the decade ahead will be to ensure that involvement with the financing of higher education does not lead to involvement with governance.

This will not be easy. The Federal government provides almost a quarter of the funds that go to support higher education, and a far greater proportion of the moneys available for research. This is a situation with considerable historical precedent. Washington raised the subject in his Inaugural Address. But only in the past three decades has Federal involvement risen to critical levels. The problem is that, as with so many Federal initiatives, we have seen a vast proliferation of programs without the formulation of any coherent policy.

Hence President Nixon first spoke on this subject in March 1969, barely nine weeks in office. In the context of the turbulence and alarm and recrimination that has so much characterized higher education in all its governmental relations in recent years, it is useful to recall that statement. The President began with the assertion that the crisis, of which I have been talking, was clearly upon us. The essence of the crisis was the preservation of intellectual freedom and the avoidance of politicization.

> Freedom—intellectual freedom—is in danger in America. The nature and content of that danger is as clear as any one thing could be. Violence—physical violence, physical intimidation—is seemingly on its way to becoming an accepted, or at all events a normal and not to be avoided, element in the clash of opinion within university confines. Increasingly it is clear that this violence is directed to a clearly perceived and altogether too conceivable objective: not only to politicize the student bodies of our educational institutions, but to politicize the institutions as well. Anyone with the least understanding of the history of freedom will know that this has invariably meant not only political disaster to those nations that have submitted to such forces of obfuscation and repression, but cultural calamity as well. It is not too strong a statement to declare that this is the way civilizations begin to die.
>
> The process is altogether too familiar to those who would survey the wreckage of history. Assault and counterassault, one extreme leading to the opposite extreme; the voices of reason and calm discredited. As Yeats foresaw: "Things fall apart; the centre cannot hold . . ." None of us has the right to suppose it cannot happen here.

Thereupon the President asserted the fundamental point of Federal policy, namely that intellectual freedom within the colleges and universities of the land was something that could only be preserved by internal efforts, that it could not be imposed by external force.

> The first thing to do at such moments is to reassert first principles. The Federal government cannot, should not—must not— enforce such principles. That is fundamentally the task and the responsibility of the university community. But any may state what these principles are, for they are as widely understood as they are cherished.
>
> First, that universities and colleges are places of excellence in which men are judged by achievement and merit in defined areas. The independence and competence of the faculty, the commitment, and equally the competence, of the student body, are matters not to be compromised. The singular fact of American

society—the fact which very likely distinguishes us most markedly from any other nation on earth, is that in the untroubled pursuit of an application of this principle we have created the largest, most democratic, most open system of higher learning in history. None need fear the continued application of those principles; but all must dread their erosion. The second principle—and I would argue, the only other—is that violence or the threat of violence may never be permitted to influence the actions or judgments of the university community. Once it does, the community, almost by definition, ceases to be a university.

This was done early. What followed was a prolonged, and as would be expected, complex effort to translate policy into program. Here the administration emerged with a fundamental conclusion: Increasingly it appeared to us that reliance on categorical aid programs as the principal source of Federal support for higher education is fundamentally subversive of the principle of noninterference. A categorical aid program is by definition a form of Federal interference in the internal affairs and priorities of the university community.

A measure of history is required here, of which the first element is the growth of higher education associated with the growth of categorical aid programs.

Between 1945 and 1970 the number of enrolled students more than quadrupled. The ratio of college and university students to the total population of the country nearly tripled, such that 3.3 percent of all Americans were enrolled for degree credit in postsecondary institutions. The total annual cost multiplied twentyfold; the amount of the Federal share went from one-sixth to almost one-fourth of the total budget. This over a period when the nation's population rose less than 50 percent (from 140 million to 200 million), when the Gross National Product rose less than fivefold, and when the total budget of the Federal government only doubled. Higher education has been one of the fastest growing sectors of our national life. In 1945, it accounted for approximately one-half of one percent of the GNP; by last year, it had more than quintupled, rising to 2.6 percent of the Gross National Product.

Let us for a moment turn to the *nature* of the Federal government's role in higher education, as it has evolved since the Morrill

Act. I should like to borrow heavily from an excellent summary prepared for the Carnegie Commission by Ronald A. Wolk. Until the Second World War, Federal aid to higher education was all but nonexistent. In the school year 1939–40, Federal sources provided about 5 percent of the total income of institutions of higher education. As I have mentioned, by 1945 that share had grown to 16 percent. This extraordinary rise, from an almost-inconsequential share to a very important one over five years time, reflects the mammoth wartime research and development effort, in which universities shared so nobly and so dramatically; and, of course, the G.I. bill, which, in Wolk's words, "paved the way for the most dramatic enrollment explosion in the history of higher education."

Aside from the large numbers of students whose way was now, for the first time, paid by the Federal government, the principal beneficiary of government spending in universities during the War was large-scale academic science. Although scientific research received its first Federal boost from the Morrill Act itself, I think most students of the history of American higher education would agree that the principal effect was on agricultural research and that, although this helped ensure the beginning of science and scientific research as we have come to understand them, they were relatively minor operations until the Second World War. The enormous expansion of chemistry, physics, biology, engineering, and their derivative fields came from the Federal government; but it is absolutely essential to remember that this expansion reflected the fact that *the Federal government wanted it to happen*. The universities were put to work on behalf of goals and activities deemed by government officials to be in the national interest.

In his 1970 message President Nixon was about as open on this point as I think a Chief Executive ought to be.

> For three decades now the Federal Government has been hiring universities to do work it wanted done. In far the greatest measure, this work has been in the national interest, and the Nation is in the debt of those universities that have so brilliantly performed it. But the time has come for the Federal Government to help academic communities to pursue excellence and reform in fields of their own choosing as well, and by means of their own choice.

The extent to which it has been the Federal government that has done the choosing of late simply cannot be overestimated. Wolk reminds us that "Some $15 million in Federal funds went to higher education for research in 1940—almost exclusively for agricultural research. In 1944 alone, a single agency (the Office of Scientific Research and Development) spent $90 million on contracts with the Universities."

Despite the postwar cutbacks, the Federal investment in university-sponsored research and development continued to grow. And after the launching of Sputnik it grew very quickly indeed. "In 1955–56, the Federal government spent about $355 million on academic research and development; a decade later, the amount reached $1.3 billion." I emphasize scientific research because it is probably the biggest example of the effect of Federal support on higher education: mammoth and rapid expansion, so big and so fast as to be quite exhilarating for all concerned; but accompanied by a clear case of Federal domination of the directions in which higher education moved. The government was still hiring the universities to do its bidding. In retrospect, this is perfectly clear. At the time, the huge amounts and rapid expansion made it look to many academics as though the Federal government was underwriting them to do as they liked. But that was an illusion; the clear fact was that the Congress and the Executive deemed the expansion and improvement of American science to be in the national interest; and that is what they hired universities to do, no matter how lax the rules may have seemed at the time.

Much the same may be said of student aid. It has come in three waves, all within the last quarter-century. First was the G.I. bill, demonstrating the nation's gratitude to its veterans and its commitment to educate and employ them after the War that they won. In the fifties was the National Defense Education Act, which gave money to people to go to college because the government felt an acute need to upgrade American education, especially school teaching; hence the teacher forgiveness provisions of NDEA. And in the sixties, of course, has come a wide assortment of programs that provide Federal aid for disadvantaged students to attend college, again because the government, reflecting a national concern, decided that this was an important national purpose.

At no point in this process would I judge that the higher-education community had control over its own destiny, at least insofar as its destiny was shaped by Federal funds. I think we in the academic community tended to absorb and assimilate each new Federal intrusion, concluding after-the-fact that we must have wanted it, and not bridling at requests that might have seemed outrageous were they not accompanied by large sums of the taxpayer's money. There are exceptions, of course, such as Harvard's refusal to undertake classified research; but only the wealthy could afford to preserve their virtue in the light of generous and repeated propositions.

Categorical aid is just about all there has been. As Wolk says, "Virtually all of the $4.6 billion in Federal aid to higher education in 1967 could be described as categorical aid, in the sense that the Federal government has categorized or designated its funds to be spent in certain areas which it has deemed to be of national concern."

I would suggest to you that back in the days when Federal aid comprised 5 percent or less of university budgets, the fact that such aid came through categorical programs had, at most, a marginal effect on higher education. But in an era when the Federal share approaches a full one-quarter of the budget, the effect is very powerful indeed. And the effect is primarily one of distortion of institutional purposes in pursuit of federally determined objectives.

That is why one is bemused when members of the academic community get upset over reductions in any one of the many categories of Federal aid. Such reductions—which are more than matched by increases elsewhere, total *Federal outlays for higher education having risen every single year since 1960*—simply reflect changed national interests, changed *priorities* if you will. When the higher-education community allowed itself to get into the business of accepting categorical grant money from the Federal government, it accepted an implicit condition, which was that no category was permanent or immutable. When a private institution allows itself to become dependent on support that is itself subject to the political process, it entangles itself in a sequence that it is largely powerless to control. And it certainly runs the *risk* of being victimized by the political forces that govern the money; but one would have to be paranoid indeed to think that the Federal government's *changes in emphasis* in recent years amounted to victimization. Let me repeat the point that total Federal outlays for higher education have grown in every one of the last ten years, and have grown dramatically, from *$1.1 billion in 1960 to about $5 billion in 1970,* thus sustaining a rising curve that has had few dips and no severe or lasting ones since the Second World War.

What has happened, of course, is that the categorical emphases have shifted; and, to be sure, the overall rate of growth has slowed in the higher-education segment of the Federal budget, as it has for the total budget and almost every other individual portion of it. During the decade of the 1960s education was the fastest-growing portion of the Federal budget; many would argue that it was only catching up to where it should be, was only receiving its due. I do not disagree. But it would be naive in the extreme to think that this "catch-up growth rate" would continue forever, particularly as the rate of growth in college enrollments has itself slowed; degree-credit enrollment in post-secondary institutions more than doubled from 1957 to 1967; although the projected increase in absolute numbers of students over the next decade, from 1967 to 1977, is about the same, the growth rate will be 50 percent rather than 100 percent.

In a political system, one man's raised priority is another man's reduced budget; one categorical program increased usually means another one diminished. It is perfectly understandable why anyone whose favorite program is cut is irritated, if not desolate. But that is the built-in risk of organizing institutions around categorical Federal support.

Not to know this is not to know how government operates. If many on the academic side of the exchange did not know much about government, the reverse ignorance has been just as much in evidence.

Higher education has been deemed important to the government only to the extent that it has accomplished particular purposes that the government deemed important, and could accomplish them more effectively, faster, or cheaper, than someone else. This sounds harsh, for we academics spend a good deal of time reassuring ourselves that universities and especially professors are vitally important to the future of the nation. But there is a crucial distinction to be made: something that is considered important to the *nation* by its proponents and beneficiaries becomes important to the *government* only insofar as those proponents and beneficiaries can convince the nation as a whole that it *is* important. And that it is worth the money—more so, at least, than competing claimants for the same funds. Even then, it does not become important in its own right, or in the terms in which its proponents view it; it becomes important to the government only in those terms that the nation has started to perceive as important. The result: another categorical program.

The three great bursts of Federal funds and categorical programs follow this pattern. During the Second World War, the nation perceived that higher education was important insofar as it could do the research and development necessary to win a modern war, and insofar as it could make veterans employable. Sputnik roused the nation to concern over the state of teaching in its schools, particularly in science, and over the state of elementary and secondary education in general. The newly awakened concern with poverty and opportunity in the early 1960s bred a sense that higher education could somehow ease the plight of the poor, the nonwhite, and the deprived. And in each case the Federal categorical programs that resulted were concentrated on these purposes, not on others. And each time the higher-education community not only accepted the money and adopted the purposes, but also came to view the programs and funds as its birthright, as something to which it was somehow entitled, rather than as a necessarily temporary response to a perceived condition.

The administration's response to this long-continued situation, which had so clearly become unviable, was to propose a fundamental shift in the form of Federal assistance to educational institutions, away from categorical aid toward general-purpose grants. A National Foundation for Higher Education was proposed, to be administered by a semiautonomous Board and Director appointed by the President. It would make grants to individual institutions, to States and communities, and to public and private agencies. The object was not simply to reverse the forms of Federal assistance, but in the measure possible to redress the imbalances that the earlier forms have wrought.

The President's message was explicit on this point.

One of the unique achievements of American higher education in the past century has been the standard of excellence that its leading institutions have set. The most serious threat posed by the present fiscal plight of higher education is the possible loss of that excellence.

But the crisis in higher education at this time is more than simply one of finances. It has to do with the uses to which the resources of higher education are put, as well as to the amount of those resources, and it is past time the Federal Government acknowledged its own responsibility for bringing about, through the forms of support it has given and the conditions of that support, a serious distortion of the activities of our centers of academic excellence.

The purposes he avowed are ones I would hope most of us might share. His concern was in no sense limited to the large or prestigious institutions. He referred also to "the community college mounting an outstanding program of technical education, the predominantly black college educating future leaders, the university turning toward new programs in ecology or oceanography, education or public administration."

To this end he proposed that the National Foundation have three principal purposes.

—To provide a source of funds for the support of excellence, new ideas and reform in higher education, which could be given out on the basis of the quality of the institutions and programs concerned.

—To strengthen colleges and universities or courses of instruction that play a uniquely valuable role in American higher education or that are faced with special difficulties.

—To provide an organization concerned, on the highest level, with the development of national policy in higher education.

Two hundred million dollars were budgeted for the Foundation's first year.

One would like to report that the response of higher education was positive with respect at least to this proposal, but I fear this was not the case either. Here and there approval was expressed. Here and there suspicion. But on balance there was no response. Quite serious efforts by the President, members of the Cabinet, and of the White House staff to explain the proposal and to elicit either support or some counterproposal came to nothing. Time after time such discussion would begin on a fairly high— and appropriate—level of general principles and within moments degenerate into a competitive and barely dignified clamor over this little categorical program or that.

Had we thought categorical aid had distorted the relations of the higher-education community to the Federal government before the program was announced, we were utterly convinced of the fact in the aftermath. Corrupted would not be too strong a term. *No one seemed able to think of the whole subject.* Few, even, seemed able to think of the interests of a single whole institution. A major presidential initiative which, right or wrong, was at very least the product of some thought and some analysis was greeted by silence on the part of precisely those institutions that are presumably devoted to thought and analysis.

Had there existed a powerful "higher-education lobby" which willy-nilly would push through great increases in existing programs, the sequence of events might be more explicable. (It is worth noting that in the course of five years the elementary and secondary school interests have created such a lobby in Washington.) But there was no such lobby, and the result was predictable. Congress did nothing. A 1970 newsletter of the American Council on Education reports that the chairman of the Subcommittee on Education had given up efforts to assemble a committee quorum to draft a comprehensive higher-education bill. "She said," the report continues, "she saw no chance of passing a higher education bill at this time because of concern over campus unrest."

And there we are left. I have hoped, earlier, to make clear a conviction that campus unrest is not going to go away. It is and will remain a condition of American society in the present era. (One would very much hope that campus violence will ebb, and that is surely a possibility. But the gulf between the campuses, especially the elite ones, and the rest of the society will persist.) The task of statesmanship would accordingly seem to be to fashion a system of Federal (and of course state and local) support for higher education which is as much as possible insulated from the political tempers of the time.

The campuses are almost surely going to continue to make quite extraordinary demands on the society at large. I repeat that this was predictable, and was predicted. The culture in this respect is extremely volatile, even in ways unstable. This is the result not of failure, but of success; not of the suppression of liberty, but of its extension. One recalls Bernard Shaw's prophecy: "Later on, liberty will not be . . . enough: men will die for human perfection, to which they will sacrifice all their liberty gladly." This is a condition we shall live with: threatening to the traditions of university and society alike. More then is the reason to address ourselves with something very like a sense of urgency to the question of how we are to preserve and expand higher education while maintaining a diverse society that will on occasion appear almost a dichotomous one.

Similarly the society will continue to make enormous demands on higher education. The circumstances that led to the categorical aid system of Federal support have not much changed. Indeed the demands for relevancy in higher education, and the presumption that university professors can do what mayors, governors, and even presidents cannot, is very much to be encountered at this time. Oscar and Mary Handlin have made unmistakably clear that this was the primordial expectation of American higher education. Higher education was to be "immediately useful and practical" if it was to receive public support. Useful in training ministers; useful in training farmers; useful in training technicians; useful in training social engineers. Indeed at times one wonders that education as such survived. All this will continue, albeit one would predict a certain withdrawal of the campuses in the period just ahead. (It was interesting to note the proposal of the Scranton Commission that "In general, we recommend an overall reduction in outside service commitments.") Here again the task of statesmanship will be to devise ways by which the services to institutions, private or public, off the campus, can be carried out in ways that maintain both the independence of the institution and its viability as a stable and creative society.

No small efforts these. Gigantic ones if they are to be combined with steady progress toward a national goal of universal higher education. New kinds of institutions will need to be invented. New forms of institutional governance, new types of teaching and new subjects to be taught. But to achieve this in, let us say, the next thirty years, would hardly involve a greater achievement, or greater change, than that of the past three decades.

There is only one respect in which the period ahead involves demands on higher education that are in ways novel. The demand is for national leadership. If there is to be fundamental reform in the relations between the national government and higher education there will have to be leadership on both sides, there will have to be negotiations, agreements, oversight, revision. The higher-education community is not now organized for any such effort. It has no such men. It seemingly comprehends no such undertakings.

This is the leap of imagination that is required. To become not just a national resource and national problem, but a national force as well. It is an effort contrary to many of the best instincts of precisely those men now in higher education that one would wish to see take up the challenge. But that is what a challenge involves. Much will depend on the outcome.*

---

* There is something gently comic about a professor on leave addressing former colleagues, quoting at great length and with scarce concealed approval passages from Presidential pronouncements which he himself has written. The scene is somehow redolent of children playing grown-ups. Still, this address to the American Council on Education was quite the most seriously—I would not object to the term "earnestly"—intended statement I made during two puzzled years in a Republican administration. Still, on occasion, I wonder why it was such a failure.

Let it be clear that it was. I asked the representatives of higher education, in Congress assembled, to interest themselves in the higher-education bill the administration had sent to Congress. They did nothing of the kind. The Democratic Congress was left almost entirely to its own in dealing with the legislation, much as the Republican administration had been in devising it. In the end the process produced the Higher Education Amendments of 1972 which, to my view, rank with the Northwest Ordinance, the Morrill Act, the G.I. Bill, and the National Defense Education Act in importance for higher education. One of five such measures in nearly two centuries. Yet higher education had almost nothing whatever to do with shaping the legislation. It was not excluded. My address was almost a plea for involvement. By its own choice it stayed aloof.

There is not another organized interest group in the nation that would have made such a choice. Let it first be clear that a choice was made. The most useful testimony came in 1972, after the legislation had been enacted, from John C. Honey, chairman of the Department of Higher Education at Syracuse University, who with John C. Crowley had been commissioned by the American Council on Higher Education to study the "Federal relations operation" of the Council. In an editorial written for Science six months after the amendments became law, Honey declared:

Basic decisions about the future of virtually all of higher education are now clearly in the hands of the federal government. The Higher Education Amendments of 1972, passed with bipartisan support and White House approval, will profoundly affect the character and quality of education beyond the high school for a long, long time. The failure of the Washington-based spokesmen for higher education to contribute significantly to the shaping of those amendments verges on the scandalous.

This failure is worth noting since there are lessons for the future. The "centerpiece" organization of higher education, the American Council on Education, had, until recently, leadership which eschewed a vigorous active role on the governmental scene. Its small staff has not been given to easy communication with public officials or with other Washington-based educational associations. There has been a good deal of in-house jockeying for domination among the associations. A paucity of solid data and an overabundance of wishfulness have characterized the representations of the spokesmen for higher education before congressional committees.

The deep-rooted reason for the ineffectiveness of higher education's Washington representatives is in the apolitical or anti-political attitudes of many academics. Do faculty members across the country know the essential features of that legislation which is bound to markedly change their lives—the Higher Education Amendments of 1972? How many of them know which way their congressmen and senators voted on the amendments? How many have expected and wanted their Washington representatives to compete effectively with other claimants for federal resources?

The essence of Honey's charge is "political naïveté." This is rather confirmed by the keynote address given to the 1972 meeting of the American Council on Education by Martha E. Peterson, president of Barnard College.

Do you remember Daniel Patrick Moynihan in St. Louis in 1970 at the A.C.E. meeting chiding leaders in higher education about their lack of interest in the new educational policies being developed in Washington? He acknowledged that everyone had been busy with internal crises, but he wondered whether or not we would not regret abdication of external responsibility to politicians and legislators.

We thought then that he spoke only of the White House proposals to the Congress for changes in financing higher education and feared we might be enticed to take sides in a partisan political battle. But have you thought of Mr. Moynihan's advice in connection with affirmative action experiences? Is it not possible that failure to take positive and strong positions on campus in support of affirmative action has made it necessary for HEW to intervene in such a way that on-campus ability to govern is eroded?

Dr. Peterson was speaking more specifically of the "disgrace of 'affirmative action' " programs in which "Through intransigence, unperceptiveness or preoccupation with other issues, the higher education community seemed unable to recognize and take action in correcting injustices until forced to do so by HEW— a dismal example of lack of internal leadership." The Federal government, she said, had "invaded the right of autonomy of the campus" and the campus had only itself to blame.

Up to a point, I agree with the charge of political naïveté. The new Republican administration of 1969 was the first in history to encounter the condition of the universities as one of the "problems" with which it had to deal. Accordingly, it was the first to try to set forth a policy concerning such matters. My address reviewed that policy and the legislation that followed from it. I would hope that most readers will find that the policy was primarily designed to stress the autonomy of the universities, and to bring about a decrease in government influence. That, at all events, was *my* purpose, and more than any other person, I devised the policy.

The universities did not see this. When the administration adopted almost word-for-word proposals such as that for a National Foundation for Education which had been formulated by the Carnegie Commission for Higher Education, they all but turned against their own proposal. Why? The main reason I can think is that they distrusted and resented the President. Even those university and college heads who did not were in effect forced to do so by their own students and faculty.

The extent and the origins of the political bias of American higher education have been the subject of measurement and analysis, and need not be reviewed here. Honey begins his *Science* editorial with something of an understatement: "It is probable that a sizable majority of academics on our campuses across the country would have preferred to see the Democrats in control of the White House." Still, one is puzzled as to why they were so clumsy at taking advantage of a Republican-controlled White House which was making pronouncements and proposing programs that, coming from a liberal Democrat, would have elicited great support. I suspect the answer lies first in the fact that the corruption of academic dogma—Nisbet's phrase—had proceeded so far by this time that the academic community was not fully comfortable with a President asserting that it ought to be left alone to run its own affairs, with government support but not direction.

The academy paid a price for this. It had been wholly possible to get a National Foundation for Higher Education established. But the effort received almost no cooperation whatever from those who were to benefit from it. (See Chester E. Finn, Jr., "The National Foundation for Higher Education: Death of An Idea," *Change*, March 1972.)

Left to itself, Congress concluded to pare the President's program down somewhat. He had asked for two new institutions to be established in HEW. First, the Foundation for Higher Education, a device modeled on the University Grants Commission in Britain for channeling "free" money to colleges and universities. Second, a National Institute of Education, modeled on the National Institutes of Health, for pursuing long-range, big-scale research in the mysteries of the education process such as turned up by the Coleman report. Although out of government by now, I was asked in Congress which should be chosen. I opted for the Institute, reasoning that there was sufficient number of persons who both wanted the NIE (since established) and knew what to do with it. By contrast, the universities were not prepared to understand and support the Foundation. In the course of the next twenty or thirty years there will surely come another chance. This time the academics might somewhere summon the sense of the political system which any soybean lobbyist brings to the smallest transaction in Washington.

There is a small, final footnote to this story. In the summer of 1972 I had occasion to call on President Nixon. As I entered the Oval Office I found him standing with a large plaque and a photographer waiting to present me the pen with which he had signed the Higher Education Amendments of 1972. He had done so in private the previous June. There had been no ceremony. It was almost as if the administration had sought to conceal the act. (A charge, to be sure, made against it in other fields!)

This was, I think, a loss. *Inter alia*, the legislation provided for the Federal stipends mentioned in the preceding article, which would "equalize" the financial support of low-income students so that no one would have fewer resources than those available to students from families of median income. Probably the legislation doesn't precisely do this, but for sheer impact there has hardly been such a bill since the New Deal. The program is known as Basic Opportunity Grants (BOGS, one regrets to report). The FY 1974 budget requests $959,000,000 for BOGS. One billion dollars for a program of great equalizing intent and probable result. In the whole of the War on Poverty nothing came near this by way of direct income redistribution. Yet I should imagine that six months after its enactment, at most a handful of Americans knew the program even existed, much less its dimension.

I offer an explanation for this. During his first administration, Nixon and his opponents joined in a strange and almost sinister symbiosis. In the main, the legislative program of the administration was at least as "advanced" as that of his Democratic predecessors. In many areas, it was more so. Some students of social policy such as Nathan Glazer have consistently pointed this out. (Glazer finding much virtue in the administration's domestic programs, while fiercely opposing its foreign policy.) It is a question capable of objective answer. Given, say, the stated goals of the Great Society, were those goals advanced or retarded by the legislative program of the succeeding administration? The answer must be: advanced. In the main, however, Nixon's opponents very much did not want him to obtain what they assumed would be the political advantage of being known to have advanced such goals, or to have tried. Accordingly, a vast, instinctive response arose similar to that which psychiatrists term "denial" in an individual. It was said—and believed—that he had not done that which he had done. *Nixon did not protest this.* To the contrary, he, or his administration, seemed almost as anxious to conceal the liberal reality as did the liberal opposition. To repeat, there was no signing ceremony for the Higher Education Amendments of 1972. LBJ would have staged a barbecue to mark the occasion.

Why this pattern? As best I can interpret, with no direct knowledge, the administration perceived that the liberal tide was running out fast and that while objective analysis may have indicated a continued effort at, for example, government programs to achieve greater equality of opportunity—new strategies, perhaps, but established goals—political analysis indicated that the less the general public knew of this, the better the next election would be. In any event (Gertrude Himmelfarb's observation) the new Republicans simply could not internalize the ethic of the modern, interventionist government which they took over in 1969. And so they could not have sung their own praises very well, even if they had been inclined to do so. But the main point, as I would put the argument, is that the Republicans sensed that at least from 1969 on the Democrats who hadn't gone to Ivy League colleges were getting pretty fed up with those who had. In 1972, of course, the Republican perception was amply confirmed. Yet when the Watergate revelations struck, the administration found itself curiously without that presumption of decent purpose and good works which comes of complying with the interventionist ethic. The opposition seemed vindicated and triumphant. The President had won an election already past; they had won the future.

The Presidency and
the Press

17

As his years in Washington came to an end, Harry S. Truman wrote a friend:

> I really look with commiseration over the great body of my fellow citizens, who, reading newspapers, live and die in the belief that they have known something of what has been passing in the world in their time.

A familiar presidential plaint, sounded often in the early years of the Republic and rarely unheard thereafter. Of late, however, a change has developed in the perception of what is at issue. In the past what was thought to be involved was the reputation of a particular President. In the present what is seen to be at stake, and by the Presidents themselves, is the reputation of government—especially, of course, Presidential government. These are different matters, and summon a different order of concern.

There are two points anyone would wish to make at the outset of an effort to explore this problem. First, it is to be acknowledged that in most essential encounters between the Presidency

"The Presidency and the Press" was first published in *Commentary*, March 1971.

314

and the press, the advantage is with the former. The President has a near limitless capacity to "make" news which must be reported, if only by reason of competition between one journal, or one medium, and another. (If anything, radio and television news is more readily subject to such dominance. Their format permits of many fewer "stories." The President-in-action almost always takes precedence.) The President also has considerable capacity to reward friends and punish enemies in the press corps, whether they be individual journalists or the papers, television networks, news weeklies, or whatever these individuals work for. And for quite a long while, finally, a President who wishes can carry off formidable deceptions. (One need only recall the barefaced lying that went with the formal opinion of Roosevelt's Attorney General that the destroyer-naval-base deal of 1940 was legal.)

With more than sufficient reason, then, publishers and reporters alike have sustained over the generations a lively sense of their vulnerability to governmental coercion or control. For the most part, their worries have been exaggerated. But, like certain virtues, there are some worries that are best carried to excess.

The second point is that American journalism is almost certainly the best in the world. This judgment will be disputed by some. There are good newspapers in other countries. The *best* European journalists are more intellectual than their American counterparts, and some will think this a decisive consideration. But there is no enterprise anywhere the like of *The New York Times*. Few capitals are covered with the insight and access of the Washington *Post* or the Washington *Evening Star*. As with so many American institutions, American newspapers tend to be older and more stable than their counterparts abroad. The Hartford *Courant* was born in 1764, twenty-one years before *The Times* of London. The New York *Post* began publication in 1801, twenty years before the *Guardian* of Manchester. What in most other countries is known as the "provincial" press—that is to say journals published elsewhere than in the capital—in America is made up of a wealth of comprehensive and dependable daily newspapers of unusually high quality.

The journalists are in some ways more important than their

journals—at least to anyone who has lived much in government. A relationship grows up with the reporters covering one's particular sector that has no counterpart in other professions or activities. The relationship is one of simultaneous trust and distrust, friendship and enmity, dependence and independence. But it is the men of government, especially in Washington, who are the more dependent. The journalists are their benefactors, their conscience, at times almost their reason for being. For the journalists are above all others their audience, again especially in Washington, which has neither an intellectual community nor an electorate, and where there is no force outside government able to judge events, much less to help shape them, save the press.

That there is something wondrous and terrible in the intensities of this relationship between the press and the government is perhaps best seen at the annual theatricals put on by such groups of journalists at the Legislative Correspondents Association in Albany or the Gridiron in Washington. To my knowledge nothing comparable takes place anywhere else in the world.* These gatherings are a kind of ritual truth-telling, of which the closest psychological approximation would be the Calabrian insult ritual described by Roger Vailland in his novel *The Law,* or possibly the group-therapy practices of more recent origin. The politicians come as guests of the journalists. The occasion is first of all a feast: the best of everything. Then as dinner progresses the songs begin. The quality varies, of course, but at moments startling levels of deadly accurate commentary of great cruelty are achieved. The politicians sit and smile and applaud. Then some of them speak. Each one wins or loses to the degree that he can respond in kind; stay funny and be brutal. (At the Gridiron John F. Kennedy was a master of the style, but the piano duet performed by Nixon and Agnew in 1970 was thought by many to have surpassed anything yet done.) A few lyrics appear in the next day's papers, but what the newspa-

---

* I am indebted to Richard O'Hagan of the Canadian Embassy in Washington for the information that the Parliamentary Press Gallery has since about 1867 been staging an annual show "markedly similar to that of the Gridiron." The Toronto press corps, comparable to that of Albany, puts on a similar fête. It may be, as Mr. O'Hagan suggests, a North American phenomenon. Its history *must* be written.

permen really said to the politicians remains privileged—as does so much of what the politicians say to them. The relationship is special.

How is it then that this relationship has lately grown so troubled? The immediate answer is, of course, the war in Vietnam. An undeclared war, unwanted, misunderstood, or not understood at all, it entailed a massive deception of the American people by their government.* Surely a large area of the experience of the 1960s is best evoked in the story of the man who says: "They told me that if I voted for Goldwater there would be 500,000 troops in Vietnam within a year. I voted for him, and by God, they were right." The story has many versions. If he voted for Goldwater we would be defoliating the countryside of Vietnam; the army would be sending spies to the 1968 party conventions; Dr. Spock would be indicted on conspiracy charges; and so on. By 1968 Richard Rovere described the capital as "awash" with lies.

The essential fact was that of deceit. How else to carry out a full-scale war, that became steadily more unpopular, with none of the legally sanctioned constraints on the free flow of information which even the most democratic societies find necessary in such circumstances? This situation did not spring full-blown from the involvement in Southeast Asia. It was endemic to the cold war. At the close of World War II official press censorship was removed, but the kinds of circumstance in which any responsible government might feel that events have to be concealed from the public did not go away. The result was a contradiction impossible to resolve. The public interest was at once served and disserved by secrecy; at once disserved and served by openness. Whatever the case, distrust of government grew. At the outset of the U-2 affair in 1960, the United States government asserted that a weather plane on a routine mission had been shot down. *The New York Times* (May 6, 1960) reported just that. *Not* that the U.S. government *claimed* it was a weather plane, but simply that it was. Well, it wasn't. Things have not been the same since.

---

* This statement was written before the Pentagon Papers appeared, and intends a quite different reference. Vietnam involved self-deception in government much more than any deliberate contrivance. Such, at least, is one view.

But there are problems between the Presidency and the press which have little to do with the cold war or with Vietnam and which—if this analysis is correct—will persist or even intensify should those conditions recede, or even dissolve, as a prime source of public concern. The problems flow from five basic circumstances which together have been working to reverse the old balance of power between them. It is the thesis here that if this balance should tip too far in the direction of the press, our capacity for effective democratic government will be seriously and dangerously weakened.

I

The first of these circumstances has to do with the tradition of "muckraking"—the exposure of corruption in government or the collusion of government with private interests—which the American press has seen as a primary mission since the period 1880–1914. It is, in Irving Kristol's words, "a journalistic phenomenon that is indigenous to democracy, with its instinctive suspicion and distrust of all authority in general, and of concentrated political and economic power especially." Few would want to be without the tradition, and it is a young journalist of poor spirit who does not set out to uncover the machinations of some malefactor of great wealth and his political collaborators. Yet there is a cost, as Roger Starr suggests in his wistful wish that Lincoln Steffens's *The Shame of the Cities* might be placed on the restricted shelves of the schools of journalism. Steffens has indeed, as Starr declares, continued "to haunt the city rooms of the country's major newspapers." The question to be asked is whether, in the aftermath of Steffens, the cities were better, or merely more ashamed of themselves. Looking back, one is impressed by the energy and capacity for governance of some of the old city machines. Whatever else, it was popular government, of and by men of the people. One wonders: did the middle- and upper-class reformers destroy the capacity of working-class urban government without replacing it with anything better so that half-a-century later each and all bewail the cities as ungovernable? One next wonders whether something not dissimilar will occur now that the focus of press attention has shifted from City Hall to the White House. (And yet a miracle of American national government is the almost complete absence of monetary corruption at all levels, and most especially at the top.) *

The muckraking tradition is well established. Newer, and likely to have far more serious consequences, is the advent of what Lionel Trilling has called the "adversary culture" as a conspicuous element in journalistic practice. The appearance in large numbers of journalists shaped by the attitudes of this culture is the result of a process whereby the profession thought to improve itself by recruiting more and more persons from middle- and upper-class backgrounds and trained at the universities associated with such groups. This is a change but little noted as yet. The stereotype of American newspapers is that of publishers ranging from conservative to reactionary in their political views balanced by reporters ranging from liberal to radical in theirs. One is not certain how accurate the stereotype ever was. One's impression is that twenty years and more ago the preponderance of the "working press" (as it liked to call itself) was surprisingly close in origins and attitudes to working people generally. They were not Ivy Leaguers. They now are or soon will be. Journalism has become, if not an elite profession, a profession attractive to elites. This is noticeably so in Washington, where the upper reaches of journalism constitute one of the most important and enduring *social* elites of the city, with all the accouterments one associates with a leisured class. (The Washington press corps is not leisured at all, but the style is that of men and women who *choose* to work.)

The political consequence of the rising social status of journalism is that the press grows more and more influenced by attitudes genuinely hostile to American society and American government. This trend seems bound to continue into the future. On the record of what they have been writing while in college, the young people now leaving the Harvard *Crimson* and the Columbia

* The Watergate exposé, pressed so indefatigably by two young reporters, Bob Woodward and Carl Bernstein of the Washington *Post*, is in the very best of this tradition, and well might the President's Press Secretary, Ronald Ziegler, apologize to them and their newspaper, as he did in the spring of 1973. I would only plead that if some of those young salesmen in the White House had read this *Commentary* article, they would have known they were going to be caught. Some consolation may be taken from the fact that the Watergate events are likely to produce, in twenty years or so, some spirited middle-class advocates of prison reform.

Spectator for journalistic jobs in Washington will resort to the Steffens style at ever-escalating levels of moral implication. They bring with them the moral absolutism of George Wald's vastly popular address, "A Generation in Search of a Future," that describes the Vietnam war as "the most shameful episode in the whole of American history." Not tragic, not heartbreaking, not vastly misconceived, but *shameful*. From the shame of the cities to the shame of the nation. But nobody ever called Boss Croker any name equivalent in condemnatory weight to the epithet "war criminal."

II

An ironical accompaniment of the onset of the muckraking style directed toward the presidency has been the rise of a notion of the near-omnipotency of the office itself. This notion Thomas E. Cronin describes as the "textbook President." Cronin persuasively argues that in the aftermath of Franklin Roosevelt a view of the Presidency, specifically incorporated in the textbooks of recent decades, was developed which presented seriously "inflated and unrealistic interpretations of Presidential competence and beneficence," and which grievously "overemphasized the policy change and policy accomplishment capabilities" of the office. Cronin cites Anthony Howard, a watchful British commentator:

> For what the nation has been beguiled into believing ever since 1960 is surely the politics of evangelism: the faith that individual men are cast to be messiahs, the conviction that Presidential incantations can be substituted for concrete programs, the belief that what matters is not so much the state of the nation as the inspiration-quotient of its people.

In his own researches among advisers of Kennedy and Johnson, Cronin finds the majority to hold "tempered assessments of Presidential determination of 'public policy.'" Indeed, only 10 percent would describe the President as having "very great impact" over such matters.

Working in the White House is a chastening experience. But it is the experience of very few persons. Watching the White

House, on the other hand, is a mass occupation, concentrated especially among the better-educated, better-off groups. For many the experience is one of infatuation followed much too promptly by disillusion. First, the honeymoon—in Cronin's terms, the "predictable ritual of euphoric inflation." But then "the Camelot of the first few hundred days of all Presidencies fades away. . . . Predictably, by the second year, reports are spread that the President has become isolated from criticism." If this is so, he has only himself to blame when things go wrong. And things do go wrong.

If the muckraking tradition implies a distrust of government, it is nonetheless curiously validated by the overly trusting tradition of the "textbook Presidency" which recurrently sets up situations in which the Presidency will be judged as having somehow broken faith. This is not just the experience of a Johnson or a Nixon. Anyone who was in the Kennedy administration in the summer and fall of 1963 would, or ought to, report a pervasive sense that our initiative had been lost, that we would have to get reelected to get going again.

Here, too, there is a curious link between the Presidency and the press. The two most important *Presidential* newspapers are *The New York Times* and the Washington *Post* (though the *Star* would be judged by many to have the best reporting). Both papers reflect a tradition of liberalism that has latterly been shaped and reinforced by the very special type of person who *buys* the paper. (It is well to keep in mind that newspapers are capitalist enterprises which survive by persuading people to buy them.) Theirs is a "disproportionately" well-educated and economically prosperous audience. The geographical areas in which the two papers circulate almost certainly have higher per-capita incomes and higher levels of education than any of comparable size in the nation or the world. More of the buyers of these two papers are likely to come from "liberal" Protestant or Jewish backgrounds than would be turned up by a random sample of the population; they comprise, in fact, what James Q. Wilson calls "the Liberal Audience." Both the working-class Democrats and the conservative Republicans, with exceptions, obviously, have been pretty much driven from office among the constituencies where the *Times* and the *Post* flourish. It would be wrong to ascribe this to the influence of the papers. Causality almost certainly moves both ways. Max Frankel of the *Times,* who may have peers but certainly no betters as a working journalist, argues that a newspaper is surely as much influenced by those who read it as vice versa.

The readers of *The New York Times* and the Washington *Post,* then, are a special type of citizen: not only more affluent and more liberal than the rest of the nation, but inclined also to impose heavy expectations on the Presidency, and not to be amused when those expectations fail to be met. Attached by their own internal traditions to the "textbook Presidency," papers like *The Times* and the *Post* are reinforced in this attachment by the temperamental predilections of the readership whose character they inevitably reflect. Thus they help to set a tone of pervasive dissatisfaction with the performance of the national government, whoever the presidential incumbent may be and whatever the substance of his policies.

III

A third circumstance working to upset the old balance of power between the Presidency and the press is the fact that Washington reporters depend heavily on more or less clandestine information from federal bureaucracies which are frequently, and in some cases routinely, antagonistic to Presidential interests.

There is a view of the career civil service as a more or less passive executor of policies made on high. This is quite mistaken. A very great portion of policy ideas "bubble up" from the bureaucracy, and, just as importantly, a very considerable portion of the "policy decisions" that go down never come to anything, either because the bureaucrats cannot or will not follow through. (The instances of simple inability are probably much greater than those of outright hostility.) Few modern Presidents have made any impact on the federal bureaucracies save by creating new ones. The bureaucracies are unfamiliar and inaccessible. They are quasi-independent, maintaining, among other things, fairly open relationships with the Congressional committees that enact their statutes and provide their funds. They are usually willing to work with the President, but rarely to the point where their perceived interests are threatened. Typically, these are rather simple territorial interests: not to lose any jurisdiction, and if possible to gain some. But recurrently, issues of genuine political substance are also involved.

At the point where they perceive a threat to those interests, the bureaucracies just as recurrently go to the press. They know the press; the press knows them. Both stay in town as Presidential governments come and go. Both cooperate in bringing to bear the most powerful weapon the bureaucracies wield in their own defense, that of revealing Presidential plans in advance of their execution. Presidents and their plans are helpless against this technique. I have seen a senior aide to a President, sitting over an early morning cup of coffee, rise and literally punch the front page of *The New York Times.* A major initiative was being carefully mounted. Success depended, to a considerable degree, on surprise. Someone in one of the agencies whose policies were to be reversed got hold of the relevant document and passed it on to *The Times.* Now everyone would know. The mission was aborted. There was *nothing* for the Presidential government to do. No possibility of finding, much less of disciplining, the bureaucrat responsible. For a time, or rather from time to time, President Johnson tried the technique of *not* going ahead with any policy or appointment that was leaked in advance to the press. Soon, however, his aides began to suspect that this was giving the bureaucracy the most powerful weapon of all, namely the power to veto a Presidential decision by learning of it early enough and rushing to *The Times* or the *Post.* (Or, if the issue could be described in thirty seconds, any of the major television networks.)

What we have here is disloyalty to the Presidency. Much of the time what is involved is no more than the self-regard of lower-echelon bureaucrats who are simply flattered into letting the reporter know how much *they* know, or who are just trying to look after their agency. But just as often, to repeat, serious issues of principle are involved. Senator Joseph McCarthy made contact with what he termed "the loyal American underground" —State Department officials, and other such, who reputedly passed on information to him about Communist infiltration of the nation's foreign-policy and security systems. President Johnson made it clear that he did not trust the Department of State to maintain "security" in foreign policy. Under President Nixon the phenomenon has been most evident in domestic areas as OEO warriors struggle among themselves to be the first to disclose the imminent demise of VISTA, or HEW functionaries reluctantly interpret a move to close some fever hospital built to accommodate an eighteenth-century seaport as the first step in a master plan to dismantle public medicine and decimate the ranks of the elderly and disadvantaged.

It is difficult to say whether the absolute level of such disloyalty to the Presidency is rising. One has the impression that it is. No one knows much about the process of "leaking" except in those instances where he himself has been involved. (*Everyone* is sooner or later involved. That should be understood.) The process has not been studied and little is known of it. But few would argue that the amount of clandestine disclosure is decreasing. Such disclosure is now part of the way we run our affairs. It means, among other things, that the press is fairly continuously involved in an activity that is something less than honorable. Repeatedly it benefits from the self-serving acts of government officials who are essentially hostile to the Presidency. This does the Presidency no good, and if an outsider may comment, it does the press no good either. Too much do they traffic in stolen goods, and they know it.

This point must be emphasized. The leaks which appear in the *Post* and *The Times*—other papers get them, but if one wants to influence decisions in Washington these are clearly thought to be the most effective channels—are ostensibly published in the interest of adding to public knowledge of what is going on. This budget is to be cut; that man is to be fired; this bill is to be proposed. However, in the nature of the transaction the press can only publish half the story—that is to say the information that the "leaker" wants to become "public knowledge." What the press *never* does is say who the leaker is and why he wants the story leaked. Yet, more often than not, this is the more important story: that is to say, what policy wins if the one being disclosed loses, what individual, what bureau, and so on.

There really are ethical questions involved here that have not been examined. There are also serious practical questions. It is my impression that the distress occasioned by leaks has used up too much Presidential energy, at least from the time of Roosevelt. (Old-time brain-trusters would assure the Johnson staff that nothing could compare with FDR's distractions on the subject.)

The primary fault lies within government itself, and one is at a loss to think of anything that might be done about it. But it is a problem for journalism as well, and an unattended one.*

IV

The fourth of the five conditions making for an altered relation between the Presidency and the press is the concept of objectivity with respect to the reporting of events and especially the statements of public figures. Almost the first canon of the great newspapers, and by extension of the television news networks which by and large have taken as their standards those of the best newspapers, is that "the news" will be reported whether or not the reporter or the editor or the publisher likes the news. There is nothing finer in the American newspaper tradition. There is, however, a rub and it comes when a decision has to be made as to whether an event really is news, or simply a happening, a nonevent staged for the purpose of getting into the papers or onto the screen.

The record of our best papers is not reassuring here, as a glance at the experience of the Korean and the Vietnam wars will suggest. Beginning a bit before the Korean hostilities broke out, but in the general political period we associate with that war, there was a rise of right-wing extremism, a conspiracy-oriented politics symbolized by the name of Senator Joseph McCarthy, and directed primarily at the institution of the Presidency. There was, to be sure, a populist streak to this movement: Yale and Harvard and the "striped-pants boys" in the State Department were targets too. But to the question, "Who promoted Peress?" there was only one constitutional or—for all practical purposes —political answer, namely that the President did. McCarthy went on asking such questions, or rather making such charges, and the national press, which detested and disbelieved him throughout, went on printing them. The American style of objective journalism made McCarthy. He would not, I think, have

* It is hardly necessary to note that this relationship led to activities on the part of the Nixon administration that were not only dishonorable but apparently criminal. I would only ask those who are appalled by these activities—and who is not?—to accept that there *is* a problem here, that it has existed for a long time and that it persists.

gotten anywhere in Great Britain, where, because it would have been judged he was lying, the stories would simply not have been printed.

Something not dissimilar has occurred in the course of the Vietnam war, only this time the extremist, conspiracy-oriented politics of protest has been putatively left-wing. Actually both movements are utterly confusing if one depends on European analogues. McCarthy was nominally searching out Communists, but his preferred targets were Eastern patricians, while his supporters were, to an alarming degree, members of the Catholic working class. The Students for a Democratic Society if that organization may be used as an exemplar, was (as least in its later stages) nominally revolutionist, dedicated to the overthrow of the capitalist-imperialist-fascist regime of the United States. Yet, as Seymour Martin Lipset, Nathan Glazer, and others have shown, its leadership, and perhaps also its constituency, were disproportionately made up of upper-class Jewish and Protestant youth. By report of Steven Kelman, who lived as a contemporary among them at Harvard, the SDS radicals were "undemocratic, manipulative, and self-righteous to the point of snobbery and elitism." Peter Berger, a sociologist active in the peace movement, has demonstrated quite persuasively—what others, particularly persons of European origin like himself have frequently seemed to sense—that despite the leftist ring of the slogans of SDS and kindred groups, their ethos and tactics are classically fascist: the cult of youth, the mystique of the street, the contempt for liberal democracy, and the "totalization of friend and foe [with] the concomitant dehumanization of the latter," as in the Nazi use of "Saujuden" ("Jewish pigs").

In any case, the accusations which have filled the American air during the period of Vietnam have been no more credible or responsible than those of McCarthy during the Korean period, and the tactics of provocation and physical intimidation have if anything been more disconcerting. Yet the national press, and especially television, have assumed a neutral posture, even at times a sympathetic one, enabling the neofascists of the Left to occupy center stage throughout the latter half of the sixties with consequences to American politics that have by no means yet worked themselves out. (It took Sam Brown to point out that one consequence was to make the work of the antiwar movement, of which he has been a principal leader, vastly more difficult.)

Would anyone have it otherwise? Well, yes. Irving Kristol raised this question in an article that appeared before the New Left had made its presence strongly felt on the national scene, but his views are doubtless even more emphatic by now. He wrote of the "peculiar mindlessness which pervades the practice of journalism in the United States," asserting that the ideal of objectivity too readily becomes an excuse for avoiding judgment. If McCarthy was lying, why print what he said? Or why print it on the front page? If the SDS stages a confrontation over a trumped-up issue, why oblige it by taking the whole episode at face value? Here, let it be said, the editorials of *The Times* and the *Post* have consistently served as a thoughtful corrective to the impressions inescapably conveyed by the news columns. But the blunt fact is that just as the news columns were open to astonishingly false assertions about the nature of the American national government during the McCarthy period, they have been open to equally false assertions—mirror images of McCarthyism indeed—during the period of Vietnam. And although it is impossible to prove, one gets the feeling that the slanderous irresponsibilities now being reported so dutifully are treated with far more respect than the old.

The matter of a policy of "genocide" pursued by the national government against the Black Panthers is a good example. By late 1969, preparing a preface to a second edition of *Beyond the Melting Pot,* Nathan Glazer and I could insist that the charge that twenty-eight Panthers had been murdered by the police was on the face of it simply untrue. Yet in that mindless way of which Kristol writes, *The Times* kept reprinting it. Edward Jay Epstein has brilliantly explained the matter in a recent article in *The New Yorker.* What he finds is an immense fraud. No such policy existed. There was no conspiracy between the Department of Justice, the FBI, and various local police forces to wipe out the Panthers. Yet that fraudulent charge has so profoundly affected the thinking of the academic and liberal communities that they will probably not even now be able to see the extent to which they were deceived. The hurt that has been done to blacks is probably in its way even greater. None of it could have happened without the particular mind-set of the national press.

If the press is to deserve our good opinion, it must do better in such matters. And it should keep in mind that the motivation of editors and reporters is not always simply and purely shaped by a devotion to objectivity. In the course of the McCarthy era James Reston recalled the ancient adage which translated from the Erse proposes that "If you want an audience, start a fight." This is true of anyone who would find an audience for his views, or simply for himself. It is true also of anyone who would find customers for the late city edition. T. S. Matthews, sometime editor of *Time*, retired to England to ponder the meaning of it all. In the end, all he could conclude was that the function of journalism was entertainment. If it is to be more—and that surely is what the Rosenthals and Bradlees and Grunwalds and Elliotts want—it will have to be willing on occasion to forgo the entertainment value of a fascinating but untruthful charge. It will, in short, have to help limit the rewards which attend this posture in American politics.

V

The final, and by far the most important, circumstance of American journalism relevant to this discussion is the absence of a professional tradition of self-correction. The mark of any developed profession is the practice of correcting mistakes, by whomsoever they are made. This practice is of course the great invention of Western science. Ideally, it requires an epistemology which is shared by all respected members of the profession, so that when a mistake is discovered it can be established as a mistake to the satisfaction of the entire professional community. Ideally, also, no discredit is involved: to the contrary, honest mistakes are integral to the process of advancing the field. Journalism will never attain to any such condition. Nevertheless, there is a range of subject matter about which reasonable men can and will agree, and within this range American journalism, even of the higher order, is often seriously wide of the mark. Again Irving Kristol:

> It is a staple of conversation among those who have ever been involved in a public activity that when they read the *Times* the next morning, they will discover that it has almost never got the story quite right and has only too frequently got it quite wrong.

Similar testimony has come from an editor of *The New York Times itself*. In an article published some years ago in the *Times Magazine,* A. H. Raskin had this to say:

> No week passes without someone prominent in politics, industry, labor, or civic affairs complaining to me, always in virtually identical terms: "Whenever I read a story about something in which I really know what is going on, I'm astonished at how little of what is important gets into the papers—and how often even that little is wrong." The most upsetting thing about these complaints is the frequency with which they come from scientists, economists, and other academicians temporarily involved in government policy but without any proprietary concern about who runs the White House or City Hall.*

This is so, and in part it is unavoidable. Too much happens too quickly: that *The Times* or the *Post* or the *Star* should appear once a day is a miracle. (Actually they appear three or four times a day in different editions.) But surely when mistakes are made they ought to be corrected. Sometimes they are, but not nearly enough. It is in this respect that Kristol is right in calling journalism "the underdeveloped profession."

Assertions that the press has a flawed sense of objectivity, or that it enjoys too cozy a relationship with the civil service, are not easily proved or disproved. But to say that mistakes are repeatedly made and not corrected is to say something which ought to be backed up with specific instances. Let me, then, offer two, taken from stories which appeared in *The New York Times* during the second half of 1970. (I was serving in the White House at the time, though I was not directly involved in any of the matters to be described.)

The first of my two examples is a long article which appeared in *The Times* on Sunday, November 15, 1970, under the headline, "Blacks Seek Tougher Equality Standards for Federal

---

* It should not, of course, be supposed that people inside government "know" what happens. The *Rashomon* effect is universal. It is, moreover, not uncommon for men in government to be doing something quite different from what they think or intend. In such cases, the more accurate the press reporting, the more baffled or enraged the officials will be. Still, the judgment Raskin reports is near universal.

Hiring and Promotion." This story was not hostile to the administration; rather the contrary. It noted that the President had earlier signed an executive order requiring each department and agency to maintain an "affirmative" equal-opportunity program, and that the number of blacks in the top grades of the civil service had gone up almost by half under the "low-key approach of the Nixon Administration." The number of black lawyers in the Justice Department had declined somewhat. There were said to have been 61 (out of a total of 1,900 to 2,000) under the Democrats. This figure had dropped under the Republicans to 45, but it also appeared that the difference was to be made up by new recruits. In the meantime the Department of Transportation was promulgating new rules, the Bureau of Prisons had eliminated the written test for correction officers, and similar activity aimed at increasing the number of blacks in the higher levels of the federal government was to be encountered elsewhere. All this, however, was going on in the context of a federal employment system whose patterns of practice were lamentably at odds with its profession of being an "equal-opportunity employer," to use the federal phrase. In the words of the *Times* story:

> The most recent figures show 137,919 blacks among the 1,289,114 Government employees covered by Civil Service regulations. That is about 10.7 percent, less than the black proportion of the population, estimated in the 1970 census as 12.9 percent.

The story went on to note that a number of black activists doubted that the federal government ever had been an equal-opportunity employer. One was particularly skeptical of executive orders: "This friendly persuasion thing has never worked in the history of our Government." Next came the question of quotas:

> Although little support for a formal quota system is evident, there is a widely held belief that Presidential statements of policy should be supplemented by more detailed instructions as to how the policies should be implemented.

There is little to take exception to in the foregoing. The official census figures for 1970 show blacks to be 11.2 percent of the population, not 12.9 percent, but newspapers routinely make such mistakes. It should also have been pointed out that blacks constitute only 10.9 percent of the civilian noninstitutional population of sixteen years of age or older, which is to say the population available for employment. In that sense, even accepting the figures used by *The Times,* blacks might be seen as having almost exactly "their" proportion of government employment, although an inadequate number of top positions.

The difficulty in this instance lies not with what was in the story, but what was not. What was not in the story was the fact that the category of federal worker—"General Schedule"—of which Negroes do indeed comprise 10.7 percent is only one of three categories. In the other two categories of federal employee, the Postal Service and Wage System employees, Negroes made up 19.5 percent and 19.7 percent respectively. In rough terms, federal jobs are about equally divided among the three categories.* Small wonder, then, that *The Times* reported an absence of much discussion about establishing racial quotas for federal employment. Altogether, blacks have more than 15 percent of federal jobs. If quotas were established according to the black proportion of the adult population, almost a third of black federal employees would have to be fired!

What all this comes to is that the very considerable achievement of blacks in qualifying for federal jobs and getting them far in excess of their proportion in the work force is in effect concealed and a legitimate source of black pride thereby denied. So too we are denied a legitimate sense of national progress in combating discrimination. And thus we are fed the tendentious allegations of those who wish to discredit the American "system" as inherently and irrevocably racist.

With respect to the role of the *Times* reporter, it must be said that it is simply not possible for him to have gotten the data on Classified Service employment from the Civil Service Commission releases on the subject without knowing that this is but

---

* These are, by the way, good jobs. In 1970, mean annual earnings of year-round full-time workers in the economy as a whole were $8,496. The average earnings of General Schedule federal employees in that year were $11,058; of Postal employees, $8,770; and of Wage System employees, $8,159. Washington, D.C. has a much higher per-capita income than any state in the union for the reason that it has so many federal employees.

one of three categories of employment, and that in the other categories blacks do exceptionally well. The truth would have made things look better than the reporter wished them to look. One fears it is as simple as that.

The second instance is rather more complicated. On September 14, 1970, a front-page story was published in *The Times* under the headline, "Negro College Heads Say Nixon Ignores Their Plight." The lead paragraph declared: "The presidents of nine financially troubled Negro colleges accused the Nixon Administration today of intensifying racial tensions by failing to support black education." The presidents felt that massive grants were needed and one was reported as saying that "It's five minutes before doomsday in this country." Dr. Vivian Henderson, president of Clark College in Atlanta, was reported as notably disturbed, asserting that "the Nixon Administration's utter lack of sensitivity on this point, purposeful or otherwise, is feeding the flames that already roar in the hearts of many black students."

All this seemed routine enough. From the onset of mass urban rioting in the mid-1960s all manner of requests for federal funds have been backed up by not especially subtle threats of violence. Nor was it unfamiliar to learn a few weeks later that the tactic had worked. On October 2, the front page of *The Times* carried a story from the Associated Press which began: "The Nixon Administration responded to complaints that it is insensitive to Negro education by announcing today a 30 percent increase in Federal aid for predominantly black colleges." The next paragraph explained: "The Secretary of Health, Education, and Welfare, Elliot L. Richardson, said in a statement the $30-million increase was ordered by President Nixon after he heard appeals from Negro educators."

The story bumped around in the press for the next few months, culminating in a way on January 3, 1971, when another *Times* story reported that the Negro colleges were not finding it possible to draw on all of the additional $30 million. Some college presidents were reportedly angry to have learned that the law provides for a 30-percent matching requirement for construction aid, which made up $20 million of the additional $30 million. But the basic theme of *The Times*'s coverage of this episode remained the same. The January 3 story began: "For two years, Negro colleges called on the Nixon Administration for substantial financial help. Last September, the Administration responded, releasing $30 million for use by the schools." There are problems of detail here. The Nixon administration had not been in office for two years in September 1970; the first *Times* report of an appeal appeared (as best I can determine) that very month, and the response came a month later, in October. Be that as it may, the January 3 story declared: "Black educators have severely criticized President Nixon for allegedly ignoring the plight of their schools. The educators charged that black schools have not shared in the money and grants that go out to American educational institutions."

To repeat, a familiar theme. The way to get something out of the federal government is to blast it out. Left to itself government would never have given these financially weak institutions a break. If you want action—especially if you are black—raise hell. Right?

Wrong.

At least wrong in this instance. The true sequence of events which made up this story was turned literally upside down by *The Times*. The initiative to aid black colleges had been voluntarily taken by the administration a year before *The Times* got on to the issue. The increased support was announced months before *The Times* reported it. Far from having denounced the administration, the black college presidents had been praising it. And, for good measure, far from getting less than their share of federal aid, the black colleges had all along been getting rather more.

There are 124 "predominantly black colleges" in America, most of them small, and most in the South. They enroll somewhat more than 2 percent of the college population, but this includes more than half of all black undergraduates.* They live with many difficulties, of which the most important—as is true of almost all colleges, large and small—is money. In 1969, they organized themselves as the National Association for Equal Opportunity in Higher Education and set out, as well they might, to get more federal funds. On October 23, 1969, a meeting on

---

* In 1969 there were 171,339 students in black colleges, or 2.14 percent of the national junior- and senior-college gross enrollment. Problems of definition complicate the statistics.

this subject was held in the Executive Office Building presided over by Robert J. Brown, a Special Assistant to the President, who as a Southern Negro was much interested in the problems of the predominantly black colleges. As a result of this meeting the Federal Interagency Committee on Education (FICE) was directed to find out what was already being done for these colleges by the considerable array of federal agencies involved in supporting education and what plans existed for the future. A preliminary report was sent to the White House in February 1970, and in June a 45-page document entitled "Federal Agencies and Black Colleges" was printed. It was a good report, full of information concerning what was being done and of recommendations for doing more. (One does not commission such reports with the expectation of being advised to do less.) In the meantime, on May 25, 1970, the President had met with a group of black college presidents, apparently the first such meeting ever to be held. In the aftermath of the Cambodian invasion Dr. James Cheek, president of Howard University, which is basically a federal institution, served temporarily in the White House as an associate of Chancellor Alexander Heard. During that time he made recommendations directly to the President on the subject of the black colleges. Much attention, then, was being given to this matter in the White House.

On July 23, 1970, a White House press conference was held by Brown and Robert Finch, formerly Secretary of HEW, now Counsellor to the President. The main purpose of the occasion was to release a statement by Heard on the completion of his advisory work on campus unrest. Obviously seeking to strike a positive note about the Heard-Cheek effort, the two White House men also brought up the subject of black colleges. The FICE report was given to the press, and Finch announced that on departing Dr. Cheek had filed a "separate document" on this "very unique" problem. He continued: "That just came in today. The President read it today. The President asked him to write such a report, and I am authorized to say, after discussing it with the President, that in HEW . . . we are going to increase [aid] . . . from $80 million to $100 million." Finch's numbers were somewhat garbled. HEW aid to black colleges at the time was $96 million for the fiscal year. The additional sum now being reallocated was between $29 million and $30 million. In any event, the *Times* report of the press conference did not mention this subject.

On July 31, Dr. Herman R. Branson, president of Central State University in Wilberforce, Ohio, and the new head of the National Association for Equal Opportunity in Higher Education, wrote the President expressing appreciation for his move. On August 10 the President replied:

> The present financial plight of many of our small and the overwhelming majority of our black colleges clearly demonstrates to me that the Federal Government must strengthen its role in support of these institutions.
>
> I have committed this Administration to the vigorous support of equal educational opportunity. At the same time, we are encouraging excellence in all of our institutions of higher education.*

In a release dated August 11, 1970, the National Association for Equal Opportunity in Higher Education formally responded to the administration's move. In the accepted and understood manner of interest groups, the Association expressed gratitude for what it had got, but assured the government that it was not, of course, enough. On the other hand, it was confident that more would be forthcoming:

> We do not view this excellent first step as adequate to all our needs but rather as a model of what all agencies can do. . . . With the forthright statement of the President in his letter to Dr. Branson, we are very much encouraged and heartened about the future.

The Times reported nothing of this statement, as it had reported nothing of the original announcement from the White House that an extra $30 million or so was being made available to black colleges. White House announcements, Presidential letters, Wash-

* The President was referring to his message to Congress on Higher Education of March 1970, which proposed a system of student aid by which the federal government would concentrate assistance on low-income students. A proposal to establish a National Foundation for Higher Education specifically referred to the problems of black colleges.

ington press conferences—all were ignored. The subject was not dealt with at all until the following month when, as noted earlier, a story depicted the black college presidents as denouncing the administration's "utter lack of sensitivity" on this matter. *This* story made the front page.

The day after it appeared Dr. Vivian Henderson, of Clark College in Atlanta, to whom the remark about "utter lack of sensitivity" had been attributed, sent the following unequivocal denial to *The Times*:

> I am deeply disturbed by the inaccurate reporting of the conference of Presidents of Negro Colleges that appeared in the September 14 issue of *The New York Times*. The following statement is attributed to me: "Instead the Nixon Administration's utter lack of sensitivity on this point, purposeful or otherwise, is feeding the flames that already roar in the hearts of many black students." This is a gross error and misrepresentation of what actually went on at the meeting. To be sure, we were concerned with the limited response of President Nixon to our problems. The fact is, however, that President Nixon has responded. He has not been silent with regard to concerns expressed by the Presidents in the meeting with him last May. Since the meeting with Mr. Nixon, about $27 million additional funds have been made available to black colleges. It would be unfair on our part not to recognize this response, limited though it is.
>
> I did not make the statement your reporter attributes to me. I do not recall such a statement being made during the course of the conference. . . .

The Times did not print this letter. Instead it went on to repeat the theme of the original story and gradually to establish it elsewhere as truth. In the end a small bit of history had been rewritten: even the wire services followed *The Times*'s version. *No one intended this.* That should be clear. It is simply that the journalistic system preferred a confrontation-capitulation model of events, and there was no internal corrective procedure to alert the editors to the mistakes being made.

There are true social costs in all this. For one thing, a paper like *The Times* is a prime medium for internal communication within the government itself. Any Washington official following this story in *The Times* would have had to assume that the administration's attitude toward black colleges was just about opposite to what in fact it was. Such a reversal of signals can have serious consequences. Similarly there are consequences to the principals involved, in this case the college presidents who had been acting with skill and discipline and reasonable success (most notably in having gained access: within hours of the appearance of the first *Times* story a black college president was in the White House seeking reassurance that the $27–30 million had not been jeopardized) but who found themselves represented as stereotypical confrontationists. Everyone in a sense lost because *The Times* got the story wrong.

VI

In the wake of so lengthy an analysis, what is there to prescribe? Little. Indeed, to prescribe much would be to miss the intent of the analysis. I have been hoping to make two points—the first explicitly, the second largely by implication. The first is that a convergence of journalistic tradition with evolving cultural patterns has placed the national government at a kind of operating disadvantage. It is hard for government to succeed: this theme echoes from every capital of the democratic world. In the United States it is hard for government to succeed and just as hard for government to appear to have succeeded when indeed it has done so. This situation can be said to have begun in the muckraking era with respect to urban government; it is now very much the case with respect to national government, as reflected in the "national press" which primarily includes *The New York Times,* the Washington *Post, Time, Newsweek,* and a number of other journals.

There is nothing the matter with investigative reporting; there ought to be more. The press can be maddeningly complacent about real social problems for which actual countermeasures, even solutions, exist. (I spent a decade, 1955–65, trying to obtain some press coverage of the problem of motor-vehicle design, utterly without avail. The press, from the most prestigious journals on down, would print nothing but the pap handed out by the automobile companies and wholly owned subsidiaries such as the National Safety Council.) The issue is not one of serious inquiry, but of an almost feckless hostility to power.

The second point is that this may not be good for us. American government will only rarely and intermittently be run by persons drawn from the circles of those who own and edit and write for the national press; no government will ever have this circle as its political base. Hence the conditions are present for a protracted conflict in which the national government keeps losing. This might once have been a matter of little consequence or interest. It is, I believe, no longer such, for it now takes place within the context of what Nathan Glazer recently described as an "assault on the reputation of America . . . which has already succeeded in reducing this country, in the eyes of many American intellectuals, to outlaw status. . . ." In other words, it is no longer a matter of this or that administration; it is becoming a matter of national morale, of a "loss of confidence and nerve," some of whose possible consequences, as Glazer indicates, are not pleasant to contemplate.

Some will argue that in the absence of a parliamentary question-time only the press can keep the Presidency honest. Here we get much talk about Presidential press conferences and such. This is a serious point, but I would argue that the analogy does not hold. Questions are put in Parliament primarily by members of an opposition party hoping to replace the one in office. Incompetent questions damage those chances; irresponsible questions damage the office. Indeed, British politicians have been known to compare the press lords to ladies of the street, seeking "power without responsibility." It would, of course, be better all around if Congress were more alert. Thus The Times has reported that the GNP estimate in the 1971 Budget Message was not that of the Council of Economic Advisors, but rather a higher figure dictated by the White House for political purposes. This is a profoundly serious charge. Someone has a lot to explain. It could be the administration; it could be The Times. Congress should find out.

Obviously the press of a free country is never going to be and never should be celebratory. Obviously government at all levels needs and will continue to get criticism and some of it will inevitably be harsh or destructive, often enough justifiably so.

Obviously we will get more bad news than good. Indeed the content of the newspapers is far and away the best quick test of the political structure of a society. Take a morning plane from Delhi to Karachi. One leaves with a sheaf of poorly printed Indian papers filled with bad news; one arrives to find a small number of nicely printed Pakistani papers filled with good news. One has left a democracy, and has entered a country that is something less than a democracy.

Nonetheless there remains the question of balance. Does not an imbalance arise when the press becomes a too-willing outlet for mindless paranoia of the Joseph McCarthy or New Left variety? Does it not arise when the press becomes too self-satisfied to report its own mistakes with as much enterprise as it reports the mistakes of others?

Norman E. Isaacs, a working journalist, has written thoughtfully about the possibility of establishing a "national press council." This, in effect, was proposed by Robert M. Hutchins's Commission on Freedom of the Press in 1947: "A new and independent agency to appraise and report annually upon the performance of the press." There are press councils in other democratic countries which hear complaints, hand down verdicts, and even, as in Sweden, impose symbolic fines. There is a case to be made here, but I would argue that to set up such a council in this country at this time would be just the wrong thing to do. There is a statist quality about many of the press councils abroad: often as not they appear to have been set up to ward off direct government regulation. Freedom of the press is a constitutional guarantee in the United States: how that freedom is exercised should remain a matter for the professional standards of those who exercise it. Here, however, there really is room for improvement. First in the simple matter of competence. The very responsibility of the national press in seeking to deal with complex issues produces a kind of irresponsibility. The reporters aren't up to it. They get it wrong. It would be astonishing were it otherwise.

Further, there needs to be much more awareness of the quite narrow social and intellectual perspective within which the national press so often moves. There are no absolutes here; hardly any facts. But there *is* a condition that grows more not less pronounced. The national press is hardly a "value-free" institution. It very much reflects the judgment of owners and editors and reporters as to what is good and bad about the country and what can be done to make things better. It might be hoped that such persons would give more thought to just how much elitist criticism is good for a democracy. Is this a shocking idea? I think not. I would imagine that anyone who has read Peter Gay or Walter Laqueur on the history of the Weimar Republic would agree that there are dangers to democracy in an excess of elitist attack. A variant of the Jacksonian principle of democratic government is involved here. Whether or not ordinary men are capable of carrying out any governmental task whatsoever, ordinary men are going to be given such tasks. That is what it means to be a democracy. We had best not get our expectations too far out of line with what is likely to happen, and we had best not fall into the habit of measuring all performance by the often quite special tastes, preferences, and interests of a particular intellectual and social elite. (Perhaps most importantly, we must be supersensitive to the idea that if things are not working out well it is because this particular elite is not in charge. Consider the course of events that led to the war in Indochina.)

As to the press itself, one thing seems clear. It should become much more open about acknowledging mistakes. *The Times* should have printed Dr. Henderson's letter. Doubtless the bane of any editor is the howling of politicians and other public figures claiming to have been misquoted. But often they *are* misquoted. At the very least, should not more space be allotted to rebuttals and exchanges in which the issue at hand is how the press performed?

Another possibility is for each newspaper to keep a critical eye on itself. In the article previously cited which he did for the *New York Times Magazine,* A. H. Raskin called for "a Department of Internal Criticism" in every paper "to put all its standards under reexamination and to serve as a public protection in its day-to-day operations." *The Times* itself has yet to establish such a department but the Washington *Post* has recently set a welcome example here by inaugurating a regular editorial-page feature by Richard Harwood entitled "The News Business." Harwood's business is to check up on what his paper runs, and he is finding a good deal to check up on. (To all editors: *Please* understand there is nothing wrong with this. It is a routine experience of even the most advanced sciences. Perhaps especially of such.) Harwood has made a useful distinction between mistakes of detail—the ordinary garbles and slips of a fast-moving enterprise—and mistakes of judgment about the nature of events:

> The mistakes that are more difficult to fix are those that arise out of our selection and definition of the news. Often we are unaware of error until much time has passed and much damage has been done.
>
> In retrospect, it seems obvious that the destructive phenomenon called "McCarthyism"—the search in the 1950s for witches, scapegoats, traitors—was a product of this kind of error. Joseph McCarthy, an obscure and mediocre senator from Wisconsin, was transformed into the Grand Inquisitor by publicity. And there was no way later for the newspapers of America to repair that damage, to say on the morning after: "We regret the error."

Which will turn out "in retrospect" to seem the obvious errors of the 1960s? There were many, but they are past. The question now is what might be the errors of the 1970s, and whether some can be avoided. One Richard Harwood does not a professional upheaval make, but he marks a profoundly important beginning. All major journals should have such a man in a senior post, and very likely he should have a staff of reporters to help him cover "the news business."

As for government itself, there is not much to be done, but there is something. It is perfectly clear that the press will not be intimidated. Specific efforts like President Kennedy's to get David Halberstam removed as a *Times* correspondent in Vietnam almost always fail, as they deserve to do. Nonspecific charges such as those leveled by Vice President Agnew, get nowhere either. They come down to an avowal of dislike, which is returned in more than ample measure, with the added charge that in criticizing the press the government may be trying to intimidate it, which is unconstitutional.

What government can do and should do is respond in specific terms to what it believes to be misstatements or mistaken emphases; it should address these responses to specific stories in specific papers and it should expect that these will be printed (with whatever retort the journal concerned wishes to make). Misrepresentations of government performance must never be allowed to go unchallenged. The notion of a "one-day story," and the consoling idea that yesterday's papers are used to wrap fish, are pernicious and wrong. Misinformation gets into the bloodstream and has consequences. *The Times* ought by now to have had a letter from the Chairman of the Civil Service Commission pointing out the mistakes in the November 15 story on minority employment, and the even more important omissions. If the first letter was ignored, he should have sent another. Similarly *The Times* ought long since have had a letter from an HEW official exposing the errors of its coverage of federal aid to black colleges. Failing that, someone should have called in the education writers of *The Times* and asked why they let other men misreport their beat. Etc. Hamilton's formulation has not been bettered: the measure of effective government is energy in the executive.

In the end, however, the issue is not one of politics but of culture. The culture of disparagement that has been so much in evidence of late, that has attained such an astonishing grip on the children of the rich and the mighty, and that has exerted an increasing influence on the tone of the national press in its dealings with the national government, is bad news for democracy. Some while ago the late Richard Hofstadter foresaw what has been happening:

> Perhaps we are really confronted with two cultures (not Snow's), whose spheres are increasingly independent and more likely to be conflicting than to be benignly convergent: a massive adversary culture on the one side, and the realm of socially responsible criticism on the other.

But given what has been happening to the press in recent years and what is likely to go on being the case if current trends should continue on their present path, where is such "socially responsible criticism" to come from? Or rather, where is it to appear in a manner that will inform and influence the course of public decision-making?*

* This article aroused much comment, and occasioned a lengthy rebuttal from Max Frankel (*Commentary*, July 1971). When I wrote it I was not, I think, sufficiently aware of the intensity of the fear of the Nixon administration on the part of the newspapers of which I wrote, a mutual mistrust that reached crisis propor-

tions following the advent of the Pentagon Papers, and the effort of the administration to prevent their publication. *The Times* and the *Post* won that legal battle, but did not let the matter rest there. Nor should they have. As the Presidential campaign came on, executives of these papers put forth their views with accustomed vigor. On October 19, 1972, Benjamin Bradlee, executive editor of the *Post*, as reported in the Boston *Globe*, "severely criticized fellow editors and publishers who have not realized that 'The Nixon Administration is committed to our destruction.'" On November 1 James Reston, Vice-President of the Times, lamented the heavy one-sided editorial support for the administration among the press of the nation: "Even in the midst of the most sustained campaign against the First Amendment rights of a free press in the last fifty years . . ." Just how much a campaign there was, and how it got started, ought to be the subject of careful inquiry. But *something* was going on—that is surely clear enough. It may be that now attention can turn to the more general issues of which I wrote.

The Deepening Schism

18

Anthropologists tell of a people so indifferent to complexity that the whole of their numerical systems consists of the terms "one," "two," and "many." And yet how close to our own reality they are. It is hard enough to keep two things in mind; more than that becomes immensely difficult. A while back, one of Harvard's great chemists was discoursing on what he called the "many-body problem," a condition in which the number of variables interacting with one another in any given situation makes that situation extraordinarily complicated and difficult to fathom. I asked in what range of numbers this "many-body problem" begins. A somewhat suspicious glance was returned. Did I really not know? Apparently not. "Three," he replied.

This is an aspect of our reality. It becomes significant with the onset of what James S. Coleman terms an "information-rich society." Such a society is not necessarily better able to handle itself. For people, as for rats, too much contradictory information is disorienting and there follows the impulse to get back to simple things. Could this be the origin of *"les terribles simplificateurs"* whose dominion Burckhardt forecast a hundred years ago? Were the great Whigs of the nineteenth century able to live with complexity because their information was so spare? Could

"The Deepening Schism" was first published in *The Public Interest*, Spring 1972, under the title "The Schism in Black America."

THE DEEPENING SCHISM / 345

our movement for "social indicators," a splendidly rational enterprise, only lead to more irrationality in politics, as the numbers reveal so many contradictory tendencies?

Political society wants things simple. Political scientists know them to be complex. This is no small matter. There is hardly a limit to the price people will pay to keep things simple. One could argue that, in part, the leftist impulse is so conspicuous among the educated and well-to-do precisely because they are exposed to more information, and are accordingly forced to choose between living with the strains of complexity or lapsing into simplism.

Social science needs a strategy for dealing with this condition. The various disciplines wish to become ever more complex in order, *inter alia,* to provide "more reliable guides to public policy." But as complexities compound themselves, the public is likely to ask for ever more simplicity. Or the elites will. Yes, more probably the latter. It may be that the issue cannot be resolved in the near future, that a period of ever greater complexity will be necessary before things start falling into place and grow simple again. It may be that things will never fall into place. In the meantime, a short-run coping strategy might be for social scientists to try to win confidence by making things as simple as they can—and then to draw upon that fund of confidence by asking for a little extra effort to accept complexity without being intimidated by it. Let me see whether this can be done with the always-troubled issue of race. I shall try to answer the question: "Are things getting better or worse?"

TWO MODELS

There are, of course, simple *moral* truths about race which most Americans embrace. We assert, foremost, the equality of the races, which is to say that there can be no question of hierarchical caste distinctions. Not all Americans, of course, assert this, but the trend of public opinion seems irreversible. Reviewing three decades of opinion survey findings, Andrew M. Greeley and Paul B. Sheatsley come firmly to this conclusion and find this process accelerating. The highest prointegrationist scores are among the young, and among these, "Young Southerners manifest the largest net rise. . . ." Desegregation of schools, they find, has "ceased to be a significant issue." Yet few persons would assert that there are equal conditions existing between the races in America. There are not. Nor would many argue that the present disparities are acceptable. They are not. Nor would many prudent men predict an era of mounting racial peace. Desegregation is one thing; busing another. It is an issue that could tear the 1970s apart.

Already simplicity is slipping away, and only a very few facts have been adduced, and these mostly involving popular attitudes. Is there anything simple to be said that can help a citizen or politician make sense of seeming chaos? Just possibly. Two propositions may help interpret events: *First, things are going in two directions at once. Some things are getting better, others worse. Second, considerable energy is devoted to denying either trend.*

Recall that this is an experiment, and promised relative simplicity—of an order such that the argument may be grasped by, say, a third of the persons who run for public office in a normal year.

Begin with the fact that there has been a great folk migration from the South to the North and West. We know something about this experience. As an immigrant group settles in the city, a process of differentiation commences. Given a rough equivalence of circumstance upon arrival, a group begins to sort itself out by a process perhaps not dissimilar to natural selection. In most instances (as I would judge) there is a general upward movement, but with some individuals moving farther and faster than others. Soon the peasant or village sameness is succeeded by the social distances that separate contractor from ditch digger, landlord from tenant, state senator from straight party voter. For *some* groups, however, the urban impact can be quite disorganizing, so that within the group there are those who *decline* in their circumstances as well as those who rise. Hence, along with contractor and ditch digger there comes into being the even greater gulf that separates those members in a group who rise from those who decline: criminal lawyer and criminal, social worker and social derelict.

Let the first process be called the "everybody up" model, the second the "up-and-down" model. Both were implicit in much that Nathan Glazer and I wrote in *Beyond the Melting Pot,* a project begun in the late 1950s. It may help to think of "everybody up" as, in simplified terms, the Jewish experience, and of "up-and-down" as that of the Irish, the latter being the first large rural-to-urban migration. In the early 1960s, I had become persuaded that the black experience would be "up-and-down."*

THE EXPERIENCE OF THE 1960s

When the "everybody up" model takes hold dramatically and when the group involved has characteristics that make it readily identifiable, efforts will sometimes be made to impose a ceiling on just how far up the group may go. Jews encountered this, briefly, in "quotas" at professional schools and the like. (They may soon encounter this again, although for quite different reasons.) This ceiling has the effect of a caste limitation not unlike that which blacks encountered in the South. An obvious defensive strategy was to forbid the imposition of such ceilings. Laws were passed designed to thwart such efforts—as, for example, by forbidding deans of admission to enquire as to the religion of an applicant, or, later, to ask for a photograph. All this much overestimated the upward pressures that would be exerted by most immigrant groups. The mobility of a few groups (notably the Jews and the Japanese) has been astonishing, but for most it has been modest. But this initial misapprehension led to the assumption, by concerned liberals, that the great problem for blacks in the North would be that their efforts to rise would be blocked. Blacks, from their experience in the South, had reason enough to agree.

Ethnic experience argued otherwise, or such at least was my judgment. A portion of the newcomers would rise: not dramatically, perhaps, but perceptibly. The politics and culture of the Northern city would, if anything, encourage this rise. No ceiling would be imposed. This was in part hunch, based on personal experience. I had grown up poor in New York and had found

* Glazer and I had thought it would be "everybody up" for the Puerto Ricans, but this remains in doubt. The present plight of the Puerto Ricans tends to reinforce my later judgment that the job market and social welfare arrangements of the 1960s and beyond would greatly reward some newcomers while punishing others.

this to be, if anything, rather an advantage as one commenced to show a little promise. Americans *like* poor kids coming along; they really do. (The preponderance of radical youth come from very well-to-do, even rich families. They have no way of knowing this about their country. It is, in a sense, a form of knowledge denied them, and suggests that they are entitled to a certain patience.)

Ethnic experience, however, also argued that for some groups the immigrant experience would be bi-modal. Up for some members of the group, down for others. I judged it would be "up-and-down" for the blacks, as it had been for the Irish (and some others). It seemed to me the real problem would be that of those falling through the floor, creating a twentieth-century equivalent of "the dangerous classes" which so preoccupied social reformers of the nineteenth century.

In the early 1960s, as an Assistant Secretary of Labor for Policy Planning and Research, watching the work force climb out of a sharp recession, I began to get a feeling from the figures that some weren't making it—that a marginal lower-working-class group was being left behind and was being transformed into a genuine lower class. I had data. I could show, for example, that, in the period roughly from 1945 to 1960, various indices of social dependency (e.g., the number of new AFDC cases) rose and fell in close relation to male unemployment rates, but that this "connection" suddenly broke up and disappeared in the late 1950s and early 1960s. I hypothesized that something had gone wrong in the situation of our urban blacks. In a policy paper prepared for the White House, I forecast sharply worsening conditions in the central cities of the North and West. At a time when the nation was preoccupied with civil-rights measures— measures having to do with the issues of race and caste—I said, in effect, that the real problem was going to be that of social class.

This, of course, set the stage for much misunderstanding. I saw the issue of caste—of plain racial discrimination—as one that would be relatively easily resolved, while the problem of social class among our urban blacks would be terribly tenacious. Others, especially perhaps middle-class blacks who had no great class problems but who had in their time encountered savage caste discrimination, almost had to hold the opposite view. They believed—and some still insist—that what was happening in the ghettos was not a new sociological catastrophe but just one more instance of the pernicious effects of discrimination. There followed a curious inversion: The assertion that a situation is not racial is taken as a racialist assertion.

It is now about a decade since my policy paper and its analysis. As forecasting goes, it would seem to have held up. There has been a pronounced "up-and-down" experience among urban blacks. That is to say, the measures of social well-being then employed have moved in the two contrary directions I forecast. This has been accompanied by a psychological reaction which I did not foresee, and for which I may in part be to blame. Allow equivocation here. I did not know I would prove to be so correct. Had I known, I might have said nothing, realizing that the subject would become unbearable, and rational discussion close to impossible. I accept that in social science some things are better not said. Those who would do good must be bound, as are doctors, by the law *primum non nocere* (first do no harm). But it is too late now. The "up-and-down" process has taken hold with a vengeance—and is being denied with a fury.

THE FAMILY

I had chosen to concentrate on family structure, believing it at that time to be the best "all-purpose" indicator of social distress. From this indicator, one could forecast that the number of dependent urban families would grow and with it, in Kenneth B. Clark's phrase—we were then reaching convergent judgments, and we shared information—a "tangle of pathology." This forecast, to repeat, was correct. The data are not to be challenged (although they can be differently interpreted). The connection between unemployed and dependency does indeed appear to have disappeared in the 1960s. Full and overfull employment (as a macroeconomic condition) was accompanied by full and overfull welfare rolls; and the process continues. New York City is now budgeting to have one person in six on welfare in its coming fiscal year.

Poverty is now inextricably associated with family structure. During the 1960s the number of children living in poverty declined sharply—*except for those in female-headed families; and this was true for white families as well as black.* (Were it not, a much more complicated hypothesis than mine would be required.) But this trend was most pronounced among blacks and other "new arrivals" in the city, as is shown in Tables 1 and 2.

Table 1. *Number (in thousands) of Related[1] Children Under 18 in* White *Low-Income Families*

YEAR	FEMALE HEAD	ALL OTHERS
1959	2,420	8,966
. . . .	. . . . .	. . . . .
1966	2,112	5,092
1967	1,930	4,799
1968	2,075	4,298
1969	2,093	3,684
1970	2,274	3,934

[1] Legally related to the head of the family.

Table 2. *Number (in thousands) of Related[1] Children Under 18 in* Negro *Low-Income Families*

YEAR	FEMALE HEAD	ALL OTHERS
1966	2,017	2,667
1967	2,265	2,293
1968	2,241	1,947
1969	2,239	1,640
1970	2,490	1,612

[1] Legally related to the head of the family.

As can be seen, the total number of poor white children drops sharply, rising only a small bit in the recent recession. But the number of poor white children in female-headed families, after declining also, begins to rise in 1967. At the outset of the 1970s it is almost as high as it was at the end of the 1950s. The black experience was similar, but more pronounced. In gross terms, the number of blacks below the poverty line declined 49.4 percent between 1959 and 1968 for families with male heads; but it increased 23.6 percent for those with female heads. Data for black children show an even more dramatic pattern in recent years. By 1968, the majority of poor black children were in female-headed families, and the proportion recently reached three fifths.

As would be indicated, the number of female-headed households has also increased. It is now large for both races. In 1971, in the central cities of metropolitan areas, it was 27.6 percent for whites and 39.3 percent for blacks. The *highest* proportion for any group of "recent arrivals" is not that of blacks, but of Puerto Ricans, an outcome at least consistent with the hypothesis that in the post-War period something went wrong with the incentive structures and economic opportunities of Northern urban areas. How else, for example, can one explain the great disparity —visible in Table 3—between the proportion of female-headed families among Mexican-Americans and that among Puerto Ricans?

Table 3. *Percent of Families with Female Head by Ethnic Origin: March 1971*[1]

WHITE	NEGRO	MEXICAN	PUERTO RICAN
9.4	30.6	12.0	33.9

[1] U.S. Bureau of the Census, *Current Population Reports*, Population Characteristics, "Selected Characteristics of Persons and Families of Mexican, Puerto Rican, and Other Spanish Origin: March 1971," Series P-20, No. 224, October 1971.

EVENTS ON THE UPSIDE

Events on the upside were, if anything, more dramatic. Simply put, during the 1960s young black husband-wife families (families with or without children in which both spouses are living together) began to approach—and in a number of important categories to reach—income parity with whites. Everywhere these younger blacks are closing the gaps. This is hardest to do in the South, where gaps were and are wider than elsewhere; but outside the South it is practically a *fait accompli*. Thus, in the noncommittal prose of the Bureau of the Census: *"There was no apparent difference in 1970 between the incomes of white and*

*Negro husband-wife families outside the South where the head was under 35 years old."**

Now this surely is an event: young couples from an oppressed minority starting their lives as full equals, in income terms at least, of their contemporaries in the "majority" group. Not only they, but their children.

This is not the end of it. In young families outside the South, *where both husband and wife worked*, incomes are *higher* than white. For those with heads under 35, black earnings were 104 percent of white. For those with heads under 25, black earnings were 113 percent of white. It would thus be reasonable to state that these young black couples, starting their lives together, beginning to send their children to school, beginning to look for a house perhaps, have the highest median family incomes ever recorded in the history of the world ($9,777 as against $8,678 for whites). Surely this says something about the recent past, and hopefully also about the future.

Qualifications are, as usual, necessary. Black wives work more often than white, and contribute a larger proportion of family income. But the difference is not great. In 1970, in the North and West, the proportion of young (under-35) husband-wife families with both spouses working was 54.1 percent for whites and 62.7 percent for blacks. For both groups the proportion of working wives grew considerably during the decade. (It is highest, for both, in the South.) Further, as Table 4 indicates, *for the youngest category of husband-wife families a higher proportion of white wives is working than black— and still there is overall income equality between the two groups.*

Table 4. *Husband-Wife Families in the North and West by Overall Income and Proportion of Wives Working. Head Under 25 Years. 1970.*

	WHITE	NEGRO
Income	$7,910	$7,540
Percent of wives working	69.6	61.0

* U.S. Bureau of the Census, *Current Population Reports*, Special Studies, "Differences Between Income of White and Negro Families by Work Experience of Wife and Region: 1970, 1969, and 1959," Series P-23, No. 39, December 1971.

The ratio of black to white income, 95.6 percent, passes for equality in Census usage. Thus, even though *more* white wives were working, there is a rough equality between the incomes of young black and white couples. (A possible explanation for this is that young Negro wives in the North and West—in families with a head under 35—earned approximately 30 percent *more* than their white counterparts, $3,900 as against $3,010 in 1970. It should also be noted that, outside the South, the black population is more urban than is the white, and would therefore tend to have higher earnings.)

Again, qualifications must be made. The young (under-35) husband-wife Negro family in the North and West in which *only* the male worked had earnings in 1970 only 76 percent of its white counterpart's. And one must remember: Half the black population still lives in the South, where the black income disadvantage is most pronounced. This is clear from Table 5.

Table 5. *Comparison of Median Family Income—North and West vs. South. 1970.*

	UNDER 35	35–44	45–54	55–64
		AGE OF HEAD		
WHITE				
Only husband worked				
North and West	$ 9,373	$11,215	$10,135	$ 9,524
South	8,210	9,787	9,738	8,169
Husband and wife worked				
North and West	$10,578	$13,651	$15,218	$14,027
South	9,948	12,139	13,292	11,467
NEGRO				
Only husband worked				
North and West	$ 7,104	$ 7,637	$ 8,269	(B)[1]
South	5,196	(B)[1]	(B)[1]	(B)[1]
Husband and wife worked				
North and West	$11,045	$12,317	$13,077	$11,384
South	7,464	8,993	8,196	7,385

[1] (B)—Base less than 75,000.

This said, it remains the case that the trend lines are consistent and powerful. If they persist, that is to say, if the present income equality of these young black/white families holds up as they grow older, one of the fundamental correlates of race in the United States—inferior earning power—will disappear.

EDUCATION AND "THE DEEPENING SCHISM"

This improvement did not "just" happen *to* blacks. It was made to happen *by* black persons working hard for things they want. It reflects also a changing reward structure. Andrew F. Brimmer, who has no peer in this area of analysis, has shown that in the 1960s the economic rewards of higher education among blacks sharply increased, but that there was little improvement for persons with less schooling. Between 1967 and 1968, the median income of Negro families headed by a person with *any* college experience rose from $8,686 to $10,704, or $2,018. In the same period, income for comparable whites rose from $11,548 to $12,356, or $808. Brimmer writes:

> Within this very short time horizon (one year) the median income of a Negro family headed by an individual with some college increased by 23.2 percent, compared to a rate of growth of only 7.0 percent for a white family headed by someone with some college education.

By contrast, he continues, the growth in income for Negro families headed by someone with only an elementary or high school education was not significantly different: For those with some high school the Negro increase was 12.1 percent; the white, 8.0 percent. For those with only eight years of education, the gap actually widened, with whites gaining 6.6 percent and Negroes only 3.0. Brimmer perceives a general pattern:

> In 1967 median family income for Negroes with a head who had four or more years of college was 55.8 percent higher than for a family headed by someone with only four years of high school. One year later this gap had widened to 74.0 percent. For white families the income increment for families with a head who had four years or more of college was 42.4 percent above those with a high school diploma in 1967, and in 1968 this gap actually narrowed slightly to 40.4 percent. . . . The income position of Negro families headed by someone with a college

degree is moving substantially closer to white families with college degrees—and progressively further away from Negro families headed by someone with only elementary or high school education.

This variance is striking in young families. In 1968 the Negro family headed by a 24-to-34-year-old person with one to three years of college had a median income 111.1 percent higher than one headed by a person with only one to three years of high school. For white families, this gap was only 29.6 percent.

In the period roughly 1964–1965, when I became persuaded that this "up-and-down" development had commenced, and would grow more pronounced, my writing concentrated upon those in trouble, the female-headed families. But the "upside" was also evident, although no one, at least not I, foresaw that it would take off nearly so dramatically as it did (as for example in black college enrollment, which increased 85 percent between 1964 and 1968). Brimmer was then an Assistant Secretary of Commerce, plying his trade of economist, and was not, as I recall, deep into this subject as yet. Since then, having become a Governor of the Federal Reserve System, he has made it his business to keep after the data, and has become most emphatic about what, in a 1970 speech at the Tuskegee Institute on "Economic Progress of Negroes in the United States," he termed "The Deepening Schism."

During the 1960s, Negroes as a group *did* make significant economic progress. This can be seen in terms of higher employment and occupational upgrading as well as in lower unemployment and a narrowing of the income gap between Negroes and whites.

However, beneath these overall improvements, another—and disturbing—trend is also evident: Within the Negro community, there appears to be a deepening schism between the able and the less able, between the well-prepared and those with few skills.

This deepening schism can be traced in a number of ways, including the substantial rise in the proportion of Negroes employed in professional and technical jobs—while the proportion in low-skilled occupations also edges upward; in the sizable decline in unemployment—while the share of Negroes among the long-term unemployed rises; in the persistence of inequality in income distribution within the black community—while a trend toward greater equality is evident among white families; above all in the dramatic deterioration in the position of Negro families headed by females.

In my judgment, this deepening schism within the black community should interest us as much as the real progress that has been made by Negroes as a group.

More recently, Michael J. Flax of the Urban Institute, using nonwhite rates of change on various social indicators for the period 1960–1968, calculated the "Approximate Year Nonwhite Levels Might Reach 1968 White Levels." His figures suggest that, in the course of the 1970s, blacks will reach the 1968 white level in a whole range of categories: percent completing high school, percent in clerical occupations, percent with incomes over $8,000 (1968 dollars), median family income, percent in professional and technical occupations, and even fertility rate.

At the bottom of Flax's scale, however, are three indices of family structure: percent illegitimate births, percent female-headed families, and percent children living with two parents. Here no date for "catching up" with 1968 white America is given. The chart reads, "Probably Never."

DENYING THE FACTS

This "up-and-down" pattern would seem by now to be sufficiently pronounced to have impressed itself on persons concerned with reporting, or analyzing, or shaping public policy. It has not. This is a difficult statement to prove, but the reader might ask himself or herself whether reading the facts so far presented does not come as something of a surprise. Professors might inquire as to how many students students are aware of these trends, or would believe them when confronted by evidence. This brings us to the second of the propositions asserted earlier: that a considerable energy is devoted to denying either trend.

As I have little more than opinion—albeit a painfully informed opinion—to offer by way of explanation of this phenomenon, the reader will be best served by a fairly brief presentation of probable-to-possible explanations. To begin with, these "up-

and-down" events have occurred in a period of mounting radical criticism of American society. This radical impulse derived, for the most part, from concerns only marginally related to poverty and race. But once a general movement to the left was under way, these issues were seized upon for understandable strategic reasons. Against relatively little resistance, radical ideologists have been insisting that almost everything is getting worse, and denying that anything is getting better. This insistence has made more of an impression on whites than on blacks. In their study, *Hopes and Fears of the American People,* Albert H. Cantril and Charles W. Roll, Jr., report than nonwhites, in sharp contrast to whites, see the nation as having progressed in recent years. Whites see only regression. Some of these whites are traditionalists, no doubt; but there is abundant and vocal evidence that large portions of the affluent, educated classes, for whom the nation has become something of an abomination, are to be found among them too.*

Denial can take the form of lying, which is common, or disputing facts, also common. (At a very good university—it must be *very* good for this test to succeed—one can come upon students who "know" that the Census rigs the data to please The Establishment.) Just as viable is the technique of redefinition. Not just among radicals, but in a more general way among affluent youth, there has developed an insistence that things previously called success are *not* success. Acquiring one wife, three kids, two cars, and a house in the suburbs can, if one wishes, be defined as disaster. The media are sensitized to this view, and hence have made much less of black success, in these "straight" terms, than they might otherwise have done.

Further, it has proved impossible to establish a reasoned discussion on family structure as a social problem. This, like the radical resurgence, is rather a phenomenon of the 1960s. A brief

---

* Observe, for example, the present rewriting of the political history of the "war on poverty" of the Kennedy-Johnson Administration in the early 1960s. That such an effort was launched is difficult to deny, but the explanation is now almost everywhere to be encountered that it was launched out of fear of an insurrectionary proletariat. Men of government *who were there*—James L. Sundquist, John C. Donovan, Adam Yarmolinsky—have written careful accounts that show nothing of the sort happened, but to little apparent consequence.

chronology may help explain. In March 1965, I finished a report for President Johnson that began, "The United States is approaching a new crisis in race relations." As remarked earlier, I felt the struggle to overcome caste discrimination in the South was all but won, but that *a new crisis of social class in the North* was coming, and that few were prepared even to understand this, much less to respond in advance with social measures that might head it off. In June, the President made this the theme of his address at Howard University. The reception was most cordial.

But two months later, hours after the Voting Rights Act was signed, the riot broke out in Watts. Victims became aggressors. Washington was startled and uncomprehending. In the midst of the crisis, the White House made public my report. Suddenly the subject of family structure came to be associated with this painful new circumstance, which is to say, riotous and self-destructive behavior on the part of a group previously (and accurately) depicted as singularly victimized. With the onset of rioting, black spokesmen were in a defensive position in America, no matter how much whites were blamed for having made it possible or inevitable. These spokesmen found it impossible to face up to what was really happening in the ghettos. Nevertheless, when the rioting subsided, the reality of self-victimization in the slums began to emerge. Central to this was the exploitation and suffering implicit in the ever-growing number of dependent families. To a community desperately declaring its unity and coherence, this was painful evidence of just the opposite. Hence the more evident it became, the less possible it was to discuss it: Black leaders took every such effort at discussion as a white, racist attempt at self-exculpation, an evasion of responsibility for the black condition. Some spokesmen went further. A literature of denial steadily accumulated on the general theme that there was nothing wrong with these family arrangements, that what was wrong was a sick society which could not see it as a "natural" and healthy adaptation. I personally came in for a good deal of abuse, although I would say that this did not become hysterical until the welfare rolls in New York City passed the one million mark.*

---

* I cannot expect the reader to be as interested in this subject as I have been—and even my interest has strayed in recent years—but the con-

A FAILURE OF ENQUIRY

The central assertion of my critics was that responsibility for the situation lay with those who pointed it out. This is common enough in human experience, and as such no cause for alarm. But there was also an edge to some of the attacks that takes one back to Hannah Arendt's depiction of the totalitarian elites of the 1930s in Europe, who maintained their positions through an

---

tinued and even growing number of books and articles taking off from this event seems most unusual. Not all this writing is hostile, and some has certainly helped my understanding. Thus Ronald Berman, in his study, *America in the Sixties: An Intellectual History*, writes:

> If the great event of the Fifties was the [*Brown v. Bd. of Education*] decision of the Supreme Court, the great event of the Sixties was, I think, the publication of the Moynihan Report. . . . The former defined the external, political limits of the problem—the latter defined its inherent character. The Report qualified the idea of progress and implicitly criticized the ideology surrounding civil rights. The sociology of civil rights, unlike its politics, argues that the realities of change are not solely matters of law; it argues that the limiting factors of change are not solely those of the white community. *The Negro Family*, with its description of social pathology, was particularly demoralizing to those who gave their faith to political action. Yet it did not initiate a new sense of the Negro condition. It was only a sad but intelligent summation.

Five years ago, I should have vigorously resisted this assessment, arguing that the Report simply called for a new direction in politics, basically one toward income redistribution. I am older, wiser, even sadder, and am no longer sure. In the fall of 1965, I published a summation of my research as the lead article in an issue of *Daedalus* devoted to "The Negro American." The President of the United States wrote an introduction to this volume. Everyone was most pleased, not least with my contribution entitled "Employment, Income, and the Ordeal of the Negro Family." I had concluded with the assertion that there was not a minute to lose, that a crisis of commitment was upon us, but clearly, I felt, we would do what had to be done. Instead, all concerned, or almost all, have since turned and attacked not the problem but the definition of it. Recently, one of the contributors to the original *Daedalus* volume, again writing in *Daedalus*, reported that there was much resentment from the moment President Johnson raised the issue of the black family at Howard University. But certainly no one gave voice to this at the time. I cannot but believe that the riots made the difference.

ability to turn every statement of fact into a question of motive. It would not be so bad were it not that so much of the literature of denial has assumed scholarly garb. One man launched an academic career with a small volume revealing in triumphant tones that, as incomes rose, black/white family structure converged. The elementary question that would be put to a sophomore—which was the dependent variable, income or family structure?—was not put to this man; he had come forward with an ideologically correct proposition. Yet the welfare rolls continued to swell. This, it was then explained, was a good thing: The new recipients had been eligible all along, but were only just coming into their rights, and welfare money would help solve their problems. That the three final social indicators listed by Flax continued to deteriorate was ignored, or even denied.

There really has been a failure of enquiry. Several years ago I had about completed a vast book on the subject, but decided not to publish it. All I had achieved was a description of the problem. Others have done this, and have done it better than I could. But causality eludes us. *Why* is this tragedy happening? Some attention is being paid the curious differential in sex ratios between American races. (For every 100 females born in 1968, there were, respectively, 105.6 Caucasian males, but only 102.6 Negro males. Oriental ratios are frequently higher than Caucasian.) This pattern has existed and has been known for some decades now. It surely has some consequences, but it is hard to see how it can explain the recent emergence of such large numbers of female-headed families. Similarly, the notion that there is an obvious historical explanation for the phenomenon—a position first advanced, I believe, by W. E. B. Du Bois in *The Negro American Family* in 1908 (although Tocqueville put forth much the same view in a report prepared for the French Senate in 1839)—is being shaken by historians. The present situation seems to be of relatively recent origin. I persist in the belief that its explanation will be found in changing relationships between employment and income, and especially in the presence of welfare income as an alternative to earnings. But, to my knowledge, little serious analysis of this question is going forward.

I take this to be a form of indifference to pain. Those children are there, and their misery is not going to be reduced by well-paid ideologues explaining that they are the product of liberated sexual mores, freed of bourgeois hypocrisy. Still, I see no prospect that this pattern of denial will change—*unless* the situation begins to improve, and the question may be posed in terms of helping it to improve even faster. A cursory look at the demographic profile suggests that this can come in the early 1980s, after having leveled off in the mid-1970s. Possibly sooner. Since none of us who write about the subject feels any of the pain, I imagine we shall summon the reserves of character required to wait.

FEEDING THE HORSE TO NOURISH THE SPARROW

In the meantime, it has apparently become necessary to deny that the condition of other blacks has improved in any respect. There is no mystery to this. There are few more valuable assets a group can possess in modern America than a belief by the larger society that it has been the victim of injustice. Blacks, who have been subjected to incredible injustice, have every reason to want to keep up the pressure on whites, and to be intensely suspicious of anything that might lead to a lessening sense of obligation—particularly if this, in turn, should lead to dismantling the enormous service programs (and their derivative organizations) which government has created to deal with problems of the poor. Recently Senator Abraham Ribicoff, a former Secretary of Health, Education, and Welfare, estimated that there are some 168 anti-poverty programs sponsored by the federal government at an annual cost of $31 billion. If one third of this amount, he notes, was given directly to the poor, there would no longer *be* any poverty in the United States (except, of course, that the poverty level would immediately be reestimated up). The Senator is right, but his very data suggest why little will come of his being right. Thirty-one billion dollars is a lot of money. Some of it goes to the poor, but a great deal also goes to the middle class, including those the programs have made middle-class. There are no direct data, but it would seem reasonable to interpret the sharp rise in the income of educated blacks during the 1960s as, *in part,* the result of the success of this group in asserting *its* right to the jobs that go with providing services to the black poor. Blacks had every reason to do this. But there now exists a tremendous *social and class interest* in maintaining these subsidies. It is not an interest of the poor but of those who minister to them. The social science of the 1960s has pretty much demolished the notion that much comes of "enriched" service programs, excepting the enrichment of the service-dispensing classes. These programs are more or less ingenious instances of that old technique: feed the horses in order to nourish the sparrows that are in the vicinity. The horses have always found this plausible.

It is not astonishing then that there was genuine fury—the fury of an important interest suddenly threatened—in a number of service organizations when the news of progress in reducing black/white income inequality began to be made known. Again, I seem to have been responsible. I first made the point in the spring of 1970, after having got the Census to break out the income figures for families in the North and West with heads under 25. It turned out that in 1968 this figure for blacks was practically level with the white figures. This seemed good news: a credit to the young black people and, for a change, no disgrace to the country. It also seemed to me to buttress the case for establishing a guaranteed income for families on the other end of the income distribution. But the revelation was not welcomed. It was resented, and the by-now familiar attacks began. When, last December, the Census published the newest data, including information on working wives, it was made—by various journalists and scholars—to seem a refutation of the earlier assertion. Where there was income equality it was only because wives worked! But this is not at all what the data say. Where *young* wives work, outside the South, there is most likely to be income inequality—in favor of blacks! Among my under 25's, fewer black wives than white wives were working in 1970—but still there was income equality. Good news? Not on your life. The media, having largely ignored the progress toward equality, now reported the new data in terms of the dispute over what equality meant.

SECOND-ORDER EFFECTS

It does not seem to me that any of these strategies give cause for concern in their first-order effects. Of course blacks should keep up the pressure. Of course they should try to get jobs being handed out to deal with black problems. But there are two possible second-order effects which need to be looked at. The first has to do with the condition of the poor. It is not good. Recently, a black professional was named Correction Commissioner of New York City, the first of his race in that position, which pays $37,500. At the time of his appointment he estimated, according to *The Times*, "that between 90 percent and 95 percent of the city's prisoners were black or Puerto Rican." The Commissioner seems a fine man, and it is altogether reasonable, given that prison population, to *expect* that there should be a black commissioner. (Typically, he replaced an Irishman, the end of a line that more or less commenced when the city's jails were disproportionately filled with Irish.) But satisfaction at this event could easily conceal the *pain* implicit in a criminal class so disproportionately drawn from two groups, and in consequence disproportionately preying on those two groups. Pain for the victim; pain for the criminal; a pathology that must be untangled, and not simply used to improve the condition of others. I say this with some force, after almost three years of watching the poverty professionals of every race, color, and creed all but systematically attempting to block the effort by the federal government to establish a guaranteed income for the poor. Power to some people corrupts.

The other of the second-order effects which come of denying improvement where it has occurred has to do with national morale. Social change is not easily achieved. When it successfully occurs, we ought to know about it, and permit it to cheer us up. There is little danger that we will grow complacent. Nothing I have written in this article provides *any* grounds for complacency. Lower-class behavior in our cities is shaking them apart. Upper-class lying—that the men in jail are political prisoners, that the fatherless child is happier, that the welfare system is a conspiracy to keep the proletariat passive—is destroying standards of discourse. The language of politics grows more corrupt. We have graduated a demi-generation of students who appear lost to reality. We are beginning to encounter middle-of-the-road politicians who will seemingly say anything. We approach a fantasized condition. All the more, then, is the need for the public to get a good hold on reassuring events when they do occur. This is especially so when the events can reasonably be

interpreted as, in part, the successful outcome of public policies
—which I believe is the case with the rising incomes of educated
young blacks.

ENVOI

To illustrate, and be done with the proposition that in our present
state good news is bad news for the generality of those who
interpret social data in this field, let me touch on the subject of
medical disqualification rates for military service. I first came
upon this subject in the summer of 1963. Kennedy's legislative
program was dead in the water. Almost the only bill of consequence to have passed the Congress was an extension of the
draft, which the Senate had debated for ten minutes. On June 30,
or thereabouts, the director of Selective Service submitted his
annual report to the President and Congress, noting that once
again about half the draftees called for preinduction examination
were found mentally or medically disqualified, or both. This
news rated two inches in the Washington *Post*, the point being it
was not news but rather the routine, recurrent finding. It struck
me, however. If half the nation's youth were not qualified for
military service, was this not an argument for the President's
Youth Employment Act, the biggest of the Labor Department's
bills that year, and one high in the President's priorities? (It
eventually became Title I of the Economic Opportunity Act.)
Was it not also the case that Selective Service might be used as
a screen to identify young people entering the work force with
educational or medical deficiencies? I proposed an enquiry. The
President's Task Force on Manpower Conservation (!) was duly
established. Much came of this. Our report, *One Third of a
Nation*, was finished by January. It was in many ways the first
profile of poverty the federal government had yet developed. The
linkage between failure on the mental tests (the Armed Forces
Qualification Test, or AFQT) with common indices of poverty—
region, race, family size, and such—was striking. It was about
the best data available to the planners just then beginning work
on the poverty program. It launched Project 100,000 in the Defense Department. It even spurred James S. Coleman, in designing his epic *Survey of Equal Educational Opportunity*, to ask

questions about family background from which emerged the central finding of his study of educational achievement.

One aspect of the Selective Service data and the report, however, was ignored at the time and has been since. *It appeared that poor persons—persons with less education, nonwhites, Southerners—were healthier than others!* Consistently, such persons had quite the lowest medical disqualification rates. I inquired about this around HEW and the Pentagon, but no one seemed to know anything—or, rather, everyone knew it could not be so. Only once thereafter am I aware of any notice being taken of it. A delegation of Black Muslims called on me in Cambridge to see if I knew anything more about these extraordinary statistics. *They* believed them.

On returning to Washington in 1969, I probed a bit further and learned that the military, in the slow but fine grinding way of bureaucracy, had been pursuing the matter. A difficulty with Selective Service data is that they not only exclude obviously disqualified persons, who are not sent forward by their draft boards, but also leave out an even larger proportion of persons who volunteer or go into the reserves or officers training, so that draft disqualification rates are higher than "true" rates. (The Director's one half became the Task Force's *One Third*.) The military had now aggregated a more representative pool, including enlistment examinations, which—while still not fully representative of the population—was quite good enough for the purpose of comparing disqualification rates by race and education level. In 1970, a summary of *preliminary* findings was prepared for me, which may as well be quoted verbatim:

I. *Whites have a higher medical disqualification rate than Negroes.* In 1969, 33 percent of the white examinees were found physically unfit for military service during preinduction examinations, compared to 24 percent of the Negroes. As shown in Table A, this white-Negro difference has persisted for many years.

2. *Better-educated men have higher medical disqualification rates than those with lesser education.* The data show that within each race, better-educated men fail the medical examination more frequently than poorly educated men. However, we still find that at each educational level the white medical disqualification rate is higher than for Negroes with the same education.

For the total population, the medical disqualification rate is

Table A. *Percent Disqualified for Medical Reasons on Preinduction Examinations—Initial Examinations Only*

	WHITE	NEGRO
July 1950—December 1965	22	13
1966	25	16
1967	28	19
1968	30	20
1969	33	24

28 percent compared to 19 percent for Negroes. When we standardize for education (by assuming that white and Negro examinees have the same educational level), the Negro disqualification rate rises to 22 percent. This indicates that the higher educational level of white examinees accounts for about one third of the white-Negro difference in medical disqualification rates.

Table B. *Percent Disqualified for Medical Reasons by Educational Level—Preinduction, Induction, and Enlistment Exams. Aug.–Sept. 1969.*

EDUCATIONAL LEVEL	PERCENT DISQUALIFIED	
	WHITE	NEGRO
Elementary School	24	17
Some High School	23	18
High School Graduate	25	18
Some College	31	26
College Graduate	38	31
Total—All Educational Levels	28	19
Total—Standardized by Education	28	22

3. *Men who score high on the Armed Forces Qualification test (AFQT) have a greater medical disqualification rate than those who receive low scores on the mental test.* For each race, men with better test scores tend to fail the medical examination more frequently. Still, at each mental group, whites have a higher medical failure rate. When we standardize for mental test score, medical disqualification rates for whites and Negroes become closer. Scores on the AFQT account for about 45 percent of the racial difference in medical disqualification rates.

Table C. *Percent Disqualified for Medical Reasons by Mental Group
—Preinduction, Induction, and Enlisted Exams. Aug.–Sept. 1969.*

AFQT MENTAL GROUP AND PERCENTILE SCORE	PERCENT DISQUALIFIED WHITE	NEGRO
I (100–93)	29	27
II (92–65)	29	27
III (64–31)	28	22
IV (30–10)	26	18
V (9–0)	26	17
Total—All Mental Groups	28	19
Total—Standardized by Mental Score	28	23

The Pentagon analysts were careful. They assumed that better-educated persons were less willing to enter the armed services, had more extensive medical histories, knew them better, and so found it easier to get themselves disqualified. It is easy to think of further possibilities (e.g., better-educated men might be older and thus more likely to be past their physical peak). In various ways the Vietnam war has surely distorted the data. Obviously, as the war grew bigger, the youth of America got "sicker" and medical disqualification rates rose. And yet—and yet the ratios persist through peace and war, high draft calls and low. In 1959, 134,601 persons were examined, and 24 percent of whites and 14 percent of blacks were medically disqualified. In 1966, 1,455,-020 persons were examined, and 25 percent of whites and 16 percent of blacks were medically disqualified. One asked about medical disqualification rates for persons who apply for enlistment. A table was prepared based on initial examinations of applicants for enlistment, men who did not receive a prior "pre-induction examination." Disparities diminished, but persisted.

Table D. *Percent Disqualified for Medical Reasons by Educational Level. Applicants for Enlistment—Initial Examinations. Aug.–Sept. 1969.*

EDUCATIONAL LEVEL	WHITE	NEGRO
Elementary School	12	8
College Graduate	13	12

What about medical separations from service "For Prior Existing Defects"—that is to say, men drafted or enlisted who are thereafter found to have been disqualified? Again a diminished pattern, but a persistent one: In Fiscal Year 1967, 1.6 percent for whites, 1.4 percent for blacks. (As to the charge that blacks were being used for cannon fodder, to the best of my knowledge at no time in the post-War period has the black proportion of the armed forces equaled the black proportion of the relevant age group.) For whatever reason, Southerners in general do best on medical tests. In the period 1953–1969, of draftees examined for military service, 35 percent of whites and 65 percent of blacks came from the South. In that period, the proportion disqualified for medical reasons on initial preinduction examinations was lowest for both blacks and whites in the South Atlantic states.

Hard to accept? Precisely. And yet is it really inconceivable? The staff paper from the Pentagon concluded:

> We cannot rule out the possibility that the differences in disqualification rates by race and education are in fact due to real differences in physical condition. . . . For example, white youths have a higher prevalence of medical disqualifications for psychiatric disorders and allergic disorders than Negroes, and for both races the rates for these disorders are higher for men with greater education.

Not entirely inconceivable. A report of the National Center for Health Statistics on "Differentials in Health Characteristics by Color" for 1965–1967 notes: "The proportion of white males with one or more chronic conditions exceeded that of nonwhite males in each age group. . . ."

Still, I cannot really bring myself to believe that blacks have better health than whites, Southerners than Northerners, grade school graduates than college graduates. I would be happy to learn it *is* so, to learn that people who get the dirty end of the stick in so much have been lucky about something. But I suspect that it probably isn't. The Defense Department study has recently been finished—it reveals a narrowing of the black/white gap—but not much more is really understood now than in 1963. One assumes that the data reflect a greater desire and ability of better-off persons to avoid military service; but one does not *know*. My point is this: *What if the data pointed in the opposite direction?*

How reluctant would we then be to accept them? The answer is obvious. If the health differentials in these data ran in the expected direction, they would be routinely accepted (as were the mental test outcomes) and incessantly cited as "proof" of how very bad things are. Since they are not useful for such "proof," they are ignored. And yet so much in our data—and in our society—runs in different and unexpected directions!

How shall we deal with the "many body" problem, which is to say, the need to keep three or more vectors in mind when assessing the state of social well-being at this time? A tentative answer would have to be that neither the will nor the capacity to do so exists in sufficient degree to make an impress on social policy. Still, resources are limited, and if we refuse to recognize situations which may be improving, we may fail to concentrate our efforts on situations which are not. This is a good formula for confirming the posture that everything *is* getting worse. It is a formula that many find so very enchanting these days.

Cui Bono?

19

A series of recent state and federal court decisions, just now reaching the Supreme Court on appeal, have held that expenditure per pupil in public schools must be equal for all students in any given state, or nearly equal, or in any event not differing in amounts clearly associated with the differing per capita wealth of different school districts. The legal arguments behind these decisions have varied somewhat, but the primary thrust has been that of "equal protection of the laws," with much owing, in almost every case, to the arguments successfully presented to the California Supreme Court in the 1971 decision of *Serrano v. Priest*. These in turn derived in considerable measure from the 1970 study *Private Wealth and Public Education* by John E. Coons, William H. Clune, and Stephen D. Sugarman.

On first encounter, these cases conform to a familiar pattern of social reform in the present age, most notably in their use of the judicial process to bring about results that apparently cannot be obtained through the political process concerning matters theretofore deemed to be within the political realm. But these events also reveal another, more recent pattern, which has only just begun to take hold in the American polity. For the judicial

"Cui Bono?" was first published in *The Public Interest*, Fall 1972, under the title "Equalizing education: in whose benefit?"

actions are self-induced, or nearly so. Almost wherever one looks, government-paid lawyers are involved on behalf of the plaintiffs. There emerges an autogamous mode of government growth: big government ordering itself to become bigger.

These actions in the area of education are probably the first of a new class of cases that will now be argued in many fields. They raise important constitutional issues having to do with the extent to which the citizen is entitled as a matter of right to have the state do certain things for him. At issue too are questions of social power which the public has a right to expect will also be taken into account as these other matters go forward. The ancient query, "*Cui bono?*" may be invoked: To whose benefit do these decisions redound?

WHAT WE SPEND ON EDUCATION

The most striking aspect of educational expenditure is how large it has become. Those who wish to argue that it is still not large enough are free to do so, and may well be right; but no one can contend that schools have been slighted in the past decade. Legislatures—in the aggregate—have levied ever-increasing amounts of money to pay for them. For the past ten years the proportion of Gross National Product expended on elementary and secondary education has risen at a rate almost half again that of the GNP itself. This education expenditure has been rising 9.7 percent annually, as against the 6.8 percent increase in GNP. The total cost of elementary and secondary education has more than doubled in the past ten years, as has expenditure per pupil. By the 1971–72 school year, current expenditure per pupil in "average daily attendance" had reached $929, and should now be near the $1000 mark. In 1971–72, some $46.8 billion was expended by public schools.

There is nothing especially notable about these rates of growth; they correspond to a general surge in public expenditure in almost every sector save defense. Writing of the ten-year period now ending, Charles L. Schultze and his colleagues at the Brookings Institution report that "in the space of ten short years, federal civilian expenditures as a percentage of GNP almost doubled."

State and local budgets, from which the great proportion of elementary and secondary school expenditure comes, rose at similar rates.

A second fact about educational expenditure is that it varies considerably by area in fairly close approximation to the wealth of the areas involved. In 1970, California, the venue of the *Serrano* decision, had the eighth highest per capita income in the nation, and the sixth highest per pupil expenditure on education. In the school year 1969–70, the average per pupil expenditure in California was $922; Mississippi spent $476. As with many of the individual school districts to which the *Serrano* class of decisions is directed, the low expenditures for education in Mississippi reflect more the low level of aggregate wealth than any manifest unwillingness to tax. In Mississippi, 4.97 percent of per capita personal income is spent on elementary and secondary education, which contrasts to a national average of 4.46 percent. New York taxes at a somewhat lower rate than Mississippi, 4.92 percent of per capita income; but this produces $1,237, almost three times the per pupil expenditure figure for Mississippi. A familiar situation.

Less familiar, but central to the thrust of these decisions, is the variation in school expenditure within states. Allowing for exceptions, a simple pattern seems to be typical throughout most of the country. Suburbs spend about the average, central cities at or slightly above the average, small towns and rural areas below the average. This is a long-standing situation. State aid programs in New York, for example, begin as a deliberate effort to "equalize" expenditure between the "rich" cities and the "poor" countryside. The wealth of New York City, as George Washington Plunkitt observed, was "pie for the hayseeds," and slice it they did; but never to the point of equality. (I write these lines in a one-room schoolhouse in upstate New York which was not closed until the year I matriculated in a veritable palace of a high school newly opened in East Harlem under the patronage of Vito Marcantonio and Fiorello La Guardia.)

A final fact, even less familiar (or more resisted), is that after a point school expenditure does not seem to have any notable influence on school achievement. To repeat, *after* a point. A school without a roof, or without books, or without teachers would probably not be a school in which a great deal of learning went on. But once expenditure rises above a certain zone, money doesn't seem to matter very much in terms of what happens to students. This "discovery" was one of the major events in large-scale social science during the 1960s (albeit one well anticipated in small-scale work), but it is of the first importance to understand that it was not unique. Something like the same thing has been "discovered" about a whole range of public services. In the main, the finding is that the influence of these mechanistic "interventions" (government programs) is distinct but limited, and often easily outdistanced by other influences of a more organic nature (family, peer group, etc.). Although a fair amount of recrimination has attended these "findings," they ought not to cause any great grief to competent persons. Indeed, if one is concerned with the expanding power of the state, evidence that its influence soon reaches an end with respect to many fundamental matters is, on the whole, cheering. Moreover, while the differential effects of state intervention may be small, they may be no less crucial for that reason.

WILL MORE MONEY DO ANY GOOD?

In the hope of evading the rancor that surrounds this subject in the United States, I submit recent data from a longitudinal study of British schoolchildren. Children born in 1958 were compared in terms of family size, social class ("I" being high; "V" low), sex, and region (England, Scotland, Wales). Here are the differences (as recounted in the journal *New Society*) children absorb from the air they breathe:

> The average difference in . . . test scores between, on the one hand, English boys in social class V who have four and more brothers and sisters, and on the other hand, Scottish girls in social class I who are only children, is equivalent to a gain in reading age of nearly four years.

If this is so, certain strategies come to mind. More youths might be shipped off to Scotland. A bonus might be paid for aborting fifth and sixth children. Mothers might be encouraged to have more girl babies. Income redistribution might help. Certain kinds of teaching might help. But, on balance, one would not conclude from the British data that increasing educational expenditure could do much to close that gap of nearly four years.

A comparable judgment would have to be made of the American situation. There are considerable regional, class, racial, and ethnic variations in certain kinds of achievement. We would like to see them eliminated, even in the knowledge that this might nudge us yet further along toward Michael Young's dilemma. But it is simply not clear that school expenditure is the heart of the matter. In 1971, the Rand Corporation carried out for the President's Commission on School Finance a review and synthesis of research findings on the effectiveness of education. The result was thoroughly predictable, but nonetheless devastating to whatever is left of conventional wisdom in this field. Simply put, in the range of current educational practice, regarding levels of expenditure, types of teaching, and such, the researchers found that no *"variant of the existing system . . . is consistently related to students' educational outcomes."** Put another way, *"research has found nothing that consistently and unambiguously makes a difference in student outcomes."* The report continues, "There is good reason to ask whether our educational problems are, in fact, school problems." And it concludes with two policy implications, each stated as gently as seemed possible:

> *Increasing expenditures on traditional educational practices is not likely to improve educational outcomes substantially.*
>
> *There seem to be opportunities for significant redirections and in some cases reductions in educational expenditures without deterioration in educational outcomes.*

A member of the President's Commission would have had to be dim indeed to fail to grasp that the Rand Corporation analysts were suggesting that with respect to school finance there is a strong possibility that we may already be spending too much.†

---

* Harvey A. Averch, *et al., How Effective Is Schooling? A Critical Review and Synthesis of Research Findings.* (Santa Monica: The Rand Corporation, January 1972), pp. xii, xiii. (All italics theirs.)

† Item: In 1966 Congress directed a nationwide program of driver education, at just that moment when it became unmistakable that no case could be made that driver training has any significant favorable effect

This thought will offend some persons, including perhaps some who have no doubt whatever that the military is spending too much. But giving offense would seem to be the role of social science at this time. And there is worse. It is no great matter that the Scarsdale school system spends extra money and gets little extra in return. But the record of compensatory education, as reported by the Rand study, is wrenching. There is small consolation to be had in articles such as "How Regression Artifacts in Quasi-experimental Evaluation Can Mistakenly Make Compensatory Education Look Harmful," to cite from the bibliography but one effort to ease the pain of unwelcome findings. These are the facts we have to live with, and they do not at this time make any case for a general increase in educational expenditure.

Certainly, they make no case for a simple-minded mandate to impose equal expenditure on the existing system. One hastens to say that men such as John E. Coons, the prime intellectual mover behind the *Serrano* decision, have nothing of the sort in mind; and it may be that the courts are well aware of the many complexities of this subject. If so, however, the courts have not let us know this. Their decisions have been couched in the simplistic language of an unreflective and uninformed progressivism. That they mean well is not to be doubted; *but will they do good?* Or, putting that question aside, will the court orders have the effect envisioned by the court? Just possibly. That is to say, just possibly there are some genuinely learned justices on those benches who do indeed understand the probable effect of their decisions but, informed by some involute theory of judicial restraint, choose not to let the public in on the secret.

The secret is simple enough. *If school expenditures are to be equalized within states, considerable sums will have to be taken away from schools attended by the lowest-income and the highest-income students and given to schools attended by students in the middle-income range.* This assertion could be wrong; it could be refuted. But all the evidence that comes to hand suggests that this

---

on driver performance. Vast sums have been expended since and will be expended hence. See my *Report of the Secretary's Advisory Committee on Traffic Safety* (U.S. Dept. of HEW, 1968); also, Harry H. Harman, *et al., Evaluation of Driver Education and Training Programs* (Princeton, N.J.: Educational Testing Service, 1969).

would be the overall effect of equalizing a fixed amount of school expenditure. This is so for the very simple reason stated by Chester Finn and Leslie Lenkowsky—that poor (low-income) students, generally speaking, do not live in "poor" school districts. The tendency is otherwise. Plunkitt's Hell's Kitchen was teeming with poverty and disadvantage, but New York County was the richest county in the state. For this reason the federal aid to education programs begun in the 1960s allocated funds on the basis of the income of students' families rather than the tax base of school districts.

There is little political likelihood that as a result of court decisions any large number of school districts will actually *lose* money. Politics does not work that way. Rather, the districts with low tax bases will be "equalized" up. The result, then, will be increased expenditure on schools and increased pressure on the national government to take on a larger share of the rising cost.*

"CUI BONO?"

Who will benefit from this? This question is easily answered: Teachers will benefit. Any increase in school expenditure will in the first instance accrue to teachers, who receive about 68 percent of the operating expenditures of elementary and secondary schools. That these are estimable and deserving persons none should doubt, but neither should there by any illusion that they are deprived. With exceptions, they are not. In general, they are deservedly well-paid professionals. Over the past two decades teachers' pay has increased at a rate roughly twice that of wages in the private economy. The average annual salary for classroom teachers in 1970–71 was $9,210. (It has since passed $10,000.) In large cities it tended to be higher, reaching $12,186 in San Francisco. The median income of men working full-time year round in 1971 was just about that of teachers—but of some 2.9

---

* In a report issued June 13, 1972, the Pennsylvania Department of Education estimated that to bring per capita expenditure throughout that state up to 80 percent of the expenditure in the highest district—a reasonable upward/downward settlement—would cost $1,052,263,235, an increase of approximately 35 percent over the 1970–71 expenditures on elementary and secondary education in the state as a whole.

million persons employed as teachers, two million were women. In that women earn only about 59 percent of the income of men when both work full-time year round, an increase in the number of teachers or an increase in teacher's pay above the general movement of wages will almost certainly increase the number of persons in higher earning brackets. Where the teacher is a married woman, family income is likely to be in the top quintile of income distribution, even the top 5 percent. Without abusing probabilities (nor asserting the existence of detailed evidence), it may be said that *increasing educational expenditures will have the short-run effect of increasing income inequality.*

Now is this what the courts intend? Possibly. The Establishment is said to do such things all the time. But the far greater likelihood is that the courts simply don't know what they are doing. This is not to insist that the analysis just outlined is correct beyond a reasonable doubt. It may yet be disproved either by events or by reanalysis of the existing data; no absolute claims are made for the dependability of each of the propositions put forward here. They represent the consensus of some knowledgeable persons; not more than that. But one has no faith whatever that the courts are even aware of such possibilities, and little faith that the plaintiffs in these proceedings are aware of them either. Rather, they appear to have seized on undeniable instances in which "rich" districts contain "rich" kids and "poor" districts, "poor" kids, and where both expenditures and outcomes are so clearly unequal that any fair-minded person would feel that something ought to be done. There *is* a Baldwin Park school district in Los Angeles, *and* a Beverly Hills school district, *and* the differences between them are probably unacceptable. *But to conceive of this disparity as prototypical simply does not accord with the known facts.*

What it does accord with is certain kinds of middle-class interest. There is, first, the peripheral but discernible interest in asserting the value of things this class values and at which it excels. This is not to be underestimated. It reflects the vigorous exercise of the middle-class citizen's desire to decide priorities. More tangibly, however, it is also a way of asserting the value, and increasing the value, of those services the middle class dispenses. There is a class economic interest at stake, and that class is pursuing its interest.

There is nothing the matter with this as such. Other groups do the same. There is hardly a more admirable group of persons than schoolteachers. Textbook manufacturers are said to be honest people also. One hears as much of bondholders. (Not *all* the money goes to teachers' salaries.) There are problems, however, of which one, again perhaps peripheral, is that there is more disguising of interest in these matters than is probably good for the integrity of public discourse. The objectives of what lawyers call "full disclosure" are not much advanced by the rhetoric of disinterested public service that attends what are often no more than raids on the Treasury. We don't presume disinterestedness on the part of persons whose interests reside in the growth and prosperity of the private sector of the economy. Why should those whose interests reside in the growth of the public sector be treated differently?

THE SELF-AGGRANDIZEMENT OF THE PUBLIC SECTOR

To be sure, the public sector is better these days at making its case. The machinery of government now routinely advances the case for more government. We take this for granted in the military, but our instinct is to exempt civilians, especially those in the "helping" professions. A routine instance comes to hand in the March–April 1972 issue of *Welfare in Review,* which includes an article on "Undergraduate Training of AFDC Caseworkers" (i.e., welfare workers in the Aid to Families of Dependent Children program). It begins with routine puffery:

> Present-day social problems and increasing public understanding of their complexity are adding importance to the social caseworker's role in our society and the training he needs for his work. A master of social work degree is usually necessary for employment as a professional worker, and social work has become institutionalized.

The findings—of a survey done in New Hampshire—are set forth in the careful and competent way of this useful publication. No distinct differences were found as between caseworkers with different undergraduate majors, but one notable fact did "fall out" of the data. Asked their reasons for becoming social workers, 71 percent of this young group (median age, 28) answered "humanitarian."

Now one would wish this. It is surely a good thing for case-workers to see themselves in this light. Or almost surely. But it tends to confuse public debate. Shoe-factory workers in Manchester, almost certainly earning considerably less than social workers in the same city, are not permitted to declare that they have chosen their profession for humanitarian reasons. In any event, nobody asks them. The result is that public policy ends up taking more money away from the factory workers to give to social workers because the latter are engaged in humanitarian pursuits, while the former pursue pedestrian enterprises geared solely for profit.

The matter would seem a bit farfetched if we had not in New York City been exposed to almost a decade of incessant statements by social-work professionals veritably urging more folks to get on welfare. In 1960, when, according to Nicholas Kisburg's calculation, there were 9.7 persons in private-sector wage and salary employment in New York City for every public welfare recipient, this posture might not have seemed unreasonable. But in 1971, with the ratio having declined to 2.6 to 1, a citizen might grow out of sorts, even to the point of associating such statements with the social work profession as a whole, which would be unjust. *And yet they do apply.* Not in the sense that this particular group of professional persons in the public sector actively desires to increase demand for its services, but in the sense that it does tend to benefit, as does any group of service-providers, from increased demand.

This is the second order of understanding that needs to be brought to bear on judicial decisions that mandate this or that increase in public services. There has been a lag in the general understanding of the relative status of the private and public sectors of the economy. For the longest time, and with the best of cases, liberals argued that while the private sector fattened, the public sector starved. Which of us has not thought that? How many of us have written articles, speeches, books, reciting the litany of unmet needs? Who has not campaigned with, contributed to, voted for candidates pledged to redress this great imbalance? Well . . . we succeeded. There are individuals such as John

Kenneth Galbraith to whom special credit is owed, but this has also been a general movement of public opinion.

If proof of our success were needed, it is best found in the continued *and accelerated* trends of civilian expenditure in recent administrations, regardless of party. Schultze, *et al.*, show this with some force, as can be seen in the following table tracing the growth in federal civilian outlays:

Growth in Federal Civilian Outlays, Fiscal Years 1955–73[1]

| PERIOD | PERCENT OF GROWTH PER YEAR | |
	REAL OUTLAYS	REAL OUTLAYS PER CAPITA
1955–60	7.6	5.8
1960–65	5.8	4.1
1965–70	9.1	7.9
1970–73	10.3	9.0

[1] Data adapted from Charles L. Schultze, Edward R. Fried, Alice M. Rivlin, and Nancy H. Teeters, *Setting National Priorities, The 1973 Budget* (Washington, D.C.: The Brookings Institution, 1973), Chapter 12.

Indeed, the only dip in this otherwise steady progression is that of the Kennedy years, brought about by a cautious administration and a hostile Congress. Otherwise the trend is steady and formidable. It is more impressive in the light of restrained military growth in the decade 1963–73, when military appropriations dropped from 53 percent of federal expenditure to 34 percent, and from 9.7 percent to 7.0 percent of GNP. Schultze, Budget Director under President Johnson, clearly had no partisan reason to call attention to these movements. They are simply unblinkable and overwhelming. That may be too strong; if they persist, they will become overwhelming.*

* In the summer of 1972, word began to come out of Washington that an "obscure" provision of a 1967 statute providing 75 percent of federal financing of "social services" for the poor was turning into a fiscal hemorrhage. The provision lay latent for several years until discovered, according to reliable reports, by an HEW official who reported it to his home state. In 1969, HEW paid out $354 million under the "program." By 1972, state applications reached $4.8 billion. In March 1972, Maryland budgeted $22.9 million in federal aid to its social services. By June the sum had risen to $417 million. Mississippi asked for an amount roughly two-thirds its entire state budget. The uses to which

THE CYCLE OF DENIAL AND DIMINISHING RETURNS

Now to the irony of it all. This kind of expenditure does *not* induce a strong perception of "unmet needs" being met. Or so it would seem. Social scientists are fully capable of investigating such questions and no doubt in time some will do so. For the moment we must do with impressions, but these are quite strong. There is a generalized perception within that part of the electorate often described as "blue-collar" that they are paying for a lot more services than they are receiving. But among the service-dispensing classes, the overwhelming perception, genuine or dissembled, is that the nation has not "reordered its priorities" and must do so. Schultze, *et al.*, calculate that "Great Society" programs in the federal budget grew from $1.7 billion in FY 1963 to $35.7 in FY 1973. This has made little impression. Frequently it is simply denied. To some extent this reflects the fact that the service-dispensing classes and their political allies are overwhelmingly Democratic, and understandably wish to believe that their interests are advanced only by a Democratic administration. (How many college professors, much less college students, would know that the size of the United States Army dropped from 1,570,000 in 1968 to some 841,000 in 1973?) But in fact the pattern has little respect for party. Johnson was damned for "slashing" programs, just as Nixon has been. As Joseph A. Schumpeter once wrote, the "technique and atmosphere of the struggle for social legislation" is no friend of truth.

---

such funds are put are presumably so varied at this point that no firm generalization should be made, but it would be fair to expect that a great deal of the money ended up with the middle-class professionals who dispense the "social services" specified by the legislation. A point to note is that, if spent on income transfers, $4.8 billion would eliminate about half the poverty in the land. This is only a little less than the sum required for the Family Assistance Plan, proposed in 1969, and in 1972 still to be acted on by Congress. $4.8 billion in "social services" will do little to eliminate poverty, but the dynamic of national politics at this time inserts the "social-services" provision and prevents even a vote on the Family Assistance Plan. It may come as no surprise to learn that the social-services professions have systematically opposed any guaranteed income plan that has had any chance of passage by the Congress.

A simple cycle is at work which anyone who has worked for social legislation will be familiar with. As government responds to a problem and the situation commences to change, those who initiated the response, and who benefit from it in one way or another, seek to ensure continued response by charging that the situation either has not improved, or has worsened, or has always been worse than originally asserted. For some, social legislation can have the effect of narcotic drugs on the addict: Ever-stronger doses are required, first to achieve the remembered euphoria of the early stages of addiction, and then merely to maintain the absence of distress.

It would, of course, be difficult to "prove" this last proposition. The Vietnam war almost surely "contaminated" all manner of public attitudes in the 1960s, especially among groups that press for social legislation and thereafter manage it. There is, however, a more general condition, certain to outlast the war, which does respond to attempts at verification by measurement. This is the condition of diminishing marginal utility of expenditure on various social services—and it feeds the cycle of denial and renewed demand. After a point, the charge that government efforts to solve a problem are not doing so begins to be true and can be shown to be such.

Public services follow production functions as do any other production processes. Typically, in an early stage increments of input have a high marginal utility which gradually diminishes until the exchange of input for output is no longer equal, and finally to the point where additional input is almost totally wasted as virtually no additional output results. It seems to be the case that, over a considerable range of public services, we are traversing a segment of a production function which is virtually asymptotic. (The Rand report puts it, with respect to education, that we are in a " 'flat' area.") The early and exhilarating days of large increments of output for small increments of input are long past. In these circumstances "trying harder" has no discernible effect, and a perverse equilibrium is attained, at least from the point of view of those whose pleasure or profit it is to demand more. No matter how hard the polity tries to produce "more," it never does, so that the posture of demanding more is never endangered by the prospect of fulfillment.

Education would seem to be a preeminent instance of this

phenomenon. As might be expected, economists have begun to discuss the subject in such terms. In 1971, Kenneth Boulding presented a paper to the American Educational Research Association entitled, "The School Industry as a Possibly Pathological Section of the American Economy." He simply noted that more input did not seem to be producing more output. The point of optimality has long been passed. A shoe factory operating in the manner of many public school systems would have long since closed down.

THE CASE FOR JUDICIAL RESTRAINT

The difficulty is that public enterprises are not subject to the discipline of the market. They can be grossly inefficient, and yet go on indefinitely. Indeed, inefficiency can become a primary source of their perpetuation, for their inability to achieve declared objectives can be taken as evidence of insufficient effort and turned into a call for yet more resource allocation. The more, then, is the need for discipline—for honesty and openness and a measure of good manners—in public discussion of such matters. It is on this ground (and for my part, *only* on this ground) that the *Serrano* family of judicial decisions seems unwarranted. We have here a troubled area of public policy. Good men and women, conscientious and learned, are uncertain what to do. Is this the time for judges, some of whom come near to flaunting their indifference to research findings, to *tell* us what to do? Are laundry workers and ditch diggers and gas pumpers to be *forced* to give up more of their wages in order to pay the wages of college graduates because of some vague notion some judge picked up at law school in the 1930s? This trifles with our democracy. One fair to pleads with the judiciary to stay out of such matters. There are other areas of justice and right in which *only* they can provide remedy, and their authority in those areas ought not to be squandered by an injudicious frolic in the maze of public finance.

Three general points in favor of judicial restraint can be made. It may be that none carries any legal weight and the courts will find themselves obliged to continue on the course they have set, in which event we will have to make the best of it. But in these final hours, while the question is not yet settled, prudence suggests several powerful counterarguments.

First, if there is injustice with respect to the allocation of educational resources, a political remedy is available, and there is abundant evidence that this remedy is both availed of and effective. More and more money goes into education, and of late more and more of this is "targeted" on groups whose educational needs seem greater than most. The trend, as in the Elementary and Secondary Education Act of 1965, has been to unequal expenditure *in favor of* students with low-income backgrounds. This has not by any means been universally achieved, but it is a trend, and the courts should be concerned lest they deflect it.

Second, the courts should at least be aware of it when, in the name of equality of access to public services, they *order* measures that must result in increased inequality of private income. This is probably the result of increased educational expenditure, although an opposing argument can doubtless be made. This is not to say that such measures constitute bad public policy. Not at all. But they should at least be *voluntary* public policy, deliberately chosen and *legitimately* enacted by the elected representatives of the people. One cannot be fully at ease when government uses tax moneys to employ middle-class professionals to persuade middle-class judges whose salaries are paid by tax moneys to hand down orders to the effect that yet more middle-class persons should be hired and paid with yet more tax moneys. This is not what the task force that drafted the Economic Opportunity Act of 1965 had in mind. Which is not to say it is for that reason wrong— and which certainly is not to question the role of poverty lawyers in so much of what they do—but they *are* part of government. A story used to be told around the State House in Albany about Al Smith's 1922 campaign for governor. He had lost out in the Harding landslide and was now running against a one-term Republican who hadn't a great deal to say but did keep harping on a bill he had signed, or refused to sign, or whatever, as a result of which he claimed the state had saved $3 million. Smith sensed that the story was catching on. He began to pursue his opponent around the state with a simple challenge: "The Governor," he would declare, "says he has saved the state $3 million. What I want to know is where is it and who's got it." Judges can ask as much.

A third general point has to do with the overall prospects for educational expenditure: They are very good. The 1970s will see almost no increase in elementary and secondary school populations. The 1972 Manpower Report of the President projects almost no increase in the number of elementary or secondary school teachers. And yet, the economy will continue to grow, making ever greater resources available to meet a stabilized set of needs. How can the outcome not be higher teacher salaries, higher per pupil expenditure, more equal expenditure where low-income children have been unfairly left behind, and more "extras" for low-income children who obviously need them more? Nor must we accept that these "extras" will have little or no consequences. If we are now in a "flat area" with respect to the "results" of educational expenditure, there is no reason to think we cannot break out of our present constraints into a new and much wider range of opportunity. I have been involved in public policy in these areas at the state and national level. I had something to do with the Elementary and Secondary Education Act of 1965. I had much to do with the creation of the President's Commission on School Finance in 1970. A fair number of hopes were dashed in that five-year interval, but not all hopes. To the contrary, as the subject came to be seen as more complex, it became more interesting, more attractive to talent. One did not have to know a great deal in 1970 to know what Rand Corporation researchers would find if asked to look into the state of knowledge on the effectiveness of schooling. One purpose of the Commission was to bring out this information in a politically neutral setting. There *is* such a thing as "the state of knowledge," and this, for the moment, is where we are at on this subject.

And that is the point! *The state of knowledge can change.* In the message to Congress proposing the School Finance Commission, President Nixon also proposed the creation of a National Institute of Education to mount a sustained and powerful effort in just this direction. Congress hesitated a moment, and then overwhelmingly concurred. The case for approaching the issue in this manner is immensely persuasive, and the new Institute was enacted with strong bipartisan support. With good luck and good management the founding of the National Institute of Education will mark a general maturing in this field and a greatly expanding federal effort extending to the whole question of school finance and the property tax. (In a recent study by the Advisory Commission on Intergovernmental Relations it was established that this is regarded as by far the worst of the general taxes levied in the nation and that there is strong support for federal intervention to reduce local property taxes.) In the meantime, the President's Commission has called for full state assumption of school costs. Are these not the signs of an active and progressive area of public policy? If so, can't the courts leave it alone? If they feel they can't, no very great harm will come. The objectives of these cases are admirable, and those who brought them have done a public service in raising the particular issue involved. But can it not be left to the normal machinery of public policy to take the hint?

THE NEW CLASS

Whatever the courts decide, a political situation has been created which will be with us a long time. One hesitates to be more than allusive, thinking back to the Danish sailor in *Billy Budd* to whom long experience had taught "that bitter prudence which never interferes with aught, and never gives advice." But a larger prudence demands that the issue be raised.

The social legislation of the middle third of the century created "social space" for a new class whose privilege (or obligation) it is to dispense services to populations that are in various ways wards of the state. A generation ago, Schumpeter described how the ideology and manifestations of early capitalism had created social space for a new bourgeois class that stood upon a foundation of individual achievement in the economic field. Even then he sensed that this private sphere—the social space created for the bourgeoisie—was facing competition from a new "public sphere," which represented a different order of values and which was occupied by different persons. In *Capitalism, Socialism, and Democracy* he wrote:

> This private sphere is distinct from the public sphere not only conceptually but also actually. The two are to great extent manned by different people—the history of local self-government offering the most conspicuous exception—and organized

as well as run on different and often conflicting principles, productive of different and often incompatible standards.

   Friction can only temporarily be absent from such an arrangement, the paradoxical nature of which would be a source of
wonder to us if we were not so accustomed to it. As a matter of
fact, friction was present long before it developed into antagonism in consequence of the wars of conquest waged upon the
bourgeois domain with ever increasing success by the men of the
public sphere.

These "wars of conquest" do not cease. The advent of new
champions is always hailed no matter what their subsequent fate.
By 1972 *The New York Times* could refer to Mayor Lindsay's
newest budget as a "bloated $10 billion monster," but these were
hardly the terms in which he was first welcomed on the scene, and
that budget, having got to $10 billion, is not going to recede. It
now amounts to an expenditure of $625 per year for every man,
woman, and child in the city. The money does not *go* to every
man, woman, and child, but it goes to enough of them so that
he who challenges the expenditure risks devastating retorts about
"human needs" and may expect no allies save such as will add
to his discredit.

   It was not always so. Interestingly, the labor movement was for
the longest time (and in many ways still is) profoundly skeptical
of eleemosynary initiatives undertaken with tax money. In a 1916
editorial in the *American Federationist,* Samuel Gompers wrote,
"There is a very close connection between *employment* as experts and the enthusiasm for human welfare." Gompers's view was
tolerant enough. His own movement was devoted to improving the
circumstances of its members, and he saw the "experts" as doing
no more than this for their own people. What he objected to was
the "experts" contention that they were doing something for the
workers. Trade unionism among public employees has necessarily
moderated the force of this view—not long ago an important
spokesman for teachers asked that the expenditure on education
as a percentage of GNP be almost doubled—but the skepticism
remains.

   Here and there in other parts of the liberal spectrum a similar
anxiety is to be encountered. Caution about "big government"
can derive from more than opposition to heavy taxes. Among
those who retain some of the qualities of an earlier liberalism there

is a discernible concern over the "ever increasing success by the men of the public sphere." The aggression is unmistakable, and seemingly irresistible, not least because the self-interest of the new class is merged with a manifestly sincere view of the public interest. This view, that the general good is served by advancing the interests of the public sphere, is apparently the dominant social view of the time, and is terribly difficult to argue against with any success.

An example from yet another area of education may help to clarify this point. It happens that I negotiated the phrasing of the 1964 Democratic platform plank which constituted agreement by the Roman Catholic hierarchy of the United States that it would support legislation for federal aid to education, an initiative it had successfully blocked for many years. In the understanding of the Bishops—or at least in my understanding—the platform plank represented a commitment that parochial schools would share federal aid with public schools on some approximate principle of equal treatment. The plank was adopted, the support was forthcoming, the legislation was passed, and the parochial schools got—nothing. Or near to nothing. Certainly they were not dealt with as they had reason to think they would be. They have not publicly complained. (Nor has anyone ever raised the 1964 "understandings" with me.) But they were nonetheless "used." Their mistake (and mine, too, as I look back) probably was in seeing the issue in terms of past prejudice against Catholic institutions. (Everyone was being very civilized in 1964. After all, did not the British government give aid to Catholic schools as to any other?) But this was not, I now think, the issue. The issue was that Catholic schools were not in the public sphere.

The 1972 Democratic party calls for equalization of school expenditure, in the *Serrano* manner. One has greater confidence that this commitment *will* be carried out, in large part with federal funds, and at federal initiative. These probabilities are symbolic of a new political situation: *Education has entered national politics.* Those of us who worked for this to happen may yet live to regret it. There was wisdom in keeping educational politics nonpartisan—as are most school board elections—and diffused. Bringing it into partisan politics at the national level makes for much ugliness. The increasingly corporate nature of the American social structure means that fierce, organized pressures will be brought to bear to raise expenditure, and that these will be supported by a civic culture that sees increased expenditure as a general public good. Anyone who on any grounds opposes such an increase opposes the interest of a class, and the preconceptions of the culture. There are energetic representatives of such interests, like Albert Shanker of the United Federation of Teachers, men and women who fight for their members, fight well, and fight clean. But the temptation to debase political language is considerable. The opponent of greater school expenditure readily becomes the enemy of children. This aspect of the changed political situation makes for a second somewhat ironical conclusion.*

STRATEGIES FOR NATIONAL EDUCATION POLICY

The increasing political influence of the public sphere will make for increasing political instability unless public services become more effective. At long last we are going to have to take public services and public administration seriously. It is not a question of efficiency but of perceived efficacy. With the fortunes of the individual declared more and more to depend on what he receives from the public sphere, the areas in which government must successfully perform are greatly expanded, while the margins of tolerance contract. A familiar prediction. But today the condition has actually come about, and it must now be attended to. A final example from education will suggest the options seemingly open to us.

Three general strategies could be pursued as a national education policy. The first would be to leave well enough alone, even to cut back on expenditures, where they are high, to the point an economist might identify as the optimal use of resources. There is a rational case for this, and a good psychological one

---

* A UPI dispatch appearing September 7, 1972, stated:

For the first time, the nation's 2.1 million elementary and high school teachers are being urged by their national organizations to take an active role in a Presidential election—to oppose President Nixon and donate funds to the campaign of Senator George McGovern.

The executive committee of the National Education Association stated the Nixon administration had "callously disregarded the crisis in education."

also. As a nation we have been generous and conscientious about education. Schools have at least processed successive cohorts of newcomers which have gone on to spectacular intellectual success. In one section of the nation one part of the population was for the longest time deliberately kept apart in segregated school systems, and there seems no question that a heavy price was paid. This calls for recompense. Such efforts can and should be made even if "things-as-they-are" is on balance accepted. (As far as *schools* go an entirely fortuitous but still spectacular compensatory event has already occurred. The pattern of ethnic succession in the cities of the North and West has been such that to a strikingly uniform degree Southern migrants have moved into previously Jewish neighborhoods. This means that one of our most educationally deprived populations is now heavily concentrated in schools which a generation earlier produced the intellectual, cultural, professional, and, to a degree, economic elite of the world's most powerful nation. If it's "good" schools we're looking for, surely these begin to approximate them.) But of course this first strategy will not be adopted. It violates the principle of autogamous growth. Politicians who espouse any such approach will be effectively driven from public life.

A second strategy would be to continue increasing educational effort in the existing mode in the expectation of getting a yet better educational "product." This means pushing more and more resources along that "flat" area in the curve, or, perhaps more accurately, jamming ever more resources into the ever-tightening angle of an asymptotic production function. Save where there are grossly unacceptable inequalities of resources (a condition that could be remedied under the first strategy), this strategy will bring about almost no changes in the standard measurements by which the existing educational system assesses results. For this reason, each new increment of resources will be demanded and justified by increasingly threatening rhetoric. Distrust and suspicion will mount.

This second strategy is the one we are now following, and it is inherently unstable. For one thing, as the public sphere expands in the announced quest for greater equality, the almost certain outcome is greater inequality deriving from the transfer of income from lower to higher social levels. This, along with the inability of services to deliver on promises beyond a certain point, leads to corruption. The public sphere begins to lie about outcomes, as by falsifying test scores—a resort so far only tentatively employed—or by manipulating outcomes through familiar devices such as social quotas.

As this is rather a dim prospect, the case becomes stronger for a third general strategy, which is to launch a serious and sustained effort to discover effective ways to achieve the goals the public has come to expect. A decade ago this would have seemed a bland enough statement. We now know it not to be. To achieve what we would wish in education, for example, is likely to require a quality of brute genius which may or may not come along. But it *could* happen; a *new* curve could be discovered. A whole new set of parameters could come into being. The education process that emerges is likely to be quite different from the schooling process we now know. A great many interests would have to be set aside to achieve such a new condition, but in the end the public interest would be served. Government has got into the business of promising more than it knows how to deliver; as there is little likelihood of cutting back on the promises, the success of the society turns on its ability to improve its performance. It is probably not a good thing to have got into this situation, but the social dynamics of an industrial society everywhere seem to lead in this direction, and to do so with special vehemence in the United States.

HOW SHOULD THE COURT PROCEED?

For the moment, the issue before the nation is not the general one of a national educational policy, nor the wide implications of the continued and self-induced expansion of the public sphere, but simply whether the courts shall order equal educational expenditure as a matter of constitutional right. One uses the phrase "before the nation" because, whatever the courts order, government at large will have to put the orders into effect, and this follow-through will in turn be shaped by public opinion.

It is not unreasonable to ask the courts to know what they are ordering. The question easily divides into two parts: First, ought there to be equal educational expenditure across school districts and—let us get it over with—across states? Second, ought there to be greater educational expenditure?

One can readily imagine that the courts, pursuing general notions of equality, might find for equal expenditure. It is difficult to see how anyone would be harmed by this. An argument could be made that present arrangements make for a certain amount of diversity and local option, with the result that parents who "care" about education can "buy" more of it by moving into selected school districts. But this argument can be countered by the equally reasonable assertion that not all parents have such options, and further that the society ought to minimize the "return" from racial and class differentiation. Equal expenditure would probably "hurt" a fair number of poor children who live in high-expenditure central city school districts, but there is no evidence that it would hurt them much, and in any event it is late in the day to think of such matters.

When the courts, or rather the Court, makes its ruling on the matter of equal expenditure, it should in all conscience acknowledge that it is getting close to the question of whether the 14th Amendment permits parents to send children to private schools, where per pupil expenditure is considerably higher than in public institutions. There is an inevitable statist quality to these decisions which must be hostile to devices for evading state control. Just as important, the Court might touch on the question of whether it is constitutional for Catholic children to be sent to schools where fragmentary but persistent evidence suggests that they are educated for a fraction of the cost of education in the public schools. (They emerge just as well, or badly, schooled, which suggests something else as well.) But in any event, the Court surely can rule for equal expenditure without doing any great injury or injustice to anyone.

On the other hand, one cannot readily imagine that the courts would knowingly order greater inequality of income distribution in the nation by mandating—or setting in motion forces that will almost surely lead to—markedly greater educational expenditure. The *Serrano* plaintiffs have not desired this. Coons and his associates have specifically argued for a formula that would permit variation in expenditure but not linked to variation in school district wealth. But one fears for the fate of any such subtlety. The issue is already discussed almost solely in the old terms of equal expenditure. In practice, this means greater expenditure.

Educational expenditure is growing, and will continue to grow, but this should be the result of political choice, not court order. For the courts to order it is to risk scandal. The scandal may be simply stated. It is that of middle-aged and elderly men imposing social nostrums which recent social science has seriously questioned, if not demolished, and doing so slothfully, without having mastered the not always simple modes of analysis by which social scientists have developed the new evidence. The legal encounters so far (if impressions may be permitted) have been rather one-sided. The state education departments, or whatever, have been represented by the kind of counsel that represents state education departments. The plaintiffs have had razor-sharp men on their side. But at the substantive level, neither the judges nor the plaintiffs have show any taste for facts. To the contrary, they have shown considerable reluctance to stir from their *confort intellectuel,* the cozy verities of thirty-year-old liberalism. It won't do. It would mean taking money from the pockets of people who need it considerably more than those into whose pockets it will be put. This is a rebuttable assertion, of course, but the courts should insist that it be rebutted before ordering anything of the sort. In the meantime there is a simple, equitable solution to the dilemma posed by the desire to bring about equality without adding to inequality. If the *Serrano* cases are to be upheld, the decision should be accompanied by an order that total expenditure not be increased as a result. That is to say, the present amount and proportion of funds expended for education should be divided up equally, raising some districts, lowering others. If overall expenditure is thereafter to be increased, it should be done through the political process, which has shown itself rather inclined in that direction. Only in this manner shall we avoid another miserable encounter between the courts and the political system of the democracy.*

* The Supreme Court case to which this passage referred, *San Antonio Independent School District* et al. v. *Rodriguez* et al., was argued shortly after this article was published and decided in March 1973. It seems to me the decision of the Court was entirely correct, with respect, at least, to the state of social science on this subject. The appellees, in the words of the majority opinion delivered by Justice Lewis F. Powell, Jr., "insist that education is itself a fundamental personal right because it is essential to the effective exercise of First Amendment freedoms and to intelligent utilization of the right to vote." The majority held otherwise; I agree. A related argument once held that ownership of land was indispensable to the responsible exercise of suffrage. Most importantly, the Court drew back from

what it viewed as an invitation to legislate in an area of great uncertainty. A key passage stated:

> Indeed, one of the hottest sources of controversy concerns the extent to which there is a demonstrable correlation between educational expenditures and the quality of education—*an assumed correlation underlying virtually every legal conclusion drawn by the District Court in this case.* Related to the questioned relationship between cost and quality is the equally unsettled controversy as to the proper goals of a system of public education. And the question regarding the most effective relationship between state boards of education and local school boards, in terms of their respective responsibilities and degrees of control, is now undergoing searching re-examination. The ultimate wisdom as to these and related problems of education is not likely to be devined for all time even by the scholars who now so earnestly debate the issues. In such circumstances the judiciary is well advised to refrain from interposing on the States inflexible constitutional restraints that could circumscribe or handicap the continued research and experimentation so vital to finding even partial solutions to educational problems and to keeping abreast of ever changing conditions. [My italics.]

This is sensible judging. I hold that Frankfurter would have approved. But not all share this view. The decision was 5 to 4, with all Democrats opposed. A story in *Time* began with a passage from Justice Powell's decision: "Education, of course, is not among the rights afforded explicit protection under our Federal Constitution." "With these chilly words," the *Time* story continued, "the Court struck down a lawsuit that aimed at greater equality of spending in education." Why "chilly"? Was the Court to apologize for the Constitution, or express its disappointment in the Founding Fathers' failure? The Court went on directly to ask whether education "is implicitly so protected"? It spoke of the "undisputed importance of education." It made every profession of concern that could be asked. Interestingly, the *Time* story noted that in Hawaii, the one state with only a single school district and strict equality of facilities and such, save where federal programs increase expenditures on poor children, there persist great differences in achievement. "Honolulu's Kahala Elementary School and Palolo Elementary School, for instance, have similar buildings (concrete blocks, carpeted floors), employ similarly skilled teachers, and use the same curriculum. Yet on uniform tests, the children in Kahala score roughly twice as high at Palolo's students." The correlates of achievement are the familiar ones. They have little to do with schools *after* a point.

On the Education of
Engineers

20

Some years ago a presidential appointee taking office in the
foreign policy maze of Washington found that part of his day's
routine was a morning intelligence briefing by a young foreign
service officer. Each day the Secretary would learn that, almost
everywhere, almost everything was going wrong, and almost
invariably the United States was to blame. It soon became routine:
in the language of game theory, an exercise of threat analysis
in worst possible case condition. At length his sanguine nature
rebelled. One morning he looked up and asked, "Don't you
have any good news?" The young man shuffled through his file
and found what he was looking for. "Mr. Secretary," he replied,
"there is an item here that the Aswan Dam is leaking."

Just how accurate this intelligence was is hard to say, although
one gathers it is clear that the dam has altered the ecology of the
southeastern Mediterranean in ways no one expected or desired.
No matter. The point has to do with what I shall call the politi-
calization of technology. This is a somewhat recent, but seemingly
inexorable, process that has large consequences for the education
of engineers.

"On the Education of Engineers" was an address delivered at Harvey
Mudd College, Claremont, California, April 1972.

Simply stated, and oversimplified, it would seem we are entering a stage of industrialism in which technologists, and their sponsors, are increasingly held politically accountable for the effects of their technology. They are held responsible, that is, not to narrowly defined groups such as might engage in lawsuits, but to an ever larger constituency which increasingly is seen as equivalent to the polity itself. This is new. Until recently technology has operated in conditions substantially like those of a free market, which is not to say that competition has been perfect, but that the outcomes of the competition have appeared to be morally neutral and socially desirable. Clearly, even the most belligerently free economy cannot sustain such conditions for very long. Big American business had at most about a half century to do as it wished. American engineers have had at least twice as long, but manifestly their *laissez-faire* phase is now on the way out also.

It was a good run. I expect it will be looked back upon as a *belle époque* of sorts. Sad. But true, and not worth too much lamenting. It is more pressing to understand what has changed and how best to respond. Engineers are, after all, preeminent realists. Their bridges do not fall down, and neither, I expect, will their morale collapse on learning that they must solve problems in the context of a somewhat new calculus of cost and benefit. This becomes, however, an immediate task for engineering education. Failing in it, the graduates of even our most distinguished schools go forth untrained for their work.

Let me pose two propositions, the first familiar, the second perhaps less so.

The first proposition is that engineers are going to have to become far more sensitive to the second- and third-order effects of what they do: because they are going to be held accountable for them. It is increasingly, and I think correctly, held that it is in the public interest that this should be so; and it is accordingly in the interest of the engineering profession to respond. Early capitalism—perhaps industrialism is the better term—placed a great premium on innovation and, as A. C. Pigou wrote in England sixty years ago, greatly encouraged the garnering of first-order profits without much assessing second- and third-order costs. In the simplest of examples, at no cost to himself the industrialist discharged his waste into the air; but thereby imposed considerable cost on the general population whose laundry bills went up. One could discourse on the sources of the transformation of values whereby society became much exercised over those laundry bills. Following Schumpeter, I don't see this as quite so rational a process as those who press this change in values tend to depict it, but inescapably there is a rational component. One recalls a theme repeated in the early sections of Carl Sandburg's biography of Lincoln: "The wilderness is careless." Civilization, by contrast, is careful, or tries to be, and at this level there is no arguing that engineers must become more sensitive to what are becoming more sensitive surroundings.

This might seem intolerably commonplace, and yet, strangely, it needs to be said. Not by such as I, but by engineers, and not as a general assertion, but with respect to specific issues. I often recall how, as a young Assistant Secretary of Labor in President Kennedy's Administration, I sat from time to time on the panel that had been established to consider the construction of a supersonic transport. The issue was assigned to then Vice President Johnson in his capacity as chairman of the space committee. The gist of the matter, as I gathered at the time, was that the military had no use for such an aircraft and accordingly a prototype would have to be developed with nonmilitary funds. Even so, the Pentagon did the calculations for us. One day we assembled to examine the cost estimates of a Mach 2 and a Mach 3 plane. It was estimated that 15 percent to 20 percent of the operating costs for the latter would be required to replace broken glass and plaster. The engineers in charge apparently had this vision of their plane swooping across the suburban approaches to the various great airports of the Nation to the accompaniment of a merry snap, crackle, and pop of picture windows and bedroom walls. Easily fixed. Nothing to worry about. Public demands speed. Well, of course, that particular public would demand the jobs of those crazy engineers; and they themselves ought to have seen this and said so. There is scarcely an end to the list one could draw of equivalent absurdity.

One could wish it were a matter only of absurdity, but, of course, it is not. We must expect that after a period in which the abuse of technology and its necessary limitations have been underattended to, they will now be overstressed. This will be an aspect of politicization, and will have its costs. Yet it comes about in the aftermath of an often outrageous indifference to the most basic human values and needs. It has seemed to me the history of the automobile encapsulates the process with great clarity. The automobile *is* technology. We can scarcely separate this machine from the civilization that produced it. Its externalities— that is to say, its second-, and third-, and fourth-, and fortieth- order effects—touch every knowable aspect of our lives, shaping them in ways we see as good, *and* ways we see as bad. Some of these influences are so subtle they are hardly noticed. Just a few years back (to repeat a point I have made before), the California State Police let it be known they passed the one-million mark in arrests for traffic violations in a calendar year. We can only admire such organizational zeal, but with an undertone of anxiety. How prudent is it for a free people to grow accustomed to being arrested by armed police? Is the marginal (if that) gain in transportation efficiency worth it? One tends to think not. And yet technology, when not watched, touches everything.

Of course, with the automobile the most immediate cost has been the death and injury resulting from crashes. A new disease made its appearance among men, and has had quite appalling consequences. Not, perhaps, as appalling as will be the long-run consequences, say, of engine wastes and meteorological phe- nomena such as smog over Los Angeles, but incomparably vivid in the effect on individual lives. Now this was a disease created by engineers. The plain fact being, as William Haddon and his colleagues wrote in 1956, "Motor vehicles are not being con- structed to crash safely under the operating conditions for which they are designed despite the foreknowledge that substantial percentages of those produced will at some time be involved in such accidents." Upwards of one automobile in three manufac- tured in the United States ended up with blood on it. Did and does. Now by this time, the 1950s, the various pieces of this puzzle were coming together. Three disciplines merged to pro- duce a soluiton. Epidemiologists defined the nature of the prob- lem. Political scientists and government executives perceived the incapacity of existing regulatory processes to change the system outcomes in any but the most trivial ways. The field of crash- impact engineering developed the technology that would make it possible to change outcomes; that is to say, to change the consequences of collision. I was among that middle group and can tell you those were exciting days. To *know* you know what to do about something that needs doing is a heady experience, one to be wished for every young person willing to acquire the disciplines that make such knowledge possible. Yet for the longest time we had no success. Industry would not respond. This is easily seen as the machinations of evil men, but I know a good deal about this subject and I don't think that: didn't then, don't now. It was a failure of business to see its best interests. A failure of business schools to advise, in a situation where, once removed, they had a better perspective. Confronted with the imbecility of entrepreneurs and the indolence of government, the engineers were the only force that might have redeemed the situation. But the engineering profession had failed to create a climate in which such considerations were automatically included in the design process—considerations, that is, of second- and third-order effects of the machine—and in which signals such as we were sending in various ways were somehow received. Henry Wakeland, one of those involved with this issue at that time—ours was by way of a small social movement—was himself an automotive engineer and made the most determined efforts to persuade the Society of Automotive Engineers that it should concern itself with such matters, but he failed, and at no little cost to himself. But one does not blame the association officers or their capitalist employers: the failing is to be found much further back in an engineering education that produced a kind of trained insensitivity to such concerns.

Of course this could not last. Government regulation was inevitable in the circumstances and came rather more quickly than any of us expected. I wrote and got issued a statement by President Kennedy on the subject during the 1960 campaign. Save that a number of the major manufacturers were making Democratic sounds in 1964, the issue would almost certainly have been injected into that campaign—I tried and almost succeeded—and the moment the campaign was over work began on legislation. When it came, the President declared: "The gravest problem before the Nation—next to the war in Vietnam—is the death and destruction, the shocking and senseless carnage, that strikes daily on our highways. . . ." Even allowing for rhetoric, that is rather a large assertion. Clearly there was something lacking in the professional formation of American engineers that they allowed matters to get to such a state.

Again, there is scarcely an end to the list one could draw up of equivalent absurdity, nor of the success of engineers in persuading not only themselves, but also the larger public, to ignore the larger consequences of what they do. It is, for example, the fashion of political liberals to declare that the Eisenhower Administration was a period barren of significant domestic initiatives. Yet this was the Administration that launched the interstate highway program, the most far-flung engineering undertaking in history. It will shape America the way the railroads shaped America. It will have more effects on cities than any so-called urban program of the middle third of the twentieth century, and for that matter any such program likely in the last third. It is scarcely possible to think where the effects of the highway program will end. But somehow the highway engineers manage to pretend that the effects are bounded by the rights-of-way, and to persuade others of this as well.

Let me be clear that I view the interstate highway system as in many respects a triumphant achievement. Not least an aesthetic achievement: portions of the system attain to genuine heights of "minimal art." But too much was at stake for those in charge to be so little concerned with matters deemed beyond the province of the simple engineer.

To be sure, there is much prudence, and probably not a little cunning, in the hard-hat approach to such tasks. If enough had been known, or stated, about the implications of the highway program, it is not likely that political agreement to build it would ever have been reached. Too many interests are affected in too many diverse ways. There are professions aplenty traumatized by the realization that "everything relates to everything," and that quintessential engineer Jay W. Forrester has not yet taught us how to measure every one of those relations. One does not ask that engineers proclaim themselves to be city planners: only that their education instill in them the realization that they *are*. They are, and by comparison almost no one else is. Somehow the professional formation should impart this awareness. Not as a sense of inadequacy or guilt, but rather as an awareness of a dimension

of opportunity that is formidably real and that makes the profession all the larger for its realization.

The second of the two propositions I would present is that just
as engineers must enlarge the area of effects which they take into
account in their decisions, and for which they must accept responsibility, so must they also learn to define what are the *limits*
of those responsibilities and to defend those limits. This poses a
genuine challenge to engineering education, for, to my knowledge, it is a matter scarcely touched upon in the present curriculum.

This is a task easily underestimated, perhaps especially by those
pressing for the larger sense of responsibility discussed in the
first proposition I have mentioned. An analogous and closely
associated situation is to be found in the movement for social
responsibility in business, an enthusiasm which has properly
many recruits, not least in the world of business, but which in its
zeal to assert what business *is* responsible for has yet to pay much
heed to those areas of public decision for which business is *not*
responsible, areas of decision in which the exercise of economic
influence would be altogether inappropriate in a political democracy.

It comes to this. The process of politicization is not self-
limiting. Once commenced, it will extend as far as the energies
of its agents can carry it.

I don't know that political science much understands this
dynamic, but certainly modern history reveals it. The great
tendency of the twentieth century is toward the total state, a
tendency legitimated and to a considerable degree sustained by
that class of persons generally known as intellectuals. Not all intellectuals, of course, but a good many; and proportionately far
more than will be found in the society generally. In the total
state all actions, all institutions, are political. Obviously, the
closer one approximates to this condition, the closer one is to
totalitarianism. The obverse holds also. This imposes a considerable strain on our judgment. Where does one draw the line? Up
to what point does one accept social controls, or even insist on
them, and at what point does one resist?

I repeat that political science has no answers, but it may have
some advice. It seems reasonably clear, for example, that those

technologies that police themselves, that are typically ahead of government and the public with respect to safeguards, counter-measures, and self-imposed restraints, are less likely to be found guilty of some wrongdoing, and thereafter presumed guilty of further malfeasance. Engineers, who are continually calculating margins of safety, ought to have no difficulty with this conception; and their education ought to implant in them a reflexive insistence upon it in the decision-making processes. What does it mean to be a profession if it is not to be self-regulating? But this requires personal standards of conduct from the men and women involved which in the main have to be taught. From the world of political science I would only add that much more is at stake than the reputation or convenience of a particular profession. There is a genuine sense in which the rest of us depend on engineers to behave in ways that retard the present tendency to ever greater government regulation. The quality of our democracy is at issue here, and those of us whose presumption it is to follow such matters do so with an increasing sense of our own incapacity to affect them.

I suppose I am saying that the eternal vigilance of engineers is the price of the liberty the rest of us enjoy—a thought that may be as troubling to engineers as it is to me, but something like that would seem to be the case. Accordingly, one urges vigilance. But a two-edged vigilance; alert to the extent of responsibility and simultaneously to the limits thereof. Here we come to problems that shade into the nonrational and sometimes even irrational realm of politics. It is necessary, for example, to be clear that the sense of well-being induced by advances in technology does not persist very long. In part there is a dynamic of capitalism which Schumpeter termed "creative destruction" that works to create dissatisfaction in order to create new demand, but it is more than that. Men can become used to anything, and in consequence bored. Consider our space program: surely the most extraordinary engineering feat in the history of human kind. As I write, April 27, 1972, Apollo 16 is on its return journey from the moon. I learn this on page 29 of *The New York Times,* having first made my way through pages of political candidates calling for a revival of American spirits from the vast depression brought on by the failure of our society to achieve its goals. There is nothing to be surprised at in this.

Technology can improve the human condition, and has done so; but it does not change it, and while this is so there will be no peace. (Any election year now one expects some candidate or other to inform an astonished public that 97 percent of the nearly 2 million Americans who will die in the coming twelve months will be victims of metabolic failure, blame the medical profession for it, and propose a kidney-machine program to put an end to the outrage.) The task of technologists faced with such assertions, and the demands that accompany them, is to assert the limits of technology, and to refuse to promise what they cannot perform. The alternative is a condition of institutionalized frenzy, which I sometimes think we approach. (I am aware, to be sure, that "social engineers" such as B. F. Skinner see little hope for this kind of rationality and insist mankind will have to condition itself to a state where it *does* accept its condition. I resist the thought, although I hardly feel qualified to reject it.)

Again, it comes to a matter of education. Technologists, who have for so long held out to us visions of what mankind *can* have, must somehow build into their discourse a feeling for limits, must somehow convey an understanding, as Oscar Handlin has noted, of what we *cannot* have. An eagerness to please can end with the greatest displeasure if this is not done. Recently Paul H. Weaver has revived our too latent memories of a distinction Aristotle made in the *Rhetoric* between three modes of public discourse: the deliberative, the forensic, and the epideictic. Deliberative discourse, as Weaver describes it, deals with the question of relative advantages and disadvantages of alternative ways of dealing with public problems, ". . . its focus is on what will happen in the future, its concern is thus with cause and effect and cost and benefit." Its method is the example. Forensic discourse seeks to establish not what will happen, but what has happened, its method is the syllogism. Epideictic speech is "speech whose purpose is to praise or blame," its method amplification. Ideally—!—political discourse ought to be deliberative; in reality it is most often epideictic. Few persons perceive these distinctions, but more are going to have to if a relatively sane politics is to survive the self-destructive impulses of late industrialism. To distinguish between deliberative discourse and moralistic speech, to prefer analysis to blame, to measure social as against ideological advantage, is almost the first order of business of the democracy at this time. It is an enterprise for which technologists are superbly equipped by disposition and to which they ought to be introduced by their education. To insist on the distinction between what can be and what ought to be, to resist the paranoid passion for the assignment of guilt, is to uphold not just the standards of a profession, but the principles of democratic society. It has been too long now since practical men who work with things have been sufficiently valued for the freedoms they create, and not a moment too soon for such men to sense the dangers to which those freedoms are now exposed.

Address to the Entering Class at Harvard College, 1972

21

It is an honor to be a member of the Freshman class of Harvard College, and not less a distinction to be asked to present one of the first of the many lectures that now await you. This is a venerable form of instruction and not, perhaps, the most efficient; but it is the way we do things here.

To be sure, other forms of instruction await you also: seminars, laboratories, above all, libraries; but lectures remain our preeminent mode of presenting ideas. They will matter most to you if you come with some information of your own on the subject to be presented so that the occasion becomes in effect an exchange: you not only listen, but respond.

Let me, then, present my first thought for the evening, which is that this rarely happens. As you know, I asked that in preparation for this lecture you each read Joseph A. Schumpeter's *Capitalism, Socialism, and Democracy*, and Lionel Trilling's *The Middle of the Journey*. I will estimate that one in ten of you has done this and that another tenth, wishing it had, imagines it has.

A show of hands indicates that the hypothesis is confirmed.

"Address to the Entering Class at Harvard College, 1972" was delivered in September of that year and was first published in *Commentary*, December 1972.

Now to the main work of the evening. Yom Kippur was over at sundown. It is in this spirit that I address you. The sins of the past are shrived, and we begin anew. And yet the past remains with us as knowledge of the future. There will be sins enough to atone for when the cycle comes round once more. There is not much in human experience that any longer appears to us as uniquely human. Those of you going into science will spend a good share of your time extrapolating the behavior of rats into that of people. Still, a sense of what will come, especially that death will come, would seem to be singular in our species.

A sense of what is coming is the central experience to be had from both Schumpeter's and Trilling's books. There is a temptation to describe this as an intellectual experience in the case of the economics text, and an aesthetic one in the case of the novel; but these are uncertain categories. It is enough to see that here are two modes of anticipation, each analytic, each rigorous, each having a claim to being considered a possible instance of social theory with true predictive qualities. Schumpeter, the economist, is absorbed with the complex impact of technology on thought; Trilling's concerns move in rather the opposite direction, as might be expected of a literary critic. But in the end, each evolves a singular vision that partakes of many disciplines. Your education at Harvard, as at any such institution, will divide up intellectual life and lead you to assume that there are profoundly different ways of knowing, and perhaps there are; and yet I would not settle too quickly into that convention.

I have asked you to read Schumpeter and Trilling because you are living in the future about which they wrote. No two men, to my thinking, have done this so well as they; but you need not share this view in order to agree that they did what they set out to do well enough for the two books to be taken as benchmarks respecting a past which has flowed into the present.

Each book is set in the late 1930s in America. (If we are to discuss them together, we will find ourselves alternating between the vocabularies of science and of literature, doing some injustice to both. But this we can claim to be a cost others have imposed on us; alternatively, a dilemma others have devised for us.) The 1930s is a period that matters to you, for it was the time when most of your senior professors were taught. (I think of the "period" as lasting into the mid-1950s.) It was the time in which your parents were taught, and so it has already pressed itself heavily upon you. But now you will encounter it as the climate in which the formative intellectual experiences of your college teachers took place, unavoidably influencing your own formation.

The fascination of that time goes beyond the intergenerational tie, for it was a period that was formative to the American political culture generally and reverberates down to this moment in much the manner that the 1920s has attained to the affective culture. Each era seems to go on repeating itself in however attenuated a manner. And why ought they not? Those are the two decades in which the present world took shape.

The world into which Joseph Schumpeter was born ended just as those decades began. There is a sense of the *douceur de vivre* of the Austro-Hungarian Empire that lent its own dimension to his detachment as a social scientist from the events and tendencies about which he later wrote. He made his way by many stages to Harvard and made a large impression when he finally arrived. I never knew him, but hanging about Cambridge on the G.I. Bill during the 1940s it was impossible not to know of him. It was said he would tell his classes that as a young man he had resolved to become three things: the world's greatest economist, the world's greatest lover, and the world's greatest horseman; but that as advancing age constricted the horizons of possibility, he was learning to accept the fact that he would not achieve his third ambition.

And yet he had: for our purposes. His book, which he described as "an effort to weld into a readable form the bulk of almost forty years' thought, observation, and research on the subject of socialism," is a work of analysis and passion on a level few can sustain; but it is more than that. It is the work of a man who has been around horses. I do not know this actually to have been true, but his stepfather is described in the *Encyclopedia of the Social Sciences* as "a high-ranking officer in the Austro-Hungarian Empire," and it ought to have been true. Schumpeter was not of the view that horses or riders are all alike. Dams counted and sires counted, training and daring counted, resolution counted, and a tenth of a second could make all the difference in life. How to explain the beginnings of capitalism? A simple matter for Schumpeter: the "Supernormal intelligence and energy" of the early entrepreneurs brought success in nine cases out of ten. How to account for the appeal of socialism? Again, simple. Socialism, in scientistic guise, formulated "with unsurpassed force that feeling of being thwarted and ill-treated which is the auto-therapeutic attitude of the unsuccessful many. . . ."

(I would assume that many of you take exception to such views, and you have every right to do so. But if you think Schumpeter wholly wrong in such matters, let me offer you at the outset what could prove the best advice you will ever get at Harvard College. Stay away from race tracks.)

Schumpeter wrote both to praise Marx *and* to bury him. His purpose was to test the scientific validity of the great Marxist thesis which has been so central to twentieth-century politics and thought. He praised Marx the Sociologist and Marx the Teacher, and was scarcely disrespectful of Marx the Economist. Even so, he thought the Marxian scenario altogether wrong. Capitalism as the organizing principle of the economy and the underlying structure of the culture would not go through the stages Marx had predicted. There would be no immiserization of the masses, no wars of colonial expansion. And yet—and here we see the daring of the man, the exuberant intellectual elegance—he concluded that Marx was right about what in the end would happen, was indeed right "that a socialist society will inevitably emerge from an equally inevitable decomposition of capitalist society." This was his "paradoxical conclusion"—that "capitalism is being killed by its achievements."

He saw this as resulting from the interaction of two phenomena. First, the very success of capitalism would lessen the importance of the entrepreneur and lessen the perceived value of the one thing capitalism indubitably creates, which is material wealth. Those men of "supernormal intelligence and energy" would gradually be replaced by managers of only marginally greater competence than the managed. One recalls Herman Wouk's description of the Navy in World War II: A system devised by geniuses to be run by morons. Further, as any good economist ought to have been able to foresee, there would come a period of diminishing utility of increased consumption *or* increased production. An economist would know this: a Schumpeter would know also that the phenomenon would first appear in the most affluent classes, thereby acquiring social prestige. Nowhere does he say so, but I choose to be confident that he quite foresaw the day when the children of the rich would go about in ragged dungarees and that on ceremonial occasions college students would bury automobiles, combining in a sense the aristocratical ways of the court of Marie Antoinette and the Kwakiutl Indians.

(Allow me, parenthetically, to note that Schumpeter was thinking in a very long time perspective. At the time he wrote it had been roughly two centuries from the period when capitalism had got going; it could well be, he judged, two centuries more before it had quite disappeared. My own estimate would be a half century from now, in part because the rate of increase in wealth has quite surpassed even Schumpeter's forecast; and he was most bullish for his time.)

The second of Schumpeter's master propositions is more subtle, and for me more difficult to follow. In essence he states that capitalism is rationalism. It began by challenging the right of kings and barons and popes and bishops to exist: it would end by challenging its *own* right. I follow *this,* and I can see how the defense would be difficult. But Schumpeter goes further. He suggests that the capitalist assault on itself will come not just from a habit of mind, a tradition of contentiousness and innovation, but also from far more ominous impulses.

He seems to argue that there is an innate contrariness in human nature—an irrational destructiveness—which far from being quelled by rationalist conditioning, merely uses it as the most effective possible device by which to attain irrational ends. Here is the key passage.

It is an error to believe that political attack arises primarily from grievance and that it can be turned by justification. Political criticism cannot be met effectively by rational argument. From the fact that the criticism of the capitalist order proceeds from a critical attitude of mind, i.e., from an attitude which spurns allegiance to extrarational values, it does not follow that rational refutation will be accepted. Such refutation may tear the rational garb of attack but can never reach the extrarational driving power that always lurks behind it. Capitalist rationality does not do away with sub- or super-rational impulses. It merely makes them get out of hand by removing the restraint of sacred or semisacred tradition. In a civilization that lacks the means and even the will to discipline and to guide them, they will revolt. And once they revolt it matters little that, in a rationalist culture, their manifestations will in general be rationalized somehow. Just as the call for utilitarian credentials has never been addressed to kings, lords, and popes in a judicial frame of mind that would accept the possibility of a satisfactory answer, so capitalism stands its trial before judges who have the sentence of death in their pockets. They are going to pass it, whatever the defense they may hear; the only success victorious defense can possibly produce is a change in the indictment. Utilitarian reason is in any case weak as a prime mover of group action. In no case is it a match for the extrarational determinants of conduct.

Now I do not fully understand this. Why is it that "Capitalist rationality does not do away with sub- or super-rational impulses"? Rather, what is the nature of these impulses, and what is the evidence for them? Hearsay, mostly, albeit impressive hearsay. One thinks of Robert Warshow's comment on the nihilism of the Marx Brothers, men who "spit on culture." They are popular among middle-class intellectuals, he writes, "because they express a blind and destructive disgust with society that the responsible man is compelled to suppress in himself."* This was written more than a quarter century ago, but is surely as true of the present. Hardly a day goes by when one or another Marx Brothers movie is not being shown somewhere within a quarter mile of Harvard Square. And this curious mixture was part also of the Greek experience. So there it is: something we see happening, even if such as I do not fully comprehend it.

I have suggested that any good man might have made these points. Schumpeter's glory lies in having identified the peculiar agent which capitalism would create for its own destruction, which is to say the intellectuals. (Of which, one could add, Marx himself was an exemplar; indeed, in the patronage of the manufacturer Engels, a prototype.) And why would it do this? Here, there is just the least touch of melancholy in a not especially sentimental man. Capitalism would create a vast intellectual class because it believed in such a class, because it derived its own vitality from intellectual processes. And so capitalism would

* Robert Warshow, *The Immediate Experience* (New York, Doubleday & Co.), 1962, p. 50.

protect intellectuals, even as they shrieked of oppression and hurled anathemas at their protectors: "any attack on the intellectuals must run up against the private fortresses of bourgeois business which . . . will shelter the quarry." Capitalism, alone of social systems, will subsidize and reward its mortal enemies: bound by its own rationale to do so. Its morale will begin to be affected.

> Perhaps the most striking feature of the picture is the extent to which the bourgeoisie, besides educating its own enemies, allows itself to be educated by them. It absorbs the slogans of current radicalism and seems quite willing to undergo a process of conversion to a creed hostile to its very existence.

Schumpeter asked no quarter of life, and yet one is glad somehow that he died in 1950 and was not on hand two decades later when one of Harvard's most distinguished officers, an avowed and courageous opponent of the Vietnam war, collapsed in the midst of a particularly brutal political demonstration just as some scion of the upper middle class was describing him on the bullhorn as a "running dog of imperialism."

I speak of melancholy because Schumpeter had a sense of what was being lost: first language, then something akin to liberty, for the collectivist society would ineluctably narrow the limits of what is permitted and what is encouraged.

> Radicals may insist that the masses are crying for salvation from intolerable sufferings and rattling their chains in darkness, and despair, but of course there never was so much personal freedom of mind and body *for all*, never so much readiness to bear with and even to finance the mortal enemies of the leading class, never so much active sympathy with real and faked sufferings, never so much readiness to accept burdens, as there is in modern capitalist society; and whatever democracy there was, outside of peasant communities, developed historically in the wake of both modern and ancient capitalism.

To this assertion he adds an equally apt footnote:

> Even Marx, in whose time indictments of this kind were not anything like as absurd as they are today, evidently thought it

desirable to strengthen his case by dwelling on conditions that even then were either past or visibly passing.

Schumpeter defined socialism as "conquest of private industry and trade by the state." He did not consider that this would have to be a precipitous sequence, nor yet that there need be a totalitarian outcome. He had no illusions about capitalism: "the civilization of inequality and of the family fortune." And yet this new State: how different a regime it would be from that of *Die Fledermaus* where Eisenstein, having insulted a government official, must go to jail for eight days, but can put it off just long enough to attend Prince Orlofsky's ball.

A quarter century later there are some things Schumpeter appears to have got wrong, but, in the main, events have gone precisely as he foresaw. The power of private enterprise remains formidable but its morale and its reputation, in places where it matters, are quite shattered. The conquest of the private sector by the public proceeds apace, abetted by the extraordinary dynamic of inflation, a point Schumpeter made in his address "The March into Socialism," delivered at the end of 1949 just eight days before his death. Wage and price controls, he forecast, would return and would "play an important part in the eventual conquest of the private-enterprise system by the bureaucracy."

What a very different mind is Lionel Trilling's. The backgrounds of the two men are not all that different; their families part of that Central European stream from which have flowed the dominant intellectual forces of American life today. With the death of Edmund Wilson, Trilling will surely be deemed the first laureate of American literary critics. His study has been that of minds, not that of markets; his endeavor has been to assess the authenticity of ideas rather than their going rate. To do this, at a middle point in his own career, he turned to the novel itself and produced his only such work, *The Middle of the Journey*. It is a novel about the two great absolutist ideas of our time and the wan possibility of maintaining a distance from either. If the world is not made by God, it is made by man: what possible position can there be in the middle? Enough perhaps for most of us to huddle there, but not very comfortably in this time, and even less in the late 1930s when the demand for commitment was greater. Each of these positions has its representatives. On the one hand, Gifford Maxim, a former Stalinist, apparently some kind of spy, who has broken with that belief and is undergoing a profound and passionate Christian conversion. He believes the Party will try to kill him, and his efforts to make this difficult by giving a public dimension to the fact that he is alive provide the structure of the narrative. Opposed, as almost, or not quite, convinced Stalinists, are Arthur and Nancy Crooms, he a rising young professional who will join the New Deal but is spending the summer in Connecticut. In the middle John Laskell, who is Lionel Trilling. One almost hesitates to note that Trilling was writing about one of the most dramatic personal, ideological encounters of American history: which hadn't happened yet. For in another sense it had happened. The ideas were there, and it was destined that men would prove their vehicles.

It is getting a bit hard to recall how dominant, then, were the ideas of the left. In the era, itself the fact was self-evident. Warshow begins his review, published in *Commentary,* of the novel with this almost casual assertion:

> For most American intellectuals, the Communist movement of the 1930s was a crucial experience. In Europe, where the movement was at once more serious and more popular, it was still only one current in intellectual life; the Communists could never completely set the tone of thinking. . . . But in this country there was a time when virtually all intellectual vitality was derived in one way or another from the Communist party. If you were not somewhere within the party's wide orbit, then you were likely to be in the opposition, which meant that much of your thought and energy had to be devoted to maintaining yourself in opposition.

The "Stalinist liberalism" of that time, he continued was "not a point of view but a psychological and sociological phenomenon." It was specifically "an experience of the middle class," centered in New York, a middle class increasingly able to summer in Connecticut.

Events lead, as they ought in a novel of ideas, which is also in ways a *roman à clef,* to an event, the death of a young girl brought about by the cruelty of her squalid lower-class—they would have used some such word: *lumpen,* perhaps—father.

Trilling's characters must face the meaning of it. Nancy Crooms knows that something evil has occurred, but there is no place for evil in her universe. "You surely know," she says to Maxim, "why it isn't his fault." "Nancy means" her husband tries to help, "that social causes, environment, education or lack of education, economic pressure, the character-pattern imposed by society, in this case a disorganized society, all go to explain and account for any given individual's actions."

No, says Maxim, the child has died; the man is bad; he is to blame. And it may be also that he is to be forgiven. He pronounced the final Christian verdict on the Communist.

> . . . You and I stand opposed. For you—no responsibility for the individual, but no forgiveness. For me—ultimate, absolute responsibility for the individual, but mercy. Absolute responsibility: it is the only way that men can keep their value, can be though of as other than mere *things*. Those matters that Arthur speaks of—social causes, environment, education—do you think they really make a difference between one human soul and another? In the eyes of God are such differences of any meaning at all? Can you suppose that *they* condition His mercy? Does He hold a Doctor of Philosophy more responsible than a Master of Arts, or a high school graduate more responsible than a man who has not finished the eighth grade? Or is His mercy less to one than another?

Laskell demurs:

> Is it really a question. . . ? I can't see it as a question, not really. An absolute freedom from responsibility—that much of a child none of us can be. An absolute responsibility—that much of a divine or metaphysical essence none of us is.

Pascal, responds Maxim said all that long ago; but there is no longer a middle way. The Renaissance idea—the day for being human in that way—was over. "Gone. Done for. Finished." The Crooms and the Maxims had inherited the future, would jointly or separately impose order. It was Laskell's hunch that "the intellectual power" had gone from the Stalinists and their power of drama also. He sensed that the Whittaker Chamberses would dominate. But he would not. Not he.

. . .

All this long ago, and yet the process proceeds. You may not think this, and assuredly you are under no obligation to do so. And yet you had best satisfy yourself why it is you think otherwise, for surely a different view would belie appearances. The appearances are those of a steady progression in the direction Schumpeter and Trilling, each in his own mode of anticipation, saw as ineluctable.

The great transformation, to my mind, although this may merely be the preoccupation of a political scientist, has been in the language and the personnel of politics. Stalinism brought the middle-class intellectual into American politics and it is vastly changed for it. Please note that I did not use the term Communism. In itself, a vigorous American Communist Party need have done no harm and possibly some good. But in the Stalinist form it was profoundly corrupting, for its fundamental thrust from the time of the popular front—that is to say the mid-1930s—was to deny that it itself existed and to make itself felt through the infiltration and manipulation of other popular movements. Deception on a massive scale became policy, while extraordinary numbers of extraordinary people submitted to *this* life of the mind. The language of politics has never recovered and confidence in politics has concomitantly declined. This happened not least because the popular reaction to these events has been led, or symbolized, by men who have only dimly grasped what really was at stake and have been easily discredited in the minds of the newer cohorts of middle-class activists coming along. Contrary to John Laskell's hunch, the point of view Gifford Maxim stood for has acquired but few advocates and less prestige, not least because so many of its ablest advocates have been, as Maxim was, converts whose conversion led them to acknowledge what all their former colleagues denied, so that they have seemed quirky at best and paranoiacal at worst. There have been times when the tiny and not very hopeful Socialist Party has seemed the sole repository of both understanding and honesty in American politics. I cite you the Hebrew: *Ha may-vin yavin.* Those who understand, understand.

Institutions have changed almost beyond recall in this process, and none so drastically as institutions such as Harvard, which was, for all its distinction, rather a sleepy and parochial institution in the 1930s. It knew little of the Crooms; nothing of the

Maxims. Indeed, there is a sense in which it knew little of intellectuals as Schumpeter understood the term, a calling that extended to that of propagandist and included that of journalist. Harvard was a place for the pursuit and the transmission of knowledge. There were, probably, few persons on the faculty who would even have thought of themselves as "intellectuals." They were scholars and might well have been offended by the other term. All that has changed in response to pressures certainly no individual can be held accountable for, and which few seem able to resist. That, perhaps, exaggerates. The *via media* that Laskell sought to follow and Maxim said was finished is not yet finished in Cambridge. It is our predominant belief, but no longer our most confident one. Professor Adam Ulam, in his compelling and necessary new book, *The Fall of the American University,* writes that for all the outward calm, "the politicization and bureaucratization of the American university have grown apace." Harvard, Professor James Q. Wilson wrote last spring, is no longer as liberal an institution as it once was. There are ideas that are not tolerated here, knowledge that is not taught. But that was predictable, wasn't it?

There are, of course, cycles in this long-term trend, and we may well be on a downward slope at the moment. Harvard became greatly involved with government in the early 1960s and came out of the experience hurt and uncomprehending. Government had seemed such great fun; but it turned out not to be fun at all, but bloody and tragic. There has been a withdrawal. The University has given fifteen honorary degrees to members of the Kennedy Administration;* but only one to a Johnson man and only one other to a Nixon man, and both of these Ivy Leaguers seem somewhat out of place in their respective administrations. It has been through, to put it gently, a chastening experience of the real world and real power.

Then, in the late 1960s, Harvard became greatly involved with the rhetoric and tactics of opposition to the government, in this case from a posture of the Left. (In both instances, of course, only a small element of the community has been involved; but that element nonetheless defined the period.) This

---

* Some of the fifteen served in earlier administrations.

movement, too, is somewhat recessive at the moment; but it persists, even as the involvement with government persists.

A CCNY man may perhaps be forgiven the impression that the University has not been equal to the strains that have been imposed on it by these movements, which Trilling described and Schumpeter anticipated, of the political culture into the scholarly community. Attack from *within* is wholly new to its experience and brings forth few of the brave and honorable qualities that so characterized the University's response to attack from *without* in the 1950s. One has the sense of a somewhat overbred community that had the instinct to bring in new blood, but did not understand that in doing so it would also bring in new conditions of argument, and resentment of its very existence. In the face of ideas that intend nothing less than the destruction of what Harvard has stood for, Harvard seems to have almost no defense save good manners. Now I do not underestimate the power of the well-behaved White Anglo-Saxon Protestant. Scenes from Eugene O'Neill's *The Hairy Ape* come quickly to mind. Yet this is a form of passive defense more appropriate to the bondholder than to the guardians of a great university tradition. The fact, as I see it, is that the ideological initiative at Harvard has been conceded to the extremists. Many ignore their views, but few contest them. An occasional Social Democrat, wandered in from CCNY, rejoins the battle of his youth; but on balance the Brahmin intellectual tradition stands uncomprehending, and not a little fearful before a still resolute politics of organized deception and violence which is a legacy of the Stalinist era in American intellectual life. There has been of late a diminishment of energy which Professor Ulam notes, but none of purpose. Mass assault has given way to "salami tactics": one professor at a time rather than one building at a time. But the institution remains trapped in its own decency, its moral authority gradually eroding, such that in the end all that will be left will be the good manners, and then it will not any longer matter.

But then there is an altogether new and quite uncertain development which takes place this week. A new class has arrived. You. It is now your University, also. It will impart some of its qualities to you, and partake of some of yours. I have dealt tonight with the foreknowledge of other men and it would be inappropriate to enter the field myself. And yet, I would wish you to know that you are well spoken of and genuinely welcome.

POSTSCRIPT

Most of the many students who attended the Freshman lecture this year were handed literature as they entered Sanders Theater by representatives of three groups, the Students for a Democratic Society (SDS), the Radcliffe-Harvard New American Movement (NAM), and the Revolutionary Communist Youth (RCY). The material was familiar enough, stressing especially that aching need for alliance with the working class which upper-middle-class radicals continue to exhibit. (One learns in the SDS pamphlet "Harvard Students under President Lowell were given course credit for breaking unions in Massachusetts by scabbing on workers' strikes. But if we really want to change things, workers must be our strongest allies.") Dean Bundy, Professors Kissinger and Huntington come in for the usual epithets. Somewhat new, however, is the identification of a "Cambridge Circle" made up of a number of professors, myself included, who are alleged to be leading an "attack on equality." It is surely "no accident" that almost without exception the specific charges leveled against the "Cambridge Circle" are lies. That is to say they are not distortions, or misreadings, but true and genuine lies. In most instances they represent the individual as holding an opinion exactly opposite of that which he does hold. This has nothing to with the correctness or incorrectness, or attractiveness, or whatever of the views the individuals do hold or those they are alleged to hold. It is merely that there has been a complete inversion of reality. I believe this to be a distinguishing quality of the Stalinoid mind-set.

In fairness to the Revolutionary Communist Youth, it shall be said they sail under their own colors. They state:

> The Revolutionary Communist Youth (RCY) is the youth section of the Spartacist League, which uniquely represents the nucleus of the vanguard party in the U.S. The RCY originated in 1969 as the Revolutionary Marxist Caucus, a left oppositional grouping in SDS which fought for Marxist clarity against both the anarcho-Maoism of the Rudd-Weatherman wing and the

crude social-workerism of Progressive Labor (which has now abandoned even a rudimentary working-class orientation for McGovern-style "anti-racist" liberalism.) In September 1971, the RCY held its Founding Conference and formally affiliated with the SL in accordance with the classic Leninist norm of youth-party relations: political subordination and organizational independence. The RCY seeks to develop young radicals into lifetime communist militants, and to build a socialist youth organization which can intervene in all social struggles with a revolutionary program based on the politics of Marx, Lenin, and Trotsky.

It is doubtless perverse to do so, but I happen to find that an honorable statement of purpose.

"Peace"

22

A decade ago most of the social scientists with whom I work and have been associated with were profoundly distressed about the directions which American society seemed to be taking. A pervasive, ominous sense of trouble shaping up could be encountered in what we wrote, in our conversations, in our talking circles. We thought things were going to become much worse than they were. We found ourselves saying this in the context of a society that didn't particularly understand, and didn't particularly welcome, such a proposition. That society—the America of the early 1960s—was much too optimistic about events, and almost in proportionate terms responded unhappily, angrily—nastily, if you will—to our glum prognoses, even as shortly thereafter it reacted in near panic when the troubles we had been anticipating came to pass.

It may be useful for those of us who went through that period of saying "Things are going to be much worse than they are," now to test our science—our weak and so uncertain science—by once again giving voice to our present presumptions which, once again, we find at odds with established opinion. Our position has reversed, although, as will be seen, our roles remain rather the same. At this moment our presumption is that "Things are going to be much better than they are." Rather the contrary

"Peace" was given as the Forty-First Alfred E. Stearns Lecture at Andover Academy, January 1973. It was first published in *The Public Interest*, Summer 1973, under the title " 'Peace'—some thoughts on the 1960's and 1970's."

view obtains in circles once so optimistic—the faculties, let us say, of those prep schools and colleges which educate the children of the upper-middle class. I don't expect such circles to be any less annoyed with us this time than they were last, even if I am not any longer as interested in what they might think as I perhaps once was. But I am worried that my friends and I may have become overconfident in the aftermath of having seen ourselves proven substantially right about a fairly serious sequence of events, such that we could fall into a lazy oppositional habit of letting our own thought be shaped by reference to the thought of others. This may be too indirect a way of putting a simple point. In the course of the 1960s we became a little contemptuous of those who had been so contemptuous of us. They had been so certain everything was bully. Then they became equally certain everything was catastrophic. *We* reacted to this by taking perhaps too much pleasure in remembering how wrong they were once, and just assuming they are wrong again. It could be that our present position is no more than reactive. It should be tested, as we should be.

We assert that things are going to be better. They are going to be different, in any event, and they are going to be different in ways that can be quantified and identified. We find ourselves, at this point, saying this not just to a skeptical elite, but also to a public now much accustomed to the thought that matters do not change for the better, but only for the worse. We are out of phase. And yet, if our science, as I say, has any validity, it is surely in this regard and in this function. I don't want to be Pollyannish. I don't want to suggest that those matters of profound concern which have so much gripped society—those public concerns which dominated the private lives of Americans in the last decade—need now concern us no longer. I mean nothing of the sort. And yet I think the situation will be different in ways that on the whole will be for the better.

There are certain essential facts, of which the first is simply that the great military involvement of the United States in Asia is at an end—possibly to resume again—but for the moment it is at an end. This was coming. The event was not sudden. It was not precisely defined. It had not the concision one had learned to expect from American history. And yet the ineluctability of it was clear enough, certainly, for me to say to Dr. Sizer* when he called late last year to ask if I would give the Stearns Lecture at Andover, to say "Yes," and to say, "I will talk about Peace."

But I would like to talk not just about peace abroad, talk not at all about that, but rather peace at home, peace within the society in which we live, following a tumultuous and rending decade which leaves us less than whole, leaves us fundamentally changed in many ways, and yet also in the aftermath of which we can see ourselves resuming the fairly well defined directions of a democracy, and doing so as a fundamentally competent people, fundamentally capable of achieving what it has undertaken to achieve.

I would like to offer you a general proposition. (Be careful when Harvard professors say such things to you, because their general propositions usually won't seem very general at all.) I'd like to state that most of the events that tore American society almost apart, or so it seemed in the 1960s, arose from conditions unique to the decade in which they occurred. They had not ever existed before. They will not ever exist again. They involve the interaction of demographic and political-cultural changes. We have more complex terms for this than perhaps need be, all derived from the Greek, and vaguely related to philosophic doctrines of the past. We use the term "synergistic," —the interaction of muscles, of chemicals, of philosophical doctrine, such that two events quite separate in their origin affect one another in such a way as to produce outcomes vastly different and greater than either could produce on its own, more amplified and in ways fundamentally different from the effect either event would have, had it occurred in isolation.

The proposition I'm going to put to you is simple. It is sufficient, I hope, at least to start a discussion of just what did happen. I'm going to say to you that the 1960s saw a profound demographic change occur in American society which was a one-time change, a growth in population vaster than any that had ever occurred before or any that will ever occur again, with respect to a particular subgroup in the population, namely those

---

* Dr. Theodore Sizer, Headmaster of Andover Academy.

persons fourteen to twenty-four years of age. This sudden increase in population interacted in a synergistic sense with a whole series of other events which originate, if you will, in the world of ideas, as distinct from the physical world in which populations increase or decrease. In the best-known example of the 1960s, people changed their minds about the requirements of justice and decent public policy concerning minority groups in American society at just the moment when the size and location of those groups were dramatically changing. But this was not the only change. People changed their minds about this, they changed their minds about that, and they changed their minds at just the point when the physical conditions of life, the ecological facts of how many people are around and where they are, were also changing. These changes interacted in such a way as to produce extraordinary differences—discontinuities —with the period immediately preceding and which I think will now be seen to be discontinuous with the period that now follows.

It started out with this fact of population. The people who cause most of the "trouble" in a society, as you probably know, are people fourteen to twenty-four. They are also the people who are most interesting, most attractive, prettiest (that's for sure), handsomest (some say), brightest, healthiest, liveliest. Your mind starts deteriorating at about twenty-four, as I understand it. In any event, everybody knows you run fastest, dance longest, and at least in my youth, drink the most in these years. Societies, no matter where they are, are mostly organized around the problem of how to get people from fourteen to twenty-four. At fourteen you are still in most respects a dependent youth, in some respects a child. At twenty-four you are an adult. In between, extraordinary turbulences take place. They are such that there was at one point, at the turn of the century, a semi-scientific quasi-Darwinian view of the whole life experience— propounded and solemnly taught for a couple of generations— that each individual is born a savage of some kind, and gradually goes through a life experience in which he evolves. At one point he's a Mede, then he's a Persian, then he's a Greek, and with any luck he ends up a citizen of the Commonwealth of Massachusetts. Whatever the merits of that argument, all agree that the transition is enormously difficult and has to be followed with great care and attention, because all kinds of turbulence occur in the process.

There is no denying, I think, that in a curious way the advanced industrial societies in which we live have found it most difficult to provide this passage for young people. Only in the last century or so, really, have we begun to perceive this fact of youth, an age in life which is neither that of infancy nor that of adulthood, but, however, the long period in between. And we have had extraordinary changes in the circumstances of youth during this century-and-a-half or so. This has been basically a phenomenon of technology.

Andover, if I may presume a knowledge that I don't entirely possess, was begun for the primary purpose of educating a very limited group of persons, the priests of the society. When Andover was begun I should think doctors were not thought a profession, or much of one; engineers were skilled craftsmen who certainly didn't go to college. There were a few persons who did mathematics and a few people who did chemistry, but by and large only ministers and, perhaps, lawyers got educated. Almost nobody else needed to be. The rest could learn what they had to know in the normal process of going to work very early in life.

We have now extended that period of learning because so much more has to be learned. Simultaneously, another fundamental biological event has occurred, probably the most important event of its kind associated with industrialism, almost not at all noticed, which is that the age of sexual maturity has been going down and down and down. In round numbers, the age of menarche was almost eighteen years in the early part of the nineteenth century. In the course of industrialization, it has dropped to below twelve years.

This, obviously, is a result of industrialization. It is perhaps the single most important impact which technology has had on the human experience. Let me not pretend to greater knowledge than I have. I say it is obviously technology because I can't think what else it could be, and I don't believe scientists have any firm theories as yet. It *could* be sunspots. But my bet is that it is a combination of clean water and abundant food. In any event, we may soon reach the point where Freud's discovery of infantile sexuality will become obsolete. People will sexualize at three and stay that way.

Thus you have a situation of a constant dropping of the age of physical maturity and you have an extension of the age of social maturity. So you might become physically mature at twelve and not be thought socially mature until you have had two years of graduate school at M.I.T. And if, in between, young people become turbulent, one is not to be surprised. Now the question is: How many such persons have been going through this experience?

This is the basic datum of my argument. Between 1960 and 1970 the size of this subgroup of the American population grew by an absolutely unprecedented amount, and it will never grow by such an amount again.

Let me give you the figures. If you go from 1890 to 1960, you find the size of this subgroup, fourteen to twenty-four, growing a little bit each succeeding decade: 10 percent, 8 percent, sometimes not at all, but usually growing a little bit. In the whole of that seventy years, 1890 to 1960, the total increase in the population of that age group, the total increase of "cohort," as we say, was 12.5 million persons. Then, in the 1960s, it grew by 13.8 million persons, an increase of 52 percent in one decade, five times the average rate of the preceding seventy years. *It grew by 13.8 million persons in the 1960s: it will grow by 600,000 in the 1970s: it will decline in the 1980s.* It's all over, it happened once, it will not ever happen again. After a 52 percent increase in the 1960s, we will see an 11 percent increase in the 1970s, we will see an 8 percent *decline* in the 1980s.*

In the terms of what we call the dependency ratios—that is, how many young people there are as against how many old people who look after the young people, pay their bills, and tell them how to behave—the ratio of persons fourteen to twenty-four to persons twenty-five to sixty-four increased 39 percent in the 1960s after either an increase of zero or a decline in every decade from the 1880s on. What happened, as we look back? (But first, let me not stand here and *tell* you what happened. I only offer a view. You may not share the view. You certainly need not . . .) What happened—in this assertion, in this

* These data are the work of Professor Norman Ryder.

hypothesis—is that suddenly a new social class was created in the United States so large in its number that it was fundamentally isolated from the rest of the society, it was isolated on campuses, it was isolated in slums, it was isolated in a way in the armed forces. It had not much contact with people younger than it, very little with people older. It was apart from the rest of society. During this period the number of males sixteen to nineteen increased by 44 percent, but the number of such persons who were *employed* grew only by 11 percent; the unemployment rates for teenagers went up enormously, as did all such signs of dislocation, of alienation, of a lack of connection. And not just for the poor, and not just for the well-to-do, but at every level of society, there emerged a sense that "We are alone and separate from them." A youth culture developed. Youth acquired its own music, its own forms of dress, clothes, its own grammar, to a degree without precedent in the United States.

For some time we have had "teenagers" around, but never with this relative lack of contact with older and younger persons and with relative intensive contact and concentration within their own ranks. The result was an extraordinary change in behavior. The curious compounding of this basic biological demographic fact with a certain number of ideas and attitudes created, as I say, a synergistic effect. Attitudes about drug use changed and interacted with a vast increase in the population given to experiment in such matters. Attitudes toward dependency on government support changed and interacted with a vast increase in the population most exposed to dependency. Attitudes about patriotism changed and interacted with a vast increase in the population for whom such attitudes are of more than hypothetical relevance, which is to say, the population which is asked, or told, to fight wars. To repeat, the population explosion interacted with quite independent developments to produce much larger consequences than would have been the case had either of those developments occurred in isolation.

Well, it's over. That time is past. We are going through a period now when we are going to have a profound change in almost all of our politics, almost all of our social relationships because this period is behind us. We are likely, for example, to see a real change in the operation of institutions. State and local government went through absolute hell in the 1960s. Why is that? It is because it has traditionally been the job of state and local government to look after young people age fourteen to twenty-four, to get them through high school and perhaps college; to see that they don't steal cars; if they have children, to provide maternity hospitals for them; to provide new housing and so on, down a long list. The crush was just too much for state and local government. But now, suddenly, it's over. In all of the 1970s we will not "need" a single additional schoolteacher if we maintain our present ratio of teachers to pupils. We have reached suddenly, and have now gone below, a "replacement" birth rate. I cannot but note, Mr. Dean, that there are a number of young persons around the Graduate School of Education at Harvard who are finding it hard to get jobs these days, and are themselves noticing that while they were out attending Zero Population Growth rallies in the late 1960s, the birth rate had already dropped to the point where we no longer "need" new schoolteachers. I can state even more ominously that in the 1980s we won't need any more professors. Think about that!

The great pressures of state and local government are now off. Revenue sharing has begun. The President signed the bill just last year. And so, for example, the 1970s and 1980s are likely to be a time when it's not so bad to be mayor, and being governor might be positively pleasant, whereas the job of President is going to be hell because in an odd way all the commitments taken up in response to the crises of the 1960s have overcommitted the finances of the national government. No matter who is President, he or she is going to spend much of his or her time during the next ten years vetoing bills passed by Congress in the confident expectation that they will be vetoed. And whereas for years we had a flow of attention and interest to the national government, simply because that was the only place large new resources seemed available, we might well see the emergence of a degree of discretionary capacity in state and local government finances, which means that interest will flow back. It will be interesting to be mayor; it will be important who gets elected. I think a movement down from the concentration, the overconcentration, of the national government is inevitable, overdue, and desirable.

Along with all this, we are going into a period of enormous personal prosperity. The "magic of compound interest" is working on us now. Our gross national product in constant dollars will go from about 1 trillion 115 billion last year to about 2 trillion in 1980. Per capita income by 1980 should reach $6,500 per person. I am soon to leave the United States to become Ambassador to India, to a country where about 140 million people live on a per capita annual income of under $20. And at the rate at which those incomes are growing, it might reach $24 by 1980.

We are going to have a level of personal opportunity associated with that kind of expenditure. We've not known its like ever before. We are not going to have the difficult experience of just keeping up with our needs that we've had to go through. Yet it should also be clear that we are not ever likely quite to be the same, certainly not in our lifetime, in the aftermath of the extraordinary decline in the confidence in American institutions which accompanied the experience of the 1960s. We shall have peace, but it will in some respects be a peace of exhaustion, and in a curiously antinomian quality, it might also be a peace of surfeit.

All of the surveys made by American public-opinion students in the last five or six years have shown an astonishingly precipitous decline in confidence in institutions. One of the curious things is the way people in different sectors, you might say of the economy, of the society, have looked at the drop of *their* confidence in *other* sectors, and have said, "Look, no one has any confidence in you," but have never looked up to note, "Alas, no one has any confidence in us either." American higher education has had a grand time explaining that nobody trusts the President, nobody trusts the Congress, nobody trusts big business, nobody trusts big labor. The best poll taken on confidence in higher education showed that in 1966 about 61 percent of the American people would express a great deal of confidence in higher education; last year it was down to 33 percent. (Mind you, the American people have not taken leave of their senses: confidence in Congress was only 21 percent, newspapers only 18 percent, and advertising was down to 12 percent.) We are none of us particularly proud of ourselves just now. We aren't particularly confident of our situation. And yet the basic ecology of national well-being is once again moving in a good direction.

I think I would predict a more "conservative" society simply on the ground that a society whose population is barely growing tends to be curiously straightened and strict in its behavior. I make no claim to any "scientific" evidence on this point (although I don't know why we can't study the question). I speak more from literary sources. If I had been asked ten years ago whom to read to find out what America was like, or was going to be like, I would unhesitatingly have said "Read Mark Twain." Mark Twain mostly tells the truth, as Huck Finn said in the opening lines of that book. He had a great sense of the ebullience, the growth, the prospects, the limitless energy and potential of this great and endless country. I don't think I would say "Read Mark Twain" today. I think I would advise a young person to read Balzac. Find out what it's like to live in a society where if you want to be a professor, you wait until the man who is professor dies. Then the fifteen of you who want the job compete in various ways. One of you gets it. The rest hope for the best for their sons.* And you won't have had many sons, you'll only have two, as it were. This doesn't mean you have a less turbulent society or a society sated with social conservatism. Ideological radicalism is just as likely. The French indeed have a phrase for it: "Think left, live right." I incline to think we're going to see a lot of both.

But we're not going to have one new institution of higher education opening every week—as we had all through the 1960s. One new president, one new provost, two new deans, five new department heads, every week, with all that such rapid expansion implied.

The population explosion of the 1960s is easily enough explained. It followed a period of fifteen years of depression and war, in which the natural progenitive qualities of the society were not given their outlet. There was a sudden increase, but it has now begun to feed back and slow down. We are getting

* The narrowing of certain kinds of opportunity may be illustrated by the changing chances of those taking the Foreign Service examination, a well-established point of entry for educated and highly motivated young persons into an elite profession. In 1971, 19,000 persons applied; 11,000 took the test, and 85 officers were appointed. In 1948 the ratio of examinees to appointees was 14 to 1. In 1960 it was 21 to 1. By 1971 it was 130 to 1. This change is almost wholly accounted for by a tenfold increase in the number taking the exam. In 1948 it was only 1,141.

back to earth, as it were. We overdid a lot of things, but we didn't go wrong; we came out a stronger society. Fifteen years ago ours was a caste society with respect to race; it no longer is. Fifteen years ago ours was a society in which the hegemony of the male, the normal presumption of male dominance, male exclusiveness in social and political and economic affairs was a given; it no longer is. Ours was a society fifteen years ago which was almost impervious to the thought that it had many problems of its own; it was much too eager to see problems in other countries and other places and to seek to deal with them. President Kennedy in his great inaugural twelve years ago made that grand statement which, in looking back, we find ourselves so extraordinarily ambivalent about. He said: "Let the word go out from this place and this time that we will pay any price, bear any burden, meet any hardship, support any friend, oppose any foe, to insure the survival and success of liberty." Well, that was not the theme of the last inaugural address. It was that we may or we may not; we are not so sure of ourselves as we were; we know the limits of our power; we have tested the limits of our will; we aren't going to take quite so many chances. And yet that too is a sign of maturity. That too, in some respects, marks the movement from that period fourteen to twenty-four into that period beyond, in which the fact of limitation of power, of energy, of integrity even, is acknowledged and learned and lived with.

And so it will be different, and it will not in every respect be better, and it will certainly in no respect be more exciting. But it will, I think, be more rewarding. I think we have come out of our time of troubles. I think the first place that will be encountered is already to be seen—it is in our institutions of education, in our elementary schools, perhaps, but most importantly in our secondary schools and in our universities. After a time of great anguish for all of us, no matter what our views, no matter what side of the arguments we are taking, I think we have come back now to a time of peace. *If* I may express hope for the future, but also in that respect predict a little bit, I think that increasingly our schools will become, in the title of Dean Sizer's brilliant, small, new book, *Places for Learning, Places for Joy*. Thank you.

About the Author

DANIEL P. MOYNIHAN, United States Ambassador to India, served in the subcabinet of Presidents Kennedy and Johnson and in the cabinet of President Nixon. He is the only person in public life to have maintained this continuity of involvement with domestic social issues through the 1960s and into the present decade.

In 1963, as Assistant Secretary of Labor for Policy Planning and Research, he began consideration of family allowances as a measure to offset the persistence of poverty in the midst of American affluence. In 1965 he was a member of the White House task force that drafted the Economic Opportunity Act of 1965. That year, for his service as "an architect of the nation's program to eradicate poverty," he received the Arthur S. Flemming Award as One of the Ten Outstanding Young Men in Government. After a period in academic life, he returned to Washington in 1969 as Assistant for Urban Affairs, later Counselor to the President. In this role he pressed an "income strategy" on social issues which was embodied in the Family Assistance Plan proposed by President Nixon in August 1969. His most recent book, *The Politics of a Guaranteed Income*, describes the events surrounding the struggle to provide such a plan.

Ambassador Moynihan has been a member of the Faculty of Arts and Sciences of Harvard University and of the John F. Kennedy School of Government. He is a member also of the board of directors of the American Association for the Advancement of Science, has received twenty honorary degrees, and is an Honorary Fellow of the London School of Economics and Political Science.

Along with *The Politics of a Guaranteed Income*, he is the co-editor of *On Equality of Educational Opportunity* and co-author of *Beyond the Melting Pot: The Negroes, Puerto Ricans, Jews, Italians and Irish in New York City*.